CONNECT FEATURES

Interactive Applications

Interactive Applications offer a variety of automatically graded exercises that require students to **apply** key concepts. Whether the assignment includes a *click and drag*, *video case*, or *decision generator*, these applications provide instant feedback and progress tracking for students and detailed results for the instructor.

EASY TO USE

Learning Management System Integration

McGraw-Hill Campus is a one-stop teaching and learning experience available to use with any learning management system. McGraw-Hill Campus provides single sign-on to faculty and students for all McGraw-Hill material and technology from within the school website. McGraw-Hill Campus also allows instructors instant access to all supplements and teaching materials for all McGraw-Hill products.

Blackboard users also benefit from McGraw-Hill's industry-leading integration, providing single sign-on to access all Connect assignments and automatic feeding of assignment results to the Blackboard grade book.

POWERFUL REPORTING

Connect generates comprehensive reports and graphs that provide instructors with an instant view of the performance of individual students, a specific section, or multiple sections. Since all content is mapped to learning objectives, Connect reporting is ideal for accreditation or other administrative documentation.

eBook

Connect Plus includes a media-rich eBook that allows you to share your notes with your students. Your students can insert and review their own notes, highlight the text, search for specific information, and interact with media resources. Using an eBook with Connect Plus gives your students a complete digital solution that allows them to access their materials from any computer.

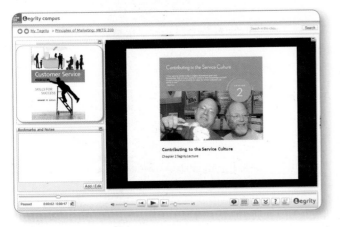

Tegrity

Make your classes available anytime, anywhere. With simple, one-click recording, students can search for a word or phrase and be taken to the exact place in your lecture that they need to review.

SIXTH EDITION

CUSTOMER SERVICE

SKILLS FOR SUCCESS

Robert W. Lucas

Principal, Robert W. Lucas Enterprises

CUSTOMER SERVICE: SKILLS FOR SUCCESS, SIXTH EDITION

Published by McGraw-Hill Education, 2 Penn Plaza, New York, NY 10121. Copyright © 2015 by McGraw-Hill Education. All rights reserved. Printed in the United States of America. Previous editions © 2012, 2009, and 2005. No part of this publication may be reproduced or distributed in any form or by any means, or stored in a database or retrieval system, without the prior written consent of McGraw-Hill Education, including, but not limited to, in any network or other electronic storage or transmission, or broadcast for distance learning.

Some ancillaries, including electronic and print components, may not be available to customers outside the United States.

This book is printed on acid-free paper.

2 3 4 5 6 7 8 9 0 DOW/DOW 1 0 9 8 7 6 5 4

ISBN   978-0-07-354546-2
MHID   0-07-354546-5

Senior Vice President, Products & Markets: *Kurt L. Strand*
Vice President, Content Production & Technology Services: *Kimberly Meriwether David*
Managing Director: *Paul Ducham*
Executive Brand Manager: *Sankha Basu*
Executive Director of Development: *Ann Torbert*
Development Editor II: *Kelly L. Delso*
Marketing Manager: *Donielle Xu*
Director, Content Production: *Terri Schiesl*
Content Project Manager: *Susan Trentacosti*
Senior Buyer: *Debra R. Sylvester*
Design: *Srdjan Savanovic*
Cover Image: *man on ladder:* © *CAP53/Getty Images; reception desk:* © *A-Digit/Getty Images*
Senior Content Licensing Specialist: *Lori Hancock*
Typeface: *10.5/13 New Century*
Compositor: *Aptara®, Inc.*
Printer: *R. R. Donnelley*

All credits appearing on page or at the end of the book are considered to be an extension of the copyright page.

Library of Congress Cataloging-in-Publication Data

Lucas, Robert W.
    Customer service : skills for success / Robert W. Lucas, Principal, Robert W. Lucas Enterprises. —
Sixth Edition.
        pages cm
    Includes index.
    ISBN 978-0-07-354546-2 (alk. paper) — ISBN 0-07-354546-5 (alk. paper)
    1. Customer services. I. Title.
HF5415.5.L83 2015
658.8'12—dc23
                                    2013046975

The Internet addresses listed in the text were accurate at the time of publication. The inclusion of a website does not indicate an endorsement by the authors or McGraw-Hill Education, and McGraw-Hill Education does not guarantee the accuracy of the information presented at these sites.

www.mhhe.com

ROBERT (BOB) W. LUCAS is the principal at Robert W. Lucas Enterprises and an internationally known author and learning and performance expert who specializes in workplace performance-based training and consulting services. He has four decades of experience in customer service, human resources development, and management in a variety of organizational environments. Throughout his career, he has lived, traveled, and worked in 25 different countries and geographic areas.

Currently, Bob is on the board for the Florida Authors and Publishers Association. In 1995 and 2011, he was the president of the Central Florida Chapter of the American Society for Training and Development (ASTD). During the past 20 years, Bob has shared his knowledge with workplace professionals from organizations such as Walt Disney World, SeaWorld, Martin Marietta, and Wachovia Bank in the Webster University Master of Arts program in Orlando, Florida. In addition, Bob has provided consulting and training services to numerous major organizations on a variety of workplace learning topics. These topics range from customer service, presentation skills, creative training and management program development, train-the-trainer, interpersonal communication, adult learning, diversity, and team building to and including employee and organizational development. Bob regularly gives presentations to various local and national groups and organizations.

Listed in *Who's Who in the World, Who's Who in America, and Who's Who in the South & Southeast,* Bob is also an avid writer. This text is the top-selling textbook on the topic of customer service in the United States. He has also written and contributed to 30 other books, including: *Please Every Customer: Providing Stellar Customer Service Across Cultures* and *How to Be a Great Call Center Representative.*

Additionally, Bob has been a contributing author for the *Annual: Developing Human Resources* series by Pfeiffer & Company since 1992 and several compilation works by various publishers.

Bob earned a Bachelor of Science degree in Law Enforcement from the University of Maryland; an M.A. degree with a focus in Human Resources Development from George Mason University in Fairfax, Virginia; and a second M.A. degree in Management and Leadership from Webster University in Orlando, Florida. Further, Bob was one of the first people in the world to attain the ASTD designation of Certified Professional in Learning and Performance (CPLP) in 2006.

BRIEF CONTENTS

CONTENTS

PART TWO   SKILLS FOR SUCCESS 86
Customer Service Interview: Scott Larsen, Auto Repair Shop Owner, Cadillac Specialists

PART THREE   BUILDING AND MAINTAINING RELATIONSHIPS   200

Customer Service Interview: Barbara Andryshak, Dunkin' Donuts District Manager

New to This Edition

Every Chapter

- New *Customer Service interviews* with service practitioners at the beginning of each topic section
- Addition of *Street Talk* segments with advice from experienced service practitioners in each chapter
- Addition of *Knowledge Check* questions at the end of each content section throughout the chapters
- Addition of *Trending Now* sections in each chapter

Chapter 1

- New *In the Real World* chapter opening case study (Zappos.com)
- New *Think About It*
- Updated research and statistics
- Expanded definitions of service technology and discussion of its use
- Updated discussion of *Global Economic Shifts* impacting customer service
- Expanded discussion of *Globalization of the Economy*
- Inclusion of *Changing Values* section that addresses the impact on customer service
- Update to *Consumer Behavior Shifts* section
- Expanded section on *Internal Customers*
- Addition of *Customer Service Competencies* section

Chapter 2

- Updated *In the Real World* chapter opening case study (Ben & Jerry's Ice Cream)
- New *Think About It*
- Updated research and statistics
- Expanded discussion of *Attitude in Service*
- Expanded discussion on *Motivators and Rewards*
- Revised *12 Strategies for Promoting a Positive Service Culture* section
- Additional *Collaborative Learning Activity*

Chapter 3

- New *In the Real World* chapter opening case study (Papa John's Pizza)
- New *Think About It*
- Updated research and statistics

- Expanded *Importance of Effective Communication* section
- Introduction and discussion of the PL.AN positive communication model
- Additional content on communicating positively
- Expanded section on *Assertive Communication*
- Expanded section on *Salvaging Relationships After Conflict*
- Additional *Search It Out* activity
- Additional *Collaborative Learning Activity*

Chapter 4

- New *In the Real World* chapter opening case study (Field's Auto Group)
- Updated *Think About It*
- Updated research and statistics
- Updated section on *Semantics*

Chapter 5

- New *In the Real World* chapter opening case study (Southwest Airlines)
- New *Think About It*
- Updated research and statistics
- Expanded *Customer-Focused Behavior* section
- Additional *Collaborative Learning Activities*

Chapter 6

- New *In the Real World* chapter opening case study (Trader Joe's)
- New *Think About It*
- Updated research and statistics
- Expanded *Characteristics of a Good Listener* section
- Additional *Search It Out* activity
- Additional *Collaborative Learning Activity*

Chapter 7

- New *In the Real World* chapter opening case study (Coca-Cola)
- New *Think About It*
- Updated research and statistics
- Updated *Identifying Behavioral Styles* section
- Additional *Search It Out* activity

Chapter 8

- New *In the Real World* chapter opening case study (Johnson & Johnson)
- New *Think About It*
- Updated research and statistics
- Updated *Impact of Diversity* section
- Expanded *Impact of Cultural Values* section
- Updated *Providing Quality Service to Diverse Customer Groups* section
- Additional *Search It Out* activity

Chapter 9

- Updated *In the Real World* chapter opening case study (Netflix)
- Updated *Think About It*
- Updated research and statistics
- Updated *The Role of Technology in Customer Service*
- Addition of *Tapping into Web-Based and Mobile Technologies* section
- Additional *Search It Out* activity
- Heavily expanded coverage of customer service and call center technologies

Chapter 10

- New *In the Real World* chapter opening case study (United Parcel Service of America, Inc.)
- New *Think About It*
- Updated research and statistics
- Expanded *The Role of Trust* section
- Addition of *Customer Loyalty* section
- Expanded *The Importance of Customer Relationship Management* section
- Updated *Small Business Perspective* section
- Additional *Search It Out* activity

An Update on a Trusted Customer Service Textbook Resource

Welcome to a brand new look for the top-selling customer service textbook in the United States. In this edition we have added four-color layout and more images to enhance the content and completely change the graphic appearance of the book. We have also updated, expanded, and reformatted much of the content.

Customer Service: Skills for Success addresses real-world customer service issues and provides a variety of updated resources, activities, examples, and tips from the author and active professionals in the industry to gain and hold readers' interest while providing additional insights into the concepts and skills related to customer service. The text begins with a macro view of what customer service involves today and provides projections for the future, then focuses on specific skills and related topics.

The sixth edition of *Customer Service: Skills for Success* contains 10 chapters divided into three parts, plus the Appendix, Glossary, and Bibliography. These parts focus on different aspects of customer service: (1) The Profession, (2) Skills for Success, and (3) Building and Maintaining Relationships. Along with valuable ideas, guidance, and perspectives, readers will also encounter interviews of real-world service providers, along with tips for implementing effective proven customer service strategies, case study scenarios, and activities to help you apply concepts learned to real-world situations in order to challenge your thinking on the issues presented. For users of previous editions, you will note the addition of several new information elements and a tie-in to today's technology through-out the chapters. If you need the chapters on Time and Stress Management and Dealing with Customers in written form, they can be found on our website, www.mhhe.com/customerservice, along with various individual and small group activities, case studies, and other support material. These can be used to engage readers and enhance content found in the book.

Learning Outcomes

Each chapter starts with behavioral-based **Learning Outcomes** to direct your focus and to help you measure your end-of-chapter success in grasping the concepts presented. You will also find a **quote** from a famous person to prompt your thinking related to the chapter topic and the text focus. Throughout the book and in the Contents, the abbreviation LO indicates the Learning Outcome that applies to that section.

LEARNING OUTCOMES

After completing this chapter, you will be able to:

3-1 Explain the importance of effective communication in customer service.

3-2 Recognize the elements of effective two-way interpersonal communication.

3-3 Project a professional customer service image through positive communication.

3-4 Provide feedback effectively.

3-5 Avoid language that could send a negative message and harm the customer relationship.

3-6 Use assertive communication techniques to enhance service.

3-7 Identify key differences between assertive and aggressive behavior.

To assist you with the content of this chapter, we have added additional review questions, activities, and other valuable resource material at www.mhhe.com/customerservice.

As you explore the chapter material, readers will find many helpful tools to enhance their learning experience and assist them in transferring their new knowledge to the workplace. These tools are outlined below.

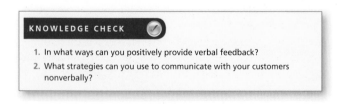

KNOWLEDGE CHECK

1. In what ways can you positively provide verbal feedback?
2. What strategies can you use to communicate with your customers nonverbally?

Knowledge Checks

Throughout the chapter, students are asked key questions in the form of a **Knowledge Check** box. This allows students to consider what they have just read and test themselves to ensure that they have grasped the concepts covered in each section of every chapter.

In the Real World

In the Real World sections, placed at the beginning of many of the chapters, provide insights into customer service in a variety of well-known businesses, industries, and organizations. These candid snapshots provide an overview of how successful businesses provide products and services and succeed in a highly competitive global world.

IN THE REAL WORLD RETAIL/MANUFACTURING—COCA-COLA

Coca-Cola is a soft drink brand that is recognized worldwide. In fact, the drink is one of the most recognized corporate logos and is sold in over 200 countries through 250 bottlers throughout the world. The company sells over 1.8 billion servings of Coke a day.

The Coca-Cola story began in Atlanta, Georgia, in 1886 when pharmacist John Pemberton was experimenting with a recipe that he later mixed with carbonated water and began to sell at his drugstore. Two years after its invention, Pemberton sold his secret formula to a businessman by the name of Asa Candler, who formed a corporation to bottle and distribute the trendy drink. He later sold the rights to two other businessmen who wanted to bottle the drink to enhance distribution. Candler sold syrup that his company produced to these distributors, but not his secret formula. They simply mixed the syrup with carbonated water and bottled it. From there, the product became a household name as more people began to take Coca-Cola home to enjoy.

As with many successful products, competitors soon emerged. To ensure that people could tell the original from these wannabes, the distributors created the trademarked contour bottle in 1916 so that customers would recognize the original product.

Candler ultimately sold his company in 1919 to a group of investors with Robert Woodruff as the president. The new group wanted to make Coca-Cola available anytime and anyplace. To accomplish this, the new company started adding bottling plants all over the world. Today, Coca-Cola owns nearly 100 trademarked brands including popular products like Dannon, Campbells, Evian, Nestea, Bacardi Mixers, Powerade, Dr. Pepper, Minute Maid, and many others. The brand was recently listed as one of the most valuable in the world at a value of $88.4 billion.[1]

The six "Ps" of the company vision statement highlight Coca-Cola's purpose and desired future objectives.

- **People.** Be a great place to work where people are inspired to be the best they can be.

- **Portfolio.** Bring to the world a portfolio of quality beverage brands that anticipate and satisfy people's desires and needs.

- **Partners.** Nurture a winning network of customers and suppliers; together we create mutual, enduring value.

- **Planet.** Be a responsible citizen that makes a difference by helping build and support sustainable communities.

- **Profit.** Maximize long-term return to shareholders while being mindful of our overall responsibilities.

- **Productivity.** Be a highly effective and fast-moving organization.[2]

To assist in accomplishing its vision, the company established the Coca-Cola Foundation in 1984. This entity focuses on helping and giving back to communities worldwide. Some of the issues supported in various countries include water stewardship (providing safe, clean drinking water), lifestyle/behavioral change programs (e.g., nutrition, exercise, and behavior modification), recycling, and education. Between 2008 and 2010 the foundation and company donated almost $700 million to these and other causes.

For more information about Coca-Cola, do an Internet search and either visit their website (www.coca-colacompany.com/) or scan the QR code with your smartphone application to get to their site.

Think About It

1. What is your opinion of the Coca-Cola Company? Explain.

2. Based on what you know or read on the Internet or through other sources, do you believe that the company is customer focused? Why or why not?

3. How does the company's community involvement potentially affect its image in the eyes of customers or potential customers?

www.coca-cola.com

Think About It

Think About It activities provide an opportunity for readers to reflect on the In the Real World scenarios that they just read, do an Internet search on those organizations, and then answer the questions provided. The goal of the activity is to cause readers to delve further into how the organization addresses customer service and to relate it to their personal knowledge and what they read about service in the book. These activities can be done individually or as a group, where answers are shared.

Quick Response (QR) Codes

You will note **Quick Response (QR) codes** inserted on the chapter openers. These optically machine-readable, two-dimension barcodes allow more tech-savvy readers with a smartphone or iPhone that has a QR application to scan the image. They are then quickly directed to a website that contains additional information about the topic just addressed in that area of the book. This element not only adds a new visual element to the text, but also precludes a reader from having to manually cut and paste or type a domain name into a computer browser to get to additional resources.

Quick Preview

Pretests called **Quick Preview** are provided at the beginning of each chapter as a self-assessment of current skills and knowledge levels before even reading the first page. This allows readers to check their topic knowledge and primes them for specific content to watch for as they read the chapter. Answers to the questions are provided at the end of the chapter.

Quick Preview

Before reviewing the chapter content, respond to the following questions by placing a "T" for true or an "F" for false on the rules. Use any questions you miss as a checklist of material to which you will pay particular attention as you read through the chapter. For those you get right, congratulate yourself, but review the sections they address in order to learn additional details about the topic.

_____ 1. Service breakdowns often occur because customer needs and wants are not met.

_____ 2. Customer expectations do not affect how service is delivered.

_____ 3. Behavioral style preferences do not affect customer needs or satisfaction levels.

_____ 4. An upset customer is usually annoyed with a specific person rather than the organization or system.

_____ 5. When you cannot comply with the demands of an angry customer, you should try to negotiate an alternative solution.

_____ 6. Competency in communicating can eliminate the need for service recovery.

_____ 7. Demanding customers often act in a domineering manner because they are very self-confident. This is a function of behavioral style.

_____ 8. Service recovery occurs when a provider is able to make restitution, solve a problem, or regain customer trust after service breakdown.

_____ 9. One key strategy for preventing dissatisfaction is to learn to think like a customer.

_____ 10. Adopting a "good neighbor policy" can help in dealings with internal customers.

_____ 11. As part of trying to help solve a customer problem, you should assess its seriousness.

_____ 12. When something does not go as the customer needs or expects, service recovery becomes a vital step in maintaining the relationship.

Answers to Quick Preview can be found at the end of the chapter.

⚙ WORK IT OUT 7.2

Service Breakdown Examples

What examples of service breakdown have you experienced or can you recall from someone else's story? List and then discuss them with classmates. After discussing your lists, brainstorm ways that the organization did or could have recovered.

Work It Out

Work It Out activities throughout the chapters challenge readers' knowledge and provide an opportunity for individual and/or small group work on a specific topic or issue.

Street Talk

Street Talk sections have been added to each chapter. These quick tips are provided by customer service professionals currently working in various organizations and industries. They provide real-world insights into strategies and techniques that people interacting with customers are using every day to enhance their service delivery.

Street Talk

When talking with a client, I try to put myself in his/her position. What is most important to her? What communicates that I understand? What is one thing I can do right now to better his situation?

PATRICIA CHARPENTIER *Owner, Writing Your Life/LifeStory Publishing*

Trending Now

Trending Now are short inserts throughout the book that provide information about new and innovative strategies being employed in companies and industries to enhance the service experience for current and potential customers.

Trending NOW

In recent years the human attention span in many developed nations has gotten significantly shorter. This can most be attributed to the faster pace at which information is delivered through technology and the resulting conditioning of the brain to receive and expect material to arrive faster and on a more regular basis. Think about how fast television commercials and movie scenes change. Also, consider the video games to which many people have spent hours playing and have become accustomed.

From an interpersonal communication standpoint, this means that you must structure messages more concisely and deliver information in "sound bites" or short spurts of information for many customers, especially those who speak another language. This is opposed to droning on with a long sales pitch or explanation. The key is to watch your customers' nonverbal cues to detect their level of attention and comprehension. If necessary, repeat what you said in a slightly different manner to ensure effectiveness of your message and understanding.

Ethical Dilemma

Ethical Dilemma boxes throughout the chapter provide a scenario and ask the reader how they might appropriately handle the situation. Potential solutions or better practices are provided at the end of each chapter.

Ethical Dilemma 6.1

A supervisor at your company who typically demonstrates high decisive-type behavior criticizes you and other employees publicly, does not seem to respect people of other races, and very rarely asks for your opinion. You perceive that when she does take the time to get your input, and that of other employees, it seems that she really does not listen to what you have to say and usually does not take your advice or suggestions. In the past, you have heard employees and external customers comment about the supervisor's behavior. You know of at least one customer who said she was defecting to a competing company because of it. Should you address your perceptions with her? Why or why not?

Ethical Dilemma Summary

Ethical Dilemma 6.1 Possible Answers

High "D" behavior, such as your supervisor is displaying, can be frustrating and create challenges in the workplace. If you have observed your supervisor exhibiting the behavior in question on numerous occasions to arrive at your conclusions, and have validated them by talking to some of your co-workers, you may be doing the supervisor and employees a good deed by bringing your perceptions to her attention. This is because most people exhibit behavior of which they are often unaware.

Such unintentional displays can create communication and relationship breakdowns if the person is not made aware or does not change them. In a service environment, this can be a real issue.

The key to providing such feedback is to do so at a nonemotional time (e.g., not immediately following an event in which the supervisor does not get input or listen and you are upset about it). Try the following approach:

Pick a time when both of you can calmly and rationally sit down to discuss the issue, perhaps over

Small Business Perspective

Small Business Perspective boxes talk about situations a small business may be faced with and ask the readers how they would deal with specific issues. These situations allow for great in-class discussion.

Small Business Perspective

Since many small business employees often deliver service face-to-face with customers and have an opportunity to get to know their customers on a more personal basis, knowledge of behavioral styles can come in handy. As noted in the chapter, by recognizing specific traits or behaviors related to the various style preferences, you can adjust your service delivery to better meet the likes of customers if you work for a small company. You might even keep an informal file on each customer that you can reference when a planned meeting is coming. In it, you can note what you believe to be the customer's primary, and any secondary, style preferences. When possible before actually meeting with the customer, refer to the file and mentally think of ways to deal with the customer. Just remember to focus on a given situation and the dynamics occurring since people can switch to other behavioral styles depending on what is happening and with whom they are dealing.

If service interactions are typically over the telephone, you can still use the strategies you read about in this chapter. Simply by listening to customer tone, timing, delivery of messages, and their reactions to what you say, you can adjust your tone, selection of words, and the approach you take to handling the interaction.

Impact on Service

Based on personal experience and what you just read, answer the following questions:

1. How might behavioral styles play an important role in dealing with fellow employees in a small company? Explain.
2. If you worked for a small business, what strategies for using what you read in this chapter might help strengthen your service to customers? Explain.

Summary and Review Questions

At the end of each chapter is a **Summary** and also **Review Questions,** which bring together the key elements and issues encountered in the chapter. These questions will test the readers' absorption level for the content they have read and highlight areas for remedial study to ensure mastery of the chapter topic.

Search It Out

Search It Out activities at the end of chapters provide the opportunity to research chapter-related skills on the Internet. In each chapter, readers will explore the Internet to obtain a variety of customer service facts, figures, and related information associated with chapter content to use in group activities, presentations, or discussions. Visit the website especially designed by McGraw-Hill for *Customer Service: Skills for Success* at www.mhhe.com/customerservice.

Collaborative Learning Activity

Collaborative Learning Activities allow one or more readers to work together with the instructor and actually address a customer service issue in order to practice their skills, find answers to various questions, and reinforce their knowledge of the chapter topic.

Face to Face

Face to Face exercises are customer service scenarios in which readers assume the role of a specified employee and use information provided to determine how they might handle a similar customer service issue if faced with it on the job.

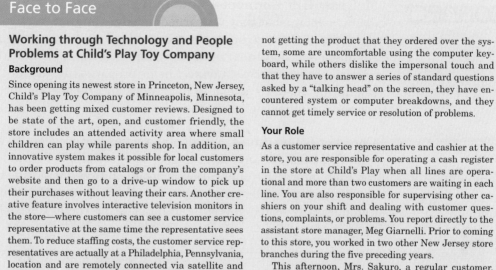

Working through Technology and People Problems at Child's Play Toy Company

Background

Since opening its newest store in Princeton, New Jersey, Child's Play Toy Company of Minneapolis, Minnesota, has been getting mixed customer reviews. Designed to be state of the art, open, and customer friendly, the store includes an attended activity area where small children can play while parents shop. In addition, an innovative system makes it possible for local customers to order products from catalogs or from the company's website and then go to a drive-up window to pick up their purchases without leaving their cars. Another creative feature involves interactive television monitors in the store—where customers can see a customer service representative at the same time the representative sees them. To reduce staffing costs, the customer service representatives are actually at a Philadelphia, Pennsylvania, location and are remotely connected via satellite and computer to all new stores. This system is used for special ordering, billing questions, and complaint resolution. Customers can also use a computer keyboard to enter data or search for product information online through the company's website while in the store.

not getting the product that they ordered over the system, some are uncomfortable using the computer keyboard, while others dislike the impersonal touch and that they have to answer a series of standard questions asked by a "talking head" on the screen, they have encountered system or computer breakdowns, and they cannot get timely service or resolution of problems.

Your Role

As a customer service representative and cashier at the store, you are responsible for operating a cash register in the store at Child's Play when all lines are operational and more than two customers are waiting in each line. You are also responsible for supervising other cashiers on your shift and dealing with customer questions, complaints, or problems. You report directly to the assistant store manager, Meg Giarnelli. Prior to coming to this store, you worked in two other New Jersey store branches during the five preceding years.

This afternoon, Mrs. Sakuro, a regular customer, came to you. She was obviously frustrated and pointed her finger at you as she shouted, "You people are stupid!" She also demanded to speak with the manager and threatened that "if you people do not want my business, I will go to another store!" Apparently, a doll that Mrs.

Planning to Serve

Planning to Serve activities provide a roadmap for planning strategies and identifying techniques from the book that can be used to provide superior customer service in the future.

Planning to Serve

In order to ensure that you are prepared to provide premium service to your customers, take some time to think about typical customer situations in which you were personally involved or that you have witnessed. Answer the following questions on the basis of situations recalled.

1. What types of behaviors does the average customer exhibit?

2. Based on what you learned about behavioral styles in general, and your preferred style, what service strategies could you use if you were involved with the behaviors identified in question 1?

3. In difficult or emotional service situations, what behaviors often manifest themselves?

4. What strategies might help you in dealing with such customer behaviors?

Quick Preview Answers and Ethical Dilemma Summary

These are the answers to the **Quick Preview** pretest at the beginning of the chapter, along with possible answers to the **Ethical Dilemma** features throughout the chapter.

Appendix

Use the **Reader Satisfaction Survey** found in the **Appendix** at the end of the text to provide the author with feedback. For doing so, readers will receive a free publication on interpersonal communication written by this book's author (Robert W. Lucas).

The Customer Service Text That Gives You More

STUDENT RESOURCES

McGraw-Hill Connect—New to This Edition!   *Connect* allows students to apply what they've learned in a dynamic, interactive way. With the purchase of *Connect*, students are provided an online assignment and assessment solution that connects them with the tools and resources they need to achieve success. *Connect* helps prepare students for their future by prompting them to complete homework in preparation for class, master concepts, and review for exams.

Connect Interactives   Students practice key concepts by applying them with these textbook-specific interactive exercises. Provided for every chapter, each interactive application is designed to reinforce key topics and further increase student comprehension. All interactive applications are automatically scored and entered into the instructor's gradebook.

QUESTION PROGRESS   Case Analysis

Case Analysis

Contributing to the Service Culture

Read the report and answer all questions.

Sam Adams is the customer service manager of a large chain store specializing in high-end toys called P-Town. Sam has been asked by his manager, the Chief Operating Officer, to come up with some ideas statements that exemplify a service culture, to be considered for use in the mission and values statement.

Sam (speaking with a small group of employees informally or in a meeting setting): As you know P-Town is in the process of reinventing itself and the higher-ups want to develop a mission statement which addresses this goal. They did a customer feedback survey, and we received very high ratings. As a result, they have asked us, since we are the ones that work with the customers every day, to come up with some ideas.

Jodi: You called us in on a Saturday morning for this? The higher-ups aren't going to use our ideas anyway. Why should we spend all of this time working on something they won't even use?

Latisha: I disagree. I think it is great they are asking for our input, and we won't know if they use our ideas unless we provide them

1. Which of the following is NOT a customer expectation?
   select ▼

2. Which of the following are good ways for customer service data collection?
   select ▼

3. Which of the following is NOT a component of a service culture?
   select ▼

LearnSmart   *LearnSmart* is the premier learning system designed to effectively assess a student's knowledge of course content through a series of adaptive questions, intelligently pinpointing concepts that the student does not understand and mapping out a personalized study plan for success. *LearnSmart* prepares students, allowing instructors to truly use valuable class time for discussion.

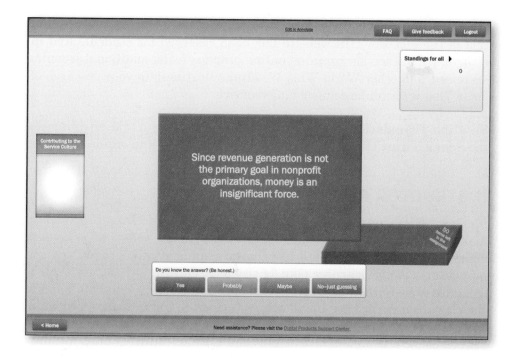

SmartBook   Fueled by *LearnSmart, SmartBook* is the first and only
adaptive reading experience available today. Distinguishing what students
know from what they don't, and honing in on concepts they are most likely
to forget, *SmartBook* personalizes content for each student in a continuously adapting reading experience. Reading is no longer a passive and lin-
ear experience, but an engaging and dynamic one where students are more
likely to master and retain important concepts, therefore coming to class
better prepared. Valuable reports provide instructors insight as to how students are progressing through textbook content, useful for shaping in-class
time or assessment. As a result of the adaptive reading experience found in
SmartBook, students are more likely to retain knowledge, stay in class,
and get better grades.

SMARTBOOK™

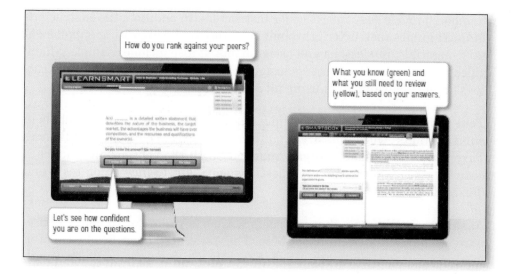

Online Learning Center (OLC)—Student Content   A separate section of the McGraw-Hill website has been reserved for students and instructors. This section contains online practice tests, additional learning exercises, and other World Wide Web links to stimulate your research efforts. Visit www.mhhe.com/customerservice.

Spanish Translations   Spanish-speaking readers can take advantage of the Spanish translations of the glossary of key terms and online quizzes.

INSTRUCTOR RESOURCES

McGraw-Hill Connect—New to This Edition!   *McGraw-Hill Connect* makes it easy for you to integrate digital resources into your course. *Connect* offers online assessment materials that are automatically graded and can provide an adaptive learning plan for students. Our Digital Success Team is available to assist instructors in implementing and using *Connect* to improve the classroom experience by allowing students to come to class prepared. Instructors will find all the resources from the Online Learning Center, described below, conveniently located in their *Connect* course as well.

Online Learning Center (OLC)—Instructor Content   The instructor's side of the Online Learning Center (OLC), also at www.mhhe.com/customerservice, serves as a resource for instructors and has several features that support instructors in the creation of lessons. Included on the OLC are the Instructor's Manual (IM), which is organized by each chapter's learning outcomes and includes page references; PowerPoint slides that include additional instructor teaching notes; the Asset Map; and other valuable materials.

Instructor's Manual   The Instructor's Manual outlines course materials, additional in-class activities, and support for classroom use of the text. It has been organized by learning outcomes to give instructors not only a basic outline of the chapter, but to assist in all facets of instruction. For every question posed in the text, the IM provides a viable answer. The text page numbers provide easy reference for instructors. In addition, the Instructor's Manual guides instructors through the process of integrating supplementary materials into lessons and assignments. It also includes sample syllabi, video notes, and student success insights. Ultimately, this will be an instructor's greatest advantage in using all materials to reach all learners.

Test Bank   Every chapter provides a series of test questions, available in our Test Bank. Questions are organized by learning outcome and Bloom's Taxonomy. A Test Table aligns questions with the content and makes it easy for you to determine the questions you want to include on tests and quizzes.

Asset Map   We know that instructors' time is valuable. To help you prepare, we have created an Asset Map. The Asset Map identifies by chapter, learning outcome, and page number exactly which supplements are available for you to use. Visit our website at www.mhhe.com/customerservice to preview how the Asset Map can help!

PowerPoints PowerPoint slides, created specifically for instructors, include additional teaching notes and are tied directly to learning outcomes. Each slide also includes a text page reference for your convenience.

Sample Syllabi Six- and sixteen-week syllabi are provided in order to tailor content to different learning programs.

Create Instructors can now tailor their teaching resources to match the way they teach! With McGraw-Hill Create, www.mcgrawhillcreate.com, instructors can easily rearrange chapters, combine material from other content sources, and quickly upload and integrate their own content, such as course syllabi or teaching notes. For those instructors needing additional information on customer service skills of stress and time management and communicating with customers in writing, there are three additional chapters available in Create. Find the right content in Create by searching through thousands of leading McGraw-Hill textbooks. Arrange the material to fit your teaching style. Order a Create book and receive a complimentary print review copy in 3–5 business days or a complimentary electronic review copy via e-mail within one hour. Go to www.mcgrawhillcreate.com_today and register.

Basis for Content

This book draws from my more than four-plus decades of real-world experience in customer service environments, management, and human resource development. I have worked in sales, retail management, and service functions for a number of organizations; owned and run all phases of operation and management for an online retail business for nearly 19 years; was a partner in a human resource performance consulting firm working with client organizations in many different industries; and taught at numerous colleges and universities through the Master's level for over two decades. Currently, I am an author, a presenter, and the principal of Robert W. Lucas Enterprises, where I self-publish and promote my own books. Part of that role involves negotiating and contracting with other businesses and organizations and providing services to them. I deal with customer issues and needs every day and know that the techniques described in this book work because I and others cited in the book have used them effectively. While there are some research and theoretical sections in the chapters, much of the information is derived from personal experience, research, and reflections of actual customer service encounters experienced by others.

Whether you are new to the service profession and have no base of customer service knowledge, or are more experienced and wish to enhance your knowledge and skills, *Customer Service: Skills for Success* and accompanying ancillary materials can provide a catalyst for your success.

I am confident that this book will assist you in reaching your goal to become a better service provider.

Bob Lucas

ACKNOWLEDGMENTS

Throughout the years, my wife, friend, and life partner, M.J., and my mother, Rosie, have sacrificed much as I have dedicated time and effort to developing tools such as this book to help others grow. Their support and love have been an invaluable asset in helping me reach my goals and are much appreciated.

A special note of appreciation also goes to Paul Ducham, Sankha Basu, Kelly Delso, Susan Trentacosti, Donielle Xu, Srdjan, Savanovic, Lori Hancock, and Debra Sylvester, and the entire McGraw-Hill team, for their expert guidance and support. Their efforts were essential in helping to create this book and add many new features to enhance its value.

Preparing any project of the length and depth of this book requires much assistance. No one person can bring together all the necessary knowledge, expertise, and insights to capture the essence of a topic.

Special thanks to the following service experts who provided *Street Talk* suggestions throughout the book:

Patricia Charpentier

Gary Goldberg

Jennifer Harper

Anne Hinkle

Stacey Oliver-Knappe

Sharon Massen

Barry Nadler

Tony Petrovich

Leilani Poland

Wendy Richard

Barbara Tanzer

Anne Wilkinson

Teri Yanovich

I also want to thank the three service experts who provided the *Customer Service Interviews* at the beginning of each section:

Ryan Eiland

Scott Larsen

Barbara Andryshak

It is with deepest gratitude that I thank to all of the following experts who took the time to read through many draft pages of the manuscript for this edition of *Customer Service: Skills for Success* and provide valuable insights, guidance, and suggestions for improvement. Without them, the final product would have proven to be of far less value to its users.

De Lena Aungst, *Sinclair Community College*

Mark P. Bader, MBA, CMPE, *Ivy Tech Community College*

Ed Cerny, *Horry-Georgetown Tech*

Toni Clough, *Umpqua Community College*

Diana Joy Colarusso, *Daytona State College*

Dan Creed, *Normandale Community College*

Yvonne Drake, *Pensacola State College*

Kelly Garland, *Tallahassee Community College*

Pearl M. Ivey, *Central Maine Community College*

Diane Kosharek, *Madison Area Technical College*

John Maier, *Northeast Wisconsin Technical College*

Todd Price, *Montcalm Community College*

Catherine Rogers, *Laramie County Community College*

Linda Rose, *Westwood College Online*

Joan Seichter, *Moraine Park Technical College*

Maria Stanko, *Ivy Tech Community College, East Chicago, Indiana*

Donna M. Testa, *Herkimer County Community College*

Nancy Warren, *Highline Community College*

Nancy Yates, *Butler County Community College*

I would also like to thank all of those reviewers who contributed by providing feedback and insightful suggestions for previous editions of the text.

Jorjia Clinger, *McCann School of Business and Technology*

Gary M. Corona, *Florida State College at Jacksonville, Kent Campus*

Michael Discello, *Pittsburgh Technical Institute*

Gordie Dodson, *Remington College Cleveland East*

Fran Green, *Everest University*

Toni R. Hartley, *Laurel Business Institute*

Richard S. Janowski, *The Butler Business School / The Sawyer School*

Diane Lolli, *Cambridge College*

Barbara VanSyckle, *Jackson Community College*

Scott Warman, *ECPI Technical College*

Joel Whitehouse, *McCann School of Business and Technology*

Special thanks also to the following educators who reviewed previous editions and offered suggestions, critique, and guidance in the refinement of the book content and format.

A. Murlene Asadi, *Scott Community College*

Blake Beck, *Idaho State University*

Claudia Browning, *Mesa Community College*

Gary Corona, *Florida Community College at Jacksonville*

Brenda Dupras, *The Saulter School*

Margaret A. Fisher, *Florida Community College at Jacksonville*

Matthew Graham, *Andover College*

Elizabeth D. Hall, *Tidewater Technical College*

Linda Harris, *Florida Metropolitan University*

DeAnn Hurtado, *Sinclair Community College*

Heidi Hutchins, *Gateway Community College*

Mark King, *Indiana Business College*

Lea Ann Kremer, *McCann School of Business & Technology*

Albert Mastromartino, *Sir Sanford Fleming College*

John Moonen, *Daytona Beach Community College*

Jacqueline Nicholson, *Holyoke Community College*

Shelly Rex, *York Technical Institute*

Paul Ricker, *Broward Community College—North Campus*

Judith Rozarie, *Gibbs College*

Dee Shields, *Indiana Business College*

Carl Stafford, *Manchester Community College*

Henry Tarbi, *Year Up*

Kathleen Wachter, *University of Mississippi*

Joyce Walsh-Portillo, *Broward Community College*

Michael Wierzbicki, *Scottsdale Community College*

Callie P. Williams, *Florida Community College at Jacksonville*

Richard Williams, *Nashville State Community College*

CUSTOMER SERVICE

SKILLS FOR SUCCESS

THE PROFESSION

1 The Customer Service Profession

2 Contributing to the Service Culture

Customer Service Interview

Ryan Eiland

Floor Manager, Fields Chrysler, Jeep, Dodge Ram

Total years' experience providing service to internal and external customers: 13

1 What are the personal qualities that you believe are essential for anyone working with customers in a service environment?

You must identify with your customers' needs and wants and most of all make a friend during this process. Really understand what he/she is trying to accomplish with this purchase. It's your job as a salesperson to identify and understand what this vehicle will do for the customer. Help the customer accomplish his or her goals, and you will have a client for life!

2 What do you see as the most rewarding part of working with customers? Why?

The satisfaction truly lies in helping a customer make the right decision for his or her family. This usually becomes a personal connection with your customer and leads to a trust and bond for future buying experiences.

3 What do you believe the biggest challenge(s) is/are in working with customers?

The biggest challenges arise with needs versus wants. Does the customer's budget reflect what his or her wants are versus his or her needs? Sometimes sensibility has to overrule emotion and what the customer's budget can allow. A great salesperson can act as a counselor to identify what is really a need versus what is a desire, and make sense of it to the consumer.

4 What changes have you seen in the customer service profession since you took your first service provider position?

The consumer has many avenues in which to voice his or her opinion today: Via Twitter, Facebook, Google Reviews, just to name a few. For this reason alone it is extremely important to make the most of every opportunity to do the very best to treat everyone with the utmost respect and dignity he or she deserves, regardless of his or her situation. If you follow this policy, the respect you will gain, and the potential customers you will have the opportunity to serve, will be exceptional. Customer service in the viral media we have today is just as good as marketing and spending company money.

5 What future issues do you see evolving related to dealing with customers in your profession and why do you think these are important?

I work for a company that truly believes in customer service and is completely transparent in negotiations . . . in all negotiations. As my general sales manager, Brian Williams, says, "We are not trying to hit home runs on car deals! We are just trying to hit base hits." I think the customer can appreciate that we are in business to make a profit and employ local residents of the community. So in answer to the question, we adapt to our customers' needs and wants all the time or we would be out of business. So I expect no future issues. We can control the future!!

6 What advice related to customer service do you have for anyone seeking or continuing a career in a customer service environment?

Be honest and sincere. Identify a need versus a want or desire. Sell on what the consumer is trying to accomplish. Most of all, identify with your customer. Put yourself in his or her shoes. Forget that you do this every day for a living!

The Customer Service Profession

"Treat every customer as if they sign your paycheck, because they do."

—Unknown

LEARNING OUTCOMES

After completing this chapter, you will be able to:

1-1 Define customer service.

1-2 Describe factors that have impacted the growth of the service sector in the United States.

1-3 Identify societal factors that have influenced customer service.

1-4 Recognize the changes in consumer behavior that are impacting service.

1-5 List the six major components of a customer-focused environment.

1-6 Explain how some companies are addressing the changes impacting the service sector.

To assist you with the content of this chapter, we have added additional review questions, activities, and other valuable resource material at www.mhhe.com/customerservice.

IN THE REAL WORLD RETAIL—ZAPPOS.COM

Zappos.com was established as ShoeSite.com but soon changed to Zappos, or "shoes" in Spanish. The company grew to be the Internet's largest shoe store with sales of $1.6 million by 2000 and $8.6 million in 2001. By 2007, they were bringing in gross sales of over $8,000 million and had expanded their product line to include clothing, eyewear, watches, handbags, and children's wear. By 2008, the company hit a mark of $1 billion in sales, a mark that owners had set to do by 2010. They also, for the first time, made the Forbes list of best companies to work for. By 2009, Amazon closed a deal to buy the company, for $1.2 billion in stock and cash, but let it continue to operate as a separate organization.

A comment made by CEO Tony Hsieh in a 2009 interview for the *Las Vegas Sun* newspaper sums up the culture of Zappos.

> Call center employees don't have scripts and are encouraged to have fun with customers; each department has its own decor and theme; every employee gets a free lunch each day, and you're just as likely to see an employee parade making its way through the company's headquarters as you are a mail cart.[1]

On the company website, there is additional insight into how they became such a powerhouse that Amazon sought them out: "We've been asked by a lot of people how we've grown so quickly, and the answer is actually really simple. . . . We've aligned the entire organization around one mission: to provide the best customer service possible. Internally, we call this our WOW philosophy."

Further evidence of the company's customer commitment can be found online if you search terms like "Zappos flowers to terminally ill" or visit the *Harvard Business Review* blog interview (http://blogs.hbr.org/ideacast/2008/05/harvard-business-ideacast-96-w.html) of *Fast Company* co-founder Bill Taylor, who relates a viral Internet story about Zappos. According to a story that Taylor relates, a woman ordered numerous pairs of shoes for her terminally ill mother and missed the then 15-day free return policy. A Zappos representative called to find out if

the shoes would be returned and was told about the woman's mother. Since the woman was preoccupied caring for her mother's affairs and could not get to a UPS Store to return the shoes, the representative arranged a UPS pickup at her home. The following day, a beautiful bouquet of flowers was delivered to the woman with an empathic note. The woman happened to be a prominent blogger and posted the story online. As one might imagine, it went viral and Zappos' stature in the eyes of current and potential customers skyrocketed.

There are many elements of the Zappos culture that make it one of the most popular retail sites on the Internet. One of these is the people who work for Zappos. After an intensive screening process that starts with completion of a crossword puzzle, new hires attend a four-week orientation program. At the end of the first week, they are given the option of quitting, being paid for their week of training, and given a bonus of $1,000 if they believe they made a bad choice in coming to work for Zappos. This is because the CEO and other leaders are so focused on getting the "right" employees who fit the culture and share the same enthusiasm and customer orientation that they feel the money to have those who do not fit in leave is a great investment. Another cultural element contributing to their success is the current 365-day, 100% satisfaction guarantee, no-questions-asked free return policy. On their website, they even state that "If you purchase on 2/29 of a Leap Year, then you have until 2/29 the following Leap Year to return those orders. That's four whole years! Woot!" What other company do you know that allows that?

Scan the QR code or visit www.about.zappos.com and do an Internet search for the term *Zappos* for articles about the company in order to learn more about this unusual organization, their history, service philosophy, policies, and customer testimonials, then answer the following questions.

www.zappos.com

5

Think About It

1. From a service perspective, how does this organization differ from other online companies that you have dealt with or heard about?

2. What do you believe are the strengths and weaknesses of this organization? Why?

3. How do you feel that Zappos compares to some of its major show and product competitors (e.g., Foot Locker, JC Penney, ShoeBuy.com, The Gap, and DSW)?

4. What role do you think the CEO's approach to creating an informal and fun corporate culture plays in the service attitude of employees?

5. As a consumer, would you now consider using Zappos in the future? Why or why not?

Quick Preview

Before reviewing the content of the chapter, respond to the following statements by placing a "T" for true or an "F" for false on the rules. Use any questions you miss as a checklist of material to which you will pay particular attention as you read through the chapter. For those you get right, congratulate yourself, but review the sections they address in order to learn additional details about the topics.

_____ 1. The concept of customer service evolved from the practice of selling wares in small general stores, off the back of wagons, or out of the home.

_____ 2. The migration from other occupations to the service industry is a recent trend and started in the late 1970s.

_____ 3. One reason for the shift from a manufacturing- to a customer service–dominated society is more stringent government regulations.

_____ 4. As more women have entered the workforce, the demand for personal services has increased.

_____ 5. Advances in technology have created a need for more employees in manufacturing businesses.

_____ 6. Because of increasing income related to service, women often now have more disposable income as consumers than they did in the past.

_____ 7. As a result of deregulation in a variety of industries, competition has slowed.

_____ 8. Quality customer service organizations recruit, select, and train qualified people.

_____ 9. Luckily, the recent recession had little impact on the service industry.

_____ 10. To determine whether delivery needs are being met, organizations must examine industry standards, customer expectations, capabilities, costs, and current and projected requirements.

_____ 11. There are two customer types with which service representatives must interact.

_____ 12. An organization's "culture" is what the customer experiences.

Answers to Quick Preview can be found at the end of the chapter.

---

customer service The ability of knowledgeable, capable, and enthusiastic employees to deliver products and services to their internal and external customers in a manner that satisfies identified and unidentified needs and ultimately results in positive word-of-mouth publicity and return business.

service industry A term used to describe businesses and organizations that are engaged primarily in service delivery. *Service sector* is a more accurate term, since many organizations provide some form of service to their customers even though they are primarily engaged in research, development, and manufacture of products.

product Something produced or an output by an individual or organization. In the service environment, products are created to satisfy customer needs or wants.

LO 1-1 Defining Customer Service

CONCEPT   Customer-focused organizations determine and meet the needs of their internal and external customers. Their focus is to treat everyone with respect and as if they were special.

Many attempts have been made to define the term **customer service**. However, depending on an organization's focus, such as retailing, medical, dental, industry, manufacturing, or repair services, the goals of providing customer service may vary. In fact, we often use the term **service industry** as if it were a separate occupational field unto itself. In reality, most organizations provide some degree of customer service. For the purposes of this text, *customer service* is defined as the ability of knowledgeable, capable, and enthusiastic employees to deliver **products** and services to their internal and external customers in a manner that satisfies identified and unidentified needs and ultimately results in positive word-of-mouth publicity and return business. By doing these

Some common characteristics for leading-edge customer-focused organizations are

- They have and support internal customers (for example, peers, co-workers, bosses, subordinates, people from other areas of their organization) and/or external customers (for example, vendors, suppliers, various telephone callers, walk-in customers, other organizations, others not from within the organization).
- Their focus is on determining and meeting the needs of customers while treating everyone with respect and as if he or she is special.
- Information, products, and services are easily accessible by customers.
- Policies are in place to allow employees to make decisions in order to better serve customers.
- Management and systems support and appropriately reward employee efforts to serve customers.
- Reevaluation and quantitative measurement of the way business is conducted is ongoing and results in necessary changes and upgrades to deliver timely quality service to the customer.
- Continual benchmarking or comparison with competitors and related organizations helps maintain an acute awareness and implementation of best service practices by the organization.
- The latest technology is used to connect with and provide service to customers, vendors, or suppliers and to support business operations.
- They build relationships through **customer relationship management (CRM)** programs.

FIGURE 1.1
Customer-Focused
Organizations

customer relationship management (CRM) Concept of identifying customer needs: understanding and influencing customer behavior through ongoing communication strategies in an effort to acquire, retain, and satisfy the customer. The ultimate goal is customer loyalty.

customer-focused organization A company that spends energy and effort on satisfying internal and external customers by first identifying customer needs, then establishing policies, procedures, and management and reward systems to support excellence in service delivery.

things, organizations can truly become **customer-focused organizations** (see Figure 1.1).

Many organizations specialize in providing only services. Examples of this category are associations, banks and credit unions, consulting firms, Internet service providers, utility companies, waste management services, county tax collectors, call centers, brokerage firms, laundries, plumbing and electrical companies, transportation companies, and medical or dental facilities. Other organizations provide both products and services. Examples are businesses such as car dealerships, brick and mortar (physical buildings) and online retail stores and manufacturers that have support services for their products, public utilities, supermarkets, theaters, and restaurants.

No matter what type of organization you work in, it is crucial for you to remember that when dealing with customers, it is not about you. Your purpose and goal should be to assist customers in meeting their needs

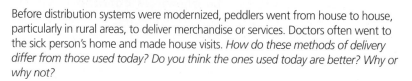

Before distribution systems were modernized, peddlers went from house to house, particularly in rural areas, to deliver merchandise or services. Doctors often went to the sick person's home and made house visits. *How do these methods of delivery differ from those used today? Do you think the ones used today are better? Why or why not?*

whenever possible. Be proactive and positive and strive to do the best you can by taking ownership of a customer contact situation. You have a vested interest to succeed since your success and that of your organization depend on it.

The term **service sector** as used by the Census Bureau and the Bureau of Labor Statistics in their reports and projections typically includes

Transportation, communication, and utilities.

Wholesale trade.

Retail trade.

Finance, insurance, and real estate.

Other services (including businesses such as legal firms, barbershops and beauty salons, personal services, housekeeping, and accounting).

Federal government.

State and local governments.

In addition, there are people who are self-employed and provide various types of services to their customers and clients.

> **service sector** Refers to organizations and individuals involved in delivering service as a primary product.

Customer Service Success Tip

Educate yourself on the service profession in general and your organization in particular by visiting service-related websites, subscribing to blogs that focus on customer service topics, and reading trade magazines, articles, newsletters, and books (e.g., *CRM Magazine*, Alexander Communications Group, or www.customerservicemanager.com). Focus on trends, improvements, and enhancements being made by organizations similar to yours. Also work to develop and expand knowledge and skills that add value to your organization.

THE CONCEPT OF CUSTOMER SERVICE

The concept or practice of customer service is not new throughout the world. Over the years, it has evolved from a meager beginning into a multibillion-dollar, worldwide endeavor. In the past when many people worked on farms, small artisans and business owners provided customer service to their neighbors. No multinational chain stores existed. Many small towns and villages had their own blacksmith, general store, boardinghouse (hotel), restaurant, tavern, barber/dentist, doctor, and similar service-oriented establishments owned and operated by people living in the town (often the place of business was also the residence of the owner). For people living in more rural areas, peddlers of kitchenware, medicine, and other goods made their way from one location to another to serve their customers and distribute various products. Further, to supplement their income, many people made and sold or bartered products from their homes in what came to be known as **cottage industries**. As trains, wagons, carriages, and stagecoaches began to cross the United States, Europe, Asia, and other parts of the world, they carried vendors and supplies in addition to providing transportation. During that whole era, customer service differed from what it is today by the fact that the owners and chief executive

> **cottage industries** The term adopted in the early days of customer service when many people started small businesses in their homes or cottages and bartered products or services with neighbors.

officers (CEOs) were also motivated frontline employees working face-to-face with their customers. They had a vested interest in providing good service and in succeeding.

When industry, manufacturing, and larger cities started to grow, the service industry really started to gain ground. In the late 1800s, as the mail services matured, for example, companies such as Montgomery Ward and Sears Roebuck introduced the mail-order catalog to address the needs of customers in the United States. In rural areas, the population grew and expanded westward, and service providers followed.

POST–WORLD WAR II SERVICE IN THE UNITED STATES

After World War II, the desire, and in some cases need, to obtain products and services started to grow throughout much of the world. In the United States there was a continuing rise in the number of people in service occupations. According to an article published on www.minnpost.com,

> Before World War II, the service sector grew because we got richer. Think about it: From domestic servants to waiters, blacksmiths to cobblers, and barbers to bankers, Americans have always been engaged in a variety of service activities. And, as the American economy grew and average incomes increase[d], Americans increased their demand for meals, repairs, grooming and financial services. Thus, more and more workers were *pulled* into the service sector by this increasing demand.[2]

THE SHIFT TO SERVICE

Today, businesses have changed dramatically as the economy has shifted from a dependence on manufacturing to a focus on providing timely quality service. The age of the **service economy** has been alive and strong for some time now. Tied to this trend has been the development of international quality standards by which effectiveness is measured in many multinational organizations. Organizations such as the International Council of Customer Service Organisations (ICCSO), www.iccso.org, work to help develop and promote service and professional excellence standards throughout the world. This is being done by setting internationally acceptable standards and certifications in an attempt to create a global atmosphere of service. For example, quality standards, such as ISO 9000 and ISO 10002:2004, were developed and are overseen by the International Organization for Standardization, www.iso.org. These are globally accepted guidelines for quality in the area of product and customer service excellence and were designed to help enhance the customer experience in affiliated organizations. In addition, to help attract and maintain a more loyal customer base, many customer-centric organizations are stepping up their enthusiasm and support for such standards. To project a more service-oriented posture, they are adding executive-level positions such as chief customer officer (CCO), or similar prestigious titles, to their hierarchy. CCOs are responsible for all operational functions

service economy A term used to describe the trend in which businesses have shifted from primarily production and manufacturing to more service delivery. As part of this evolution, many organizations have developed specifically to provide services to customers.

FIGURE 1.2

From Pre–World War II
Occupations to Service
Occupations

Typical Former Occupations	Typical Service Occupations
Farmer	Salesperson
Ranch worker	Insurance agent
Machinist	Food service
Engineer	Administrative assistant
Steelworker	Flight attendant
Homemaker	Call center representative
Factory worker	Repair person
Miner	Travel professional
Tradesperson (for example, watchmaker)	Child care provider
Railroad worker	Security guard

that influence or relate to customer relations and add a new dimension to the customer service career path.

As shown in Figure 1.2, since the end of World War II, people have moved from other occupations to join the rapidly growing ranks of service professionals.

KNOWLEDGE CHECK

1. Why is "service sector" a more appropriate term than "service industry" when describing customer service?

2. What are common characteristics of leading edge customer-focused organizations?

3. How has the concept of customer service evolved since its origin?

LO 1-2 Growth of the Service Sector

CONCEPT   Technology has affected jobs in the following ways: quantity of jobs created, distribution of jobs, and quality of jobs. The service sector is projected to have the largest job growth.

According to the U.S. Bureau of Labor Statistics, assuming a full-employment economy by the year 2020, the United States is projected to add 20.5 million new jobs by that year. Their research suggests that the fastest growth will be in personal care, healthcare, and community and social service occupations.[3] Further projections are that "Jobs requiring a master's degree will grow fastest while those requiring a high school diploma will experience the slowest growth. The employment shift in the U.S. economy away from goods-producing in favor of service-providing industries is expected to continue. Service-providing industries are anticipated to generate nearly 18 million new wage and salary jobs. As with goods-producing industries, growth among service-producing industries will vary."[4] (See Figure 1.3.)

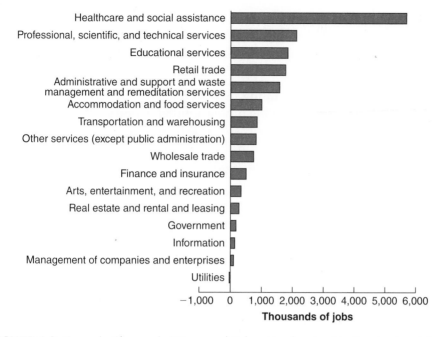

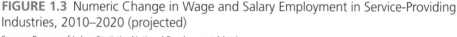

FIGURE 1.3 Numeric Change in Wage and Salary Employment in Service-Providing Industries, 2010–2020 (projected)

Source: Bureau of Labor Statistics National Employment Matrix.

The impact of these numbers can be seen as technology replaces many production line workers and increasing numbers of service jobs are created. This comes about because, as greater numbers and greater varieties of goods are produced, more service people, salespeople, managers, and other professionals are needed to design and market service delivery systems that support those products. Technology-related service jobs such as those of database administrators, computer support specialists, computer scientists, computer engineers, and systems analysts are expected to continue to grow at a rapid pace.

Other data from the Bureau of Labor Statistics[5] that apply the changes in the service industry include (see Figure 1.4)

- The U.S. labor force, comprised of all persons age 16 and older in the civilian noninstitutional population who are either employed or unemployed but seeking work, is growing slower than in the past, becoming more diverse and aging. The result is that the civilian labor force is projected to reach 164.4 million by 2020, an increase of 6.8 percent.

- By 2020, projections are that the U.S. workforce will become even more diverse than it is now. Blacks, Asians, and other groups will assume a greater share of workforce positions while whites will continue to shrink as job shareholders. Among ethnic groups, Hispanics are projected to increase from 14.8 to 18.6 percent of the workforce.

Street Talk Adopt an Internal Client Mentality

One company I used to work with instilled in me the mentality that my hiring managers were my internal candidates, thus making me treat them as a customer. This does not mean they walked all over me or got everything they wanted. Focusing on others in your organization as customers helps make you more responsive. I remember a manager who had a very detail-oriented spreadsheet that he wanted completed on a weekly basis . . . much to my chagrin and that of his other direct reports. One such manager asked me if it drove me crazy to always have to update the form. My response to him was, "He's my manager and if he wants it, he will get it."

ANNE WILKINSON

⊙ **WORK IT OUT 1.1**

Improving Service Quality

Take a moment to list some of the changes related to service that you have personally witnessed in the business world during your lifetime. Are these changes for better or worse? Why do you believe this to be true? With these changes in mind, what do you—or would you—do to improve service quality as a customer service professional in your own chosen industry or position?

- Overall employment in goods-producing industries is expected to increase by 1.7 million new jobs, driven largely by rapid growth in construction. However, projected growth among the remaining goods-producing industries is expected to be slow or negative.

- Productivity gains, automation, and international competition are projected to reduce the demand for labor in most manufacturing industries, causing job growth in manufacturing to decline by 1 percent. Computer and electronic product manufacturing jobs are anticipated to decline by 14 percent by 2020; positions in machinery manufacturing, apparel manufacturing, and chemical manufacturing also are expected to decline. Even so, jobs in other manufacturing industries are projected to increase.

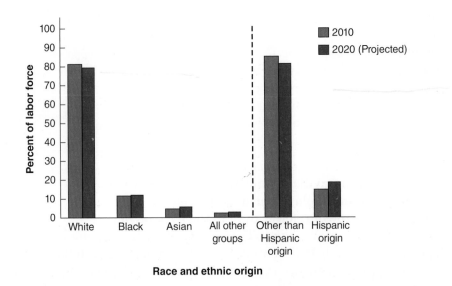

FIGURE 1.4 Percent of Labor Force by Race and Ethnic Origin

Note: The four race groups add to the total labor force. The two ethnic origin groups also add to the total labor force. Hispanics may be of any race.

Source: Bureau of Labor Statistics Division of Industry Employment Projections.

IMPACT OF THE ECONOMY

According to leading economists, today's economy is affecting jobs in three ways: (1) overall quantity of jobs created; (2) the distribution of jobs among industries, occupations, geographic areas, and organizations of different sizes; and (3) the quality of jobs, measured by wages, job security, and opportunities for development.

Quantity of Jobs Being Created

A variety of factors, including prevailing interest rates and consumer demand, typically cause companies to evaluate how many people they need and which jobs will be established or maintained. In addition, the advent of technology has brought with it the need for people with many new technical skills in the areas of computer hardware and software operation and maintenance. At the same time, technology has created an opportunity for organizations to transfer to automation tasks previously performed by employees.

According to the U.S. Department of Labor,

> Of the 20 occupations with the largest growth, one-fifth are in the office and administrative support services group. Together, these four occupations—bookkeeping, accounting, and auditing clerks; customer service representatives; general office clerks; and receptionists and information clerks—are expected to grow by 1.3 million jobs, accounting for about 18 percent of job growth among the 20 occupations with the largest growth.[6] (See Figure 1.5.)

Distribution of Jobs

Two parallel trends in job development are occurring. The first comes about from the need for employees to be able to have regular access to personal and professional networks and to engage in collaborative exchanges. This trend means that more jobs are likely to develop in major metropolitan areas, where ease of interaction with peers and suppliers, high customer density, and access to the most current business practices exist. Training and technology resources are also available in these areas. Access to technology resources helps ensure continued learning and growth of employees and also aids organizations in achieving their goals and objectives.

The second trend in job development arises from the ease of transmission and exchange of information by means of technology. It is called **telecommuting** and various other terms to describe it (e.g., e-work, telework, and work shifting). The practice does not include people who are self-employed and employees who work at home after hours without additional pay. With enhanced phone technology, **broadband Internet access** facilitates more personal communication with customers, suppliers,

telecommuting A trend seen in many congested metropolitan areas and government offices. To reduce traffic and pollution and save resources (e.g., rent, telephone, and technology systems), many organizations allow employees to set up home offices and from there electronically communicate and forward information to their corporate offices.

broadband Internet access Refers to a very fast connection to the Internet that is made possible by technology that can communicate up to 40 times the amount of data or information possible with the old phone dialup Internet connections. With broadband, users can download images, video clips, and music; send e-mail; and perform other functions at a much faster speed.

Today, many employees work from their homes all or part of the time. Telecommuting, as this is called, is used frequently by companies in large cities, such as Los Angeles, to decrease travel time. Do you think you would need different skills or abilities to telecommute? Why or why not?

FIGURE 1.5 Occupations with the Largest Numeric Growth, Projected 2010–2020

Occupation	Number of New Jobs Added	Percent Change	Wages (May 2010 Median)	Entry-Level Education	Related Work Experience	On-the-Job Training
Registered Nurses	711,900	26	$64,690	Associate's degree	None	None
Retail Salespersons	706,800	17	20,670	Less than high school	None	Short-term on-the-job training
Home Health Aides	706,300	69	20,560	Less than high school	None	Short-term on-the-job training
Personal Care Aides	607,000	70	19,640	Less than high school	None	Short-term on-the-job training
Office Clerks, General	489,500	17	26,610	High school diploma or equivalent	None	Short-term on-the-job training
Combined Food Preparation and Serving Workers, Including Fast Food	398,000	15	17,950	Less than high school	None	Short-term on-the-job training
Customer Service Representatives	338,400	15	30,460	High school diploma or equivalent	None	Short-term on-the-job training
Postsecondary Teachers	305,700	17	62,050	Doctoral or professional degree	None	None
Nursing Aides, Orderlies, and Attendants	302,000	20	24,010	Postsecondary nondegree award	None	None
Childcare Workers	262,000	20	19,300	High school diploma or equivalent	None	Short-term on-the-job training
Bookkeeping, Accounting, and Auditing Clerks	259,000	14	34,030	High school diploma or equivalent	None	Moderate-term on-the-job training
Cashiers	250,200	7	18,500	Less than high school	None	Short-term on-the-job training
Elementary School Teachers, Except Special Education	248,800	17	51,660	Bachelor's degree	None	Internship/residency
Receptionists and Information Clerks	248,500	24	25,240	High school diploma or equivalent	None	Short-term on-the-job training
Sales Representatives, Wholesale and Manufacturing, Except Technical and Scientific Products	223,400	16	52,440	High school diploma or equivalent	None	Moderate-term on-the-job training

Source: Bureau of Labor Statistics Occupational Employment Statistics and Division of Occupational Outlook.

distributors, and colleagues. With visual imaging and collaboration software like **Skype** and GoToMeeting, **instant messaging**, **social media**, e-mail, and other technology, employees can now work from their homes or satellite office locations worldwide. Government agencies, technology-focused organizations, and many companies with large staffs in major metropolitan areas that experience traffic congestion (for example, Los Angeles, Boston, Chicago, and Washington, DC) have used telecommuting for a number of years to eliminate the need for employees to travel to work each day and to reduce corporate overhead, such as office space and technology, utility, and equipment costs.

Small businesses are also using the telecommuting strategy as a way to hold down costs of hiring full-time employees and using a network of people from remote locations who have the specialized skills that are needed to provide service to customers. For example, the author of this book has run several small businesses and worked from a home office since 1999 while contracting with a bookkeeper, webmaster, marketing and graphics associate, and product suppliers in other parts of the country and staying connected with them almost exclusively through technology. In fact, he has only met his webmaster one time face-to-face in over 10 years. As a performance consultant, he typically saw his business partner one or two times a week and conducted a majority of their business via technology. Similarly, much of the contact he has had with customers and clients has been through technology.

According to Global Workplace Analytics,

> Federal employees have been required to telework to the maximum extent possible since 2000 (though only 5.2% do so). However, the current administration's proposed budget for 2011 calls for a 50% increase in telework. Both the House and Senate have passed bills aimed at enforcing federal telework mandates. More than two dozen federal, state, and local laws aimed at encouraging this practice have been proposed, and in many cases enacted.[7]

Even though many organizations have experienced savings in terms of time and money and increases in productivity, some companies (e.g., Yahoo in 2013) have reversed their use of telecommuters and brought their employees back to the organizational worksite after indicating discontent with the results of the efforts to have people work independently. Some pundits think that the lack of success experienced by Yahoo might have been the result of a poorly instituted telecommuting policy rather that a shortcoming in the process itself.

From an industry perspective, workers employed in professional and business services, in financial activities, and in education and health services are among the most likely to work at home. Technology, such as the telephone, fax, smartphone, and computer, makes it possible to provide services from almost any remote location. For example, telephone sales and product support services can easily be handled from an employee's home if the right equipment is used. To do this, a customer calls a designated toll-free number and a switching device at the company dispatches the call to an employee working at home or even in another country. This is seamless to the customer, who receives the service needed and has no idea where the call was answered. This also makes it easier for many

Skype Refers to a software application that is a division of Microsoft® and provides free or paid service that allows people to connect with other Skype subscribers anywhere in the world with voice, videos, or text messages.

instant messaging Refers to a form of Internet communication where users can transmit text messages or chat in real-time via the Internet to one or more people. More advanced forms allow voice calling, video chat, and hyperlinks to various media.

social media Provide technology where people network and share information, images, and ideas virtually through technology or social networking sites like Facebook, LinkedIn, Twitter, blogs, Wikipedia, or Pinterest.

companies to outsource some functions, thus saving money by relocating those jobs to geographical areas worldwide where wages and benefits may be less competitive.

> ### Customer Service Success **Tip**
>
> Make yourself indispensable to your employer by building a strong internal network of associates within the organization in order to reduce your chances of layoff during **downsizing.** This will help you share information and resources and add to your personal power base because you will have information that co-workers potentially do not have. Also, become thoroughly educated on the products and services that your organization provides and continually volunteer ideas and assistance to improve the organization.

downsizing Term applied to the situation in which employees are terminated or empty positions are left unfilled once someone leaves an organization.

Quality of Service Jobs

The last decade of the twentieth century saw increasing economic growth, low interest rates, and new job opportunities. Unemployment rates reached a historic low in 1999, then rose dramatically as the worst recession (2007–2009) or downturn in the economy since the Great Depression occurred and resulted in unemployment rates of 6 to 14 percent or more in most areas of the United States and around the world. As many people continue to struggle to find meaningful employment, social and workplace demographics continue to shift and people move around in a more mobile society. A major result is that job security has been affected and it is likely that competition for desired prime service jobs will continue to become much more intense into the foreseeable future.

Employees who do obtain and maintain the better customer service jobs that provide good working conditions, security, and benefits will be better educated, trained, and prepared. They will also be the ones who understand and have tapped into the concept of professional **networking**. This is the active process of building relationships inside and outside the organization through meetings, interpersonal interactions (face-to-face or via technology), and activities that lead to sound relationships and sharing of resources. Practices such as joining and becoming actively involved in committees and boards of governors or directors for professional associations or groups that support your industry will prove to be invaluable. Additionally, creating and maintaining an ongoing professional social media presence is crucial in finding jobs and developing links to other service providers and workplace professionals. Many good books have been published on the subject of networking. The Internet (for example, Amazon.com and Barnes&Noble.com) can provide such resources. Additionally, an abundance of technology (e.g., smartphones, wireless communication devices, and computers) can allow access, organization, and storing of information and provide a gateway to social networking sites like Facebook and LinkedIn. All of this will enhance the job search process and provide valuable information and opportunities for those attempting to prepare and position themselves for key jobs in the service sector.

networking The active process of building relationships and sharing resources.

Customer Service Success Tip

Social media can be a powerful tool in your effort to find a new job. Unfortunately, some people fail to realize that, just as technology can be an asset, it can also be a detriment if users fail to act responsibly, post unprofessional-sounding comments that are laden with profanity, or post inappropriate comments about peers, supervisors, and their organizations. Many job recruiters and employers actively scour Facebook, LinkedIn, and other social networking sites to see what they can find about candidates and current employees. There are many stories on the Internet about people who were turned down or lost jobs because of their poor judgment in posting comments or images. Also, keep in mind that your customers also use social media.

KNOWLEDGE CHECK

1. What is customer service?
2. In what three ways is today's economy affecting jobs?

LO 1-3 Societal Factors Affecting Customer Service

CONCEPT Many factors caused the economic shift from manufacturing to service. Increased technology, globalization of the economy, deregulation, and many government programs are a few factors. You will read about these and others in the following paragraphs.

The economies of America and many geographic areas are being dramatically changed by the forces that are shaping the world. Declining economic conditions, demographic shifts in population, constant technological change, globalization, deregulation of industries, geopolitical changes, increases in the number of white-collar workers, socioeconomic program development, and more women entering the workplace are some of the major shifts that continue to occur each year around the world.

You may wonder what factors have impacted the service industry. Some of the more important elements are identified in the following sections.

GLOBAL ECONOMIC SHIFTS

Not since the 1980s have economic indicators (e.g., stock trades, home sales, purchases, international transactions, and construction) been in such turmoil worldwide. Many people have lost jobs, personal savings are dwindling, people are losing their homes, and spending is down greatly around the world. As the economy took a downward spiral in the latter part of the first decade on the twenty-first century, consumer confidence shifted, many organizations struggled to provide quality service levels with reduced staff, and budgets and revenue from products and services slipped for most organizations as consumers held onto precious cash.

In addition to governmental policy and economic changes, new legislation impacting healthcare and taxes, job elimination in the government sector, and shifts in consumer spending have significantly impacted many organizations, forcing downsizings and in many cases closures. This is especially true in small businesses where a Gallop Poll of small business owners found that "30 percent of owners say they are not hiring because they are worried they may no longer be in business in 12 months." Further, 66 percent of those interviewed said they were worried about the current state of the economy and its impact on business. Obviously, this has long-term implications for hiring in the service industry and for consumers who have been curtailing their buying habits since the start of the recession out of the same fears that business owners are experiencing.

According to an interview comment by Phil Rist, executive vice president of BIGinsight, a consumer-centric information portal,

> Events that have transpired over the past four years have forever changed consumers, and this is evidenced in what they deem expendable and untouchable purchases. The financial meltdown, natural disasters, and the threat of terrorism have sent shock waves through consumers and impacted their priorities. The added layer of advancing technology has changed how they research and make purchases . . . the retail landscape will likely never be the same.[8]

Overall, consumers do business as never before. Large numbers of customers search and do their homework for products and services online and often use retail outlets as a showroom to physically examine things they are interested in potentially purchasing. The result is that sales in brick-and-mortar stores are down for many retailers and suppliers. Best Buy instituted a price-matching strategy in March 2013 to combat this shop-around practice. They decided to match prices for all product categories against all local retail competitors and major online operations such as Apple.com, Dell.com, hhgregg.com, homedepot.com, Lowes.com, and other highly recognized retailers.

Another important factor related to the changes in the economic environment that have occurred in recent years is that many companies have made dramatic shifts in the way they do business and attempt to attract and hold customers. The approach to customer service in many instances is no longer "business as usual." Instead of viewing it as something that should be done well, most organizations now see it as something that must be done.

Because of the financial meltdown that occurred during the high point of the recession, many organizations that have been household names for decades and had international presence have cut back severely on the size of their workforce and sold off, merged, or closed operations. They have also have taken dramatic steps to attract and keep customers. Companies like Chrysler, General Motors (GM), Citigroup, Goldman Sachs, and American Express received funds through the Emergency Economic Stabilization Act of 2008 from the U.S. federal government to remain financially solvent. In addition, companies struggled (and still do in many instances) to find a balance between profitability and providing quality service. For example, companies like Sears, JC Penney, Best Buy, Dell, Borders Books, Hollywood Studios, Blockbuster, and other notable companies have continually juggled their retail and service policies since 2010 in an effort to remain competitive and stay in business. Some succeeded while others did not. All of this turmoil and change has had an adverse impact on the economy, the service industry, and ultimately employees and potential employees.

SHIFTS IN THE POPULATION AND LABOR FORCE

There are a number of important factors impacting the future of the labor force in the United States. Today's labor force is older, more racially and ethnically diverse, and composed of more women than in the past. Additionally, it is expected to grow at a slightly slower rate than in previous decades. In fact, research by the U.S. Department of Labor indicates that "The labor force is projected to increase by 10.5 million in the next decade, reaching 164.4 million in 2020. This 6.8-percent increase in the size of the labor force is lower than the 7.9-percent increase posted over the previous 10-year period, 2000–2010, when the labor force grew by 11.3 million."[9]

According to U.S. Census data, the U.S. resident population will grow from 308.7 million in 2010 to 341.4 million in 2020, an increase of 32.7 million people in 10 years. Several significant factors will shape the future demographics of the U.S. population. The first is that there will be a significant increase in the older population. By 2020, the 55-years-and-older age group is expected to number 97.8 million, or 28.7 percent of the resident population, compared with 24.7 percent in 2010. A second pivotal factor is that immigration will continue to play a major role in the growth and makeup of the racial and ethnic composition of the U.S. population. Every race and ethnicity is projected to grow through 2020. However, the *share* of white non-Hispanics in the total resident population is expected to decrease.[10]

The upside of this growing and aging population is that there will be a need for more consumer goods and services to provide for the needs and expectations of customers. This will also lead to an expansion of jobs to fill the positions needed to produce products and serve customers.

Figure 1.6 shows how the labor force is projected to look by 2020.

Since the size of the labor force is the most important factor related to the size and makeup of the available pool of workers, organizations that

FIGURE 1.6 Median Age of the Labor Force, by Gender, Race, and Ethnicity, 1980, 1990, 2000, 2010, and Projected 2020

Group	1980	1990	2000	2010	2020
Total	34.6	36.4	39.3	41.7	42.8
Gender:					
Men	35.1	36.5	39.2	41.5	42.4
Women	33.9	36.2	39.3	42.0	43.3
Race:					
White	34.8	36.6	39.6	42.3	43.3
Black	33.3	34.8	37.4	39.3	40.4
Asian	34.1	35.8	37.9	41.2	44.0
Ethnicity:					
Hispanic origin	32.0	31.2	33.7	36.9	38.7
White non-Hispanic	35.2	37.1	40.5	43.6	44.8

hire service representatives will have to make some adaptations related to the way they recruit and hire in order to obtain quality candidates for open positions. This may include seeking viable candidates from other geographic areas if qualified ones cannot be found locally.

INCREASED EFFICIENCY IN TECHNOLOGY

The development and increased sophistication of machines, service equipment, and computers have caused an increase in production and quality. Three results of this trend have been acquisition of equipment that enhances the service experience for customers, an increased need for service organizations to take care of the technology, and a decrease in manufacturing and blue-collar jobs.

An advantage of this change is that machines and equipment can work 24 hours, seven days a week with few lapses in quality, with no need for breaks, and without increases in salary and benefits. They also potentially enhance the ease of service delivery and provide faster processing. For example, instead of having to direct customers to a cash register or central customer service desk in a store where they often have to stand in long lines to check out, individual sales representative can be given a portable data collection device that looks similar to an iPad screen and that they can carry with them. When a customer is ready to make a purchase, the sales representative simply scans the product bar code, takes the customer's credit card and swipes the magnetic strip through the device, and then has the customer sign the screen with his or her fingertip. If the customer desires a receipt, it can be sent to an e-mail address the customer enters into the device. When customers get to their computer, their receipt is waiting for them. The author of this book uses an alternative method to process book sales in the back of the room at his presentations. He uses a Wi-Fi-connected iPad with a small portable scanner called the Square, which plugs into the top of the device. Inventory items are already entered into the iPad, so once the appropriate item is selected on the screen, the customer's credit card is scanned, he or she signs on the display screen, and the transaction is completed much the same as described above.

All of this makes technology extremely attractive to profit-minded business and corporate shareholders and managers who are concerned with service delivery and how it impacts sales. Although technology can lead to the loss of some jobs, technological advances in the computer and telecommunications industry alone have created hundreds of service opportunities for people who install, monitor, and run the machines and automated services. Everything from point-of-sale transactions, toll-free numbers, and telemarketing or teleselling to shopping and service via the Internet, television, and telephone has evolved and continues to expand.

A major factor driving implementation of technology-based service is that, according to U.S. Census figures, over 228 million adults over the age of 18 have Internet access and use it at home and in other locations (e.g., work, library, or school). In addition, 76.7 percent of U.S. households reported having a computer of some sort and using Internet access in the home.[11] This number is sure to increase as the U.S. government focuses on enhancing its technology capabilities and giving citizens access to the

Customer Service Success Tip

Knowledge is power. Learn as much about as many software packages and pieces of equipment used by your organization as possible. Stay abreast of emerging technology trends in your industry. Volunteer to attend training and to work on committees tasked with identifying and implementing new service technology in your organization and professional organizations to which you belong.

Internet. One step toward the goal set by President Barack Obama that Internet access would be available to 98 percent of the population in the future was that $7 billion in the Recovery Act was targeted toward upgrading and expanding broadband access nationwide in order to provide access to rural areas and increase Internet capacity in schools, libraries, public safety offices, and other community buildings.

An impact of expanded Internet access is that more people will have access to products and services via computers, smartphones, iPads, and similar devices. They can shop and buy from the convenience of their home and other locations without ever visiting retail organizations. This means the need for fewer sales associates and other in-house service providers but opens the door for call centers and technology support people.

Globalization of the Economy

Beginning in the 1960s, when worldwide trade barriers started to come down, a variety of factors have contributed to expanded international cooperation and competition. This trend has been termed **globalization**, with many companies focusing on **business-to-business (B2B)** initiatives, as well as individual consumers. Since the 1960s, advances in technology, communication, and transportation have opened new markets and allowed decentralized worldwide access for production, sales, and service. To survive and hold onto current market share while opening new gateways, U.S. firms need to hone the service skills of their employees, strengthen their quality, enhance their use of technology, and look for new ways of demonstrating that they can not only meet but exceed the expectations of customers. All of this means more competition and the evolution of new rules and procedures that they have not been able to obtain in the past. Sometimes the deciding factor for the customer on whether to purchase a foreign or domestic product will be the service you provide.

At some point, many companies make staffing and/or production decisions based on bottom-line figures. When this happens, companies can, because of recent changes in the law, take their production or call center functions "offshore" (**offshoring**) to other countries (Mexico, India, etc.). In doing so, companies often save money on costs such as production, wages, and benefits. This is becoming more and more common in technology-oriented companies. Unfortunately, in some industries (e.g., high-tech, manufacturing, and telecommunications) there are simply not enough qualified job candidates to fill positions. For that reason, businesses look to alternate sources overseas. One point to remember about offshoring is that while many politicians and citizens demean offshoring as detrimental to the economy, the reality is that it is just one of the strategic decisions that help to keep companies that participate in the practice profitable and can actually add to the economy by generating profits for investors. In turn, they might put some of

globalization The term applies to an ongoing trend of information, knowledge, and resource sharing around the world. As a result of a more mobile society and easier access to transportation and technology, more people are traveling and accessing products and services from international sources than ever before.

business-to-business (B2B) Refers to business-to-business customer service.

offshoring Refers to the relocation of business services by an organization from one country to another (e.g., services, production, and manufacturing). The work may be kept in another entity of the organization that is located in another country or contracted (outsourced) to a third party. Typically, this is done to cut costs with cheaper worker salaries and/or tax savings.

For many customer service jobs, skill in using technology will increase your value as a source of information for current and future customers. How can you keep abreast of changes in technology?

that money into other companies and ventures and buy products that further stimulate the economy. Like any other corporate decision, there are pros and cons with the practice of offshoring.

In addition to offshoring, many organizations are also **outsourcing** job functions that have been traditionally handled internally (e.g., recruiting, payroll, benefits, training, marketing, manufacturing, and distribution) to third-party companies that specialize in these areas.

outsourcing Refers to the practice of contracting with third-party companies or vendors outside the organization (often in another country) to deliver products and services to customers or to produce products.

An advantage of outsourcing jobs, especially to other geographic locations where salaries are not as high, is that it can help keep costs low, increase profit margins, and aid companies in their efforts to be globally competitive. A major disadvantage is that the practice potentially takes jobs away from local workers.

According to research done by business and accounting firm BDO USA,

> manufacturing is leading the charge overseas, as the most heavily outsourced function for more than 60 percent of U.S. technology firms. Research and development, distribution, and IT services and programming are the other company functions outsourced most frequently. In spite of supply chain interruptions that plagued the region over the past few years, Southeast Asia is the leading outsourcing destination for U.S. tech companies. The businesses are also moving parts of their operations to India, Eastern Europe and Russia.[12]

insourcing The opposite of outsourcing, this occurs when organizations decide to have internal employees assume functions and perform work instead of contracting it out to third parties or outsourcing it.

Related to offshoring and outsourcing, **insourcing** is an interesting trend started in recent years after many countries suffered severe unemployment and drops in their economies. With a glut of skilled employees available in the job market, organizations have been able to recruit highly talented candidates for relatively lower salaries and benefit packages. In some cases, this has negated the need for companies to seek cheaper alternatives overseas while bolstering their image in their home countries because they appear to be supporting local workers. While this has not reversed the offshoring or outsourcing initiatives of some major companies, it does hold potential promise for some skilled unemployed workers seeking new opportunities in the production and service industries on a local level.

DEREGULATION OF MANY INDUSTRIES

deregulation Occurs when governments remove legislative or regulatory guidelines that inhibit and control an industry (e.g., transportation, natural gas, and telecommunications).

Over the years, the United States has witnessed the deregulation of a number of industries (e.g., airline, telephone, railroads, and the utility industries from the later 1970s to the early 2000s). **Deregulation** is the removal of government restrictions on an industry. The continuing deregulation of major U.S. public services has caused competition to flourish. However, deregulation has also brought major industry shakeups, sometimes leading to breakdowns in service quality in many companies and, in some instances, closure or restructuring of the company. An example of this was the breakup of AT&T ("Ma Bell") into many smaller communication companies ("Baby Bells") in 1984. For a good overview of how deregulation has impacted life in the United States, see www.howstuffworks.com/10-effects-of-deregulation.htm#page=0.

These events have created opportunities for newly established companies to step in with improvements and innovations to close the gaps and better serve customers. For example, smaller low-cost carriers (e.g., Southwest

Airlines and Jet Blue) came into existence and provided cheaper fares to cities not traditionally covered by larger carriers or where demand is not normally as great. They even challenged the traditional internationally known airlines (American, United, Continental, Northwest, and Delta) on traditional routes to larger cities in the United States.

GEOPOLITICAL CHANGES

Events such as economic embargoes, political unrest, and conflicts and wars involving various countries have reduced U.S. business access and competition within some areas of the world (for example, Cuba, Vietnam, Iran, Iraq, Myanmar, and Venezuela) while companies from some countries have free access in those areas. These circumstances not only limit access to product, manufacturing, and distribution channels, but also reduce the markets to which U.S. businesses can offer products and services. In effect, every closed port or country border has a negative effect on travel industry professionals, such as reservationists, air transport and manufacturing employees, cruise operators, tour guides, suppliers, and border-area retail businesses.

Other positive and negative historical changes have occurred that—like it or not—have affected the way companies do business and will continue to do so into the twenty-first century. The passage of the **North American Free Trade Agreement (NAFTA)**, which was a trade agreement between the United States, Canada, and Mexico that eliminated a number of trade and investment barriers between the three countries, made it easier for many U.S.-based companies to relocate and send jobs across borders (offshoring) in order to find less-expensive labor forces, increase profits, and avoid unions and federal taxes. Like many such political arrangements, there are pros and cons to this agreement that impact a number of industries.

North American Free Trade Agreement (NAFTA) A trade agreement entered into by the United States, Canada, and Mexico to help, among other things, eliminate barriers to trade, promote conditions of fair trade across borders, increase investment opportunities, and promote and protect intellectual property rights.

Further events such as trade agreements with China and the thawing of relations with Vietnam in recent years have opened new political and economic doors. The shift in relations with Iran, Iraq, Afghanistan, and several other nations as the result of human rights violations, violence, terrorism, and military-related actions have created obstacles to international trade and commerce in a variety of ways in areas of the Middle East, Asia, and South America.

Geopolitical events such as these will lead to more multinational mergers and partnerships and a need for better understanding of diversity-related issues by all employees and managers. As a service provider, it is your responsibility to research these major world events and the cultures of others in order to better understand and relate to people with whom you come into contact in the workplace. Failure to do so can lead to breakdowns in service and relationships and ultimately the loss of business. From a personal standpoint, this could limit your ability to travel internationally and secure meaningful employment in the service industry and your opportunities (e.g., training, pay, enhanced benefits) in your organization.

With increased ease of transportation and communication, companies cannot afford to ignore international competitors. For years, North American firms viewed Japan as their chief economic and business rival. Now other countries are challenging Japan (e.g., Taiwan, South Korea, Vietnam,

Pakistan, China, and India) and are becoming firmly entrenched in the marketplace. An example of this was the introduction of the South Korea–made Kia car line into the U.S. market in the 1990s. Initially, many people did not view that company as a significant economic threat and the car was sometimes called the "poor person's automobile." Kias were even compared to the ill-fated Russian Yugo that was manufactured in Yugoslavia in the mid-1980s and introduced into the U.S. market. That brand quickly faded from existence due to its terrible quality. To the surprise of many, Kia has begun to turn its reputation around and has built a series of vehicles that are starting to rival the quality of larger U.S. manufacturers. Some of their models now win national awards and recognition from major car reviewers.

Another geopolitical event that has impacted many organizations was the formation of the European Union. This alliance of neighboring countries formed an economic market made up of 28 states that subscribe to a standardized system of laws that ensure free movement of people, goods, services, and capital. The majority of member states adopted the euro as a common currency and accepted it at a standard exchange rate. They also eliminated the requirement for a passport from the people of member countries traveling throughout the Union. The last step has positive economic implications because it encourages more use of travel-related services.

CHANGING VALUES

Values are internalized and a result of individual life experiences and societal mores. As the world changes, so do individual values in some instances. Such changes can have an impact on what people view as valuable and important, what they want and desire, and how they approach relationships with others around them. For example, many people in the United States value such things as personal control, equality, individualism, action, and competition. People from other parts of the world might value traditionalism, group cohesiveness, societal ownership, and acceptance of hierarchy, status, and birthright.

Throughout the world, there has been a tremendous amount of dynamic change in recent decades due to economic instability, quickly expanding and enhanced technology, global mobility where people move quickly and frequently, and other factors outlined in this chapter. The result has been a gradual shift in what many consumers hold near and dear.

Because different societies view what is important from different perspectives, clashes can sometimes result when service providers encounter customers who have differing values. The important thing to remember in such situations is that neither the customer nor the provider has the "right" set of values; they are simply different and each much respect and honor those of the other party.

As a result of societal values, companies often change their approach to doing business as a competitive strategy and to one of attracting and holding customers. This often includes shifting the way they do business, the products that they deliver, and their manner of service.

Because many consumers are now cost-conscious, are ecologically aware, and value sustainability, many automobile manufacturers are developing vehicles that are more energy efficient, use ecologically sensitive fuels, and cost less. Examples of this trend are the Chevrolet Volt, Toyota Prius, and

---

⚙ WORK IT OUT 1.2

Personal Exposure to the Global Trend

To help you recognize the impact this global trend has on you and your family as consumers, think about all the products you own (for example, car, clothing, microwave oven, television, portable electronic devices, game systems, computer). List five major products that you or your family members own, along with their country of origin (you can find this on the warranty plate along with the product's serial number, usually on the back or bottom of the product).

Nissan Leaf. Another example involving service enhancement is a move by the fast-food chain McDonald's in 2013. After seeing their market share slip to Subway, Wendy's, and other competitors, executives met with franchisee owners to discuss ways to enhance and speed up slipping service. They had found that one in five complaints from customers involved "friendliness" of service providers. To address this and other issues, the organization decided to focus on customer service as the real driver for branding the organization and increasing sales. To counter negative consumer perceptions related to service, McDonald's is looking at ways to increase staffing at crucial periods of the day. They also rolled out a "dual point" ordering system nationwide to personalize service. Under it, a customer places an order at the register and receives a receipt with a number. Once that number shows up on a screen indicating the order is complete, the customer picks it up at the other end of the counter from a "runner" whose sole purpose is to hand out cups, condiments, and other items to customers and thank the customer for coming into the store, thus freeing up cashiers to take orders correctly.

INCREASE IN THE NUMBER OF WHITE-COLLAR WORKERS

With the movement out of factories and mines and off the farm, more people find themselves working at a traditional nine-to-five office job or providing service on a variety of work shifts (telephone and technical support centers). This trend has led to the creation of new types of service occupations. Office workers need to have someone clean their clothes, spruce up their homes (inside and out), care for their children, do their shopping, run their errands, and feed their families. In effect, the service phenomenon has spawned its own service trend.

MORE WOMEN ENTERING THE WORKFORCE

The fact that more women are in the workplace means that many of their traditional roles in society have shifted, out of necessity or convenience, to service providers such as cleaners, cooks, and child care providers. The

A population made up of women, ethnically different people, older people, and those with other diverse characteristics contribute to a better understanding of various groups essential for service success. How can you improve your own knowledge of different groups so that you can better serve?

tasks previously handled by the stay-at-home wife and mother are now being handled by the employees of various service companies.

The Department of Labor has published statistics showing that women will comprise 57.1 percent of the labor force by 2020.[13] As women have become a larger part of the workforce, they have slowly seen their income levels rise compared to those of their male counterparts, but have not yet reached equality in workplace compensation. Even so, the direct impact of increasing income related to service is that many women often now have more disposable income as consumers than they did in the past.

A MORE RACIALLY AND ETHNICALLY DIVERSE POPULATION IS ENTERING THE WORKFORCE

As with the entrance of women into the workforce, the increase in numbers of people from different cultures entering the workforce will have a profound impact on the business environment. Not only are the members of this expanded worker category bringing with them new ideas, values, expectations, needs, and levels of knowledge, experience, and ability, but as consumers themselves they bring a better understanding of the needs of the various groups that they represent.

By 2020, the U.S. civilian labor force age 16 and over is expected to number 164.4 million. Among the major race and ethnicity groups, labor force participation rates according to race are projected to be whites, 79.4 percent; blacks, 12.0 percent; Asians, 5.7 percent; and all other groups, 2.9 percent. People of Hispanic origin are expected to total 18.6 percent of the total workforce makeup. That percentage is up 3.8 percent over 2010.[14]

You will explore these trends, and other diversity factors, further in Chapter 8.

MORE OLDER WORKERS ENTERING THE WORKFORCE

Think about the last time you went to a fast-food restaurant or a retail store like McDonald's, Wendy's, Burger King, Walmart, Kmart, or Target. Did you notice the number of people serving and assisting you who seemed to be older than people you usually see in those roles? This evolving phenomenon is the result of a variety of social factors. The most significant factor is that the median age of people in the United States is

FIGURE 1.7
2010–2020 Workforce Percent of Labor Force by Age

In 2020, baby-boomers will be age 56 to 74 years, and this age group will be the largest age group in the workforce, comprising 25.2 percent. Other age groups comprise the remainder of the workforce in the following percentages:

45–54 years = 20.1

35–44 years = 21.4

25–24 years = 22.2

16–24 years = 11.2

Source: Bureau of Labor Statistics Division of Industry Employment Projections, www.bls.gov/ooh/About/Projections-Overview.htm

rising because of the aging of the "baby-boom" generation (those born between 1946 and 1964).

From a workplace perspective, this means that more of the people in this age group will stay in the workplace or return once they leave (see Figure 1.7). This may be caused by pure economic necessity, since many people may have not prepared adequately for retirement and cannot be certain that the Social Security system will support them. Some people return to the workplace for social reasons—they miss the work and/or the opportunity to interact with others and feel useful. Whatever the reason for the desire or willingness of older workers to reenter the workforce, many organizations have realized that they often have an admirable work ethic. Also, since there are not enough entry-level people in the traditional pool of younger workers (because of lower birthrates during the 1970s), companies are actively recruiting older workers.

Ethical Dilemma 1.1

With all the competition for customer service jobs in your organization, you are concerned that you might not be able to get a promotion that you feel you deserve. You have heard that there are three other employees being considered for a job opening for which you want to apply. You know all three people and their work habits. Each has a "skeleton in the closet" related to performance issues in the past of which you are aware, but your supervisor is not. Your supervisor will be screening applicants soon.

1. Should you inform your supervisor of what you know to ensure that she makes an educated choice based on qualifications? Why or why not?

2. What could be the potential result of any action that you take about this issue?

See possible responses at the end of the chapter.

Customer Service Success Tip

Diversity is here to stay. Network with people from different cultures; visit ethnic restaurants; travel to other countries; read books and articles about different countries; learn a second language; and explore research on the Internet about different cultures, gender issues, age groups, religions, ability issues, and other factors that each person brings to the workplace. All this will help you more effectively interact with and maximize the potential of others while enhancing your opportunities for success as a customer service professional.

GROWTH OF E-COMMERCE

e-commerce An entire spectrum of companies that market products and services on the Internet and through other technology, and the process of accessing them by consumers.

The past two decades have been witness to unimagined use of the personal computer and the Internet by the average person. As an example of the impact of **e-commerce**, the retail trade sector (e.g., motor vehicles and parts, furniture, electronics, food, sporting goods, and mail order houses) had sales of nearly $1,106.8 billion in the fourth quarter of 2012. Nearly $59.5 billion of that amount was in e-commerce sales.[15] Almost any product or service is available at the click of a mouse, press of a key, or voice command. Consumers regularly "surf the net" for values in products and services without ever leaving their homes or offices. For example, many people do business with others all over the world without ever meeting them face to face or even talking to them on the telephone. Entire business-to-business customer relationships occur every day between people who are strangers but who provide key products and services to their customers electronically (e.g., computer programmers, accountants, book editors, graphic artists, and website designers). This new way of accessing goods and services through technology has been termed e-commerce.

Armed with a password, site addresses, and credit cards, shoppers use this virtual marketplace to satisfy needs or wants that they likely did not know they had before logging onto their computer and connecting with the Internet. And, with so many options available for just a small investment of time, they can comparison-shop simply by changing screens. No wonder the twentieth century saw the establishment of more millionaires and billionaires than any of its predecessors.

The creators and owners of the most innovative sites and products can provide products, services, and information worldwide without ever physically coming into contact with a customer, and yet can amass huge reserves of money. Examples of these success stories and popularity are eBay (an online auction service), Craig's List (an online listing of items for sale, services, personal announcements, local classifieds, and forums for jobs, housing, and events), Microsoft (software products), and Amazon.com (an online book and product seller and auction line), which have become household names and are used by millions of shoppers yearly.

Street Talk We All Have Customers

Even if you don't directly serve external customers, you always have customers. You probably serve an internal client. It could be co-workers, a manager, another team, or even another division within your organization. Learn as much as you can about those customers and identify the service you actually provide to them. Learn how you fill their needs. That helps you better identify the skills you need to improve, the industry knowledge you need to have, and potentially other ways you can support these clients. Enhancing these skills will create a stronger value for you as a team member.

BARRY NADLER

KNOWLEDGE CHECK

1. Of the eleven societal factors that have affected customer service, which do you think has the biggest impact? Why?

2. What other societal factors do you believe have affected the customer service sector? Why?

LO 1-4 Consumer Behavior Shifts

CONCEPT Americans and people in many parts of the world are now struggling to make ends meet financially due to some of the worst economic conditions in recent memory. They are looking for ways to maintain their desired standard of living without too many sacrifices. The result has been a shift in the ways people approach buying and obtaining the necessities and desired products and services.

DIFFERENT MINDSET

In the past, many consumers took a "money is no object" approach to shopping because, if they did not have cash readily available, they had several pieces of plastic in their wallet that allowed them to spend (often beyond their means). This was possible because financial institutions were doling out these instruments of commerce in a very haphazard manner to virtually all who looked like they could potentially repay what they spent. Unfortunately, that practice proved to be highly flawed. As a result, the financial institutions that let credit practices run rampant fell like proverbial dominos and took along the world's economy with them. In the aftermath of this economic carnage, many consumers have had a reality check and have learned that prudence is an important element of commerce. Plainly speaking, if you do not have the money, do not spend it!

A majority of consumers who formerly acted on impulse and bought whatever they desired are now taking a very cautious approach. Initially, the shock of having credit severely curtailed or cut off totally by their banks and credit unions sent many people into panic mode. As jobs disappeared, savings and bank accounts dwindled, and many people became homeless, a sense of panic spread throughout the United States and the world.

Economic reports are now starting to show that people have begun to shift from a "cutting back" mentality to a slightly more optimistic "cautious spending" approach. Part of their new strategy is to reevaluate their paradigm, or the way they look at products. Where they might have only gone for the nationally known brand or reputation in the past, they now evaluate and consider generic or store brands with comparable options and services offered by local providers. They are also being more conscientious about their spending and instead of seeking chic, top-of-the line products, they are shopping at discounters like Ross, TJMaxx, dollar stores, and BIG Lots; comparison-shopping more; bargaining with retailers; bartering; and renting versus buying items. The sales advertisements and coupons that they overlooked in the past are often sought out and acted upon. Online, they frequent www.eBay.com and similar auction sites or product clearance sites like www.overstock.com. Sites like www.pricegrabber.com that allow online product and price comparison are also very popular.

Another interesting outcome of the recession and massive job losses is that many consumers, especially younger ones, want to have less financial obligation in the event something traumatic happens in their life related to employment and financial security. A larger number of consumers are opting to rent rather than buy homes, cars, furniture, and even clothes. An article on the Bloomberg.com website emphasized how companies are moving to address this trend toward temporary usage versus ownership.

Customer Service Success Tip

If your goal is to ultimately have your own service-oriented business, start planning today. Take college courses on business-related topics, network with others in your industry through professional groups like the International Customer Service Association (ICSA), and conduct research on how to start a small business effectively through the Small Business Association.

Enterprise Holdings Inc. and Hertz Global Holdings Inc. . . . are expanding in what the Santa Monica, California–based research firm IBISWorld estimates to be the $1.8 billion hourly car-rental business, a segment dominated by younger drivers. . . . Startups such as Rent the Runway Inc. are supplying high-fashion apparel to satisfy those who want to rent, not own. CORT, a unit of Warren Buffet's Berkshire Hathaway Inc. . . ., is increasing its furniture-rental marketing efforts to college students and fledgling households. . . ."[16]

Today's consumers are also looking to save money in other ways. Instead of jumping in their car and driving around to numerous stores to compare sale prices and products, they often sit at their computer and do their research and buying there. They also look to consolidate trips in order to save on the amount of gas they expend. This is why stores like Walmart and Target Super Stores have become so popular and powerful.

EXPECTATION OF QUALITY SERVICE

Most customers expect that if they pay a fair dollar, in return they will receive a quality product or service. If their expectations are not met, customers simply call or visit a competing company where they can receive what they think they paid for.

An even more powerful example of a new trend where consumers are getting what they want via technological means was highlighted in an article on www.trendwatching.com. When consumers or others band together to send a message online, the results can be powerful and businesses line up to compete. Examples of the result of combined buying power that many people have come to use and trust include www.priceline.com and www.hotwire.com. The site dubbed the trend "crowd clout." An example of the full potential of such clout was seen in the efforts to get Barack Obama elected as the 44th president of the United States. Websites such as www.moveon.org act as a rallying point for civic and political action.

The expectation of quality service that most consumers have also creates a need for better-trained and better-educated customer service professionals. Not only do service professionals need up-to-date product information in order to be at the top of their game when interacting with customers, they also need to be abreast of current organizational policies and procedures, what the competition offers, and the latest techniques in customer service and satisfaction. Companies recognize that if they do not meet the service expectations of customers, they lose business and revenue. Thus, the superior service providers invest large amounts of money in training employees.

ENHANCED CONSUMER PREPARATION

Customers today are not only more highly educated than in the past, they are also well informed about the price, quality, and value of products and services. This has occurred in part through the advertising and publicity by companies competing for market share and by the activities of consumer information and advocacy groups that have surfaced. With the advent of the Internet, consumers are really in a power position when it comes to dealing with organizations providing products and services that they want.

For example, in the past, car buying was a painful experience for consumers, who were literally at the mercy of car salespeople who had all the knowledge about the industry, sales process, inventory, and pricing data. That has all changed for people who are Internet savvy and take the time to do their homework. Now, sites such as www.edmunds.com, www.kelleybluebook.com, www.usaa.com, and others have all sorts of pricing tools, interest calculators, invoice information, and articles on how to effectively shop for, negotiate, and buy a new or used car. Having the same information and tools salespeople have available evens the playing field.

Armed with knowledge about what they should receive for their money, consumers make it extremely difficult for less-than-reputable businesspeople to prosper or survive. With consumers now on the defensive and ready to fight back, all business owners find that they have to continually prove the worth of their products and services. They must provide **customer satisfaction** or face losing customers to competitors.

customer satisfaction The feeling of a person whose needs have been met by an organization.

KNOWLEDGE CHECK

1. What are the societal factors affecting customer service?
2. In what ways have recent worldwide economic events caused a shift in consumer behavior?

LO 1-5 The Customer Service Environment

CONCEPT In this section, the six components that make up a service environment and contribute to customer service delivery are discussed. Use these factors to ensure that a viable customer service environment is the responsibility of every employee of the organization—not just the customer service representatives.

COMPONENTS OF A CUSTOMER SERVICE ENVIRONMENT

Let's take time to examine the six key components of a **customer service environment**, which will illustrate many factors that contribute to customer service delivery:

customer service environment An environment made up of and influenced by various elements of an organization. The key components are the customer, organizational culture, human resources, products, delivery systems, and service.

1. The customer
2. Organizational culture
3. Human resources
4. Products/deliverables
5. Delivery systems
6. Service

Many factors affect your customers and what they perceive as quality service. With the exception of the customer, all of these factors are under the control of the service provider and staff.

FIGURE 1.8
Components of a Customer-Focused Environment

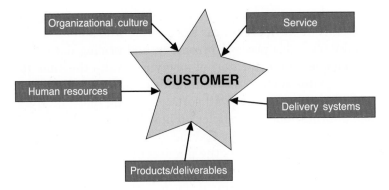

THE CUSTOMER

As shown in Figure 1.8, the central component in a customer-focused environment is the customer. All aspects of the service organization revolve around that crucial entity. Without the customer, there is no reason for any organization to exist. And since all employees have two types of customers with whom they must interact, either internal or external, there must be a continuing consciousness of the need to provide exceptional, enthusiastic customer service. As Karl Albrecht and Ron Zemke say in their classic book on customer service, *Service America*, "If you're not serving the customer, you'd better be serving someone who is." This is true because if you aren't providing stellar support and service to internal customers, external customers usually suffer. And, if you are not providing exception service to your external customers, your internal customers will suffer because revenue for salaries, benefits, training, equipment, and other important elements required to function will shrink.

External Customers

external customers Those people outside the organization who purchase or lease products and services. This group includes vendors, suppliers, people on the telephone, and others not from the organization.

External customers may be current or potential customers or clients. They are the ones who actively seek out; research; and buy, rent, or lease products or services offered by your organization. This group can sometimes involve business customers who purchase your product to include with their own for resale. It can also involve an organization that acts as a franchise or distributor. Such an organization buys your products to resell or uses them to represent your company in its geographic area.

Internal Customers

internal customers People within the organization who either require support and service or provide information, products, and services to service providers. Such customers include peers, co-workers, bosses, subordinates, and people from other areas of the organization.

Many employees in the workplace will tell you that they do not have "customers." They are wrong. Anyone in an organization has customers. They may not be traditional customers who contact you to buy or use products or services. Instead, they are **internal customers** who are co-workers, employees of other departments or branches, and other people who work within the same organization. They also rely on others in their organization to provide services, information, and/or products that enable them to do their jobs. The interesting thing about internal customers is that there is typically a symbiotic relationship between you and them for information, products, or services. That is because in addition to them obtaining things from you, you also depend on them for information, products, and services.

⚙ **WORK IT OUT 1.3**

Who Are My Internal Customers?

Take a few minutes to think about your current organization or select any organization with which you have been associated and create two lists: one of your internal customers and another of your suppliers. Then compare your lists to see which customers also act as suppliers and help you better serve the external customers of your organization.

Mc Graw Hill Education **connect**

Examples of internal customers include

Cafeteria workers. You are their customer because they provide products and services to you and they depend on you to buy food and drinks that they prepare or sell, thus providing them employment.

Human resources staff. Managers and other employees depend on human resources staff to support hiring and staff management functions and to manage employee benefits. The HR staff also depend on the managers and others to provide them with information and feedback in the form of employee surveys, updated job descriptions, forms, and other job-related information that they use to manage the HR function.

Print shop employees. These are the employees who provide printed and promotional materials used by various departments to support and market to their customers. They depend on department staff to provide them with business that keeps them employed.

Security personnel. These are the employees who all other employees depend upon to oversee safety and keep them safe. They depend on the other employees to provide feedback on how they are doing their job, to report hazards and safety or security violations, and to use their services (e.g., escorting employees to their cars in dark areas of the property after dark).

Recognizing this formidable group of customers is important and crucial to everyone in the organization for on-the-job success. That is because, in the internal customer chain, an employee is sometimes a customer and at other times a supplier. At times, you may call a co-worker in another department for information. Later that same day, this co-worker may call you for a similar reason. Only when both parties are acutely aware of their role in this customer-supplier relationship can the organization effectively prosper and grow to full potential.

The important point to remember related to your internal customers is that you must take care of them, just as you do your external customers. They must be serviced effectively and treated with respect in order to allow them to provide exceptional service to their customers. Without the information, products, and services that you provide them, they do not have the tools needed to do their job.

ORGANIZATIONAL CULTURE

Without the mechanisms and atmosphere to support frontline service, the other components of the business environment cannot succeed. Put simply, **organizational culture** is what the customer experiences. This culture is made up of a collection of subcomponents, each of which contributes to the

organizational culture Includes an element of an organization that a customer encounters.

⚙ **WORK IT OUT 1.4**

Types of Service

Take a minute to think about customer service. In what ways do organizations typically provide service to external customers?

overall service environment. Typically, culture includes the dynamic nature of the organization and encompasses the values and beliefs that are important to the organization and its employees and managers. The experiences, attitudes, and norms cherished and upheld by employees and teams within the organization set the tone for the manner in which service is delivered and how service providers interact with both internal and external customers.

HUMAN RESOURCES

human resources Refers to employees of an organization.

To make the culture work, an organization must take great care in recruiting, selecting, training, and retaining qualified people—its **human resources**. That's why, when you apply (or applied) for a job as a customer service professional, a thorough screening process will be (or was) likely used to identify your skills, knowledge, and aptitudes. Without motivated, competent workers, any planning, policy, and procedure change or systems adaptation will not make a difference in customer service.

Many organizations go to great lengths to obtain and retain the "right" employees who possess the knowledge, skills, and competencies to professionally serve customers (see Figure 1.9). Job candidates who are skilled, motivated, and enthusiastic about providing service excellence and who possess all or a majority of the requisite skills needed to perform required job responsibilities are often hard to find, expensive to recruit, and appreciated by employers and customers. As noted earlier, organizations now rely on all employees to provide service excellence to customers; however, they also maintain specially trained "elite" groups of employees who perform specific customer-related functions. Depending on their organization's focus, these individuals have a variety of titles (for example, a customer service representative in a retail organization might be called a *member counselor* in an association, but these employees often perform similar functions).

A challenge for many organizations is finding a way to attract and keep qualified employees. In years past, it was not unusual for someone to spend an entire career with one or two employers. Times have changed for many reasons. One of the biggest is that there is often no loyalty toward the organization by employees or vice versa by the organization toward employees. One U.S. Bureau of Labor Statistics study found the following:

In January 2012, median employee tenure (the point at which half of all workers had more tenure and half had less tenure) for men was 4.7 years, little changed from January 2010. For women, median tenure in January 2012 was 4.6 years, up from 4.2 years in January 2010. Among men, 30 percent of wage and salary workers had 10 years or more of tenure with their current employer; among women, the figure was 28 percent.

The median tenure for employees age 65 and over was 10.3 years in January 2012, over three times the tenure for workers age 25 to

FIGURE 1.9 Typical Titles and Functions Performed by Customer Service Personnel in Organizations (Median Incomes in Washington, DC, Area)

Receptionist/Front Desk Clerk

Salary average: $16.00 per hour

Employees performing this function in organizations have the primary role of meeting, greeting, and offering initial assistance to customers and visitors. This is a crucial role that starts setting the tone for how others view the organization. Whether in a doctor's or attorney's office, gym, car dealership, homeless shelter, or office building, these frontline service representatives are the standard bearer for an organization and should be adequately trained and empowered to assist those with whom they come into contact.

Customer Service (CS)/Member Support Clerk

Salary average: $17.00 per hour

This is typically an entry-level position requiring strong organizational ability; an ability to follow instructions, listen, and manage time; and a desire to help. A key function is clerical support, which includes filing, researching information, typing, and similar assignments. Deal with customers via the telephone, e-mail, correspondence, and face-to-face.

Customer Service (CS) Representative/Member Counselor

Salary average: $16.00 per hour

This position is an entry-level position into the customer service field (although many people have years of experience in the job). Since these employees interact directly with customers and potential customers, they need strong interpersonal (communication, conflict management, listening) skills as well as a desire to help others, a fondness for working with people, a knowledge of organizational products and services, and a thorough understanding of what a CS representative does. Key functions include interacting face-to-face or over the telephone with customers, receiving and processing orders or requests for information and services, responding to customer inquiries, handling complaints, and performing associated customer contact assignments.

Data Entry/Order Clerk I

Salary average: $14.00 per hour

The data entry/order clerk is an entry-level position requiring knowledge of personal computers and software, ability to work on repetitive tasks for long periods of time, and an eye for accuracy. Key functions include verifying and batching orders received from customer service representatives for input by computer personnel. In organizations that have personal computer systems connected by networks, data entry/order clerks enter data and generate and maintain reports.

Senior Customer Service (CS) Representative/Member Counselor

Salary average: $22.00 per hour

This position is usually staffed by personnel with experience as a CS representative. A position like this one requires a person with a sound understanding of basic supervisory skills, since job duties may include providing feedback, training, and support and administering performance appraisals to other representatives or counselors.

Service Technician or Professional

Salary range varies by specialty. For example, an Auto Service Technician/Mechanic with less than 1 year of experience can earn between $10.00–18.00 per hour.

This group provides many different types of services and carries a variety of titles (for example, air-conditioning technologist, plumber, automotive specialist, office equipment technician, law enforcement officer, firefighter, or sanitation worker). Each specialized area requires specific knowledge and skills.

Inbound/Outbound Call Center Representative

Salary range: $14.00–$16.00 per hour

Customer service representatives may perform some or all of the functions of this job, but often specially hired or trained employees fill the position. They make and receive phone calls with the intent of promoting or selling company products or services. In many organizations these employees are full-time or part-time sales personnel whose job is to use the telephone to call customers or potential customers or receive orders or questions from customers. Employees in these positions need strong self-confidence because of the number of rejections to offers and irate calls they receive, sound verbal communication and listening skills, a positive attitude, good knowledge of sales techniques, an ability to handle people who are upset, and a desire to help others through identification and satisfaction of needs. Key functions include placing and/or receiving calls, responding to inquiries with product and service information, asking for and recording orders, and following up on leads and requests for information.

(Continued)

FIGURE 1.9 (*Concluded*)

Help Desk Computer Analyst

Salary average: $24.00 per hour

Typically responsible for providing hardware or software support via an automatic call distributor (ACD) system (see Chapter 9) or e-mail to callers in various geographic locations for their desktop PCs, laptops, and peripheral devices. They answer calls, log all incidents into their call-tracking database, and provide technical assistance.

Counter and Rental Clerk

Salary average: $17.00 per hour

These employees work in a variety of organizations receiving orders for services such as repairs, car and equipment rentals, dry cleaning, and storage. They are typically responsible for estimating costs, accepting payments, and, in some cases, completion of rental agreements.

Other Service-Related Functions

In addition to these positions, many organizations have supervisory, manager, director, and vice president positions in most of the job areas indicated or in the service area as a whole. The existence of higher-level positions provides opportunities for upward advancement and learning as experience is gained.

Note: Salaries vary greatly in any occupation and industry and are often dictated by an employee's experience, education, knowledge, initiative, and ability to quickly assume more responsibility or perform at a higher level. Salary examples shown here are from www.monster.com. To get an idea of salaries for various types of service jobs in your area, visit www.monster.salary.com or www.payscale.com.

34 (3.2 years). More than half of all workers age 55 and over were employed for at least 10 years with their current employer in January 2012, compared with 13 percent of workers age 30 to 34.

Among the major race and ethnicity groups, 20 percent of Hispanics had been with their current employer for 10 years or more in January 2012, compared with 31 percent of whites, 26 percent of blacks, and 23 percent of Asians. . . . The shorter tenure among Hispanics can be explained, in part, by their relative youth. Almost half of Hispanic workers age 16 and over were age 16 to 34, compared with just over a third of whites, blacks, and Asians.

Younger workers are more likely than older workers to be short-tenured employees. For example, among 16- to 19-year-old workers, 73 percent had tenure of 12 months or less with their current employer in January 2012, compared with 9 percent of workers age 55 to 64.[17]

Figure 1.10 Lists some common competencies needed by successful customer service professionals.

FIGURE 1.10 Competencies of Customer Service Professionals

There are many things that make one successful in the service profession and life. Many skills and competencies that someone possesses can carry over into other situations throughout life. The following are some general competencies or qualities that can make you successful when interacting with internal and external customers:

Adaptability	Communication: oral, listening, and written	Judgment	Reliability
Attention to detail		Negotiation	Resiliency
Business acumen	Continuous learning	Organizational knowledge	Self-awareness
Caring	Creative thinking	Problem solving	Service orientation
Collaboration	Diversity	Professionalism	Technical expertise
Communication: open	Drive for results	Quality	Time management
	Initiative		

WORK IT OUT 1.5

Attracting and Training Employees

Think about organizational strategies aimed at recruiting and training service employees. What are some things you have heard or read about that companies are doing to attract, hire, and keep qualified service employees?

DELIVERABLES

The fourth component of a service environment is the **deliverables** offered by an organization. A deliverable may be a tangible item manufactured or distributed by the company, such as a piece of furniture, or a service available to the customer, such as pest extermination. In either case, there are two potential areas of customer satisfaction or dissatisfaction—quality and quantity. If your customers receive what they perceive as a quality product or service to the level that they expected, and in the time frame promised or viewed as acceptable, they will likely be happy. On the other hand, if customers believe that they were sold an inferior product or given an inferior service or one that does not match their expectations, they will likely be dissatisfied and could take their business elsewhere. They may also provide negative word-of-mouth advertising for the organization.

deliverables Products or services provided by an organization.

DELIVERY SYSTEMS

The fifth component of an effective service environment is the method(s) by which the product or service is delivered. In deciding on **delivery systems,** organizations examine the following factors.

delivery system The method(s) used by an organization to provide services and products to its customers.

Industry standards: How is the competition currently delivering? Are current organizational delivery standards in line with those of competitors?

Customer expectations: Do customers expect delivery to occur in a certain manner within a specified time frame? Are alternatives acceptable?

Capabilities: Do existing or available systems within the organization and industry allow for a variety of delivery methods?

Costs: Will providing a variety of techniques add real or perceived value at an acceptable cost? If there are additional costs, will consumers be willing to absorb them?

Current and projected requirements: Are existing methods of delivery, such as mail, phone, and face-to-face service, meeting the needs of the customer and will they continue to do so in the future?

SERVICE

Stated simply, service is the manner in which you and other employees treat your customers and each other as you deliver your company's deliverables. Effective use of the techniques and strategies outlined later in this book is required in order to satisfy the needs of your customers.

KNOWLEDGE CHECK

1. What are the six components of a customer service environment?
2. Which customer service environment element do you believe is most important? Why?
3. Do you believe that there should be a difference in the way you deal with internal and external customers? Explain.

LO 1-6 Addressing the Changes

CONCEPT   All customer-based organizations must provide excellence in service and an environment in which customer needs are identified and satisfied.

With all the changes, developing strategies for providing premium service that will attract and hold loyal customers has become a priority for most organizations. All customer-based organizations have one focus in common—they must provide service excellence and an environment in which customer needs are identified and satisfied—or perish.

learning organizations A term used by Peter Senge in his book *The Fifth Discipline* to describe organizations that value knowledge, education, and employee training. They also learn from their competition, industry trends, and other sources, and they develop systems to support continued growth and development in order to remain competitive.

To this end, organizations must become **learning organizations**, a term made popular by author Peter Senge in his book *The Fifth Discipline*. Basically, a learning organization is one that uses knowledge as a basis for competitive advantage. This means providing ongoing training and development opportunities to employees so that they can gain and maintain cutting-edge skills and knowledge while projecting a positive can-do customer-focused attitude. A learning organization also ensures that there are systems that can adequately compensate and reward employees on the basis of their performance. In such an organization, systems and processes are continuously examined and updated. Learning from mistakes, and adapting accordingly, is crucial.

In the past, organizations took a reactive approach to service by waiting for customers to ask for something or by trying to recover after a service breakdown. Often, a small customer service staff dealt with customer dissatisfaction or attempted to fix problems after they occurred. In today's economy, a proactive approach of anticipating customer needs is necessary and becoming common.

To excel, organizations must train all employees to spot problems and deal with them before the customer becomes aware that they exist. Every employee must take personal responsibility for customer care.

service recovery The process of righting a wrong or correcting something that has gone wrong involving provision of a product or service to a customer. The concept involves not only replacing defective products, but also going the extra step of providing compensation for the customer's inconvenience.

If a service breakdown does occur, managers in truly customer-focused organizations should empower employees at all levels to do whatever is necessary to satisfy the customer. For this to happen, management must educate and train staff members on the techniques and policies available to help serve the customer. They must then give employees the authority to act without asking first for management intervention in order to resolve customer issues. This concept, known as **service recovery**.

KNOWLEDGE CHECK

1. What are the six components of a customer service environment?
2. What is a learning environment and what role does it play in helping create a competitive advantage?

Small Business Perspective

Customer service is equally or more important in small businesses because those organizations do not have the deep pockets possessed by their multinational competitors. Because of limited staff and resources, these organizations must excel at identifying and addressing the needs of current and potential customers. They must then depend on every employee to put forth 110 percent effort to help satisfy customer needs and expectations. Smaller companies do not have the luxury of a large human resource team to support employees. The owners must get creative to figure out ways to effectively train staff in order to provide them with the knowledge, skills, and attitudes needed to excel and to aid employee retention.

The law defines a small business as "one that is independently owned and operated and is not dominant in its field of operation." According to the **Small Business Administration (SBA),** small business is big business in the United States. This is because

- The 23 million small businesses in America account for 54% of all U.S. sales.
- Small businesses have provided 55% of all jobs and 66% of all net new jobs since the 1970s.
- The 600,000 plus franchised small businesses in the U.S. account for 40% of all retail sales and provide jobs for some 8 million people.
- The small business sector in America occupies 30–50% of all commercial space, an estimated 20–34 billion square feet.

Furthermore, the small business sector is growing rapidly. While corporate America has been "downsizing," the rate of small business "start-ups" has grown, and the rate for small business failures has declined.

- The number of small businesses in the United States has increased 49% since 1982.
- Since 1990, as big business eliminated 4 million jobs, small businesses added 8 million new jobs.[18]

Nationally, these small businesses make up more than 70 percent of all businesses. They may be run by one or more individuals, can range from home-based businesses to corner stores or construction contractors, and often are part-time ventures with owners operating more than one business at a time.

The Center for Women's Business Research (CWBR) states that one in 11 adult women is an "entrepreneur," and that nearly half of all privately held U.S. businesses are 50 percent or more woman-owned. The CWBR also states that 10.6 million firms are at least half owned by women, and that "these firms employ 19.1 million people and generate nearly $2.5 trillion in sales. Between 1997 and 2004, the number of companies 50% or more women-owned increased at nearly twice the rate of all companies—as did employment rates."[19]

Small Business Administration (SBA) U.S. governmental agency established to assist small business owners.

(continued)

Impact on Service

Based on your experience and what you just read, answer the following questions.

1. What level of customer service have you experienced from small businesses in your local area? Explain.
2. In what ways have you seen service providers in small businesses excel from a service standpoint?
3. In what ways have you seen service providers in small businesses fail from a service standpoint?

Key Terms

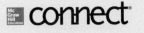

broadband Internet access

business-to-business (B2B)

cottage industries

customer-focused organization

customer relationship management (CRM)

customer satisfaction

customer service

customer service environment

deliverables

delivery system

deregulation

downsizing

e-commerce

external customers

globalization

human resources

insourcing

instant messaging

internal customers

learning organizations

networking

North American Free Trade Agreement (NAFTA)

onshoring

organizational culture

outsourcing

product

service economy

service industry

service recovery

service sector

Skype

Small Business Administration (SBA)

social media

telecommuting

LEARNSMART

Summary

As many organizations move toward a more quality-oriented, customer-focused environment, developing and fine-tuning policies, procedures, and systems to better identify customer needs and meet their expectations will be crucial. Through a concerted effort to perfect service delivery, organizations will be able to survive and compete in a global economy. More emphasis must be placed on finding out what the consumer expects and going beyond those expectations. Total customer satisfaction is not just a buzz phrase; it is a way of life that companies are adopting in order to gain and maintain market share. As a customer service professional, it is your job to help foster a customer-oriented service environment.

Review Questions

Either on your own or in discussion with someone else review what you have learned in this chapter by responding to the following questions:

1. What is service?

2. Describe some of the earliest forms of customer service.

3. What are some of the factors that have facilitated the shift to a service economy?

4. What have been some of the causes of the changing business environment in recent decades?

5. Describe the impact of a company's culture on its success in a customer-focused business environment.

6. What role does the human resources element of the customer service environment play in customer satisfaction?

7. What two factors related to an organization's products or deliverables can lead to customer satisfaction or dissatisfaction?

8. When organizations select a delivery method for products or services, where do they get information on the best approach to take?

9. What are the six key components of a customer service environment?

10. Why are many organizations changing to learning organizations?

Search It Out

www.mhhe.com/customerservice

Searching the Web for Salary and Related Information

1. To learn more about the history, background, and components of customer service occupations, select one of the topics below, log on to the Internet, and gather additional research data. One valuable site is the U.S. Department of Labor at http://stats.bls.gov. You can also type in the term "salaries" on a search engine to identify other sources of income information. Report your findings to your work team members, peers, or students, depending on the setting in which you are using this book.

   Research the projected salaries and benefits for customer service providers in your industry or in one that interests you.

   Search for information on organizational behavior and organizational culture and share your findings with the class. Discuss how behavior and culture impact service delivery.

Develop a bibliographic listing of books and other publications on topics introduced in this chapter. The resources should be less than five years old. You can do this by going to sites such as:

   www.amazon.com
   www.bn.com
   www.glencoe.com/ps
   www.mhprofessional.com

Find the websites of at least three companies that you believe have adopted a positive customer service attitude and are benefiting as a result. Select any issue raised in this chapter and research it further.

Note: A listing of websites for additional research on specific URLs is provided on the *Customer Service* website at www.mhhe.com/customerservice.

2. Visit the McGraw-Hill website for this textbook for additional activities, study materials, and resources related to book content at www.mhhe.com/customerservice.

Collaborative Learning Activities

Emphasizing Education

1. Team up with several other people to form a discussion group. Spend some time talking about what you believe the role of schools is today and how well schools are preparing young people for the work world. Share specific personal examples from your own educational background or that of someone you know.

2. Form groups of three to five members and discuss the impact of study results obtained by American Pulse™ when they asked: "What is the #1 issue facing you and your household going into 2013?" Their survey results follow:

Top 10 Issues Facing Americans Going into 2013 (Adults 18+)

Money—32.3%

Employment—8.2%

Economy—7.5%

Cost of Living—5.9%

Health/Illness—5.5%

Healthcare—5.1%

Taxes—4.4%

Housing—3.8%

Debt—3.4%

Government—3.0%

Source: American Pulse, January 2013, www.ProsperDiscovery.com.

As a group, discuss the following questions and be prepared to share your views with the rest of the class.

Based on what you read in this chapter, what factors might be affecting survey recipients?

How do the statistics shown in this study analysis potentially impact service organizations?

How do you see these responses personally impacting you in the future?

3. Form small groups and revisit the competencies list in Figure 1.9. What additional competencies do you feel are necessary to be successful when working with customers? Do you believe each of these competencies is crucial or not? Discuss your beliefs.

Face to Face

Getting Ready for New Employee Orientation at PackAll
Background

PackAll is a packing and storage company headquartered in Minneapolis, Minnesota, with franchises located in 21 cities throughout the United States. Since opening its first franchise in Minneapolis in 1987, the company has shown great market potential, ending its first year with a profit and growing every year since.

The primary services of the organization are packaging and preparing nonperishable items for shipment and mailing via parcel post. Air-conditioned spaces for short-term storage of personal items and post office boxes are also available to customers.

To ensure consistency of service at all locations, specific standards for employee training and service delivery have been developed and implemented. Before owners or operators can hang up their PackAll sign, they must sign an agreement to comply with standards and must successfully complete a rigorous eight-week management-training program. The program focuses on the key management and business skills necessary to run a successful business and educates employees on corporate philosophy and culture. In addition management offers tips for guiding employee development. At intervals of three and six months after opening their operation, owners or operators are required to participate in a retreat during which they share best practices, receive additional management training, and have an opportunity to ask questions in a structured setting.

Your Role

Today, you joined a Pack All franchise in Orlando, Florida, as a customer service representative. New-employee orientation will be held tomorrow. At that time, you will learn about the service culture, policies and procedures, techniques for handling customers, and specific job skills and requirements.

Before being hired, you were told that your primary duties would be to service customers, provide information about services offered, write up customer orders, collect payments, and package and label orders.

Critical Thinking Questions

1. What interpersonal skills do you currently have that will allow you to be successful in your new position?

2. What general questions about handling customers do you have for your supervisor?

3. If a customer asks for a service that PackAll does not provide, how will you handle the situation? Exactly what will you say?

Planning to Serve

Working alone or with others, create a list of the major issues facing the service industry or your organization (if you are working) and that directly impact you. Also, list strategies that you can implement to personally address these issues.

To do this, draw a line down the center of a sheet of blank paper. On the left side write the word "Issues" and on the right side, the word "Strategies."

Here is an example of one issue with strategies to address it:

Issue	Strategies
Service industry is growing quickly.	Do Internet research to gather statistics on an occupation that I am currently in or in which I am interested. Identify geographic areas of opportunity, possible salary and benefits, and specific targeted employers.

Quick Preview Answers

1. F   3. F   5. T   7. T   9. F   11. T

2. T   4. F   6. T   8. T   10. T

Ethical Dilemma Summary

Ethical Dilemma 1.1 Possible Answers

1. Should you inform your supervisor of what you know to ensure that she makes an educated choice based on qualifications? Why or why not?

   This is a touchy issue. If a candidate's performance (or lack of it) is affecting you, other employees, the organization, and customers, then you should probably approach your supervisor in a confidential manner to inform her of what is going on. The downside of taking such action is that your supervisor might question your timing and motives for doing so, especially since there are three different people involved and you have not come forward earlier.

2. What could be the potential result of any action that you take about this issue?

   In such situations, when you witness inappropriate activities or behavior of others that impacts the organization, you should discreetly point it out to them, and, if necessary, to someone in charge. It is unwise to save such information for an opportune time when you can use it in retaliation or to gain personally. This could affect how they, your supervisor, and peers view you and could impact trust in the future, thus negatively affecting your future opportunities. (See also customer service environment related to dealing with internal customers.)

Contributing to the Service Culture

"Your earning ability today is largely dependent upon your knowledge, skill and your ability to combine that knowledge and skill in such a way that you contribute value for which customers are going to pay."
—BRIAN TRACY

LEARNING OUTCOMES

After completing this chapter, you will be able to:

2-1 Explain the elements of a successful service culture.

2-2 Define a service strategy.

2-3 Recognize customer-friendly systems.

2-4 Implement strategies for promoting a positive service culture.

2-5 Separate average companies from exceptional companies.

2-6 Identify what customers want.

To assist you with the content of this chapter, we have added additional review questions, activities, and other valuable resource material at www.mhhe.com/ customerservice.

IN THE REAL WORLD RETAIL—BEN & JERRY'S ICE CREAM

Ben & Jerry's Homemade, Inc. is one of the twentieth century's fabled success stories. The company was founded in 1978 by two childhood friends—Ben Cohen and Jerry Greenfield. The two met in gym class on Long Island in 1963 and have been lifelong friends since.

Being children of the 60s, both Ben and Jerry concluded that college was a wise decision. This epiphany was driven in no small part by the fact that Vietnam was at a high point and the military draft was in full swing.

The two conducted extensive, yet rudimentary, research. Among other things, they visited libraries, stood on the corner and counted foot traffic, and brainstormed a lot. With their newly acquired knowledge, they decided to open an ice cream store. This decision was based on the realization that it was a simple business that did not require large amounts of start-up capital or experience. Also, Jerry had worked in his college cafeteria scooping ice cream, while Ben had several jobs driving an ice cream truck and managing freezer boxes for an ice cream company (counting product and loading/unloading trucks). With such in-depth experience, the two were destined to succeed in the ice cream business.

After searching for a location, facility, and equipment for their new enterprise, they settled on a rundown gas station building in Burlington, Vermont. Realizing that they had much to learn about the ice cream industry and would need more investment capital to get their business off to a sound start, they sought additional industry knowledge. Before they applied for a small business loan, they decided to enroll in a correspondence course on ice cream making from Penn State University. Since they could not afford the tuition ($5), they split the cost and sent in one fee, then jointly completed the mail-in materials.

From the beginning, Ben & Jerry's embodied the 60s "for the people" philosophy. Their free-wheeling, let-it-all-hang-out personas helped them succeed by endearing them to their local customers. They capitalized on the image that they were just two guys trying to make it in the business world. By developing a "people's ice cream" concept and using high-quality, locally produced ingredients, they built a loyal customer base. They also used low-cost, unorthodox marketing strategies, which continue to this day. For example, they priced their ice cream so the ordinary person could afford it (originally 52¢ per cone). Next, they started a free outdoor movie festival where they projected movies onto the outside wall of their store in the summer. They also started a tradition in which anyone can get a free ice cream cone on Ben & Jerry's anniversary date. The latter promotion is still in effect and each year they give away nearly half a million free cones nationwide.

The business philosophy of Ben & Jerry's is summed up in its Mission Statement, which comprises three parts: a Social Mission, a Product Mission, and an Economic Mission. (www.benjerry .com/activism/mission-statement/). As a result of Ben & Jerry's philosophy, the organization's community involvement and philanthropy through its Ben & Jerry's Foundation have brought international recognition over the years. In 1988, the company was awarded the Corporate Giving award for donating 7.5 percent of its pretax profits to nonprofit organizations. Also in that year, Ben Cohen and Jerry Greenfield were named Small Business Persons of the Year and received their award from President Reagan at the White House. From the beginning of their operation, Ben & Jerry's emphasis has been on quality products, affordable pricing, and supporting the local community. These factors have served the company well and gave a sound base for what has become a multimillion-dollar, international organization.

To get to the point that they are today, Ben and Jerry have used many unique marketing strategies and an approach that business should be fun and "real." From scraggy beards, jeans, and pith helmets, the two have strived not to be the typical corporate executives in a traditional work environment. As in the beginning, employees at

www.benjerry.com

45

Ben & Jerry's still enjoy a casual working environment where fun and activities are commonplace.

Some of the unusual marketing approaches used by Ben & Jerry's include

- Outdoor movie festival with free ice cream.
- Free ice cream cones for mothers on Mother's Day.
- Carnival-like performances by Ben and Jerry in which Ben (aka Habeeni-Ben-Coheeni) is carried aloft on a board, dressed in a bed sheet. Once on a stage, he assumes a trancelike state in which his body becomes rigid and he is suspended between two wooden chairs. At that point, Jerry places a cinder block on Ben's stomach and proceeds to smash it with a sledgehammer.
- The Cowmobile (an RV) that travels around the country to major locations and events distributing free ice cream samples.
- Pictures of Ben and Jerry that appear on their packaging with the phrase "two real guys."
- Sponsorship of the Newport Folk Festival in Newport, Rhode Island.
- Elvis Day celebration (on Elvis Presley's birthday).
- Products with unusual and memorable names (e.g., Cherry Garcia, Zsa Zsa Gaboreo, Rainforest Crunch, Norieggnog, and Peace Pops).
- The One Sweet Whirled Campus Tour of colleges and universities. The intent of the initiative was to raise the awareness of young people about global warming and the need to reduce CO_2 release.

In 2000, Ben & Jerry's was acquired by British-Dutch multinational food giant Unilever. Although the founders are still engaged with the company, they do not hold any board or management position and are not involved in day-to-day management of the company. Their efforts are more focused on the promotional aspects, "waving the flag" and speaking at events, and staying involved in philanthropic ventures.

Ben & Jerry's franchises and PartnerShops can be found in 27 different countries with nearly 500 in North America (United States and Canada). The latter types of franchises are ones in which Ben & Jerry's provides special incentives to qualified nonprofit organizations that open ice cream scoop shops. They are part of Ben & Jerry's social initiative to help nonprofit organizations generate revenue and to provide training in the food industry to otherwise unemployable young people.

Keeping up with pop culture is something that Ben & Jerry's has done from its inception. In 2012, the company introduced its own version of Greek frozen yogurt to tap into the societal trend to eat more healthy foods like yogurt. Also, it continues to work toward fostering a better world through partnerships with various environmental organizations and movements.

Think About It

Visit the Internet and library to learn more about the Ben & Jerry's organization. Based on what you learn and read above, answer the following questions and be prepared to discuss your responses in class.

1. Do you have personal experience with this company? If so, describe your impressions.
2. How does this organization differ from other similar successful companies of which you are aware?
3. How is this organization similar to other successful companies of which you are aware?
4. What does Ben & Jerry's do that encourages customer support and loyalty?
5. Does the organization do anything that might cause a negative impression in the mind of customers? Explain.
6. Would you want to work for this company? Why or why not?

Quick Preview

Before reviewing the chapter content, respond to the following questions by placing a "T" for true or an "F" for false on the rules. Use any questions you miss as a checklist of material to which you will pay particular attention as you read through the chapter. For those you get right, congratulate yourself, but review the sections they address in order to learn additional details about the topic.

_____ 1. Service cultures include such things as policies and procedures.

_____ 2. To remain competitive, organizations must continually monitor and evaluate their systems.

_____ 3. Advertising, service delivery, and complaint resolution are examples of customer-friendly systems.

_____ 4. To better face daily challenges and opportunities in the workplace, you should strive to increase your knowledge, build your skills, and improve your attitude.

_____ 5. Some of the tools used by organizations to measure service culture include employee focus groups, mystery shoppers, and customer lotteries.

_____ 6. By determining the added value and results for me (AVARFM), you can develop more personal commitment to service excellence.

_____ 7. Use of "they" language to refer to management when dealing with customers helps demonstrate your commitment to your organization and its culture.

_____ 8. Communicating openly and effectively is one technique for working more closely with customers.

_____ 9. Even though you depend on vendors and suppliers, they are not your customers.

_____ **10.** Business etiquette dictates that you should return all telephone calls within four hours.

_____ **11.** Your job of serving a customer should end at the conclusion of a transaction so that you can switch your attention to new customers.

_____ **12.** Customers want value for their money and effective, efficient service.

Answers to Quick Preview can be found at the end of the chapter.

LO 2-1 Defining a Service Culture

CONCEPT Many elements contribute to a service culture.

What is a **service culture** in an organization? The answer is that it is different for each organization. No two organizations operate in the same manner, have the same focus, or provide management that accomplishes the same results. Among other things, a culture includes the values, beliefs, norms, rituals, and practices of a group or organization. Any policy, procedure, action, or inaction on the part of your organization contributes to the service culture. Other elements may be specific to your organization or industry. A key point to remember about service culture is that you and every other employee plays a key role in communicating the culture of your organization to your customers. You may communicate the culture through your appearance, your interaction with customers, and your knowledge, skill, and **attitude**. The latter element is crucial in your success and that of your organization. As a service provider, if you take a job just to have a paycheck without buying into the service culture and supporting the goals of the organization, both you and the organization will lose. For you to be successful in the service industry (or any other for that matter), you must take ownership of your roles and responsibilities and show commitment to doing the best you can every day that you go to work. Even further, you must project a positive attitude when you are not at work as well. Think about the number of times you have heard friends "bad mouth" their boss, organization, products, and services. Did their attitude toward their job inspire you to want to patronize their workplace or apply for a job there? If you were to take the same approach in sharing information about your organization or the people in it, there can be a negative effect on you and the organization. Such actions can lead to lost customers and revenue that goes to pay salaries and benefits, and to provide the tools and environment necessary to conduct business and deliver effective customer service. What you do or say around others in any environment sends a powerful message about you, your level of professionalism, and your organization. If you cannot support your employer, quit and find a job where you can. To do less is being unfair to yourself and your organization.

Culture also encompasses your products and services, and the physical appearance of the organization's facility,

service culture A service environment made up of various factors, including the values, beliefs, norms, rituals, and practices of a group or organization.

attitude Emotional responses to people, ideas, and objects. They are based on values, differ between individuals and cultures, and affect the way people deal with various issues and situations.

Organizations that have a solid customer service culture that projects a customer-focused attitude typically generate positive feedback from their customers. _What can you do as a service provider to contribute to your organization's service culture?_

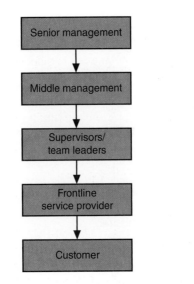

FIGURE 2.1 Typical Hierarchical Organization

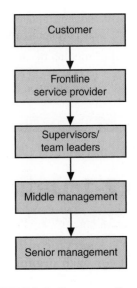

FIGURE 2.2 Customer-Centric Organization

customer-centric A term used to describe service providers and organizations that put their customers first and spend time, effort, and money identifying and focusing on the needs of current and potential customers. Efforts are focused on building long-term relationships and customer loyalty rather than simply selling a product or service and moving on to the next customer.

equipment, or any other aspect of the organization with which the customer comes into contact. Unfortunately, many companies are top-down–oriented (with upper management at the top of their hierarchy and customers as a final element or afterthought) or product-centered and view customers from the standpoint of what company products or services they use (Figure 2.1). Successful organizations are customer-centered or **customer-centric** and focus on individual needs (Figure 2.2).

An organization's service culture is made up of many facets, each of which affects the customer and helps determine the success or failure of customer service initiatives (Figure 2.3). Too often, organizations over-promise and underdeliver because their cultural and internal systems (*infrastructure*) do not have the ability to support customer service initiatives. For example, suppose that management has the marketing department develop a slick piece of literature describing all the benefits of a new product or service provided by a new corporate partner. Then a special toll-free number or website is set up to handle customer responses, but no additional staff is hired to handle the customer calls or current service providers are not given adequate information or training to do their job. The project is likely doomed to fail because adequate service support has not been planned and implemented.

In the past, organizations were continually making changes to their product and service lines to try to attract and hold customers. Often this has been their primary approach to customer satisfaction. Now, many major organizations have become more customer-centric and stress relationships with customers. They realize that it is cheaper, and smarter, to keep current customers rather than subscribe to a revolving-door approach of continually trying to attract new customers to replace the ones that they lost to competitors. Advertising campaigns often reflect this new awareness as companies try to communicate that they are focused on their customers.

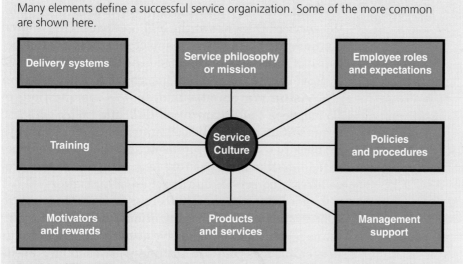

Many elements define a successful service organization. Some of the more common are shown here.

FIGURE 2.3
Elements of a Successful Service Culture

Service philosophy or mission: The direction or vision of an organization that supports day-to-day interactions with the customer.

Employee roles and expectations: The specific communications or measures that indicate what is expected of employees in customer interactions and that define how employee service performance will be evaluated.

Delivery systems: The way an organization delivers its products and services.

Policies and procedures: The guidelines that establish how various situations or transactions will be handled.

Products and services: The materials, products, and services that are state of the art, are competitively priced, and meet the needs of customers.

Management support: The availability of management to answer questions and assist frontline employees in customer interactions when necessary. Also, the level of management involvement and enthusiasm in coaching and mentoring professional development.

Motivators and rewards: Monetary rewards, material items, or feedback that prompts employees to continue to deliver service and perform at a high level of effectiveness and efficiency.

Training: Instruction or information provided through a variety of techniques that teach knowledge or skills, or attempt to influence employee attitude toward excellent service delivery.

The following are some familiar slogans used by companies in their promotional materials:

"You can do it; We can help"—Home Depot

"Like a good neighbor"—State Farm Insurance

"When you're here, you're family"—Olive Garden Restaurants

"You're in good hands"—Allstate Insurance Company

"We'll leave the light on for you."—Motel 6

"Think what we can do for you."—Bank of America

SERVICE PHILOSOPHY OR MISSION

Generally, an organization's approach to business, its **mission** or its **service philosophy**, is driven from the top of the organization. Upper management, including members of the board of directors, when appropriate, sets

mission The direction or focus of an organization that supports day-to-day interactions with customers.

service philosophy The approach that an organization takes to providing service and addressing the needs of customers.

mission statement An organization's mission statement defines its purpose or objectives and *how* it will attain them. It is committed to writing and is publicly shared with employees and customers.

vision statement A vision statement communicates an organization's values and purpose and explains *what* the organization wants to be.

There are many factors that influence service outcome when dealing with customers. *What role do you play in the customer-provider relationship and what might you do to improve your performance in the future?*

the vision or tone and direction of the organization. Without a clearly planned and communicated vision, the service ethic ends at the highest levels. This is often a stumbling block where many organizations falter because of indecision or dissension at the upper echelons.

Most successful organizations have written **mission** and **vision statements** that answer the questions of "What does the organization do?" and "Why does the organization exist?" Mission statements should always tie back to the vision statement and should be incorporated into the infrastructure (e.g., HR policies and procedures) and service culture of an organization.

Leadership, real and perceived, is crucial to service success. In successful organizations, members of upper management make themselves clearly visible to front-line employees and are in tune with customer needs and expectations. They also "walk the talk" and continually drive and communicate the mission and vision of the organization through their words, actions, and decisions. Ultimately, these measures set the tone for a more ethical, productive, and customer-conscious organization. If all employees are aware of what their organization stands for, how it accomplishes its mission, and where it is headed in the future, they can play a crucial role in creating a service culture that strives to identify and meet customer needs, wants, and expectations. Part of ensuring that everyone in the organization is working toward the same goals is to ensure that all policies, infrastructure, and actions support the mission and vision statements. For example, performance appraisals should have language that addresses how supervisors, managers, and employees are doing at addressing established goals and objectives and actions taken to uphold ethical standards. Additionally, all individual and department goals should be tied to the organizational mission and goals.

Although it is wonderful when organizations go to the trouble of developing and hanging a nicely framed formal mission or vision statement on the wall, if they are not a functional way of life for employees, they serve little purpose.

EMPLOYEE ROLES AND EXPECTATIONS

Many tasks and responsibilities are assigned to frontline service providers. People who perform direct customer support functions are some of the most crucial in an organization. That is because customers and other people contact them for information, compliments, and complaints and to purchase products and services.

Depending on your job, the size and type of your organization, and the industry involved, the **employee roles** and **employee expectations** may be similar from one organization to another, and yet they may be performed in a variety of different ways. Such roles and expectations are normally included in your job description and in your performance goals. They are updated as necessary during your tenure in the job position. Where goals are concerned, you are typically measured against them during a given performance period. Subsequent decisions on any rewards for which you are eligible are made based on your performance and your organization's policy.

As a service professional, you are the "face" of your organization in interactions that start with a customer contact. Your primary function is to listen actively and gather the information needed in order to make a decision on what course of action is needed to best serve the customer in any given situation. This typically requires a polite, professional demeanor and effective and efficient answers to questions or resolutions to problems.

employee roles Task assignments that service providers assume.

employee expectations Perceptions about positive and negative aspects of the workplace.

Rumba

For you and your organization to be successful in providing superior service to your external and internal customers, your roles and expectations must be clearly defined and communicated in terms of the following characteristics, sometimes referred to as **RUMBA** (**R**ealistic, **U**nderstandable, **M**easurable, **B**elievable, **A**ttainable).

RUMBA An acronym for five criteria (realistic, understandable, measurable, believable, and attainable) used to establish and measure employee performance goals.

Customer Service Success Tip

Meet with your supervisor to discuss your organization's service philosophy and mission statement and what your role is related to helping accomplish this. If there are policies or other standards in place that make your job difficult or impossible to successfully achieve, propose and discuss possible alternatives. Make sure that you have researched the options that you plan to propose and have examples of situations and organizations in which they have been successful. Also, approach the discussion from a positive, proactive approach rather than from an emotional, negative one in which you appear to be simply complaining or making excuses for performance that is not meeting current standards.

Realistic Your behavior and responsibilities must be in line with the reality of your particular workplace and customer base. Although it is possible to transfer a standard of performance from one organization, and

> ## ⚙ WORK IT OUT 2.1
>
> ## Organizational Culture
>
> **Think about your own organization's service culture or, if you're not actively working as a customer service professional, the culture of an organization with which you are familiar.**
>
> 1. What do you believe the service philosophy of this organization to be? Why?
> 2. Are there things that make the organization unique? If so, what are they?
> 3. What factors (positive or negative) about employee performance in this organization stand out in your mind?
> 4. Are there factors about the culture that detract from effectiveness? If so, what are they?
> 5. If you were managing this organization, what service culture aspects would you change? Why?

even industry, to another, modifications may be necessary to fit your specific situation. For example, is it realistic that all customer calls must be handled within a specified time period? Many managers set specific goals in terms of "talk time" for their customer service representatives. Can every angry customer be calmed and handled in a two- to three-minute time frame? If not, then a standard such as this sets up employees for failure.

After a performance goal has been set for you, evaluate it fairly and objectively for a period of time (possibly 30 days). This allows time for a variety of opportunities to apply it. At the end of the specified trial period, if you think the goal is unrealistic, go to your supervisor or team leader and discuss modifying it. In preparation for this discussion, think of at least two viable alternatives to the goals. Also, recognize that performance goals are often driven by organizational goals that may be passed down from upper management. Although they might be modified, it may take some time for the change to come about, so be patient. Ultimately, if the goal cannot be modified, do your best to perform within the established standard so that your professional image does not suffer.

Understandable You must have a sound understanding of your performance goals before you can act appropriately and effectively, just the way you need to understand how to do your job or how to communicate with others in the workplace. You should first try to participate in the establishment of your performance goals and those of your department or team. To do this, set up a meeting with your supervisor or team leader to discuss goals. Once goals are in place, you and everyone else affected must have a clear understanding of them so that you can effectively reach the assigned goal. If questions or doubts exist about a goal or your role in accomplishing it, make sure to clarify your understanding with a supervisor or team leader since you will ultimately be held accountable if you fail to reach a performance goal. This may impact professional opportunities and personal earning potential.

Measurable Can your performance be measured? The answer is yes. Typically, factors such as time, productivity, quantifiable results, revenue, and manner of performance (how you accomplish your job tasks in terms of following an established step-by-step formula) are used to determine your accomplishment of goals. In a production environment, or in certain sales environments, performance can be measured by reviewing the number of products made or sales completed. In a purely customer-focused environment, **service measurement** can be in terms of factors such as talk time on the telephone, number of customers effectively served, customer feedback surveys and satisfaction cards, and letters or other written correspondence—or, on the negative side, by customer complaints.

service measurement Techniques used by organizations to determine how customers perceive the value of services and products received.

Ethical Dilemma 2.1

Assume that your organizational philosophy states in part that your purpose is "to provide quality products at a competitive price in a low-pressure customer atmosphere." Even so, your supervisor establishes a goal that requires you to have "x" number of sales per shift as an outbound sales representative. Based on your research, this number is two more than the typical industry average for a salesperson during a work shift. You recognize that to achieve this goal, you will have to be more "persuasive" than you usually are when dealing with customers or than you feel comfortable in doing.

1. What ethical issue(s) do you face in this situation?
2. How might these impact service delivery?
3. What impact might this situation have on your performance?
4. How might this situation be addressed?

See possible responses at the end of this chapter.

Whatever the measure, it is your responsibility to be sure that you know the acceptable level and do your best to perform to that level. If something inhibits your performance, or if organizational obstacles such as conflicting priorities, overburdening multiple assignments, policies, procedures, equipment, or other employees stand in your way, you should immediately discuss the difficulties with the appropriate authority.

Believable For any goal to be attained, it must be believable to the people who will strive to reach it and to the supervisors or team leaders who will monitor it. The biggest issues in developing goals are to make them worthy of belief and faithful to the values of the individual and organization, and to ensure that they make sense and tie in directly with the established overall departmental and organizational goals. Too often, employees are given assignments that are contrary to the ultimate purpose or mission and overall values or beliefs of the organization. This can create confusion about what is important and the direction to be taken and ultimately can impact the level of trust that service providers have with their supervisor and/or organization.

Attainable Given the right training, management support, and organizational environment in which the tools, information, assistance, and rewards are provided, you can attain your goals. The determining factor, however, is you and your attitude toward achieving agreed-upon levels.

Managers should always attempt to set up win/win situations in which you, your organization, and, ultimately, the customer benefit from any service encounter. However, you should be aware that in the "real world" this does not always happen—systems break down. In such cases, it is up to you to ensure that service continues to be delivered to customers in a seamless fashion. They should not hear about internal problems, and, quite honestly, the customers probably do not care about these problems. They should be able to expect that the products and services they paid for are delivered when promised, in the manner agreed upon, and without inconvenience to them. Anything less is unacceptable and is poor service.

Employee Roles in Larger Retail and Service Organizations

As customers have matured in their knowledge of service standards and what they expect of providers, they look for certain qualifications in those who serve. They gain knowledge from numerous sources that help them be more savvy in their dealings with businesses (for example, *Consumer Reports* magazine; Internet research; and television shows such as *20/20, Dateline*, and *60 Minutes*). Many times, these customers become sticklers about service and when they do not get the level of service they expect, they take their business elsewhere and/or take legal action. In some cases, they might give the organization a second chance by complaining. This benevolent initiative, allowing organizations to "fix themselves," is often done as a test. If you or your peers fail, several things can occur. You may not only lose a customer, but you may also "gain" an onslaught of negative word-of-mouth publicity that can irreparably damage an organization's image as a whole, and yours specifically.

Customers expect service employees to typically have at least the following qualifications and competencies in both large and small organizations:

- Broad general knowledge of products and service.
- Interpersonal communication skills (e.g., verbal, nonverbal, and listening along with cross-gender and cross-cultural communication).
- Technical expertise related to products sold and serviced.
- Positive, customer-focused, "can-do" attitude.
- Initiative.
- Motivation.
- Integrity.
- Loyalty (to the organization, to products, and to customers).
- Team spirit.
- Creativity.
- Sound ethics.

Employees of both small and large organizations contribute to their service cultures through interactions with customers. *What are some things that they can do to project a positive service image?*

- Time management skills.
- Problem-solving capability.
- Conflict resolution skills.

Such skills and capabilities are crucial, whether you are operating a cash register, polishing a car, handling a returned item, repairing a sink, questioning a crime witness or suspect, coaching an executive or technical manager (for example, a consultant who offers seminars on enhancing interpersonal skills), or dealing with a negative situation (for example, a shoplifter or disgruntled customer). If you fail to possess and/ or exhibit any or all of these factors, the end result could be a breakdown in the relationship between you and your customer, with ultimately negative repercussions.

Employee Roles in Smaller Retail and Service Organizations

The growth of small businesses since the early 1990s skyrocketed, especially women- and minority-owned businesses, until the recession hit. Many small business entrepreneurs started out of necessity (because of layoffs or downsizing) or out of frustration caused by limitations within a larger structure (lack of promotion opportunity, low salaries, actual or perceived discrimination, poor management, or continual changes). As a result of the recession, hiring by small business owners dropped because they either did not need more employees, were unsure that sales would cover costs, and had major concerns with having to pay for healthcare and deal with other government policies.

Even so, the growth of sole proprietorships (one-owner businesses) and small businesses has an upside in that they provide more choices for customers. On the downside, this growth also created problems for people making the transition from large to small organizations. This is because, in addition to having to possess all the qualifications and characteristics listed earlier, employees in small businesses perform greatly varied tasks. Typically, the human resources and technical systems they might call upon for support are limited. If something goes wrong, they cannot "bump the problem upstairs," nor can they obtain immediate, on-site assistance. This often causes customer frustration or anger.

The types of jobs that fall into this struggling category run the gamut of industries. Some examples are

- Administrative assistant (freelance)
- Accountant
- Consultant
- Automotive mechanic
- Computer technician
- Salesperson
- Caterer
- Tailor
- Personal shopper
- Office support staff
- Hair stylist
- Masseuse/masseur
- Office equipment repairperson
- Office cleaning staff
- Child care provider
- Gardener
- Electrician and plumber
- Electronics repairperson
- Visiting nurse or nurse consultant
- Driver
- Temporary worker

To stave off failure and help ensure that customer needs are identified and satisfied, owners and employees in such establishments must continually strive to gain new knowledge and skills while working hard to deliver a level of service equal to that offered by the bigger organizations. The public is generally unforgiving and, like an elephant, has a long memory—especially when service breaks down.

If you work in this type of environment, look for opportunities to provide stellar service and really go out of your way to practice your people skills. Get back to the basics of how to effectively deal with people—listen, ask questions, provide feedback, communicate well—and do not miss an opportunity to let your customers know that they are special, that you are there to serve their needs, and that you appreciate them.

Employee Roles in Nonprofit Organizations

An option to working for a for-profit company is to seek employment in a nonprofit organization. Even though revenue generation is not the primary goal in such organizations, money is a significant force. Without donations, grants, and other fund-raising efforts, these organizations cannot provide the crucial services, products, and deliverables to their customer/client base (often lower-income and older people or others who have few other alternatives for attainment of needed items and services). In such organizations, administrators, staff, and volunteers provide a wide degree of services and support. Unless these workers maintain a cheerful, positive, and professional attitude, revenue and service levels might plummet. They must never forget that everyone with whom they come into contact is either a potential donor or recipient of products and services.

WORK IT OUT 2.2

Think about the two return policies in Figure 2.4.

What is your reaction to policy example 1? Why?

What is your reaction to policy example 2? Why?

The following qualifications and competencies are very helpful for anyone working in a nonprofit environment.

- Specific knowledge of the organization and products and services it provides.
- Interpersonal communication skills.
- Positive, customer-focused "can do" attitude.
- Initiative.
- Motivation to succeed.
- Integrity.
- Commitment to others.
- Volunteer spirit.
- Team orientation.
- Sound ethical attitude.
- Time management skills.
- Problem-solving ability (ability to think "outside the box").
- Entrepreneur spirit (ability to work in an environment in which free thinking and creativity are encouraged and needed).

Policies and Procedures

Although there are a lot of local, state, and federal regulations with which you and your organization must comply, many policies are flexible. For example, if you go to your bank to deposit a fairly large check that exceeds the maximum amount the bank will accept, the teller may inform you that there will be a seven-day hold put on the check until it clears the sender's bank. In this case, you might petition the branch manager and possibly get this period modified since you are dealing with a "bank" policy.

Many customers negatively meet organizational culture directly when a service provider hides behind "company policy" to handle a problem. The goal should be to respond to policy customer requests and satisfy needs as quickly, efficiently, and cheerfully as possible. Anything less is an invitation for criticism, dissatisfaction, potential customer loss, and employee frustration.

Return policies in a retail environment are a case in point. Even though customers may not always be "right," they must be treated with respect and as if they are right in order to effectively provide service and generate future relationships. An effective return policy is part of the overall service process. In addition to service received, the return policy of an organization

Owners and employees in sole proprietorships must work hard to deliver service equal to that given by larger organizations. *How can an owner make his or her organization special or different?*

is another gauge customers use to determine where they will spend their time and money. The return statements shown in Figure 2.4 were received by the author of this book in the past and send specific messages about the organizational culture of both organizations. Notice the tone or service culture that radiates from each example. Think about your "gut" reaction as a customer when you read both policies.

Organizations often hang up fancy posters and banners touting such claims as "The customer is always right," "The customer is No. 1," or "We're here to serve YOU!" But at the moment of truth, when customers come into contact with employees, they frequently hear, "Please take a number so we can better serve you," "I can't do that," or (on the phone) "ABC Company, please hold—CLICK." Clearly, when these things occur, the culture is not customer-focused and service has broken down. The important question for organizations is, "How do we fix our system?" The answer: make a commitment to the customer and establish an environment that will support that commitment. That's where you come in as a customer service professional. Through conscientious and concerned assistance to customers, the organization can form a solid relationship with the consumer through its employees.

Ethical Dilemma 2.2

Your organization's return policy stresses that "Our goal is your total satisfaction," yet you have been told by your supervisor that returns cost the organization money and negatively impact her quarterly bonus. For that reason, she has instructed you and other employees that you should find a reason not to accept returns and provide refunds whenever possible (e.g., a package was opened, it has been more than seven days since purchase, a receipt is not provided, or the item is being discontinued and the manufacturer will not take it back). She has even suggested that you lie to a customer or make up an excuse rather than accept a return. Further, she instructed you that all returns and refunds must be approved by her, yet when she is paged over the intercom, she typically does not respond and leaves you and other service employees to face an escalating negative customer situation.

1. How does such a service atmosphere potentially impact customers? Employees?
2. What message does this approach to service say about the organization?
3. What are potential outcomes of such practices by the supervisor?
4. What can you and other employees do to address the situation?

PRODUCTS AND SERVICES

The type and quality of products and services also contribute to your organizational culture. If customers perceive that you offer reputable products and services in a professional manner and at a competitive price, your organization will likely reap the rewards of loyalty and positive "press." On the other hand, if products and services do not live up to expectations or

FIGURE 2.4

Sample Return Policies

Policy 1

To err is human; to return is just fine . . .

Already read the book? Pages printed upside down? The package arrived bruised, battered, and otherwise weary from the trip? Actually, the only reason you need to return an item bought from us is this: You're not satisfied . . .

Having the chance to talk with our customer helps us learn and improve our service. It is also an opportunity to demonstrate the [organization's name] customer policy: YOU'RE RIGHT!

Policy 2

Return policy

Returns must meet the following criteria:

1. Books must be received within thirty (30) days of the invoice date. Please allow one week for shipping.

2. Books must be received in salable condition. Damaged books will not be accepted for credit.

3. Refunds will not be made on videotapes and software unless they were defective at the time of purchase. Please notify [organization's name] of any such defects within ten (10) days of the invoice date.

Return shipping information

Returns must be shipped to [organization's name and full address].

Any returns not shipped to the above address will not be credited and FULL PAYMENT for shipping will be the responsibility of the shipper.

All charges incurred in returning materials, including customer's charges, if any, are the responsibility of the shipper.

Ensure that your returns are not lost or damaged.

Comments and feedback

We value your opinion! If you need to return any of the enclosed material, please take a minute to let us know why. Your comments and suggestions will help us better meet your needs in the future.

Customer Service Success Tip

To get the information you need, you may have to take the initiative. Your customer does not want to hear you say, "Nobody showed me how," "I can't," "I don't know," or "It's not my job." Remember what you read earlier about seamless service. Here are some questions you might ask your supervisor related to job responsibilities:

• What are my exact duties? (Get a copy of your job description in writing, if possible.)

• What are your expectations of me?

• How do I handle [name specific] situations?

• Who should I see about _____?

• Where are [materials, policies, equipment] located?

• Who is in charge when you are not available?

• What is my level of authority?

---

promises, or if your ability to correct problems in products and services is deficient, you and the organization could suffer adversely.

MOTIVATORS AND REWARDS

In any employee environment, people work more effectively and productively when their performance is recognized and adequately rewarded.

Whether the rewards are in the form of monetary or material items, or a simple verbal pat on the back by the manager, most employees expect and thrive on some form of recognition.

As a way of managing your own motivation level, it is important to remember that there will be many times when your only motivation and reward for accomplishing a goal or providing quality service will come from you. The reality is that every time you do something well or out of the ordinary, you may not receive a financial or any other kind of reward for it. On the other hand, many companies and supervisors go out of their way to recognize good performance. Many use public recognition, contests, games, employee activities (sporting or other events), financial rewards, incentives (gifts or trips), employee-of-the-month or -year awards, and a variety of other techniques to show appreciation for employee efforts (see Figure 2.5). Whatever your organization does, there is always room for improvement and you should take time to make recommendations of your own on ways to reward employees.

FIGURE 2.5

Types of Employee Rewards

Organizations are getting creative in their efforts to recognize and reward positive service practices. By using incentives, they can reward positive behavior and encourage repeat actions by the employee receiving the reward and their peers. The following are some typical forms of recognition being used by various organizations:

Compensation

Commissions paid for representatives or sales staff members who successfully up-sell or encourage customers to buy new or additional products or services are one form of compensation. A tiered system is often used where higher percentages are paid based on the number or level of sales made by the employee during a given performance period. Another form of compensation is a guaranteed annual raise when an employee meets or exceeds established service standards—for example, number of dissatisfied customers or members "saved" when they contact the organization with an issue and threaten to defect to a competitor (e.g., cable, phone, or lawn care customers). Another example of how incentives or awards apply can be found in most call centers. Representatives are often compensated based on meeting standards like "call or contact time" (how long they were on a call or interacted with a customer) or numbers of calls or customers handled in a given period of time.

Flexible Time or Time Off

In a stressful world where many people now value time with their families, many organizations are becoming more lenient in their approach to allowing employees time off to take care of personal activities or just relax.

There are different ways that companies institute flexible work schedules depending on an organization's structure, size, and mission:

- Flexible start and end time for the workday (based on approved scheduling).
- Compressed workweek (e.g., four 10-hour workdays with an additional day of the week off).
- Telecommuting, where employees work part of their week from home and the other portion in their office or other designated worksite.
- Project- or results-oriented scheduling, where employees have no set number of hours per week but must reach an established level of productivity or meet required deadlines for project completion.
- Two or more part-time employees sharing a job and required to work specific days/hours.

Many small businesses use a flextime strategy to attract qualified workers and compete effectively for talent that they might not otherwise be able to afford. Larger organizations use flextime as a way to enhance employee morale.

Of course like any other policy, there are downsides to flextime. When companies use this work strategy heavily, employees and supervisors may lose a degree of regular contact,

FIGURE 2.5
(*Concluded*)

and it adds to the burden of scheduling for supervisors. Additionally, some employees do not handle flextime well and disciplinary issues arise that might actually cause an employee to become disgruntled and morale could suffer for them and their peers.

Employee Recognition

One of the easiest and least expensive means of rewarding employees is to acknowledge them as people and applaud their accomplishments. Ways to accomplish this can cost little or no money. There are many inexpensive and effective ways for supervisors to recognize their staff. Some of these include

- Having a buffet breakfast or pizza party once a month to celebrate employees' birthdays that occur during the period.
- Giving a round of applause for accomplishments.
- Giving a handwritten note or card from the CEO or other high-ranking member of management along with a gift card.
- Passing around a "floating trophy" of some sort that is retained by the employee who meets an announced performance goal during a specific period and then moves on to the next person during the following period.
- Providing employee-of-the-month parking spaces for the person who excels and meets established criteria for the slot. This often means an indoor parking spot or one closer to the building entrance.

The important thing about rewards is that they be perceived as being given fairly and in a timely fashion near the completion of an event that precipitated the reward.

MANAGEMENT SUPPORT

You cannot be expected to handle every customer-related situation that develops. In some instances, you will have to depend on the knowledge and assistance of a more experienced employee or your supervisor or manager and defer to his or her experience or authority. A key role played by your manager, supervisor, and/or team leader is to provide effective, ongoing coaching, counseling, and training to you and your peers. By doing this, supervisors can pass on valuable information, guide you, and aid your professional development. Also, it is their job to be alert to your performance and ensure that you receive appropriate rewards based on your ability to interact effectively with customers and fulfill the requirements of your job. Unfortunately, many supervisors have not had adequate training that would enable them to provide you with the support you need. They were probably good frontline service providers, with a high degree of motivation, initiative, and ability. As a result, their management promoted them, often without providing the necessary training, coaching, and guidance to develop their supervisory skills. In other instances, they may be as overwhelmed with job responsibilities as you are. Even they may recognize the importance of coaching and intend to do so; they may simply not have the time.

If you find that you are not receiving the support you need, there are some things you should consider doing in order to ensure that you have the information, skills, and support to provide quality service to your customers.

Strive for Improvement

Customer service can be frustrating and, in some instances, monotonous. You may need to create self-motivation strategies and continue to seek fulfillment or satisfaction. By remaining optimistic and projecting a can-do image that

---

⚙ WORK IT OUT 2.3

Managing Customer Encounters

Take a few minutes to respond to the following questions. Then your instructor may group you with others to discuss responses.

1. Have you ever witnessed or experienced a customer service situation in which a supervisor or manager became involved in an employee-customer encounter? If so, what occurred?
2. How do you feel the supervisor handled the situation?
3. Could the supervisor's approach have been improved? If so, how?

---

makes customers enjoy dealing with you, you can influence yourself and others. Smile as an outward gesture of your "I care" philosophy. Many self-help publications and courses are available that can offer guidance in this area.

The reality in many of today's work environments is that organizations have downsized and are struggling to come back from the worst economic recession in recent memory. This has impacted productivity, revenue, employee morale, customer perceptions, and overall societal values. The new business norm is what it is today for many organizations and their employees. The result is that employees and their supervisors are learning to adapt to the changing face of customers related to their needs, wants, and expectations. That means that you on an individual level must step back and analyze your job and role in the service culture so that you can better prepare to meet the challenges and opportunities that you will surely encounter.

Look for ways to improve your skills and to raise the level of service you provide to your customer. Whether it is through formal training, mentoring, or simply observing positive service techniques used by others and mimicking them, work to improve your own skills. The more you know, the better you can assist customers and move your own career forward.

Look for a Strong Mentor in Your Organization

Many organizations have realized that to provide succession planning for the future, they must create a system whereby frontline employees, junior supervisors, and managers or future leaders are guided in their personal and professional development by those with more expertise, tenure, and contacts. This is going to become even more crucial in the future because of the coming "brain drain" in which thousands of older workers will retire and exit the workplace in virtually every industry and type of organization. When they go, they will take decades of experience and knowledge and leave behind a huge gap in many organizations, especially those that have not created an effective exit strategy or prepared others to step into key roles and positions. One viable strategy is to put into place a strong organizationally sponsored and supported mentoring program.

If your organization does not have a system in place to pair newer employees in the profession with those more knowledgeable and skilled, try to find someone who is a superior customer service professional and get to know him or her. As your relationship grows, become a sponge and soak up as much of his or her knowledge as possible. Additionally, do an Internet search for professional organizations that cater to your profession (e.g., customer service representatives, call center representatives, sales professionals, or whatever your job title). Often they offer networking opportunities on a regular basis locally where you can attend meetings to hear guest speakers who share their expertise in the field. Through such events, you can likely identify other professionals who are looking to share best practices and information while growing their knowledge and skills.

Mentors are people who are well acquainted with the organization and its policies, politics, and processes. They are well connected (inside and outside the organization), communicate well, have the ability and desire to assist you (the **protégé**), and are capable and experienced. Ask these people to provide support and help you grow personally and professionally. Many good books on the topic of mentoring are available. Figures 2.6 and 2.7 list some characteristics of a mentor and protégé.

mentors Individuals who dedicate time and effort to befriend and assist others. In an organization, they are typically people with a lot of knowledge, experience, skills, and initiative, and have a large personal and professional network established.

protégé Typically less-experienced recipients of the efforts of mentors.

Avoid Complacency

Anyone can go to work and just do what he or she is told. The people who excel, especially in a service environment, are the ones who constantly strive for improvement and look for opportunities to grow professionally. They also take responsibility or ownership for service situations. Take the time to think about the systems, policies, and procedures in place in your organization. Can they be improved? How? Now take that information or awareness and make recommendations for improvements. Even though managers have a key role, the implementation and success of cultural initiatives (practices or actions taken by the organization) rest with you, the frontline employee. You are the one who interacts directly with a customer and often determines the outcome of the contact.

When searching for someone to mentor you, look for these characteristics:

- Willingness to be a mentor.
- Experience in the organization or industry and/or job you need help with.
- Knowledgeable about the organization and industry.
- Good communicator (verbal, nonverbal, and listening skills).
- Awareness of the organizational culture.
- Well-connected inside and outside the organization.
- Enthusiastic.
- Good coaching skills and a good motivator.
- Charismatic.
- Trustworthy.
- Patient.
- Creative thinker.
- Self-confident.
- Good problem solver.

FIGURE 2.6

Characteristics of an Effective Mentor

Since mentoring is a two-way process, you should make sure that you are ready to have a mentor. You should have the following characteristics:

- Willingness to participate, listen, and learn.
- Desire to improve and grow.
- Commitment to working with a mentor.
- Self-confidence.
- Effective communication skills.
- Enthusiasm.
- Openness to feedback.
- Adaptability.
- Willingness to ask questions

FIGURE 2.7

Characteristics of a Successful Protégé

⚙ **WORK IT OUT 2.4**

Training for Service

Take a few minutes to think about and respond to these questions. Once you have responded, your instructor may form groups and have you share answers.

1. What type of skills training do you believe would be valuable for a customer service professional? Why?

2. What types of training have you had or do you need to qualify for a service position?

Some people might throw up their hands and say, "It wasn't my fault," "Nobody else cares; why should I," or "I give up." A special person looks for ways around roadblocks in order to provide quality service for customers. The fact that others are not doing their job does not excuse you from doing yours. You are being paid a salary to accomplish specific job tasks. Do them with gusto and pride. Your customers expect no less. You and your customers will reap the rewards of your efforts and initiative.

EMPLOYEE EMPOWERMENT

empowerment The word used to describe the giving of decision-making and problem-resolution authority to lower-level employees in an organization. This precludes having to get permission from higher levels in order to take an action or serve a customer.

Employee **empowerment** is one way for a supervisor to help ensure that service providers can respond quickly to customer needs or requests. The intent of empowerment is a delegation of authority where a frontline service provider can take action without having to call a supervisor or ask permission. Such authority allows on-the-spot responsiveness to the customer while making service representatives feel trusted, respected, and like an important part of the organization. Empowerment is also an intangible way that successful service organizations reward employees. Often someone who has decision-making authority feels better about himself or herself and the organization.

Customer Service Success Tip

If your supervisor empowers you to make decisions, that means he/she trusts your ability to handle various issues. Do not take this trust lightly. Before taking action, stop, weigh alternatives, and then resolve the situation to the best of your ability in order to send a message of competency and professionalism.

As a service provider, think of customer situations in which you have to get approval from a supervisor or manager before making a decision or taking action to serve your customers. If you feel having to do so is causing a delay in serving your customers, approach your supervisor and suggest having decision-making authority given to you.

Some examples of possible empowerment situations include the following:

- A cashier has to call a supervisor for approval of a customer's personal check.
- A cable television installer has to call the office for approval before adding a hookup for another room.
- A computer technician cannot comply with a customer's request that she make a backup CD-ROM of her hard drive before running a diagnostic test because policy prohibits it.
- A call center service representative does not have the authority to reverse late payment charges on the account of a customer who explained that he was in the hospital for three weeks with surgery complications.

- A bank representative cannot waive returned check fees even though she acknowledges the bank created the error that resulted in bounced checks in the first place.
- An assistant cruise purser cannot correct a billing error until the purser returns from lunch.
- A volunteer coordinator must check with the director before allowing a volunteer worker to implement a new process that she recommends to expedite service delivery to a client.

TRAINING

The importance of effective training cannot be overstated. To perform your job successfully and create a positive impression in the minds of customers, you and other frontline employees must be given the necessary tools. Depending on your position and your organization's focus, this training might address interpersonal skills, technical skills, organizational awareness, or job skills, again depending on your position. Most important, your training should help you know what is expected of you and how to fulfill those expectations. Training is a vehicle for accomplishing this and is an essential component of any organizational culture that supports customer service.

Take advantage of training programs offered by your organization. Check with your supervisor and/or training department, if there is one. If you work in a small company or nonprofit organization, have a limited budget for training, or do not have access to training through your organization, look for other resources. Many communities have lists of seminars available through the public library, college business programs, high schools, chambers of commerce, professional organizations, and a variety of other organizations. The Internet also offers a wealth of articles and information in the form of free podcasts or YouTube training videos on a variety of topics. Go to www.YouTube.com and search for "customer service training" and see what comes up. Tap into these resources to gain the knowledge and skills you will need to move ahead. Also, your training and skill level will often determine whether you keep your job if your organization is forced to downsize and reduce staff.

KNOWLEDGE CHECK

1. What are the elements included in a successful service organization?
2. What does the acronym RUMBA stand for and how does it relate to your service roles and expectations?
3. What part do rewards and management support play in successful customer service?

Trending NOW

Social media are impacting organizational culture as never before. Tech-savvy customers are reaching out to organizations and communicating with those who have adopted technology and created a social presence on sites like Pinterest, Facebook, and Twitter to gather information, communicate complaints, and post compliments. This inexpensive means of connecting with current and potential customers is reducing costs and enhancing product and service awareness, while potentially generating revenue for forward-thinking organizations.

LO 2-2 Establishing a Service Strategy

CONCEPT A service provider helps determine approaches for service success.

The first step a company should take in creating or redefining its service environment is to make sure it knows who its customers really are and how it plans to attract and hold those customers. Many organizations do not even consider this crucial step when creating a business plan or developing their culture.

Next, the organization should periodically conduct an inspection of its systems and practices (e.g., policies, procedures, service and product delivery mechanisms, customer care strategies, and practices for identifying potential customer dissatisfaction in advance and correcting it) to decide where the company is now and where it needs to be in order to better serve customers and to be competitive in a global service economy. The manner in which internal (co-workers and supervisors) and external (anyone outside the organization) customer needs are addressed also should be reviewed. For example, are surveys, focus groups, or customer-provider meetings/forums conducted?

It is not just your organization's responsibility to ensure the success of customer service. As a service professional, you have to be familiar with the organization's goals and work toward helping make them successful. A simple way to accomplish this is to give thought to your role in the service process and continually reevaluate what you do on a daily basis when dealing with customers. If you have a positive experience, recognize what made it so and strive to repeat that behavior with other customers. If something went wrong when serving a customer, objectively evaluate the situation and decide what role, if any, you played in a less-than-successful outcome. If you determine that you could have done better, decide on a more positive approach for the future. If you are unsure how to prevent a recurrence of the service breakdown, ask advice from co-workers or your supervisor.

As a service provider, you should do your part in determining needed approaches for service success. From the perspective of a customer service professional, ask yourself the following questions to help clarify your role:

- Who is my customer?
- What am I currently doing, or what can I do, to help achieve organizational excellence?
- Do I focus all my efforts on total customer satisfaction?
- Am I empowered to make the decisions necessary to serve my customer? If not, what levels of authority should I discuss with my supervisor?
- Are there policies and procedures that inhibit my ability to serve the customer? If so, what recommendations about changing policies and procedures can I make?
- When was the last time I told my customers that I sincerely appreciated their business?
- In what areas of organizational skills and product and service knowledge do I need additional information?

LO 2-3 Customer-Friendly Systems

CONCEPT System components are advertising, complaint resolution, and delivery systems.

A service culture starts at the top of an organization and filters down to the frontline employee. By demonstrating their commitment to quality service efforts, managers lead by example. It's not enough to authorize glitzy service promotional campaigns and send out directives informing employees of management's support for customer initiatives; managers must get involved. Further, employees must take initiative to solve problems and better serve the customer. They must be alert for opportunities and make recommendations for improvement whenever appropriate. Only in these situations can changes and improvements in the culture occur.

TYPICAL SYSTEM COMPONENTS

Part of the effectiveness in serving customers can be accomplished through policies and practices that say, "We care" or "You're important to us." Some **customer-friendly systems** that can send positive messages are advertising and complaint or problem resolution.

Advertising

Advertising campaigns should send a message that products and services are competitive in price and that the quality and quantity are at least comparable to those of competitors. Otherwise, customers will likely go elsewhere. An advertisement that appears to be deceptive can cost the organization customers and its reputation. For example, if an advertisement states that something is "free" (a cup of coffee; a buy-one, get-one-free item; tire rotation; or a consultation), but somewhere in the advertisement (in small print) there are restrictions ("with a purchase of $20 or more," "while supplies last," "if you buy two new tires," or "if you sign a one-year contract"), then it may be viewed as deceptive.

To prevent misunderstandings as a service provider, make sure that you point out such restrictions to customers when they call or ask questions. If you notice that an advertisement sounds a bit "tricky," inform your supervisor immediately. Possibly the ad was not proofread carefully enough before it was printed and/or aired. Remember, you have a vested interest in your organization's success. Take ownership.

Complaint or Problem Resolution

The manner in which complaints or problems are handled can signal the organization's concern for customer satisfaction. If an employee has to get approvals for the smallest decisions, the customer may have to wait for a supervisor to arrive (a supermarket cashier has to call for a manager to approve a check for $10, but when

customer-friendly systems
Refers to the processes in an organization that make service seamless to customers by ensuring that things work properly and the customer is satisfied.

Customer Service Success Tip

Unhappy people are still your customers or potential internal or external customers when they contact you at work. Your goal should be to try and appease them so that they return for future products or services. If you fail at this goal, you and your organization will potentially suffer financial and prestige loss.

The best way to create a service culture is to get everyone in the organization involved in planning and brainstorming. Everyone should be encouraged to share ideas about how and where internal changes need to be made and to be more responsive to customer needs. *How do you think these ideas can be shared most effectively?*

the supervisor arrives, he or she doesn't even look at the check before signing and walking away). This can lead to customer and employee frustration and irritation and makes the organization, and the service provider, look inept.

As a service professional, you should make recommendations for improvement whenever you spot a roadblock or system that impedes provision of service excellence.

SERVICE DELIVERY SYSTEMS

service delivery system The means by which an organization effectively gets its products and services to customers.

Service delivery systems are a combination of people, technology, and other internal and external elements that make up your organization's method of getting its products and services to customers. Your organization must determine the best way to deliver quality products and service and to provide effective follow-up support to its customers. There should be an ongoing and continuous reevaluation of system success to ensure that it keeps up with the changing needs of your customers. As part of that system, everything that you do is crucial in positioning your organization to be the "go to" source for the types of products and services that are offered to current and potential customers. This includes the way information is made available to customers, initial contacts and handling of customer issues, sales techniques (hard sell versus relationship selling), order collection and processing, price quotations, product and service delivery, processing of paperwork, invoicing, and follow-up. Customers should not have to deal with internal policies, practices, or politics. They should be able to contact you; get the information they need; make a buying decision, where appropriate; and have the products or services they have selected flawlessly delivered in a timely, professional manner. Anything less is poor service and may cost your organization in terms of lost business, customers, or reputation. These concepts also apply to your dealings with your internal customers who request information or services.

Customers also expect value for their money. Part of this is professional, easy-to-access service. For example, if you are in a retail organization and do not have a toll-free number with online customer support, extended hours of operation, top-quality merchandise, and effective resolution of problems, your customers may rebel. They can do this by complaining, speaking negative word-of-mouth publicity, writing letters to consumer advocacy groups (television or radio stations; Better Business Bureaus; local, state, and federal government agencies), and/or going elsewhere for their needs. Additionally, if your company's website is not kept up to date (or if your company has no web presence), or if the website is difficult to navigate, customers may go elsewhere. Customers want to quickly "click" for their information. Websites that are hard to navigate or that take a long time to load up will often be abandoned by customers.

There are many ways available for delivering service to customers. Two key factors involved in delivery are transportation modes (how products and services are physically delivered—by truck, train, plane, U.S. Postal Service, courier, or electronically) and location (facilities located centrally and easily accessible by customers). The location can be crucial to nonprofit organizations and medical or dental care providers since many clients or patients do not have access to dependable transportation. They often have to depend on friends, family, and public transportation to access services and products.

Customer Service Success Tip

Successful customer service results from relationships that you forge with others. By taking the time to slow down and let your customers take the lead and discover what they need or want, you increase the opportunity to better meet or exceed their expectations. In doing so, you are contributing to a positive service culture and helping secure your organization's reputation as a customer-focused entity.

Direct or Indirect Systems

The type of delivery system used (direct or indirect contact) is important because it affects staffing numbers, costs, technology, scheduling, and many other factors. The major difference between the two types of systems is that in a direct contact environment, customers interact directly with people, whereas in an indirect system their needs are met primarily with self-service through technology (possibly integrated with the human factor in customer contact/call centers) integrated with Internet services.

There is a delicate balance in selecting a service delivery system. This is because each customer is unique and has personal preferences. While many prefer a hands-off self-service approach, others resent it and often view it as a loss of caring. Many banks discovered this fact in recent years. They saw technology as a cost-saving strategy to deliver service. Branches were closed as money was spent to upgrade automated phone systems and add automatic teller machines (ATMs). Many customers rebelled. The result is that companies like Chase Bank are now increasing their branch locations and retrofitting their branches and ATMs. Other banks are looking for ways to send a message that they are customer-oriented. For example, BankUnited, which was in receivership as a result of failed financial policies during the recession, has gone on to be listed by the FDIC as one of the most profitable banks in Florida, where it is headquartered. Some of their turnaround and growth is an emphasis on reaching its customers and providing customer-friendly service. The organization focused on opening new branches across the state and started a process called "bank on wheels" where they sent mobile branches, in the form of large, specially equipment recreational vehicles, into remote areas not served by their brick-and-mortar branches. These mobile branches include ATMs, walk-up tellers, flat-screen video, a small lobby, and two office spaces to meet with employees. Customers are able to get most of the services available in a standard branch. In addition, like many organizations, these companies use automated attendant phone systems that allow callers to speak or manually enter information with their telephone touchpad.

Figure 2.8 shows some ways by which organizations are providing service to customers and prospective customers.

Third-Party Delivery (Outsourcing/Offshoring)

In recent years, as companies strive to reduce costs, increase profit, and stay ahead of the competition, an interesting trend has occurred. Many companies are eliminating internal positions and delegating, assigning, or hiring outside (third-party) organizations and individuals to assume eliminated and newly created roles (call center customer support functions, human resource benefits administration, accounting functions, and marketing) for an agreed-upon price (normally without the extra cost of benefits). Typically, outsourced (within your country) and offshored (outside your country) positions are noncore (e.g., call center support, manufacturing, or product design/development). Many third-party providers and the jobs outsourced or offshored are located in India, Mexico, Pakistan, Philippines, and a number of other developing nations where the labor supply is large and the wages and cost of doing business are much lower than

FIGURE 2.8

Direct and Indirect Service Delivery Systems

Many industries are using technology to provide service that has traditionally been obtained by a customer going to a supplier and meeting face to face with an organization's representative. The following lists compare the traditional (direct) and technological (indirect) approaches.

Direct Contact	Indirect Contact
Face to face	Toll-free telephone number
Bank tellers	Automated teller machines or online banking
Reservationists (airlines, hotels)	Online computer, smartphone, or tablet reservations
Front desk staff (hotels)	On-screen, in-room television checkout and bill viewing
Ticket takers (theme parks)	Ticket scanning kiosks
Customer service representatives	Online viewing or telephone automated attendant to provide balance or billing information (credit card companies)
Lawyers	Telephone tip lines or e-mail
Photo developers	Self-service film kiosk or Internet transmission of digital images
Supermarket clerks	Online ordering and delivery
Towing dispatchers	In-car navigation and notification systems
Cashiers	Self-service checkout cash registers

they would be in a developed nation. For example, major U.S. companies like American Express, Citigroup, Microsoft, and others have found this strategy of exporting job assignments and processes to other countries to be a lucrative practice. They save millions of dollars in taxes and revenue by distributing call center and service functions outside their own borders.

This practice of outsourcing jobs to a third party provides multiple benefits while also bringing with it some downsides. On the positive side, companies can save money by

- Eliminating large ongoing salaries.
- Reducing health benefits, retirement, and 401(k) payments.
- Avoiding the need to purchase and update computers and related equipment and a myriad of other equipment.
- Increasing workforce size without necessarily doing likewise to the budget.
- Bringing in new, fresh expertise, ideas, and perspectives from outside the organization.

And, on the negative side:

- Long-term employee expertise is lost.
- Employee loyalty to the organization suffers.
- Succession planning opportunities and the potential to groom and hire from within an enculturated workforce is reduced.
- The organization's reputation in the eyes of local citizens is potentially tarnished due to sending jobs away.

- The morale of the "survivors" (employees whose jobs were not eliminated) is potentially adversely affected.
- Managing becomes more complex.
- Customers must deal with "strangers" with whom they cannot build a long-term relationship because their provider may be gone the next time they call or stop by.
- Response time in getting a job or task completed may increase because of distance or other factors.
- Quality of work is not always up to expectations internally or for customers (e.g., dealing with service representatives who have hard-to-understand accents or do not fully understand the customer's culture or expectations).

An alternate cost-saving measure that many organizations have adopted is the practice of redesignating job positions as either part time or shared by two employees who are both part time. As a result of their status, these employees do not qualify for all benefits because of the number of hours they work. Another common strategy is to fill positions with "temporary" employees contracted through a temporary staffing agency that assumes responsibility for staff benefits like healthcare. All of this is done in an effort to reduce rising employee costs (especially benefits) while providing the necessary customer support.

TOOLS FOR SERVICE MEASUREMENT

In a customer-oriented environment, it is important for organizations to constantly gauge their service effectiveness as perceived through the eyes of their customers. There are many ways to find out how well you and your peers are doing in serving customers. Once the results of organizational self-assessments are obtained, they will likely be shared with you and other employees in an effort to determine ways to reduce shortcomings and enhance strengths. If your supervisor fails to share such results, simply ask. Again, you have a vested interest in improvement and if he or she forgets to include you in the improvement loop—or intentionally omits you—you should take the initiative to demonstrate that you do care and are concerned with customer service delivery. From a selfish standpoint, having this developmental knowledge will allow you to identify resources and work toward improving your knowledge and skills. By doing so, you self-empower and make yourself more marketable inside and outside the organization.

Here are some of the typical techniques or tools available to organizations for customer service data collection:

- *Employee focus groups.* In such groups, you and others might be asked to comment or develop ideas on various topics related to customer service or employee and organizational issues. Although you will be providing interesting and valuable insights from your own perspective, remember that your views may differ significantly from those of your customers. For this reason, if your ideas are not implemented, do not be discouraged. Overriding organizational and customer issues to which you are not privy may be the reason.

1. **Partner with customers.** Probably the most important strategy for an organization to adopt in order to create a positive customer-centric service culture is to form a solid relationship with its customers. After all, customers are the reason you have a job and the reason your organization continues to exist. With that in mind, you should do whatever you can to promote a positive, healthy customer-provider relationship. This can be done in a number of ways, many of which will be addressed in detail in later chapters. Here are some simple techniques:

   - Communicate openly and effectively.
   - Smile—project a positive image.
   - Listen intently, and then respond appropriately.
   - Facilitate situations in which customer needs are met and you succeed in win/win situations helping accomplish organizational goals.
   - Focus on developing an ongoing relationship with customers instead of taking a one-time service or sales opportunity approach.

2. **Explore your organization's vision.** By working to better understand the focus of the organization and asking yourself, "What's the added value and results for me?" (AVARFM), you can develop your own commitment to helping make the organization successful. An example of AVARFM might occur when a new policy is implemented that requires you to answer a phone by the third ring.

   A "mystery caller" system is in place as a means of monitoring compliance. Also, to each employee who meets the three-ring standard, rewards are given. You now have a reason or added value associated with compliance.

3. **Help communicate the culture and organizational vision to customers—daily.** Customers have specific expectations. It does no good for the organization to have a vision statement with a future objective in mind if you do not help communicate and demonstrate it to the customer. Many companies place slogans and posters throughout the workplace or service area to communicate the vision. Although these approaches reinforce the message, a more effective means is for you to deliver quality customer service regularly. Through your attitude, language, appearance, knowledge of products and services, body language, and the way you communicate with your customers, they will feel your commitment to serve them. You will read more about techniques for presenting yourself professionally in later chapters.

ethics The term comes from the Greek word "ethos," meaning character. Ethics is involved with right and wrong or good and evil and is illustrated by the way one responds to situations or acts.

ethical behavior Acting in a manner that sends a message of positive morality and good values when confronted with a customer situation or problem.

4. **Demonstrate ethical behavior.** The **ethics** of your organization are intertwined with its culture. **Ethical behavior** is based on values—those of the society, organization, and employees. These values are a combination of beliefs, ideologies, perceptions, experiences, and a sense of what is right (appropriate) and wrong (inappropriate) and are demonstrated through your words and actions and those of your peers and supervisors. All aspects of organizational and employee conduct come into focus when ethical or moral issues arise. It is how you and others around you handle problems or other situations that arise on a daily basis that paint a picture of the organization's overall ethical values, and, in some cases, your own.

   Successful demonstration of ethical behavior is often determined by the values of the customer and how he or she perceives your behavior, and the customer often holds you and your organization to high standards. Thus, it is crucial for you to be aware of your words and actions so that you do not inadvertently send a negative ethical message to your customers.

How do you know which values your organization holds as important? Many times, they are communicated in an employee manual distributed during new hire orientation. Sometimes they are emblazoned on a plaque on the wall, possibly as part of the mission or philosophy statement or next to it. However, the reality test or "where the rubber meets the road" related to your organization's values comes in the day-to-day operational actions of you and your organization.

From an ethical standpoint, it is often up to you and your frontline peers to assess the situation, listen to your customers' requests, scrutinize your organizational policies and procedures, consider all options, and then make the "right" decision. This decision is fair—to your customer and your organization—and it is morally and legally right. The 1999 movie *The Insider* (with Al Pacino and Russell Crowe) epitomized the issues of ethical behavior. The movie is based on the true story of a tobacco industry insider who blew the whistle on his company, which publicly denied the harmful side effects of smoking. Even though the man stood to lose everything, possibly even his life, he acted out of conscience in an effort to help others. Another movie, *Erin Brockovich*, demonstrated what can happen if unethical behavior is not immediately caught and corrected by an organization. In that movie, Pacific Gas & Electric (PG&E) dumped chemicals into the soil and water of Hinkley, California, for years. They then covered up the pollution even though many of the local residents developed serious health problems and died. The company even paid medical bills for some residents to give the appearance of a good corporate neighbor. Ultimately, Erin was able to piece together the details while working for a small legal firm; the subsequent lawsuit resulted in the largest class-action lawsuit payment in history at the time and severe damage to the reputation of PG&E.

The key to ongoing customer relations is trust. Without it, you have no relationship and cannot win customer loyalty.

5. **Identify and improve your service skills.** Take an inventory of your interpersonal and customer service skills; use the strengths and improve the weaker areas. By continually upgrading your knowledge and skills related to people, customer service, and products and services offered, you position yourself as a resource to the customer and an asset to the organization. There is a list of different websites offering various behavioral style surveys at www.mhhe.com/customerservice if you wish to pursue learning more about yourself. Some sites periodically offer a shortened or beta test version of surveys they develop.

6. **Become an expert on your organization.** As the frontline contact person with customers, you are likely to receive a variety of questions related to the organization. Typical questions involve organizational history, structure, policies and procedures systems, products, or services. By being well versed in the many facets of the organization and its operation, related industry topics, and your competition, you can project a more knowledgeable, helpful, and confident image that contributes to total customer satisfaction.

> **Customer Service Success Tip**
>
> One way to better position yourself for success in your organization is to become known as a service champion. Go out of your way to learn policies, procedures, and your corporate culture, then become an advocate for demonstrating ethical behavior, meeting organizational goals, and helping co-workers to do the same.

As a frontline contact with customers, you will be asked a variety of questions about the company and its products. *What skills will you need and what information should you give customers in this situation?*

7. **Demonstrate commitment.** As an employee with customer contact opportunities and responsibilities, you are the organization's representative. One mistake that many frontline employees (and many supervisors) make in communications with customers is to intentionally or unintentionally demonstrate a lack of commitment or support for their company and a sense of powerlessness. A common way in which this occurs is with the use of "they" language when dealing with customers. This can be in reference to management or policies or procedures; for example, "Mrs. Howard, I'd like to help but our policy (they) says . . ." or "Mrs. Howard, I've checked on your request, but my manager (they) said we can't . . ."

An alternative to using "they" language is to take ownership or responsibility for a situation by telling the customer what you can do, not what you cannot do. Customers are not interested in internal strife or procedures; they want to have their needs satisfied. To try to involve customers in situations that are out of their control and that do not concern them is unfair and unwise. Positive language and effort on your part can reduce or eliminate unnecessarily dragging the customer in. Here's one approach: "Mrs. Howard, I'm terribly sorry that you were inconvenienced by our mistake (policy or omission). What I can do to help resolve this situation is . . ."

8. **Work with your customer's interest in mind.** Think to yourself, "If I were my customer, what type of service would I expect?" Then, set out to provide that service.

9. **Treat vendors and suppliers as customers.** Some customer service employees view vendors and suppliers as salespeople whose only purpose is to serve them. In fact, each contact with a vendor or a supplier offers a golden opportunity to tap into a preestablished network and potentially expand your own customer service base while providing better service to existing customers. People remember how they are treated and often act in kind.

10. **Share resources.** By building strong interpersonal relationships with co-workers and peers throughout the industry, you can develop a support system of resources. Sometimes customers will request information, products, or services that are not available through your organization. By being able to refer customers to alternative sources, you will have provided a service, and they are likely to remember that you helped them indirectly.

11. **Work with, not against, your customers.** Customers are in the enviable position of being in control. At no time in recent history has the cliché "it's a buyer's market" been more true, and many consumers know it. To capitalize on this situation, many organizations have become very creative and proactive in their efforts to grab and hold customers. One large Colorado-based national supermarket, Albertson's,

developed a series of commercials touting "Albertson's—it's your store" and stressing that corporate efforts were focused on customer satisfaction. Your efforts should similarly convey the idea that you are working with customers to better serve them.

12. **Provide service follow-up.** Providing follow-up is probably one of the most important service components. Service does not end when the service encounter or sale concludes. There are numerous follow-up opportunities to ensure that customer satisfaction was attained. This can be through a formal customer satisfaction survey or telephone callback system or through an informal process of sending thank-you cards, birthday cards, special sale mailings, and similar initiatives that are inexpensive and take little effort. Think of creative ways to follow up, and then speak to your supervisor about implementing them. These types of efforts reinforce service commitment to customers and let them know that you want to keep them as your customers.

KNOWLEDGE CHECK

1. In your opinion, what is the most important strategy for communicating a positive service culture? Why?

LO 2-5 Separating Average Companies from Excellent Companies

CONCEPT Ask questions to determine the service environment in a company in which you seek employment or are currently employed.

Whether you are currently working in an organization or are seeking employment, the following factors can demonstrate an organization's level of service commitment. They also can be used as a basis for questions you might ask supervisors or interviewers in order to determine what type of service environment exists.

- Executives spend time with the customers.
- Executives spend time talking to frontline service providers.

TRENDING NOW

Self-service is in vogue in the twenty-first century. In a world driven by instant gratification, customers expect that they can have what they want when, how, and where they want it. Interactive voice response systems, web-based e-commerce, and self-help interactive touch-screen kiosks have shown customers that they can be served without having the annoyance of standing in long lines or sitting on hold waiting for the "next available agent." With the advent of technology that can speak to and understand customers, provide visual images, transact business processes, anticipate what customers want based on choices they make on a touch screen, and much more, people have come to expect that every organization will use the latest technology in its business activities. Organizations that fail to embrace and invest in equipment and software that meet customer wants and expectations will fall by the wayside.

- Customer feedback is regularly asked for and acted upon.
- Innovation and creativity are encouraged and rewarded.
- Benchmarking (identifying successful practices of others) is done with similar organizations.
- Technology is widespread, frequently updated, and used effectively.
- Training is provided to keep employees current on industry trends, organizational issues, skills, and technology.
- Open communication exists between frontline employees and all levels of management.
- Employees are provided with guidelines and empowered (in certain instances, authorized to act without management intervention) to do whatever is necessary to satisfy the customer.
- Partnerships with customers and suppliers are common.
- The status quo is not acceptable.

KNOWLEDGE CHECK

1. How can you determine what type of service environment exists in an organization when speaking to supervisors or interviewers?

LO 2-6 What Customers Want

CONCEPT   Customers expect effective, efficient service and value for their money. Customers also expect certain common things that service providers can furnish.

what customers want Things that customers typically desire but do not necessarily need.

Most customers are like you. And **what customers want** is value for their money and/or effective, efficient service. They also expect certain intangible things during a service encounter. Here are seven common things that customers want and expect if they are to keep doing business with you and your organization:

1. **Personal recognition.** This can be demonstrated in a number of ways (sending thank-you cards or notes or birthday cards, returning calls in a timely fashion, or taking the time to look up information that might be helpful even if the customer did not ask for it). A simple way to show recognition to a customer who enters your work area, even if you cannot immediately stop what you are doing to serve him or her, is to smile and acknowledge the person's presence. If possible, you might also offer the customer the option of waiting, having a seat, and so on.

2. **Courtesy.** Basic courtesy involves pleasantries such as "please" and "thank you," as there is no place or excuse for rude behavior in a customer service environment. Even though customers may not always be right, you must treat them with respect. If a situation becomes too intense and you find yourself "losing it," call upon someone else to serve that customer. This is especially important in stressful environments where customers are truly suffering and not likely to be in the mood for poor attitudes or delays (e.g., hospital waiting rooms and doctors' or dentists' offices).

3. **Timely service.** Most people don't mind waiting briefly for service if there is a legitimate reason (as when you are waiting on another customer or

obviously serving another customer on the phone), but they do not like to spend what they believe is undue amounts of time waiting to be served.

Your challenge as a customer service professional is to provide prompt yet effective service. It is important to remember that customers value their time as much as you and your managers/bosses do.

Work diligently to stay on schedule and at least explain when delays do occur so that the customer understands the reason for the wait (e.g., in a doctor's office when scheduled appointments are running behind because of a medical emergency or the doctor was delayed while in surgery). If extensive delays are likely to occur, offer the customer an option of possibly rescheduling. Customers probably will not want to, but the gesture of allowing them some decision in the situation is psychologically soothing in many cases.

4. **Professionalism.** Customers expect and should receive knowledgeable answers to their questions, service that satisfies their needs and lessens effort on their part, and service personnel who take pride in their work. You can demonstrate these characteristics by exemplifying the ethics talked about earlier, and the communication behaviors outlined in later chapters of this book.

5. **Enthusiastic service.** Customers come to your organization for one purpose—to satisfy a need. This need may be nothing more than to "look around." Even so, they should find a dedicated team of service professionals standing by to assist them in whatever way possible.

By delivering service with a smile, offering additional services and information, and taking the time to give extra effort in every service encounter, you can help guarantee a positive service experience for your customer.

6. **Empathy.** Customers also want to be understood. Your job as a service provider is to make every effort to be understanding, and to provide appropriate service.

To succeed in the service profession, you must be able to put yourself in the customer's position or look at the need from the customer's perspective as much as possible. This is especially true when customers do not speak English well or have some type of disability that reduces their communication effectiveness.

When a customer has a complaint or believes that he or she did not receive appropriate service, it is your job to calm or appease in a nonthreatening, helpful manner and show understanding.

A common strategy for showing empathy is the **feel, felt, found technique.** When using it, a service provider is demonstrating a compassionate understanding of the customer's issue or situation. For example, a customer is upset because the product desired is not in stock. A service provider might respond by saying: "Mr. Philips, I know how you feel. I've felt the same way when I had my heart set on a specific item. Many customers have actually found that the alternative product I described to you has the same features and performs several other functions as well."

feel, felt, found technique A process for expressing empathy and concern for someone and for helping that person understand that you can relate to the situation.

Your Customer Expectations

Now that you know what goes into making a customer environment "customer-friendly," think about your own expectations when you patronize a company. Share your answers with others in the class.

Drawing on your own experiences, list four or five expectations that you feel are typical of most customers.

McGraw Hill Education **connect**

7. **Patience.** Customers should not have to deal with your frustrations or pressures. Your efficiency and effectiveness should seem effortless. If you are angry because of a policy, procedure, management, or the customer, you must strive to mask that feeling. This may be difficult to do when you believe that the customer is being unfair or unrealistic. By suppressing your desire to speak out or react emotionally, you can remain in control, serve the customer professionally, and end the contact sooner.

As an additional resource, there is a chapter on stress management available to you at www.mhhe.com/customerservice.

KNOWLEDGE CHECK

1. What do you believe is the most important strategy for communicating a positive service culture? Why?

2. What are some strategies for giving personal recognition to your customers?

3. How might you exhibit enthusiastic service to your customers?

4. What is the feel, felt, found technique and what does it potentially communicate to a customer?

Small Business Perspective

No matter what size organization you work for, having great leaders who are visionary and think from a customer perspective will make the organization successful. In small business, such leadership is crucial for success because such organizations do not typically have "deep pockets" with large amounts of expendable resources available. In such companies, every dollar counts. For that reason, it is very important that everyone from the owner or CEO down to frontline employees embraces the concepts that you read about in this chapter. All must go above and beyond what their job description requires and take personal ownership for the company every day. Employees and management must pull together to share knowledge and skills and create a customer-centric atmosphere.

Typically, employees in successful small companies tend to bond as "family" and really get to know one another. As a result, they are more likely to pitch in when needed without an expectation of reward. This does not mean that if you work for a small company you should not expect to get paid for what you do. It simply means that by getting to know the strengths and areas for improvement of other employees and management, you can help fill gaps if you possess knowledge and skills that they do not have. In the long run, such behavior normally results in a higher payout for the organization because customers hear about you and are attracted to do business with the firm. When this occurs, revenue comes in that can fund salary increases, new equipment, and employee functions (e.g., family picnics and celebrations for special occasions or holidays).

In small organizations, effective communication and feedback are powerful and needed. Unlike many large organizations where you might be able to avoid someone and get assistance and information needed to do your job elsewhere, in a small organization, resources are limited and everyone has to do his or her part and work cohesively together. If a disagreement or misunderstanding occurs, you must work together to resolve and get past it, just as you should with your own family members.

Successful small business employees typically possess many of the following attributes:

- **Self-initiative or ability to recognize what needs to be done.** By identifying potential issues that need to be addressed and accomplishing them without a lot of direction or guidance from others, service providers in small companies aid the overall effectiveness of the organization and address customer expectations.

- **Strong powers of persuasion.** There may be no one else around when a customer calls or comes by your office in a small company. For that reason, you must be able to share an opinion, idea, or information in a convincing manner so that your customers believe and trust what you are saying. Strong oral, nonverbal, and written skills will often make the difference in whether you succeed when dealing with customers.

- **Flexibility.** Unlike larger organizations where there may be written policies and procedures and a Human Resources department to consult for various issues, small business employees often have to be able to "think on their feet" and come up with appropriate solutions when dealing with customers. This comes from having sound knowledge and skills related to products and service procedure.

- **Creativity.** There will be many times when working for a small business where you will have to come up with a solution to a customer question or issue on the spur of the moment. To do this, you must be able to use the products, services, and tools offered by the organization to best satisfy the needs or wants of your customers.

- **Problem-solving ability.** Since you will be working with limited resources in many instances, you must be able to gather data and information about a customer issue (see Chapter 3 for ideas on effective questioning), quickly analyze what you learned, and make an appropriate decision.

Before going to work for a small organization, read Chapter 6 and decide if you have the right temperament or behavioral style preference to succeed in such an environment.

Impact on Service

Based on personal experience and what you just read, answer the following questions:

1. What characteristics or traits do you feel that many employees in small companies lack that causes service problems? Explain.

2. From a service perspective, do you think it is better to work for a small company or large one? Why?

3. To what degree do you feel service providers in small companies differ from their large organization counterparts? Explain.

> **Customer Service Success Tip**
>
> In addition to any specifics you would like to learn for yourself, ask the following questions of those with whom you interact regularly:
>
> - Do I tend to smile when I speak?
> - Do I spontaneously smile and greet people who pass me in the workplace?
> - What body cues (nonverbal signals) do I use regularly when I speak?
> - How would you categorize my overall presence when I speak (confident, uncertain, timid, relaxed)? Why do you perceive that?
> - What "pet" words or phrases do I use regularly?
> - When I speak, how does my tone sound (assertive, attacking, calming, friendly, persuasive)? What examples of this can you provide?
> - When I am frustrated or irritated how do you know it?

KNOWLEDGE CHECK

1. What are two key elements can make your customer interactions more successful?

LO 3-2 Ensuring Two-Way Communication

CONCEPT Two-way communication involves a sender and a receiver, each of whom contributes to the communication process. Part of the communication process is deciding which is the best channel to ensure clear message delivery.

As a customer service professional, one of your primary roles is to ensure that a meaningful exchange of information takes place each time you interact with a customer. By accepting this responsibility, you can perform your job more efficiently, generate goodwill and customer loyalty for the organization, and provide service excellence. Being aware of the elements of **two-way communication** and the importance of each will help facilitate your communication success. Figure 3.1 shows a communication model that helps the interpersonal communication process.

two-way communication An active process in which two individuals apply all the elements of interpersonal communication (e.g., listening, feedback, positive language) in order to effectively exchange information and ideas.

INTERPERSONAL COMMUNICATION MODEL

Environment

The environment (office, call center, store, and group or individual setting) in which you send or receive messages affects the effectiveness of your message. For example, in a busy business environment, you are likely

> **Street Talk**
>
> Using jargon or unfamiliar vocabulary when explaining a procedure to a student or other customer will leave the listener confused or totally misinformed. Know your audience when explaining any new technique or procedure.
>
> SHARON MASSEN, PH.D., CAP *Massen and Associates*

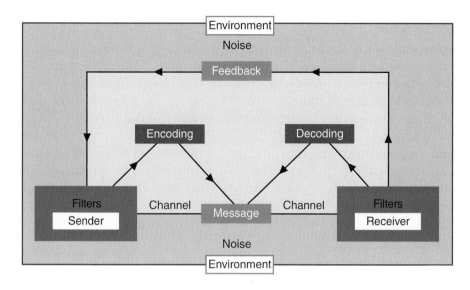

FIGURE 3.1
Interpersonal Communication Model

to be making an effort to meet deadlines, serve all customers, or create a positive experience for each customer. In such an environment, you or others may take shortcuts in communicating and send what might be perceived as curt or abrupt verbal and nonverbal messages. This could potentially cause a service breakdown. The key to success in such instances is to take a deep breath when things get hectic, remember to use a calm and professional tone, and think before speaking or responding nonverbally. If things get so stressful that you feel like you are going to "lose it," you might want to take a short break if possible before encountering your next customer. Otherwise, you may inadvertently allow your frustration to carry over from one customer to the next and could come across as being rude or unprofessional to the second person.

sender One of the two primary elements of a two-way conversation. He or she selects a communication channel and then creates and encodes the intended message to the receiver. This starts the communication process.

receiver One of the two primary elements of a two-way conversation. The receiver gathers the sender's message, decodes the message based on his or her interpretation, and then decides how to react to it.

Sender

You take on the role of **sender** as you initiate a message with your customer. Conversely, when customers respond, they assume that role. As the sender, you have a responsibility to think of the message that you want the customer to receive, decide the best way to communicate it (channel), and then use words and nonverbal cues that effectively convey that message.

Receiver

Initially, you may be the **receiver** of your customer's message; however, once you offer feedback, you switch to the sender role. As the receiver, you must effectively listen in order to receive and effectively comprehend what the customer has said. If unsure, you should either paraphrase (repeat the customer's message in your own words) or ask questions that will clarify the meaning for you.

Two-way communication is the foundation of effective customer service. *How can you be sure that you are listening to the customer?*

Message

message A communication delivered through speech or signals, or in writing.

The **message** is the idea or concept that you or your customer wishes to convey. Often our messages get lost in the delivery. Because we choose inappropriate words or nonverbal cues, the customer misinterprets or does not understand our intended point. This can lead to a breakdown in communication and service. In order to prevent this from occurring, it is important to think before speaking. Consider factors such as the customer's gender, age, culture, primary language, experience and knowledge level, ability to hear, and any other factor that might affect the way in which the customer might receive and analyze your message. Then, formulate a message that is clear and concise and communicates your intended meaning.

Channel

channel Term used to describe the method through which people communicate messages. Examples are face to face, telephone, e-mail, written correspondence, and facsimile.

The method you choose to transmit your message (over the phone, in person, by fax, by e-mail, or by other means) is the **channel**. In an ideal world, it is typically best to communicate face to face, with a secondary preference being over the telephone. Through these two channels, you and your customer are able to hear words, inflections, tone, and other voice qualities that impact message meaning or, in the case of face to face, see the nonverbal cues that accompany the words. When you revert to written communication there is the potential for misunderstanding of words, lost opportunity to supplement the words with verbal and nonverbal cues, and the potential feeling of the message being impersonal.

Encoding

encoding The stage in the interpersonal communication process in which the sender decides what message will be sent and how it will be transmitted along with considerations about the receiver.

Encoding occurs as you evaluate what must be done to effectively put your message into a format that your customer will understand (language, symbols, and gestures are a few options). Failing to correctly determine your customer's ability to decode your message could lead to confusion and misunderstanding. As mentioned under the "message" section above, you must consider many personal factors about your recipient in order to ensure that she gets the message that you intend.

Decoding

decoding The stage in the interpersonal communication process in which messages received are analyzed by a receiver in an effort to determine the sender's intent.

Decoding occurs as you or your customer converts messages received into familiar ideas by interpreting or assigning meaning. Depending on how well the message was encoded or whether personal filters (e.g., gender, background, age, language, or cultural differences) interfere, the received message may not be the one you originally intended. This can lead to a service breakdown and potential conflict.

Feedback

feedback The stage of the interpersonal communication process in which a receiver responds to a sender's message.

Unless a response is given to messages received, there is no way to determine whether the intended message was received. **Feedback** is one of the most crucial elements of the two-way communication process. Without it, you have a monologue. Feedback typically comes in the form of nonverbal reactions or verbal responses or questions during face-to-face or telephonic communication. When you are using e-mail, texting, or other written

WORK IT OUT 3.1

Communication Reality Check

To better plan your own future service strategy, think about your own past service experiences. Think of your reaction when you walked into a store that used a greeter and the person either did or said nothing other than eyed you up and down or said something like, "Welcome to . . ." in a robotic fashion and without smiling, then handed you an advertisement flyer, which you likely did not want in the first place. What was your reaction? What message about the organization did their words or actions send to you? On a scale of 1–5 (5 being highest), how would you rate their level of service? If you were them, what could be done differently in the future to change the rating you gave?

formats, you have to wait for a response. In such instances (or when no response is forthcoming), it is a good idea to clarify receipt and proper understanding of your original message based on the type of feedback that you receive. Never assume that someone got and interpreted your message the way you intended. Read the response well before leaping to any potential negative conclusions. There have been too many instances in which people have sent an inappropriate emotional response, which they later regretted, because they initially misinterpreted feedback they received.

Filters

Filters are factors that distort or affect the messages you receive. They include, among other things, your attitude, interests, biases, expectations, experiences, education, beliefs and values, background, culture, and gender. These factors can cloud our perception and judgment and can sometimes result in communication and service breakdowns. Consider your own filters when sending or interpreting messages.

filters Psychological barriers in the form of personal experiences, lessons learned, societal beliefs, and values through which people process and compare information received to determine its significance.

Trending NOW

In recent years the human attention span in many developed nations has gotten significantly shorter. This can most be attributed to the faster pace at which information is delivered through technology and the resulting conditioning of the brain to receive and expect material to arrive faster and on a more regular basis. Think about how fast television commercials and movie scenes change. Also, consider the video games to which many people have spent hours playing and have become accustomed.

From an interpersonal communication standpoint, this means that you must structure messages more concisely and deliver information in "sound bites" or short spurts of information for many customers, especially those who speak another language. This is opposed to droning on with a long sales pitch or explanation. The key is to watch your customers' nonverbal cues to detect their level of attention and comprehension. If necessary, repeat what you said in a slightly different manner to ensure effectiveness of your message and understanding.

Noise

noise Refers to physiological or psychological factors (physical characteristics, level of attention, message clarity, loudness of message, or environmental factors) that interfere with the accurate reception of information.

Noise consists of physiological factors (e.g., health or physical characteristics and abilities) or psychological factors (e.g., level of attention, mood, mental health, or emotional condition) that interfere with the accurate reception of information. It can also include environmental factors (e.g., external sounds or room acoustics) that inhibit communication and listening.

KNOWLEDGE CHECK ✓

1. What are the 10 elements of the interpersonal communication model?
2. Which of the model elements is one of the most crucial in the two-way communication process?

LO 3-3 Communicating Positively

CONCEPT A positive approach to addressing customers can be productive.

You should think out everything from your greeting to your closing statements before you come into contact with a customer. Know what you want and need to say, avoid unnecessary details or discussion, and be prepared to answer questions about the organization, its products and services, and the customer's order. To maximize your potential and create a positive outcome with customers, use the PLAN acronym as a guide to effective communication with those with whom you come into contact. The model stands for

Prepare for Positive Customer Interactions.

Let Your Customers Know They Are Important.

Address Your Customer's Expectations Positively.

Nurture a Continuing Relationship.

Just as you can turn customers off with your word choice, you can also win them over. Figure 3.2 contains some tips.

PREPARE FOR POSITIVE CUSTOMER INTERACTIONS

The first element of the PLAN acronym is all about getting into a mental state of mind to effectively provide quality service to your customers.

Too often service providers wait for something to happen and then react to the situation. This is a formula for disaster, especially if they do not have the knowledge or skills to address a customer's needs. To prevent this from happening to you, consider the types of potential customer situations you might encounter. Next, get training, discuss possible scenarios and solutions with peers and your supervisor, and role-play handling potential customer issues so that you have in mind possible actions to take should an actual situation arise.

Some phrases can assist you in strengthening relationships with your customers. Such language reinforces your integrity and encourages customers to trust you. How do you or could you use these words? Which ones do you use the most?

Please.	May I . . . ?
Thank you.	Have you considered . . . ?
I can or will . . .	I'm sorry (I apologize) for . . .
How may I help?	However, and, or yet (instead of but).
I was wrong.	It's my (our) fault.
I understand (appreciate) how you feel.	Would you mind . . . ?
Situation, issue, concern (instead of problem).	What do you think?
Often, many times, some (instead of global terms).	I appreciate . . .
You're right.	Use of customer's name.

FIGURE 3.2

Words and Phrases That Build Customer Relationships

Identify Pet Peeves

One way to prepare to serve your customers is to do a quick mental assessment before they arrive or contact you. Part of this analysis revolves around you and your personal preferences.

Most people have something that bothers them about how others communicate or behave. These "hot buttons," or **pet peeves**, can lead to customer relationship breakdowns if you are not aware of what your pet peeves are and how you come across to others. By identifying and acknowledging your potential irritants, you can begin to modify your behavior in order to prevent problems with customers. You may also be able to avoid situations in which such behaviors are present or might manifest themselves and cause problems for you.

Your customers also likely have a list of things that they dislike about service providers. If you exhibit one of their pet peeves while serving them, you could find yourself opposite a disgruntled person who is not afraid to voice his or her displeasure. They may even escalate their complaint to your supervisor or elsewhere.

Some typical behaviors that service providers exhibit, and that might bother customers, include

Disinterest in serving.

Excessive wait times.

Unprofessional service provider appearance (in the customer's mind).

Lack of cleanliness (environment or service provider).

Abruptly putting someone on telephone hold without their permission.

Failing to answer telephone within four rings.

Eating or chewing while dealing with a customer.

Lack of knowledge or authority.

Poor quality of service.

Condescension (taking an air of superiority to the customer).

Rudeness or overfamiliarity (using first names without permission).

pet peeves Refers to factors, people, or situations that personally irritate or frustrate a service provider and that, left unchecked, can create a breakdown in effective service.

WORK IT OUT 3.2

My Pet Peeves

Take a few minutes to think about irritating behaviors that service providers have exhibited when helping you in the past. Make a list of these behaviors and strive not to exhibit similar ones, since your customers will likely also be irritated by them. After you create your list, compare it with others in the class.

As an alternative, your instructor may form groups of four or five learners and do this as a group activity.

LET YOUR CUSTOMERS KNOW THEY ARE IMPORTANT

The second element of the PLAN acronym deals with making your customers feel as if they are the most important people in the world at the moment they contact you. To do this, you must consider each person who calls, texts, comes into your place of business, or contacts you through a computer or other communication tool to be a guest of your organization. Treat him or her with respect, dignity, and hospitality as you likely would a family member or good friend. Many companies have adopted the term "guests" to describe their customers or visitors as a way to remind employees of this concept.

The following are some proven strategies to help you accomplish the goal of making people feel welcome by you and your peers when they contact the organization.

Make Customers Feel Welcome

Personalize your greeting a bit. If appropriate, shake hands, smile often, and offer a sincere welcome, not the canned, "Welcome to . . . ." Instead, use whatever your organizational policy dictates, such as, "Good morning/afternoon, welcome to . . . . My name is . . . . How may I assist (or help) you?" Even on the telephone you should smile and verbally "shake your customer's hand" because your smile can definitely be heard in your voice. Be conscious of the need to sound approachable and receptive.

Most people like to feel as if they belong, to be recognized as special, and to be seen as individuals. To help enhance your service delivery, get to know your customer's name when possible and use it in greeting him or her. Also use it where appropriate throughout the conversation and when closing the encounter. Try to avoid using negative-sounding "you" messages as a primary means of addressing your customer. For example, instead of, "You'll need to fill out this form before I can process your refund," try, "Mr. Renaldi, can you please provide some information on this form while I start processing your refund? That way, we'll have you out of here quickly." The latter approach makes it sound as if you recognize customers as being important and puts them psychologically in control of the situation as opposed to being told what to do. You are also showing respect for their time. This can often mean the difference between a smile from your customer and a confrontation and demand to speak to a supervisor.

Many companies go out of their way to send the message of "family." For example, the Olive Garden restaurant advertises that "When you're here, you're family." Similarly, CarMax and several other national automobile chains go to great lengths to make the customer feel welcome and special. For example, they drape a huge ribbon over a newly purchased vehicle in a well-lit garage, available sales representatives gather with the customer to congratulate him or her on being part of the "family," and photographs are taken of this "special moment." While some customers might view the latter as "hokey" or not sincere, others might appreciate the special treatment.

Focus on the Customer as a Person

Strive to let customers know that you recognize them as individuals and appreciate their time, effort, patience, trust, and business. This is important. To deliver quality service effectively, you must deal with the human being before you deal with his or her needs or business concerns.

For example, if someone has waited in a line or on hold for service, as soon as this person steps up or you come back on the line, smile warmly, thank him or her for being patient, apologize for the wait, and ask what you can do to assist him or her. Often in such situations the service provider says something like, "Next" (sounds canned and not customer-focused) or "Can I help the next person?" (better, but it still goes straight to business without an apology or without recognizing the customer's inconvenience or wait). On the phone the service provider goes straight to, "This is Jean; how may I help you?" (with no recognition of the customer's inconvenience).

Another opportunity to focus on the customer occurs at the end of a transaction or call. If your organization does not have a standard parting comment to use with customers, simply smile and say something like, "Mr. Rinaldi, thank you for coming to (or calling) ABC Corporation. Please come back (or call) again." The key is that you must sound sincere. You may even want to modify your parting statement for subsequent customers so that it sounds more personal—and so the next person in line doesn't hear you parrot the same words with each customer.

- *Offer assistance.* Even if a problem or question is not in your area of responsibility, offer to help get answers, information, or assistance. Your customer will likely appreciate the fact that you went out of your way to help.

- *Be prepared.* Know as much as possible about the organization, its products and services, your job, and, as appropriate, the customer. Also, make sure that you have all the tools necessary to serve the customer, take notes, and do your job in a professional manner. This allows you to deliver quality information and service while better satisfying customer needs and expectations.

- *Provide factual information.* Don't express opinions or speculate why something did or didn't, or will or will not, occur. State only what you are sure of or can substantiate. For example, if you are not sure when a delivery will take place or when a co-worker who handles certain functions will return, say so, but offer to find the answer or handle the situation yourself. Don't raise customer expectations by saying, "This should be delivered by 7:30 tomorrow morning" or "Sue should be back from lunch in 10 minutes." If neither event occurs, the customer is likely to be irritated.

- *Be helpful.* If you cannot do something or don't have a product or service, admit it but be prepared to offer an alternative. Do not try to "dance around" an issue in an effort to respond in a manner that you feel the customer expects. Most people will spot this tentative behavior, and your credibility will suffer as a result. Do not insult your customer's intelligence by taking this approach. You and the organization will lose in the long run.

> **Customer Service Success Tip**
>
> Look for ways to celebrate your customers and make them feel special and valued. For example, congratulate them on special events of which you are aware (e.g., weddings or anniversaries, birthdays, birth of children, graduation from school, and other successes). This will return dividends of increased customer satisfaction, higher levels of customer trust in the organization, and reduced stress for you because you will have fewer instances of unhappy customers with whom you have to deal.

- *Accept responsibility.* Take responsibility for what you do or say and, if necessary, for actions taken by someone else that failed to satisfy the customer. Don't blame others or hide behind "they said" or "policy says" excuses. When something goes wrong, take responsibility and work to resolve the problem positively and quickly. If you don't have the authority needed, get someone who does, rather than refer the customer to someone else.
- *Take appropriate action.* You should go to great lengths to satisfy the customer. Sometimes this may mean bending the rules a bit. In such cases, it may be easier to ask forgiveness from your supervisor than to explain why you lost the organization a good customer. If a request really cannot be honored because it is too extreme (a customer demands a free $100 item because he or she had to return one that did not work properly), explain why that specific request cannot be fulfilled and then negotiate and offer alternatives.

ADDRESS YOUR CUSTOMER'S EXPECTATIONS POSITIVELY

The third element of the PLAN acronym focuses on the area of interpersonal communication with your customers.

Communication is a major portion of your job and has a definite impact on the relationships and impressions that you forge with your customers or clients. Each time you interact with a current or potential customer, he or she is assessing you from many standpoints, which plays a large part in how the customer sees and interprets you and your organization.

The following sections provide some guidance on ways that you can project a positive customer service attitude and image.

WORK IT OUT 3.3

Analyzing Your Verbal Communication Skills

To help you determine how you sound to others, try a bit of objective self-analysis. To do this, place a cassette or digital voice recorder nearby, either at home or in the office, and leave it on for about 45 minutes to an hour while you interact with other people. Then play the cassette or recorder to hear what your voice sounds like when you communicate verbally with others. Be especially alert for verbal cues that send a negative message or seem to be misinterpreted by the other people involved. Also, listen carefully to the manner in which others respond to you. Do their words or voice tone seem different from what you expected? Did they seem to respond to your comments in a way that shows confusion, frustration, or irritation because of what you said or how you said it? If you answer yes to these questions, and this occurs several times on the tape or recorder, go back to the people involved in the conversation and ask them to help you interpret what's on the recording. You may find that your communication style is doing more to hurt than help in gathering information and building relationships with others.

Use Customer-Centric Language

A mistake by many service providers is to communicate as if they are the important element of a transaction. In reality, it is the customer upon whom a message should be focused. The following examples show the difference in focus:

Provider-Centered

- As soon as I have time . . .
- I'll send out a form that we need you to complete and sign.
- Let me explain the benefits of this product.

Customer-Centered

- I'll take care of that right away.
- To make sure that we have all the information needed to ensure you the best service, once you get the form, please complete and sign it.
- As a savvy consumer, you'll appreciate the benefits of this product. May I explain?

Another important thing to remember in communicating with customers is to use easily understood words or communication style, especially when interacting with those who speak a primary language other than your own. This does not mean you have to "dummy down" your speech or appear to talk down to someone. Instead, it means that you watch your customer's nonverbal body language for signs of confusion or frustration as you speak, and frequently ask for feedback and questions. This also applies when you are selling or servicing a customer in a technical area where they might not have your level of knowledge or expertise and do not recognize the terminology you might use to describe something.

If you are on the telephone, listen for sounds of confusion or pauses that may indicate that the customer either did not understand something you said or has a question.

> **Customer Service Success Tip**
>
> When the telephone rings, mentally "shift gears" before answering. Stop doing other tasks, clear your head of other thoughts, focus on the telephone, then cheerfully and professionally answer the call.

Here is an example of how your customer might feel if you use language with which customers are not familiar:

Many interpersonal impartation decompositions can be ascribed to one singular customer service professional fallacy—that all customers can discern the significance of the service provider's vernacular.

How did that statement feel to you? Remember that feeling the next time you are tempted to communicate inappropriately with customers.

Simply stated, what you read means: *Many customer service professionals fail to use language their customers can understand.*

> ### Customer Service Success Tip
>
> Technology has increased the options and speed at which you can communicate with your customers. Even so, there is still a need to stay personally connected with others. There is no substitution for face-to-face or telephone contact with your customers. This format allows you to "read" their tone of voice and body language, which you cannot do via other technology.
>
> Chances are that you really cannot overcommunicate with your customer, especially when problems exist. It is important that you stay in touch with customers periodically to stay in the forefront of their memory and to demonstrate that you value them. The key is to read their reactions to your efforts and, in those instances when someone might want less contact, act accordingly.

Use "Small Talk"

Look for opportunities to communicate on a personal level or to compliment your customer. If you promptly establish a professional relationship with your customers, they are less likely to attack you verbally or complain. Listen to what they say. Look for specific things that you have in common. For example, suppose your customer mentions that she has just returned from Altoona, Pennsylvania, where she visited relatives. If you grew up in or near Altoona, comment about this and ask questions. By bonding with the customer, you show that you recognize the customer as more than a nameless face or a prospective sale.

One thing to keep in mind about **small talk** is that you must listen to your customer's words and tone. If it is obvious he or she is impatient or in a hurry, skip the small talk and focus on efficiently providing service.

small talk Dialogue used to enhance relationships, show civility, and build rapport.

Use Positive "I" or "We" Messages

In addition to avoiding the "you" statements that you will read about later in this chapter, focus on what "I" or "we" can do for or with the customer. In addressing the customer, state the specific service approaches you will take; for example, "I'll handle this personally," as opposed to "I'll do my best" or "I'll try." Expressions like "I'll handle this personally" sound proactive and positive. **"I" or "we" messages** go a long way in subtly letting the customer know that you have the knowledge, confidence, and authority to help out.

"I" or "we" messages Messages that are potentially less offensive than the word "you," which is like nonverbal finger-pointing when emotions are high.

Ask Positively Phrased Questions

Sometimes the simplest things can cause problems, especially if someone is already irritated. To avoid creating a negative situation or escalating

Look for ways to create a positive message exchange between you and your customer. *What are potential outcomes when a service provider communicates a "can do" attitude with a customer?*

customer emotions when things are already amiss, choose the wording of your questions carefully. Consider these two specific techniques.

The first technique is to find a way to rephrase any question that you would normally start with "Why?" The reason is that this word cannot be inflected in a way that doesn't come across as potentially abrasive, intrusive, or meddlesome. Don't believe it? Get a recorder and attempt to say the word without an inflection that sounds challenging or questioning.

As with many experiences you have, the origin of negative feelings toward the word likely stem from childhood. Do you remember when you wanted to do something as a child and were told no? The word that probably came out of your mouth (in a whiney voice) was "Why?" This was a verbal challenge to the person who was telling you that you couldn't do something. And the response you probably heard was, "Because I said so" or "Because I'm the mommy (or daddy); that's why." Most likely, you didn't like that type of response then, and neither did your customers when they were children. The result of this early experience is that when we hear the word *why* as a question, it can sound like a challenge and can prompt a negative emotional reaction (blame a flashback to memories for this). To prevent this from occurring, try rewording your "Why" question or asking questions that might not be perceived as arrogant, rude, or directive.

Examples

Instead of	Try
Why do you feel that way?	What makes you feel that way?
Why don't you like . . . ?	What is it that you don't like about . . . ?
Why do you need that feature?	How is that feature going to be beneficial to you?
Why do you want that color?	What other colors have you considered?

The second technique to consider regarding question phrasing is to ask ones that do not create or add to a negative impression. This is especially important if you have a customer who is already saying negative things about you, your product or service, or the company. By asking questions that start with a negative word and trying to lead customers to an answer, you can be subtly adding fuel to an emotional fire.

For example, suppose your customer is upset because he ordered window blinds through the mail and did not get the color he wanted. He has called you to complain. You have asked a few questions to determine the color scheme of the room in which the blinds will be installed. You say, "Based on what you have told me, don't you think the color you received would work just as well?" Your customer now launches into a tirade. He probably thinks that you were not listening to him, were not concerned about his needs, and presumed you could lead him to another decision.

Examples of Alternative Questioning Strategies

Here are some more examples of questions that could cause communication breakdowns, along with some suggested alternatives.

Instead of	Try
Why?	What prevents . . . ? or Could you please provide an alternative suggestion to _____?
Don't you think . . . ?	What do you think . . . ?
Wouldn't this work as well?	How do you think this would work?
Couldn't we do . . . instead?	Could we try . . . instead?
Aren't you going to make a deposit?	What amount would you like to deposit?
Don't you have two pennies?	Do you have two pennies?
Shouldn't you try this for a week before we replace the part again?	How do you feel about trying it for week to see how it works before we replace the part again?

Be Specific

Whenever you have to answer questions, especially details relating to costs, delivery dates, warranties, and other important areas of customer interest, give complete and accurate details. If you leave something out, possibly because you believe it isn't important, you can bet that the customer may feel it was important, and will be upset.

Examples

If deliveries are free, but only within a 50-mile radius, make sure that you tell the customer about the mileage policy. (The customer may live 51 miles away!)

If a customer calls to ask for the price of an item and your quote does not include tax, shipping, and handling, say so. Give the total cost, so that there are no surprises when the customer drives to the store to make the purchase or orders from your website and ends up paying more.

Listen Carefully and Respond Appropriately

Active listening is a key element of two-way verbal communication. The manner in which you listen and respond often determines the direction of the conversation. When customers feel that they are not being listened to, their attitude and emotions can quickly change from amiable to confrontational.

One technique to ensure that you have received your customer's message correctly is to use a technique called **paraphrasing**. To ensure that you got the message that your customer intended to communicate, take time to ask him or her for feedback. Do this by repeating to the customer the message you thought you heard, but in your own words—paraphrase. As an example of this technique, assume that a customer called to complain that a toy that she had purchased for her grandson was defective and missing parts. She went on to describe how she has been a loyal customer of the store since her children were small and that while she normally has no complaints about products and services she receives, she is disappointed by this defective toy. In response, you should thank her for her continued business and personalize by commenting on the length of her patronage. Next, you should paraphrase what you heard by saying something like, "Mrs. Hawthorne, I apologize for the inconvenience that this has caused you. I know that you must be very frustrated. If I understand the problem correctly, you bought this item on June 28 as a present for your grandson and when he tried to assemble it, two parts were missing; is that correct?" Once she confirms, apologize again, assure her that you can help resolve the issue and pursue questions to find out if she would like to exchange the item, just get the missing parts, or return it for a refund.

paraphrasing The practice of a message receiver giving back in his or her own words what he believes a sender said.

NURTURE A CONTINUING RELATIONSHIP

The final element of the PLAN acronym deals with how well you close a transaction, encourage your customers to return, and have them say positive things about their experience.

In order to maintain an ongoing business relationship with customers, each person in the organization has to take responsibility for leaving a positive impression on those with whom they come into contact throughout the day. It is not enough to simply do your job as a service provider. You also have to cement the transaction and relationship by demonstrating such traits as credibility, trustworthiness, conscientiousness, and other characteristics that many customers expect from a service professional. The following are some easy-to-apply strategies that might help you accomplish this and encourage customers to return and spread positive word-of-mouth publicity about you and your organization.

Ask Permission

Get customer approval before taking action that was not previously approved or discussed, such as putting a telephone caller on hold or interrupting. By doing so, you can raise the customers to a position of authority, boost their self-esteem, and empower them (to say yes or no). They'll likely appreciate all three.

Agree with Customers

Like most other people, customers like to hear that they are right. This is especially true when a mistake has been made or something goes wrong. When a customer has a complaint or is upset because a product and/or service does not live up to expectations, acknowledge the emotion he or she is feeling and then move on and help resolve the issue. Defusing by acknowledgment is a powerful tool.

However, listen carefully for the level of emotion. If the customer is very angry, you may want to choose your words carefully. For example, suppose you have a customer who has called or returned to your store on four occasions to address a single problem with a product. She has been inconvenienced, has not gotten satisfaction in the previous encounters, and has spent extra time in an effort to correct the problem. When she calls or arrives, her voice tone and volume are elevated and she is demanding that you get a supervisor. In this situation, your best approach probably is to let her vent and describe the problem without interrupting, apologize as often as appropriate, and do everything you can to resolve the issue fairly (assuming that she has a legitimate complaint). You would not want to use a statement that could further enflame her.

Although phrases such as "You sound upset Ms. O'Malley" or "I can understand how you feel" can help diffuse some tense situations, they can come across as patronizing and insincere when someone is really angry (such as in the above example). Instead of using such terminology, try looking for something she is saying that you can agree with. Also, remember that when customers get angry, raise their voices, and say certain things, they are not typically angry with you—they are frustrated and angry with the organization and/or system. Try not to become defensive or sound irritated, since this will likely only escalate the customer's emotions.

For example, suppose Ms. O'Malley says something like, "You people are a bunch of idiots. I've been coming in here for years and I always have problems. Why don't you hire someone with brains to serve your customers?" A normal human response would be to become defensive or to retaliate. However, think back on what happened when you were a child at the playground and similar situations occurred. When someone pushed you or called you a name and you responded with name-calling or pushed back, emotions escalated until someone either struck out at the other person or ran away crying. No one won. The relationship was damaged, possibly irreparably.

In the case of Ms. O'Malley, if you strike back with similar comments, neither of you will win. Moreover, you will likely lose a valued customer who will tell her story to many friends—and you will have to explain to your boss why you acted the way you did. Instead, try a defusing technique in which you seek something to agree upon. For example, you might reply, "I know this is frustrating, especially when it seems we haven't done a good job solving your problem." After this, assuming she doesn't launch back in with another tirade, you might then offer, "Let me help you take care of this right now." If she does verbally attack again, let her vent and then try another calm agreement response, followed by another apology and a second offer to assist. The key is to remain professional and in control of your emotions so that you can find a suitable resolution to the issue.

The value in this approach is that in letting Ms. O'Malley vent, you are discovering her emotions and possibly the history of the problem by listening actively. If you need more information, you can ask questions once you have defused her emotions and she calms down a bit. Typically, if you remain calm and objective and look for minor things with which you can agree, the customer will back off. Also, the customer may likely start to see that she is the one out of control and that you are being professional while trying to help her. If the customer truly wants the problem to be solved, she soon realizes that cooperation with you is necessary.

In many cases, if you resolve the customer's problem professionally, he or she will often apologize for his or her actions and words once the emotion of the moment passes.

Elicit Customer Feedback and Participation

Make customers feel as if they are a part of the conversation by asking questions. Ask opinions, find out how they feel about what you're doing or saying, and get them involved by building **rapport** through ongoing dialogue. Acknowledge their ideas, suggestions, or information with statements such as, "That's a good idea (or suggestion or decision)." This will foster a feeling that the two of you are working together to solve a problem while putting the customer in psychological control of the situation. The beauty of such an approach is that if the customer comes up with an idea and you follow through on it, he or she feels a sense of ownership and is less likely to complain later or feel bad if things don't work out as planned.

rapport The silent bond built between two people as a result of sharing common interests and issues and demonstrating a win-win, I care attitude.

Close the Transaction Professionally

Instead of some parroted response used for each customer like, "Have a nice day," offer a sincere "Thank you" and encourage the customer to return in the future. Remember, part of a service culture is building customer loyalty.

Customer Service Success Tip

The techniques and strategies discussed in this chapter are important in nonretail environments as well; for example, a library, dentist's office, nonprofit organization, or government agency.

KNOWLEDGE CHECK

1. For what does the PLAN acronym stand?
2. How can you plan for positive customer interactions?
3. What are some strategies that can be used to let customers know they are important?
4. What can be done to positively address customer expectations?
5. How can you continue to nurture customer relationships?

LO 3-4 Providing Feedback Effectively

CONCEPT Your feedback could affect the relationship you have or are building with your customers. The effect may be positive or negative, depending on the content and delivery.

Feedback is a response to messages a listener receives. This response may be transmitted verbally (with words) or nonverbally (through actions or inaction). Depending on the content and delivery, your feedback could positively

⚙ **WORK IT OUT 3.4**

FEELING SPECIAL

Think of times when you have been put on hold or stood in a line.

1. How did the service provider address you when it was your turn for service?

2. Did you feel special or did you feel like the next in a long line of bodies being processed? Why?

3. When the service provider simply picked up the phone and offered to assist you or shouted, "Next," while you waited in line, what thoughts went through your mind about the provider and the organization?

4. What could service providers do or say to eliminate negative customer feelings in such situations?

STREET TALK

Do not just complain about the bad things that you experience when dealing with customers. Look for positive aspects of any interaction. People are used to hearing bad things, but it seems that they rarely hear good feedback about what they do. Say something positive; it will make their day. I recently applied this concept when I was at a Major League Baseball game. There was a family with three children under the age of 10 who were well behaved. I was able to talk with their mother and grandmother before I left the game. I told them how well behaved I thought the children were. They seemed very pleasantly surprised.

ANNE WILKINSON

or negatively influence your relationships with your customers. Figure 3.3 offers some tips on providing feedback effectively; the two types of feedback are discussed in the following sections.

VERBAL FEEDBACK

The words you choose when providing feedback to your customers are crucial to interpretation and understanding. Before providing feedback, you should take into consideration the knowledge and skill level of your customer(s). This is part of the "encoding" discussed earlier in the interpersonal communication model. Failure to consider the customer could result in breakdowns in understanding. For example, if you choose words that are not likely to be part of your customer's vocabulary because of the customer's education and/or experience, your message may be confusing. Also, if you use acronyms or technical terms (jargon or words

Trending NOW

With the expansion of globalization come millions of people shifting to new geographic locations throughout the world. This means that the likelihood of you encountering someone who is from another country or culture is pretty high. This is a good reason for you to take the time to do some research on various countries and cultural groups related to backgrounds, values, customers, and other facets of daily life and to also consider learning another language.

Here are 10 tips for effectively providing feedback:

1. When appropriate, give feedback immediately when communicating face to face or over the telephone.
2. Communicate in a clear, concise manner.
3. Remain objective and unemotional when providing feedback.
4. Make sure that your feedback is accurate before you provide it.
5. Use verbal and nonverbal messages that are in congruence (agree with each other).
6. Verify the customer's meaning before providing feedback.
7. Make sure that your feedback is appropriate to the customer's original message (active listening helps in getting the original message).
8. Strive to clarify feedback when the customer seems unclear of your intention.
9. Avoid overly critical feedback or negative language (as described in this chapter).
10. Do not provide feedback if it could damage the customer-provider relationship.

FIGURE 3.3
Guidelines for Providing
Positive Feedback

unfamiliar to the customer), the meaning of the message could get lost. When providing **verbal feedback,** you should also be conscious of how your customer is receiving your information. If the customer's body language or nonverbal cues (gestures, facial expressions) or words indicate misunderstanding, you should pause and take any corrective action necessary to clear up the confusion.

verbal feedback The response given to a sender's message that allows both the sender and receiver to know that a message was received correctly.

NONVERBAL FEEDBACK

Nonverbal feedback can be more powerful than the spoken or written word because it is often subject to interpretation based on the customer's background, culture, gender, age, and many other factors. Depending on the way that you sit, stand, move, gesture, make or fail to make eye contact, speak, or even the amount of time you allocate to a customer, you can either send unintended messages or reinforce positive verbal communication. Other factors related to you such as the appearance of your work area, clothing, jewelry, body art, hairstyle, or makeup can send powerful messages.

nonverbal feedback Messages sent to someone through other than spoken means. Examples are gestures, appearance, and facial expressions.

Manage Body Language

The ways in which you sit, stand, gesture, position your body (face to face or at an angle), or use facial expressions can all send positive or negative messages. Think about times when someone has looked at you and you responded with, "What are you looking at?" This is likely because something about their glance sent a message that triggered something in your brain that either caused alarm or raised your concern. This is why you should consciously think about your nonverbal cues when interacting with customers.

Use Eye Contact Effectively

In addition to greeting the customer, make regular eye contact (normally no longer than three to five seconds at a time) and assume a positive approachable posture throughout your interaction with a customer. Also, be careful about giving customers the "evil eye" or showing your displeasure with them through your eyes when emotions are high or you are struggling with a difficult situation.

Use Positive Facial Expressions

Over the years, various sources have reported that it takes more muscles to frown than to smile. With that in mind, spend more time (and less facial energy) projecting a pleasant, positive image with your face, rather than one that might send a negative message to your customers. Since customer service is about building relationships with customers and people generally prefer to be around someone who is happy rather than unhappy, be conscious of the power of your face. Smile often, even if you are having a bad day. The bottom line is that your customers really do not care what kind of day you are having. They do care about how you communicate with and treat them.

Customer Service Success Tip

To check your perception of nonverbal cues received from others so that you can respond appropriately, use the following process:

1. Identify the behavior observed.

   Example: "Mr. Warlinkowski, when I said that it would be seven to ten days before we could get your new sofa delivered to your home, your facial expression changed to what appeared to be one of concern."

2. Offer one or two interpretations.

   Example: "I wasn't sure whether you were indicating that the time frame doesn't work for you, or whether something else went through your mind."

3. Ask for clarification.

   Example: "Which was it?"

By asking for clarification, you reduce the chance of causing customer dissatisfaction. You also send a message that you are paying attention to the customer.

KNOWLEDGE CHECK

1. In what ways can you positively provide verbal feedback?
2. What strategies can you use to communicate with your customers nonverbally?

LO 3-5 Avoiding Negative Communication

CONCEPT Use positive words or phrases, rather than emphasizing the negative.

You can squelch customer loyalty and raise customer frustration in a number of ways when communicating. Your choice of words or phrasing can often lead either to satisfaction or to confrontation, or it can destroy a customer-provider relationship. Customers do not want to hear what you can't do; they want to hear how you're going to help satisfy their needs or expectations. Focus your message on how you can work with the customer to accomplish needs satisfaction. Don't use vague or weak terminology.

A good metaphor for avoiding negative communication is the old adage of "see no evil; hear no evil; speak no evil." *What are possible outcomes if you apply this concept with your customers?*

Instead of "I'm not sure . . ." or "I'll try . . .", say, "Let me get that answer for you . . ." or "I can do. . . ."

Another pitfall to watch out for is the use of **global terms** (all-encompassing or inclusive expressions such as *always, never, everyone, all*). If your customer can give just one example for which your statement is not true, your credibility comes into question and you might go on the defensive. Suppose you say, "We always return calls in four hours," yet the customer has personally experienced a situation when that did not happen. Your statement is now false. Instead, phrase statements to indicate possible variances such as, "We attempt to return all calls within four hours" or "Our objective is to return calls within four hours." Be careful, too, about "verbal finger pointing," especially if your customer is already upset. This tactic involves the use of the word *you*, as in, "You were supposed to call back to remind me" or "You didn't follow the directions I gave you." This is like pointing your finger at someone or using a patronizing tone to belittle them. People are likely to react powerfully and negatively to this type of treatment. See Figure 3.4 for a list of words and phrases that can damage relationships.

global terms Potentially inflammatory words or phrases used in conversation. They tend to inappropriately generalize behavior or group people or incidents together (e.g., always, never, everyone, everything, all the time).

FIGURE 3.4

Words and Phrases That Damage Customer Relationships

Here are some words and phrases that can lead to trouble with your customers. Avoid or limit their use.

You don't understand.	You aren't listening to me.
You'll have to . . .	Listen to me.
You don't see my point.	I never said . . .
Hold on (or hang on) a second.	In my opinion . . .
I (we, you) can't . . .	What's your problem?
Our policy says (or prohibits) . . .	The word *problem*.
That's not my job (or responsibility).	Do you understand?
You're not being reasonable.	Are you aware . . .
You must (or should) . . .	The word *no*.
The word *but*.	Global terms (always, never, nobody).
What you need to do is . . .	Endearment terms (honey, sweetie, sugar, baby).
Why don't you . . . ?	Profanity or vulgarity.
I don't know.	Technical or industry-specific jargon.
You're wrong or mistaken.	

WORK IT OUT 3.5

Perceptions Are Reality

To emphasize that different people often have different perceptions of what they see, and the importance of appearance, look at the photographs of the people below. Each one of the individuals in these photos will come into your workspace today for service and you will have to interact with them. Number a sheet of paper 1–8 and honestly describe your reactions to and perceptions of the people shown. From a service-provider perspective, answer all three questions below about the people in each photo. Once finished, compare your responses to those of fellow students.

1. What are your perceptions about this person?
2. Explain why you have these perceptions.
3. How might your perception affect your ability to effectively serve this person?

KNOWLEDGE CHECK

1. What are global terms and why should you avoid them?

LO 3-6 Dealing Assertively with Customers

CONCEPT Express ideas simply without weakening your position.

Assertiveness is a learned skill. Your level of **assertiveness** is directly tied to your style of behavior and your culture. Some people are direct and to the point; others are calm and laid back or come across as being passive or nonassertive. Neither style is better or worse than the other. What is important is to be able to recognize which style to call upon in various situations.

There are going to be times when you and your external customer, coworker, or supervisor disagree. This is normal when humans interact. The important thing to remember is that you want to maintain the relationship and, if necessary, simply agree to disagree and negotiate a solution that both parties can live with. The goal of assertive communication is to disagree or express dissatisfaction in a manner that does not create a breakdown in the relationship.

Communicating assertively involves elements of self-respect and respect for others. Generally, assertive communication deals with expressing ideas positively and with confidence. An example would be for someone in a Western work environment to stand or sit erect, make direct eye contact, smile, listen empathetically, and then calmly and firmly nod and explain what you can do to assist the customer. This approach is sometimes a challenge for people entering a new culture or dealing with a different gender or someone on a higher social, economic, or business level. In such instances because of differing beliefs or because they do not want to potentially offend, they tend to be less assertive in sharing ideas, giving feedback, or asking questions that may seem to challenge or discredit what someone else has said. The key to being effective, if you are from a different culture and find yourself in such situations, is to listen effectively and to give carefully thought-out candid responses. Planning ahead by researching the cultures, genders, and other diversity factors related to customers with whom you interact can better prepare you for such inevitable contacts. In this diverse world, it is not a question of if, but when, you will meet someone with different values.

Figure 3.5 lists several examples of nonassertive and assertive language and behaviors. Additional resources are listed in the Bibliography.

assertiveness Involves projecting a presence that is assured, confident, and capable without seeming to be aggressive or arrogant.

KNOWLEDGE CHECK

1. What is the goal of assertive communication?

⚙ WORK IT OUT 3.6

Standing Up Assertively

To stress the need to speak up assertively when others take advantage of you. The following are examples of customer situations that you might encounter and a possible means of assertively addressing them.

Scenario 1

An irate customer calls you and starts ranting, yelling, and swearing and will not let you get a word in. What action would you take?

Scenario 2

You depend on a co-worker to provide data for a report that you must complete by the end of the month. Even though you have asked for and been promised it several times, the report is due tomorrow morning and you still do not have the information. What should you do?

Scenario 3

Your co-worker just stopped by your desk and asked if you can work late to cover for her because she has to leave early to pick up her son from daycare. You have promised your own son that you would take him shopping after work to get materials he needs for a school project that is due tomorrow. How will you handle this situation?

FIGURE 3.5

Nonassertive and Assertive Behaviors

The following list contains examples of nonassertive and assertive language and behaviors, along with tips for increasing your assertiveness. Keep in mind that some of the behaviors in both columns are potentially indicative of cultural or gender values and have been learned.

Nonassertive	Assertive
• Poor eye contact while speaking.	• Look customer in the eye as you speak (depending on the cultural background of the other person).
• Weak ("limp fish") handshake.	• Grasp firmly without crushing (web of your hand against web of the other person's hand).
• Use of verbal paralanguage (ah, um, you know).	• Stop, gather thoughts, speak.
• Apologetic in words and tone.	• Apologize if you make a mistake (I'm sorry, please forgive me), then take control and move on with the conversation.
• Soft, subdued tone.	• Increase volume; sound firm and convincing.
• Finger-pointing; blaming others.	• Take responsibility; resolve the problem.
• Nervous gestures, fidgeting.	• Hold something; grasp a table or chair; fold your hands as you talk.
• Indecisive or unsure.	• Know your products and services. If possible, prepare a list of points, comments, or questions before calling or meeting with your customer(s).
• Rambling speech, not really stating a specific question or information.	• Think, plan, and then speak.

LO 3-7 Assertive versus Aggressive Service

CONCEPT Assertive service is good for solving problems; aggressive service may escalate them.

Do not confuse assertive with aggressive service. Why is the distinction so important in customer service? What's the difference? The answer: Assertiveness can assist in solving problems; aggression can escalate and cause relationship breakdowns. Asserting yourself means that you project an image of confidence, are self-assured, and state what you believe to be true in a self-confident manner. Some ways in which assertiveness might be demonstrated when dealing with customers include

- Interact in a mature manner with customers who may be offensive, defensive, aggressive, hostile, blaming, attacking, or otherwise unreceptive to what you are trying to explain to them. Do not become defensive or confrontational.

- Use appropriate eye contact. Make positive eye contact as you speak. In Western cultures this is expected in order to demonstrate truthfulness, confidence, and friendliness. Maintain intermittent eye contact as you smile. Avoid squinting or glaring.

- Listen openly and use affirmative acknowledgments of what the customer is saying (e.g., "I understand what you are saying" or "Uh huh").

- Use an open body posture if you are face to face (e.g., uncross your arms and keep hands off your hips). Stand or sit erectly, but not rigidly. Occasionally lean forward to emphasize key points. Use open gestures with arms and hands. Gesture with open palms, as opposed to pointing.

- Avoid blaming or judging your customer. Simply give your views or explain what you can do to help remedy the situation. Express your feelings when it's appropriate, after you have allowed your customer to vent or state her issue or provide feedback.

- Use "I" statements, where you let customers know how you feel about the situation or something the customer said. Acknowledge that your message comes from your frame of reference and your perceptions ("I feel that this situation is the result of . . . ." or "In my opinion, the issue has been caused by . . . ." You can also demonstrate ownership of a situation with statements such as, "I don't agree with what I just heard you say" (as compared to "You're wrong"). Blaming statements, such as the latter, or "you" statements are like verbal finger pointing and can irritate and escalate emotions. This will likely foster resentment and resistance rather than understanding and cooperation.

- Ask for feedback and then listen carefully to the other person. For example, "Am I being clear?" "Does that make sense?" or "How do you see this situation?" Asking for feedback can indicate that you are open to dialogue and invite the customer's views or thoughts rather than trying to control the situation or conversation. Through discussion, you can correct any misperceptions either of you have.

- Learn to say no to unreasonable requests in a confident, yet nonthreatening manner. Use the word "no" and offer an explanation if you choose to.

- When appropriate, paraphrase the customer's point of view. This will let him know that you hear and understand his point or request.

- You don't have to say, "I'm sorry" every time anything goes wrong. Of course, if something occurred and it was your fault, you should apologize and try to make it right immediately. Many women sometimes tend to put themselves down by saying things like "I'm only a doing my job" or "I just work here." There's no need to apologize to customers for what might be viewed by some of them as a job that lacks stature. Everything you do has an importance of its own. Without you, customers would not be able to transact their business effectively with your organization.

- Strive for win-win solutions. Work toward mutual understanding and the attainment of resolutions that allow the organization and the customer to succeed. Try to identify a "win-win" solution in handling customer problems or service breakdowns. Some service providers take a "you win and I lose" passive approach where they give up things unnecessarily to appease the customer without first attempting to negotiate an acceptable alternative. The "you lose and I lose" solution is a total passive solution where both you and the customer give up. In this instance, the customer goes away and you lose business for your organization. On the other hand, a "you lose and I win" solution is an aggressive solution where you ignore the customer's needs in order to get your way.

Your goal should be to achieve an assertive "you win and I win" solution where both you and the customer retain respect for one another and both parties gain something from the compromise.

Aggression involves hostile or offensive behavior, often in the form of a verbal or even physical attack. Aggressive people send messages verbally and nonverbally that imply that they are superior, want to dominate, or are in charge. They often do this through behavior and language that is manipulative, judgmental, or domineering. An assertive person states (verbally and nonverbally), "Here's my position. What's your reaction to that?" An aggressive person sends the message, "Here is my position. Take it or leave it."

Aggressive behavior can lead to relationship failure. When someone verbally attacks another, the chances of emotions escalating and relationships failing increase significantly. Another possibility in a stressed-out world is that violence could result in response to aggressive behavior.

Obviously, the two modes of dealing with customers create very different service experiences. The manner in which you nonverbally or verbally approach, address, and interact with customers may label you as either assertive or aggressive. Consider the following interactions between a customer and a service provider:

Assertive Behavior Example

Customer (returning an item of merchandise): Excuse me; I received this sweater as a present and I'd like to return it.

Service Provider (smiling): Is there something wrong with it?

Customer (still smiling): Oh no. I just don't need another sweater.

Service Provider (still smiling): Do you have a receipt?

Customer (not smiling): No. As I said, it was a gift.

WORK IT OUT 3.7

Improving Feedback Skills

To strengthen your ability to provide feedback, work with two other people (one partner and one observer) to practice your skill in delivering feedback.

Select a topic for discussion (e.g., a vacation, career goals, or positive or negative customer experiences).

Spend 10 minutes talking about your selected topic with your partner.

During the conversation, you and your partner should use verbal and nonverbal feedback.

At the end of the 10 minutes, ask your partner, and then the observer, the following questions.

1. How did I do in providing appropriate verbal feedback? Give examples.

2. How well did I interpret verbal and nonverbal messages? Give examples.

3. What questions did I ask to clarify comments or feedback provided? Give examples.

4. What could I have done to improve my feedback?

Service Provider (handing over a form): That's all right. To help me process your refund a bit faster for you, could you please provide a bit of information and sign this form?

Customer (not smiling): Does this mean I have to get out of line and then wait again? I've already been in line for 10 minutes.

Service Provider (smiling): Well, rather than delay the line, if you could step over to that table to fill out the form, and then bring it back to me, I'll take care of you. You won't have to wait in line again.

Customer (smiling): Okay, thanks.

In this example, the service provider is trying to assure the customer through words and body language that he or she is there to assist the customer.

Aggressive Service Example

Customer (returning an item of merchandise): Excuse me; I received this sweater as a present and I'd like to return it.

Service Provider (not smiling): What's wrong with it?

Customer (smiling): Oh nothing, I just don't need another sweater.

Service Provider (still not smiling): Do you have a receipt?

Customer (not smiling): No. As I said, it was a gift.

Service Provider (handing over a form): Well, our policy requires that you'll have to fill out this form since you don't have a receipt.

Customer (not smiling): Does that mean I have to get out of line and then wait again? I've already been in line for 10 minutes.

Service Provider (not smiling and looking to the next customer in line): The line's getting shorter. It shouldn't take long. Next . . . .

In this example, the service provider is not doing well on service delivery, nor is he or she projecting a positive image. The nonverbal and verbal messages convey an almost hostile attitude. This type of behavior can easily escalate into an unnecessary confrontation.

RESPONDING TO CONFLICT

conflict Involves incompatible or opposing views and can result when a customer's needs, desires, or demands do not match service provider or organizational policies, procedures, and abilities.

Conflict should be viewed as neither positive nor negative. Instead, it is an opportunity to identify differences that may need to be addressed when dealing with your internal and external customers. It is not unusual for you to experience conflict when dealing with someone else. In fact, it is normal and beneficial as long as you stay focused on the issue rather than personalizing and internalizing the conflict. When you focus on the individual, or vice versa, conflict can escalate and ultimately do irreparable damage to the relationship. Figure 3.6 describes various forms of conflict.

CAUSES OF CONFLICT

There are many causes of conflict. The following are some common ones.

- *Conflicting values and beliefs.* These sometime create situations in which the perceptions of an issue or its impact vary. Since values and beliefs have been learned over long periods of time and are often taken personally at face value, individuals get very defensive when their foundations are challenged. For example, you have been taught that stealing is not only illegal, but also morally wrong. One of your co-workers regularly takes pens, paper, and other administrative supplies home for his child to take to school. His logic is that "they (the organization) are a big company and can afford it." You disagree.

- *Personal style differences.* Each person is different and requires special consideration and a unique approach in interactions. For example, your supervisor has a high D style (decisive), is very focused, and typically wants to know only the bottom line in any conversation. You have a high E (expressive) style and find it difficult to share information without providing a lot of details in a highly emotional fashion. When the two of you speak, this can lead to conflict unless one or both of you are aware of the other's style and are willing to adapt your communication style.

- *Differing perceptions.* People often witness or view an incident or issue differently. This can cause disagreement, frustration, and a multitude of other emotional feelings. For example, an employee (Sue) tells you that she is upset because a deadline was missed because another employee

FIGURE 3.6

Forms of Conflict

Conflict typically results when you and someone else disagree about something. The following are examples of five forms of conflict that might occur in your organization.

- Between individuals. You and your supervisor (or another employee) disagree on the way a customer situation should be handled.
- Between an individual and a group. You disagree about a new customer procedure created by your work team.
- Between an individual and an organization. A dissatisfied customer feels that your organization is not providing quality products or services.
- Between organizational groups. Your department has goals (for example, the way customer orders or call-handling procedures are processed) that create additional requirements or responsibilities for members of another department.
- Between organizations. Your organization is targeting the same customers to sell a new product similar to one that an affiliate organization markets to that group.

(Fred) did not effectively manage his time. Fred later commented to you that your supervisor pulled him off the project in question in order to work on another assignment. This resulted in his missing the original assignment deadline and a perception by Sue that he could not manage time.

Ethical Dilemma 3.1

You might have been taught that it is always ethically and morally wrong to lie to a customer, yet your supervisor tells you that it's okay to tell a little white lie (slight exaggeration) to explain a missed delivery.

1. How would you react to or feel about your supervisor's position?
2. Would this cause any change in your relationship with your supervisor? Why or why not?
3. Would you lie to your customer? Why or why not?

See end of chapter for possible answers.

- *Inadequate or poor communication.* Any time there is inadequate communication, the chance for conflict escalates. For example, a co-worker (Leonard) confides to you that he may have forgotten to tell a customer about limitations on your organization's return policy. As a result, when the customer brought a product back to return it, another co-worker had to deal with a frustrated and angry customer.

- *Contrary expectations.* When one party expects something not provided by another, conflict will likely result. For example, your company offers a 90-day parts-only warranty on equipment that you sell; however, when it breaks down within that period, the customer expects free service also. If that expectation is not met, you have to deal with conflict and the customer is potentially dissatisfied.

- *Inadequate communication.* People generally like to know what to expect and do not want a lot of surprises from their supervisor. When they get mixed signals because of inconsistency, frustration and conflict could result. For example, your supervisor told the entire service staff that in the future, each employee would have an opportunity to earn bonuses based on how many customers he or she could convince to upgrade their membership in the organization. You believe that you have sold the most for the month, yet when you point this out to your supervisor, he tells you that the bonus applies only if you have high sales for two months in a row.

- *Goals that are out of sync with reality.* Frustration and resentment can result from misaligned efforts. For example, you have been working as a service technician for over a year and have learned that, on average, it takes about 1½ hours to install a new telephone line. Your supervisor regularly counsels you because you do not accomplish the feat within the goal of 1 hour.

- *Opposition over shared resources.* When two people or groups vie for the same resources, conflict usually results. For example, all monies for employee training are lumped into a central training budget in your organization. You have been requesting to go to a customer service training skills program for the past six months; however, you are told that there is only enough money to train people from the technical staff to learn new computer software.

- *Outcomes dependent on others.* Whenever you have two or more people, departments, teams, or organizations working jointly toward goal attainment, the potential for conflict exists. For example, your department receives customer orders over the telephone and then forwards them to the fulfillment department for processing and order shipment. If the fulfillment process breaks down, a customer has your name and number, and he or she typically contacts you. If the customer is unhappy, it is you who have to placate him or her and spend time resolving the conflict.

- *Misuse of power.* Resentment, frustration, and retaliation often result when employees believe that their supervisor is abusing his or her authority or power. For example, you overhear your supervisor telling an attractive employee that unless certain sexual favors are granted, she will not receive a desired promotion.

There are various ways you can deal effectively with conflict. Figure 3.7 gives some guidelines.

FIGURE 3.7

Guidelines for Effective Conflict Management

Even though each situation and person you deal with will differ, there are some basic approaches that may help in resolution of disagreement(s). Try the following strategies.

- *Remain calm.* You cannot be part of the solution if you become part of the problem. If you are one of the factors contributing to the conflict, consider getting an objective third party to arbitrate, possibly a co-worker or your supervisor.

- *Be proactive in avoiding conflict.* As a customer service representative for your organization, you must try to recognize the personalities of those with whom you come into contact daily. If you are dealing with co-workers or peers, try to identify their capabilities and the environments most conducive to their effectiveness. If you are interacting with a customer, use verbal and nonverbal techniques discussed here and in Chapter 4 to help determine the customer's needs. Approach each person in a fashion that can lead to win-win situations; do not set yourself or others up for conflict or failure.

- *Keep an open mind.* Be cautious in order to avoid letting your own values or beliefs influence your objectivity when working toward conflict identification and resolution. As you will read later, this can cause damage to your long-term relationship(s).

- *Identify and confront underlying issues immediately.* Because of the emotional issues often involved in dealing with problem situations, few people enjoy dealing with conflict. However, if you fail to acknowledge and confront issues as soon as they become known, tensions may escalate.

- *Clarify communication.* Ensure that you elicit information on the causes of the conflict and provide the clear, detailed feedback necessary to resolve the issue. This effort can sometimes test your patience and communication skills, but it is a necessary step in the resolution process.

- *Stress cooperation rather than competition.* One of your roles as a service provider is to ensure that you work toward common goals with your co-workers, supervisor, and customers. When one person succeeds at the expense of another's failure, you have not done your job. Encourage and develop teamwork and cooperation when dealing with others.

- *Focus resolution efforts on the issues.* Do not get caught up in or allow finger-pointing, name calling, or accusations. Keep all efforts and discussions directed toward identifying and resolving the real issue(s). Stay away from criticizing or blaming others.

- *Follow established procedures for handling conflict.* It is easier to implement a process already in place than to have to quickly come up with one. That is why most customer service organizations have set customer complaint handling procedures.

SALVAGING RELATIONSHIPS AFTER CONFLICT

Managing conflict involves more than just resolving the disagreement. If you fail to address the emotional and psychological needs of those involved, you may find the conflict returning and/or severe damage to the customer-provider relationship may occur. Often poorly handled service recovery efforts result in such things as complaints to a service provider's supervisor, complaints to consumer agencies, bad word-of-mouth publicity, and lost customers.

Depending on the severity of the conflict and how it was handled at each step of the resolution process, it may be impossible to go back to the relationship as it was before the disagreement. The key to reducing this possibility is to identify and address conflicting issues as early as possible. The longer an issue remains unresolved, the more damage it can cause. Make the effort to help protect and salvage the relationship between you and your customers.

Often, customers are rational once they can get past their need for emotional ownership of the situation. If you can apply some basic emotion-reducing communication strategies (e.g., empathize, agree with the customer, lower your volume, and monitor your voice tone), the situation may become more manageable. Just remember that your customers are human just like you and human behavior is sometimes volatile. Allow them to vent and calm down, then focus on recovering and rebuilding the relationship. The following strategies can assist in your service recovery efforts:

- *Reaffirm the value of the relationship.* You cannot assume that others feel the same as you or understand your intent unless you communicate it. Apologize sincerely and tell them how much you value the relationship between them and the organization. Also stress that your goal is to assist them in whatever manner possible.

  Customers typically tell others about the bad experiences they have. The result is that damage can be done to your organization's reputation. This is a strong reason for you to do whatever you can to resolve the issue and appease your customer.

- *Demonstrate commitment.* You must verbalize and demonstrate your desire to continue or strengthen your relationship. The way to do this with customers is through sound interpersonal communication efforts (e.g., active listening, empathy, and positive verbal and nonverbal messages). Once you have smoothed things over a bit emotionally with the customer, take definitive action to positively address the service or product breakdown. If that means involving a co-worker or supervisor, then do that.

- *Be realistic.* Because of cultural, gender, generational, and behavioral style differences, it is difficult for some people to "forgive and forget." You have to systematically help restore their trust. It can take a while to accomplish this, but the effort is well worth it. Take the time to follow up with your customer after a recovery initiative. Send a card, discount, or gift certificate or take some other proactive measure to show the customer that you are truly sorry for the breakdown in communication and that you are willing to work to regain his or her trust.

- *Remain flexible.* A solid customer-provider relationship involves the ability to give and take. It is especially crucial that you and the other people involved make concessions following conflict. Avoid any references to policy or organizational standard procedure. If you cannot meet a

body language Nonverbal communication cues that send powerful messages through gestures, vocal qualities, manner of dress, grooming, and many other cues.

you will communicate with them more effectively. The key to "reading" **body language** is to realize that your interpretations should be used only as an indicator of the customer's true message meaning. This is because background, culture, physical condition, communication ability, and many other factors influence whether and how well people use body cues. Placing too much importance on nonverbal cues could lead to miscommunication and possibly a service breakdown. Some typical forms of body language are discussed in the following sections.

Eye Contact

It has been said that the eyes are "the windows to the soul." Eye contact is very powerful. This is why criminal investigators are often taught to observe eye movement in order to determine whether a suspect is being truthful or not. In most Western cultures, the typical period of time that is comfortable for holding eye contact is 5 to 10 seconds; then an occasional glance away is normal and expected. Looking away in some cultures can often send a message of disinterest, or dishonesty, or lack of confidence (e.g., United States, Canada, and United Kingdom). If either the length or the frequency of eye contact differs from the "norm," many people might think that you are being rude or offensive. They might also interpret your behavior as an attempt to exert power or as flirting. Additionally, looking down before answering questions, glancing away continually as your customer talks, blinking excessively, and other such eye movements can create a negative impression. In any case, your customer might become uncomfortable and may react in an undesirable manner (for example, becoming upset or ending the conversation) if you use eye contact in what they perceive as an inappropriate manner. As with all other aspects of workplace interaction in a multicultural environment, do not forget that cultural values and practices often influence the way in which people communicate and interpret message signals.

Just as you send messages with your eyes, your customer's eye contact can also send meaningful messages to you. A customer's lack of direct eye contact with you could send a variety of messages, such as lack of interest, confidence, or trust, or dishonesty, depending on how you interpret those cues. For example, if you are watching a customer shop and notice a quick loss of eye contact each time you try to engage the customer visually, the customer might be nervous because he or she is shoplifting, or the customer simply might not want your attention and assistance.

Another aspect of nonverbal communication has to do with the size of the pupils. Much research has been done on the correlation between a person's interest in an item or object being viewed and the size of the person's pupils. Typically, when a customer is interested in an item, his or her pupils will dilate (grow larger). This fact might be parlayed into increased sales and customer satisfaction because an astute and experienced salesperson can watch for dilation as a customer looks over merchandise. For example, even if a customer displays interest only after asking the price, and then moves on to another, the salesperson who has observed the customer's interest as revealed by dilation of the pupils might be able to influence the customer's buying decision. As with all nonverbal communication, if you are using this technique, remember that there is room for misinterpreting a cue. According to research on **pupilometrics** (the study of pupil reaction to stimuli), other factors such as drugs or a person's physical attraction to someone can also

pupilometrics The study of pupil reaction to stimuli.

Nonverbal cues such as eye contact, proximity, smiling, and gesturing send powerful messages. *What cues do you regularly send that impact the way customers perceive you and your organization?*

cause dilation. To avoid misinterpreting a customer's intent, listen carefully to tone of voice and observe other nonverbal signals so that you do not appear to be pushy or take the wrong action in dealing with a customer.

Facial Expressions

The face is capable of making many expressions. Your face can signal excitement, happiness, sadness, boredom, concern, dismay, and dozens of other emotions. By being aware of the power of your expressions and using positive ones, such as smiling, you can initiate and sustain relationships with others. In fact, smiling seems to be one of the few nonverbal cues that has a universal meaning of friendship or acceptance. Smiling typically expresses a mood of friendship, cheerfulness, pleasure, relaxation, and comfort with a situation. Even so, like any other nonverbal cue, you have to be cautious of "reading into" the intent of someone's cue because some people smile to mask nervousness, embarrassment, or deceit.

In some situations, smiling (yours and a customer's) may even lead to problems. For example, suppose that you are a male receptionist working at a walk-in care clinic. A male patient from the Middle East and his wife step up to your desk. You smile and greet the husband, and then turn your attention to the wife and do likewise, possibly adding, "That's a very pretty dress you have on." She smiles and giggles as she looks away in an embarrassed effort to avoid eye contact. At this point, you notice that the husband looks very displeased. A cultural element may be involved. Although your intention was to express friendliness and openness and to compliment the wife, because of his cultural attitudes, the husband may interpret your words and smiling as flirtatious and insulting.

Don't think that this means you should ignore the wives of your customers. Rather, be conscious of cultural and personal differences that people may have, and take your cue from the customer. As the world grows smaller, it is more crucial than ever that you expand your knowledge of different cultural attitudes and recognize that your ways are not the ways of everyone.

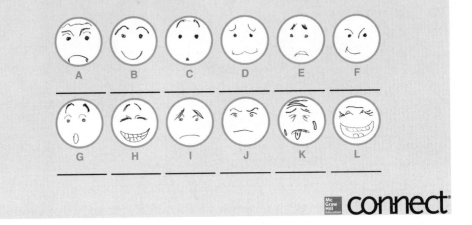

WORK IT OUT 4.1

Facial Expressions

Take a few minutes to look at each of the faces shown below. Write the emotion that you believe each image portrays and then compare your response to those of others. Did each person have the same reaction to each nonverbal cue?

A _____ B _____ C _____ D _____ E _____ F _____

G _____ H _____ I _____ J _____ K _____ L _____

Posture

posture Refers to how one sits or stands in order to project various nonverbal messages.

Posture (or stance) involves the way you position your body. Various terms describe posture (for example, formal, rigid, relaxed, slouched, awkward, sensual, and defensive). In Western-oriented cultures, by sitting or standing in an erect manner, or leaning forward or away as you speak with customers, you can send a variety of messages. By standing or sitting with an erect posture, walking confidently, or assuming a relaxed, open posture, you might appear to be attentive, confident, assertive, and ready to assist your customer. On the other hand, slouching in your seat, standing with slumped shoulders, keeping your arms crossed while speaking to someone, shuffling or not picking up your feet when walking, or averting eye contact can possibly signal that you are unsure of yourself, are being deceitful, or just have a poor or indifferent customer service attitude.

In addition, your nonverbal behavior when listening to a customer speak can affect his or her feedback and reaction to you. For example, if you lean forward and smile as the customer speaks, you can signal that you are interested in what is being said and that you are listening intently. Leaning away could send the opposite message.

Nodding of the Head

Nodding of the head is often used (and overused) by many people to signal agreement or to indicate that they are listening to a speaker during a conversation.

You must be careful when you are using this technique and, when you are watching others who are doing so, to occasionally pause to ask a question for clarification. Stop and ask for or provide feedback through a paraphrased message. A question such as "So what do you think of what I just said?" will quickly tell you whether the other person is listening and understands your meaning. The answer will also make it clear if the other person is simply politely smiling and nodding—but not understanding. The latter sometimes happens when there are cultural differences or when someone speaks a native language other than yours.

If you are a woman, be careful not to overuse the nodding technique. Some research has shown that many North American women often nod and smile more than men during a conversation. Doing so excessively might damage your credibility or effectiveness, especially when you are speaking to a man. The interpretation may be that you agree or that you have no opinion, whether you do or not.

Although nodding your head generally signals agreement, if you nod without a verbal acknowledgment or **paralanguage** (a vocal effect such as "uh huh," "I see," "hmmm"), a missed or misinterpreted cue could result. For example, suppose that you want to signal to a customer that you are listening to and understand her request. You may nod slowly, vocalize an occasional "I see" or "uh-huh," and smile as she speaks. She might interpret this to mean that you are following her meaning and are nonverbally signaling acceptance of it. But if she is stating something contrary to your organization's policy or outside your level of authority, she might misinterpret your signals thinking that you *agree* with her, not that you are merely signaling *understanding*. Later, she might be upset, saying something like, "Well, earlier you nodded agreement when I said I wanted a replacement."

paralanguage Consists of voice qualities (e.g., pitch, rate, tone, or other vocal qualities) or noises and vocalizations (e.g., "hmmm" or "ahhh") made as someone speaks that let a speaker know that his or her message is being listened to and followed.

Ethical Dilemma 4.1

You joined the Federal Emergency Management Agency (FEMA) several months before the catastrophic Hurricane Katrina made landfall along the Gulf Coast from Florida to Texas. At the time, you worked in an agency office in Pearl, Mississippi. Within months after the disaster, you were transferred to Baton Rouge, Louisiana, where you could work with partner emergency management agencies to assist in processing victim claims and help set up low-cost loans and grants to get businesses back into operation in the New Orleans area. After arriving at the office, you set about identifying key resources and communicating with flood victims. There are 25 other specialists performing similar tasks. The work hours are long and stressful, but the job is fulfilling and you really enjoy the opportunity to make a difference in the lives of people whom you are helping get their life back together.

Recently, you were in the corner of the break room, partly hidden by a vending machine as you read a book, when two other employees came in and stood by the coffee machine. From their conversation it was obvious that they were friends and you later found out that they were sisters-in-law. The two were jokingly discussing the amount of money that they dealt with every day and one made a comment to the other that there is really no sound paper trail to track the money. She went on to tell the other woman, "We could very easily 'create' some victims on paper and funnel money to ourselves. Nobody would even notice." The second woman agreed; they laughed and then left the room. As a result of what you heard, you started paying more attention to the two, since one of your jobs was to coordinate claims from the office and track the total amount of money being spent. Within months you noticed that the claims for replacement equipment and rentals from these two increased significantly over the previous quarter compared to those of other representatives in the office.

1. Do you think that these women are doing anything illegal? Explain.
2. Should you take any type of action at this point, based on what you know? If so, what?
3. What are possible consequences if you do take action? Explain.

Gestures

The use of the head, hands, arms, and shoulders to accentuate verbal messages can add color, excitement, and enthusiasm to your communication. Using physical movements naturally during a conversation with a customer may help make a point or result in added credibility.

Typically, such movements are designed to gain and hold attention (for example, waving a hand to attract the attention of someone), clarify or describe further (for example, holding up one finger to indicate the number 1), or emphasize a point (for example, pointing a finger while angrily making a point verbally).

Open, flowing gestures (gesturing with arms, palms open and upward, out and away from the body) encourage listening and help explain messages to customers. On the other hand, closed, restrained movements (tightly crossed arms, clinched fists, hands in pockets, hands or fingers intertwined and held below waist level or behind the back) could send a message of coolness, insecurity, or disinterest.

The key is to make gestures seem natural. If you do not normally use gestures when communicating, you may want to practice in front of a mirror until you feel relaxed and the gestures complement your verbal messages without distracting. Figure 4.1 summarizes positive and negative communication behaviors discussed in this chapter.

VOCAL CUES

vocal cues Qualities of the voice that send powerful nonverbal messages. Examples are rate, pitch, volume, and tone.

Vocal cues, that is, pitch, volume (loudness), rate, quality, and articulation, and other attributes of verbal communication can send nonverbal messages to customers.

Pitch

pitch Refers to the change in tone of the voice as one speaks. This quality is also called **inflection** and adds vocal variety and punctuation to verbal messages.

Changes in voice tone (either higher or lower) add vocal variety to messages and can dramatically affect interpretation of meaning. These changes are referred to as inflection or **pitch** of the voice or tone. **Inflection** is the "vocal punctuation" in oral message delivery. For example, a raised inflection occurs at the end of a question and indicates a vocal "question mark."

FIGURE 4.1

Positive and Negative Nonverbal Communication Behaviors

Positive	Negative
Brief eye contact (3 to 5 seconds)	Yawning
Eyes wide open	Frowning or sneering
Smiling	Attending to matters other than the customer
Facing the customer	Manipulating items impatiently
Nodding affirmatively	Leaning away from customer as he or she speaks
Expressive hand gestures	Subdued or minimal hand gestures
Open body stance	Crossed arms
Listening actively	Staring blankly or coolly at customer
Remaining silent as customer speaks	Interrupting
Gesturing with open hand	Pointing finger or object at customer
Maintaining professional appearance	Casual unkempt appearance
Clean, organized work area	Disorganized, cluttered work space

Some people have a bad habit of raising inflection inappropriately at the end of a statement. This practice can confuse listeners for they hear the vocal question mark, but they realize that the words were actually a statement. To rectify this communication error, be sure that your inflection normally falls at the end of sentence statements. Another technique is to use a vocal "comma" in the form of a brief pause as you speak.

Simple nonverbal cues like smiling at a customer send powerful messages that a service provider is customer-focused. *How do you feel when a service provider smiles at you?*

Volume

The range in which vocal messages are delivered is referred to as the degree of loudness or **volume**. Be aware of the volume of your voice, for changes in volume can indicate emotion and may send a negative message to your customer. For example, if a communication exchange with a customer becomes emotionally charged, your voice may rise in volume, indicating that you are angry or upset. This may escalate emotions and possibly lead to a relationship breakdown.

Depending on surrounding noise or your customers' ability to hear properly, you may have to raise or lower your volume as you speak. Be careful to listen to customer comments, especially on the telephone. If the customer keeps asking you to speak up, check the position of the mouthpiece in relation to your mouth, adjust outgoing volume (if your equipment allows this), and try to eliminate background noise, or simply speak up. On the other hand, if he or she is saying, "You don't have to shout," adjust your voice volume or the positioning of the mouthpiece accordingly or lower your voice.

volume Refers to loudness or softness of the voice when speaking.

Rate of Speech

Rate of speech varies for many people. This is often a result of the person's communication abilities, the region of the United States in which he or she was reared, or his or her country of origin. An average rate of speech for most adults in a workplace setting in Western cultures is 125 to 150 words per minute (wpm). You should recognize this because speed of delivery can affect whether your message is received and interpreted correctly. Speech that is either too fast or too slow can be distracting and cause loss of message effectiveness.

rate of speech Refers to the number of words spoken per minute. Some research studies have found that the average rate of speech for adults in Western cultures is approximately 125–150 words per minute (wpm).

Voice Quality

Message interpretation is often affected by the sound or quality of your voice.

The variations in your **voice quality** can help encourage customers to listen (if your voice sounds pleasant and is accompanied by a smile) or could discourage them (if it is harsh-sounding), depending on their perception of how your voice sounds. Some terms that describe unpleasant voice quality are *raspy, nasal, hoarse,* and *gravelly.* Such qualities can be a problem because others are less likely to listen to or interact with you if your voice quality is irritating. If you have been told, or you recognize, that your voice exhibits one or more of these characteristics and know that it is not a physiological issue, you may want to meet with a speech coach who specializes in

voice quality Refers to the sound of one's voice. Terms often attributed to voice quality are raspy, nasal, hoarse, and gravelly.

WORK IT OUT 4.2

Gesture Practice

To see what you look like when you gesture and communicate nonverbally, stand in front of a mirror or videotape yourself as you practice expressing nonverbal cues that demonstrate the following emotions. Once in class, pair up with another student and each of you select four emotions from the list. Take turns and demonstrate each emotion without telling the other person the intended message. After each attempt, discuss how your partner interpreted the emotion and what message you were actually trying to send. If the two differed, discuss why that might be the case and the potential impact on customer service.

1. Sadness
2. Frustration
3. Disgust
4. Happiness
5. Love
6. Fear
7. Anger
8. Excitement
9. Boredom
10. Frustration

helping improve vocal presentation of messages. Most local colleges and universities that have speech programs can supply the name of an expert, possibly someone on their staff. By taking the initiative to improve your voice quality, you can enhance your customer service image.

Articulation

articulation, enunciation, or pronunciation Refers to the manner or clarity in which verbal messages are delivered.

Articulation, enunciation, or pronunciation of words refers to the clarity of your word usage. If you tend to slur words ("Whadju say?" "I hafta go whitja") or cut off endings (goin', doin', gettin', bein'), you can distort meaning or frustrate listeners. This is especially true when communicating with customers who do not speak your native language well and with customers who view speech ability as indicative of educational achievement or your ability to assist them effectively. If you have a problem articulating well, practice by gripping a pencil horizontally between your teeth, reading sentences aloud, and forcing yourself to enunciate each word clearly. Over time, you will find that you slow down and form words more precisely.

Pauses

pauses A verbal technique of delaying response in order to allow time to process information received, think of a response, or gain attention.

interferences Noises that can interfere with messages being effectively communicated between two people.

verbal fillers Verbal sounds, words, or utterances that break silence but add little to a conversation. Examples are uh, um, ah, and you know.

silence Technique used to gain attention when speaking, to allow thought, or to process information received.

Pauses in communication can be either positive or negative depending on how you use them. From a positive standpoint, they can be used to allow a customer to reflect on what you just said, to verbally punctuate a point made or a sentence (through intonation and inflection in the voice), or to indicate that you are waiting for a response. On the negative side, you can irritate someone through the use of too many vocal pauses or **interferences**. The latter can be audible sounds ("uh," "er," "um," "uh-huh") and are often used when you have doubts or are unsure of what you are saying, not being truthful, or nervous. They are sometimes called **verbal fillers**. Interferences can also be external noises that make hearing difficult.

Silence

Silence is a form of tacit communication that can be used in a number of ways, some more productive than others. Many people have trouble dealing with silence in a conversation. This is unfortunate because silence is a good way to show respect or show that you are listening to the customer while he or she speaks. It is also a simple way to indicate that the other person should say something or contribute some information after you have asked a question. You can also indicate agreement or comprehension by using body language and paralanguage, as discussed earlier. On the negative side, you can indicate defiance or indifference by coupling your silence with some of the nonverbal behaviors listed in Figure 4.1. Obviously, this can damage the customer-provider relationship.

Semantics

Semantics has to do with choice of words. Although not nonverbal in nature, semantics is a crucial element of message delivery and interpretation because people interpret your intentions or meanings based on their understanding of word definitions. Think about times when you or someone has inappropriately used the wrong word in a conversation (a **malapropism**) and the result was potentially humorous or confusing to the other person. For example, imagine that you are a server in a restaurant and your male customer says, "Be sure they do not put any of those neutrons on my salad." Obviously he is referring to bread croutons. Another example might be a customer who says that she does not want any cheese on her burger when you ask her because she is "lack toast intolerant." More likely, she is lactose intolerant and cannot effectively digest milk or dairy products.

You can add to or detract from effective communication depending on the words you use and how you use them. This can happen if you use a lot of jargon (technical or industry-related terms) or complex words that customers may not understand because of their background, education, culture, or experience. In such instances, you run the risk of irritating, frustrating, or dissatisfying them and thus damaging the customer-provider relationship.

The bottom line related to semantics is that you always want to come across as being intelligent and professional when interacting with your customers. Think before you speak and work to hone your communication skills.

APPEARANCE AND GROOMING

The way you look and present yourself physically (hygiene and grooming) and your manner of dress (clothes clean, pressed, well-maintained, and professionally worn and shoes shined) send a message of either professionalism or indifference. Even though you provide attentive, quality service, the customer will typically form an opinion of you and your organization within 30 seconds based on your appearance and that of your workspace. This opinion may make the difference in whether the customer will continue to patronize your organization or go to a competitor. For example, your clothing, grooming, and choice of jewelry or other accessories could send a negative message to some people. It is crucial to be able to distinguish between what is appropriate for the workplace and what is inappropriate for a business setting. A good starting point in determining this is to ask your supervisor about the organization's dress policy and adhere to it.

Customer Service Success Tip

Sit up straight when speaking, since doing so reduces constriction and opens up your throat (larynx) to reduce muffling and improve voice quality.

semantics The scientific study of relationships between signs, symbols, and words and their meaning.

malapropism The unintentional misuse or distortion of a word or phrase that sounds somewhat like the one intended but with a different context. This often has humorous results.

Customer Service Success Tip

Occasionally spend some time scrolling through a dictionary and the many books on the market related to essential words that you should know in order to be successful. Continue to add to your vocabulary and knowledge throughout your life to become a better communicator and service provider.

⚙ **WORK IT OUT 4.3**

Adding Emphasis to Words

To practice how changes in your vocal quality affect the meaning of your message, try this activity. Pair up with someone. Take turns verbally delivering the following sentences one at a time. Each time, place the vocal emphasis on the word in boldface type. Following the delivery of each sentence, stop and discuss how you perceived the meaning based on your partner's enunciation and intonation of the key word in the sentence. Also, discuss the impact that you believe such emphasis could have on a customer interaction.

I said I'd do it.

I **said** I'd do it.

I said **I'd** do it.

I said I'd **do** it.

I said I'd do **it**.

---

appearance and grooming
Nonverbal characteristics exhibited by service providers that can send a variety of messages that range from being a professional to having a negative attitude.

hygiene The healthy maintenance of the body through such practices as regular bathing, washing hair, brushing teeth, cleaning fingernails, and using commercial products to eliminate or mask odors.

Through your **appearance and grooming** habits, you project an image of yourself and the organization. Good personal hygiene and attention to your appearance are crucial in a customer environment. Remember, customers do not have to return if they find you or your peers offensive in any manner. And without customers, you do not have a job.

Hygiene

Effective **hygiene** (regular washing and combing hair, bathing, brushing teeth, using mouthwash and deodorant, washing hands, and cleaning and trimming fingernails) is basic to successful customer service. This is true even when you work with tools and equipment, or in other skilled trades in which you get dirty easily.

Most customers accept that some jobs are going to result in more dirt and grime than others. However, they often have a negative feeling about someone who does not take pride in his or her personal appearance and/or hygiene. Such people are often perceived as inconsiderate, lazy, or simply dirty. If you failed to wash your hair, bathe, or shave prior to reporting to work, you could be offensive in appearance to customers and co-workers (you might even have an unpleasant odor) even if you work in a job that requires manual labor. The latter is no excuse for poor hygiene. Think about the times you have encountered such service providers. What was your reaction to them personally? Failing to adhere to these basic commonsense suggestions could result in people avoiding you or complaining about you. Naturally, this would reduce your effectiveness on the job and lower customer satisfaction.

A number of grooming trends have been prompted by many Hollywood actors. One is for men to appear with a one- or two-day beard stubble. While this may look sexy in movies, it has little place in most professional work environments. Likewise, many studies show that prominent tattoos and visible piercings are becoming more commonplace. Still, in many instances they not only can raise some eyebrows, but also can cause a negative customer reaction based on stereotypes of people who have such things. Often, these reactions are from older customers, for example, older baby boomers. Since this group is one of the largest market forces in many countries, their views should be considered if you want to be a successful service provider. Covering tattoos or not wearing body jewelry while at work is a simple "fix" to prevent negative reactions from some customers.

Although good hygiene and grooming are important, going to an extreme through excessive or bizarre use of makeup, hair coloring, cologne, or perfume can create a negative impression and may even cause people to avoid you. This is especially true of people who have allergies or respiratory problems, who think conservatively, or with whom you work in confined spaces.

Clothing and Accessories

For a number of years, casual dress, "dress-down days," and business casual have been buzz words in many organizations in North America as management tries to adapt to the changing values of today's workforce. For example, many hi-tech and graphic work environments often have employees in jeans, t-shirts, and sandals. This trend toward being a bit too lax is now

Many car owners are capitalizing on a trend to sell advertising spaced on their vehicles. *How does this trend tie to nonverbal communication for companies?*

starting to slowly reverse in many companies because some employees have taken the concept of "casual" to an extreme. As a result, they have begun to negatively affect the workplace and the opinions that many customers have of some organizations. In an economy where every customer counts, organizations are definitely looking for ways to attract and keep this precious commodity. Part of that is rethinking the image that is being presented to the public.

Work clothing does not have to be expensive, but it should be well-maintained and appropriate to your work setting. No matter what type of clothing is designated in your organization, clean and pressed clothing, as well as polished shoes (where appropriate), help to project a positive, professional image. Certain types of clothing and accessories are acceptable in the work environment, but others are inappropriate. If your organization does not have a policy outlining dress standards, always check with your supervisor before wearing something that might deviate from the standards observed by other employees or might create an unfavorable image to the public. For example, very high heels and miniskirts, or jeans, bare midriffs, T-shirts, pants with holes or tattered cuffs, or that hang low on the

Trending NOW

For years, buses, trains, airplanes, trucks, and other vehicles have been used as advertising venues. Companies are now constantly looking for ways to connect and send messages to current and potential customers by paying car owners to allow them to entirely wrap their personal vehicles. In effect, they are turning cars into driving billboards. In exchange for this nonverbal message board, people are able to afford a new car and have someone else pay for it or take a business tax deduction. Search online for more information about this trend.

Being aware of how people may react to violations of their space is necessary for those in customer service. Depending on the circumstances, there might be misperceptions of intentions and harassment claims. *What have been your reactions when someone violated your "personal space" in the workplace?*

hips, and tennis shoes might be appropriate for a date or social outing, but they may not be appropriate in most workplaces. They could actually be distracting or cause customer disapproval and/or complaints and lost business to your organization.

If you are in doubt about appropriate attire, many publications and videos are available on the subject of selecting the right clothing, jewelry, eyeglasses, and accessories. Check with your company's human resources department, your local public library, or the Internet for more information.

SPATIAL CUES

Each culture has its own **proxemics** or **spatial cues** (zones or distances in which interpersonal interactions take place) for various situations (Figure 4.2). When you violate co-workers' spatial preferences based on their culture, their comfort level is likely to decrease, and they may become visibly anxious, move away, and/or become defensive or offended.

Each culture has unwritten rules about contact and interpersonal proximity of which you should be aware and that should be respected when dealing with people from a given culture. In the United States and many Western cultures, studies have resulted in definitions of approximate comfort zones. These may vary, for example, when someone has immigrated to a Western environment and still retains some of his or her own culture's practices related to space.

proxemics Relates to the invisible barrier surrounding people in which they feel comfortable interacting with others. This zone varies depending on the level of relationship a person has with someone else.

spatial cues Nonverbal messages sent on the basis of how close or far someone stands from another person.

Intimate Distance (0 to 18 inches)

Typically this distance is reserved for your family and intimate relationships. Most people will feel uncomfortable when a service provider intrudes into this space uninvited.

Personal Distance (18 inches to 4 feet)

This distance is used when close friends or business colleagues, with whom you have established a level of comfort and trust, are together. It might also occur if you have established a long-term customer relationship that has blossomed into a semifriendship. In such a situation, you and the customer may sometimes exchange personal information (about vacation plans, children, and so forth) and feel comfortable standing or sitting closer to one another than would normally be the case.

Social and Work Distance (4 to 12 feet)

This is usually the distance range in face-to-face customer service situations. It is also typically maintained at casual business events and during business transactions.

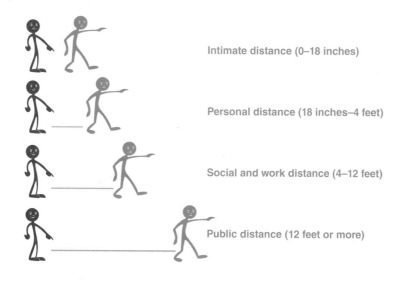

FIGURE 4.2 Typical Spatial Distances in Western Cultures

Intimate distance (0–18 inches)

Personal distance (18 inches–4 feet)

Social and work distance (4–12 feet)

Public distance (12 feet or more)

Public Distance (12 or more feet)

This distance range is likely to be maintained at large gatherings, activities, or presentations where most people do not know one another, or where the interactions are formal in nature.

An important thing to remember about spatial distances in the service environment is how others might perceive your actions. For example, suppose you have an intimate or friendly spatial relationship with a co-worker or with someone who regularly comes into your place of business. Outside the workplace, you and this person might typically engage in interactions from zero to four feet (joking around, touching, kissing, and holding hands). However, if you exhibited similar behavior in the workplace, you could create a feeling of discomfort in others, especially customers or other people who do not know you. Even if they are aware of your relationship with this person, the workplace is not the appropriate place for such behavior. Any touching should be restricted to standard business practices (e.g., a firm business handshake). In fact, touching other than this can lead to claims of a hostile work environment and could lead to a lawsuit according to numerous federal and state laws in the United States.

> **Customer Service Success Tip**
>
> The bottom line regarding touch in the workplace is keep it professional (e.g., firm handshake) or do not touch others. Respect the personal space preferences and norms of others.

ENVIRONMENTAL CUES

The **environmental cues** of the surroundings in which you work or service customers also send messages. For example, if your work area looks dirty or disorganized—with tools, pencils, files, and papers scattered about; outdated or inappropriate information or items tacked to a bulletin board; or stacks of boxes, papers stapled or taped to walls, and trash or clutter visible—customers may perceive that you and the organization have a lackadaisical attitude or approach to business. This perception may cause customers to question your ability and commitment to serve. Granted, in some professions keeping a work area clean all the time is difficult (service station, construction site office, manufacturing environment). However, that is no excuse for giving up on cleanliness and

environmental cues Any aspect of the workplace with which a customer comes into contact. Such things as the general appearance of an area, clutter, unsightly or offensive items, or general disorganization contribute to the perception of an environment.

organization of your area. If each employee takes responsibility for cleaning his or her area, cleaning becomes a routine event during work hours and no one has to get stuck with the job of doing cleaning tasks at a specific time. Also, by straightening and cleaning up after a task or project, the chance that an external customer may react negatively to the work area is reduced or eliminated.

To help reduce negative perceptions, organize and clean your area regularly, put things away and out of sight once you have used them (calculators, extra pencils, order forms, extra paper for the printer or copier, tools and equipment, supplies). Also, clean your equipment and desk area regularly (telephone mouthpiece, computer monitor and keyboard, cash register and/or calculator key surface, tools). In particular, all should do their part in cleaning common areas (break rooms or departmental refrigerators) so that co-workers (your internal customers) do not have to pick up a mess that you created. This often causes resentment and can affect the perception that others have of you.

It is also important to remove any potentially offensive items (photos of or calendars displaying scantily clad men or women; cartoons that have ethnic, racial, sexual, or otherwise offensive messages or that target a particular group; literature, posters, or objects that support specific political or religious views; or any item that could be unpleasant or offensive to view). These items have no place in a professional setting. In addition to sending a negative message to external customers who might see them, failure to remove such material might result in legal liability for you and your organization and create a hostile work environment.

MISCELLANEOUS CUES

miscellaneous cues Refer to factors used to send messages that impact a customer's perception or feelings about a service provider or organization. Examples are personal habits, etiquette, and manners.

Other factors, such as the **miscellaneous cues** discussed in the following sections, can affect customer perception or feelings about you or your organization.

Personal Habits

If you have annoying or distracting habits, you could send negative messages to your customer. For example, eating, smoking, drinking, or chewing food or gum while servicing customers can lead to negative impressions about you and your organization. Any of the following habits can lead to relationship breakdowns:

- Touching the customer (other than a professional handshake upon greeting and at the conclusion of a transaction, if appropriate).
- Scratching or touching certain parts of your body typically viewed as personal.
- Using pet phrases or speech patterns excessively ("Cool," "You know," "Groovy," "Am I right?" "Awesome," "Solid," "Whatever").
- Talking endlessly without letting the customer speak.
- Talking about personal problems.
- Complaining about your job, employer, co-workers, or other customers.

⚙ WORK IT OUT 4.4

Spatial Perceptions

Pair up with someone and stand facing him or her from across the room. Start a conversation about any topic (for example, how you feel about the concepts addressed in this chapter or how you feel about the activity in which you are participating) and slowly begin to move toward one another. As you do so, think about your feelings related to the distance at which you are communicating. Keep moving until you are approximately one inch from your partner. At that point, start slowly backing away, again thinking about your feelings. When you get back to your side of the room, have a seat and answer these questions:

1. How did you feel when you were communicating from the opposite side of the room (what were your thoughts)?
2. At what distance (moving forward or back) did you feel most comfortable? Why?
3. Did you feel uncomfortable at any point? Why or why not?
4. How can you use the information learned from this activity in the customer service environment?

Ethical Dilemma 4.2 ✳

Assume that you are a receptionist in a hospital emergency room waiting area and an older homeless male who is dirty, with cutoff jeans, sandals, and a t-shirt with holes in it, comes up to your desk. He has a dirty bloody rag wrapped around his hand and complains that he has cut himself with a rusty can lid. You greet him without a smile, hand him a clipboard with paperwork, and tell him to have a seat and complete the forms. At the same time that the indigent patient arrived, a well-dressed older woman wearing a suit arrives with a small crying girl and states that the child fell out of a tree and hurt her shoulder. You greet her warmly with a smile and proceed to engage her in conversation and assist attentively. Meanwhile the injured homeless patient waits to have a question answered about his paperwork.

1. How do you think you would feel if you were the homeless patient? Why?
2. Why do you think you might have used different standards of service for the two patients?
3. Do you think this approach to service is appropriate? Why or why not?
4. What could you have done differently/better to improve the service delivery in this situation?
5. How do you think other waiting patients might react to the difference in service that you provided?
6. What is the likely impact of the service delivery outlined in this situation?

> **Customer Service Success Tip**
>
> To determine if you have any annoying or potentially distracting personal habits that could cause relationship issues, ask someone who knows you well to be alert to gestures, movements, habits, or phrases that you repeat or use often. Once identified, make a conscious effort to reduce or eliminate the habits.

Time Allocation and Attention

Some organizations have standards for servicing customers within a specific time frame (for example, returning phone calls within four hours), but these **time allocations** should be targets because customer transactions cannot all be resolved in a specified period of time. The key is to be efficient

time allocation Amount of attention given to a person or project.

Street Talk

It is how a problem is perceived by the parties that is reality.

SHARON MASSEN, PH.D., CAP *Massen and Associates*

and effective in your efforts. Continually reevaluate your work habits and patterns to see whether you can accomplish tasks in a more timely fashion. The amount of time you spend with customers often sends subliminal messages of how you perceive their importance. If your organization has service standards that dictate how much time to spend with customers and it is adversely affecting your ability to provide quality service, consider discussing your concerns in a positive manner with your supervisor or manager. Make realistic suggestions for change. If nothing else, taking the opportunity to do this can open up communication between the two of you. You might also learn the logic behind such a policy in the event that you do not already know.

Follow-Through

Trust is the basis for any sound relationship. Without it, you really have no relationship.

When you deal with your customers, it is crucial that they can depend on you. Follow-through, or lack of it, sends a very powerful nonverbal message to customers. If you tell a customer you will do something, it is critical to your relationship that you do so. If you can't meet agreed-upon terms or time frames, get back to the customer and renegotiate. Otherwise, you may lose the customer's trust. For example, suppose you assure a customer that an item that is out of stock will arrive by Wednesday. On Tuesday, you find out that the shipment is delayed. If you fail to inform the customer, you may lose the sale and the customer's trust and potential future business. Also, the customer may view you and your organization negatively and then share that perception with others.

Proper Etiquette and Manners

etiquette and manners
Include the acceptable rules, manners, and ceremonies for an organization, profession, or society.

People appreciate receiving appropriate respect and prefer dealing with others who have good **etiquette and manners**.

Tied to nonverbal messages, the polite things you do (saying "please" and "thank you," asking permission, or acknowledging contributions) go far in establishing and building relationships. Such language sends an unspoken message that says, "I care" or "I respect you." In addition, behavior that affects your customer's perception of you can also affect your interaction and ability to provide service (interrupting others as they speak, talking with food in your mouth, pointing with your finger or other items such as a fork, or resting elbows on the table while eating lunch with a customer). Many good books are available on business manners and dining etiquette if you are unsure of yourself. Additionally, there are dozens of blogs and other Internet resources that address the dos and don'ts of providing service to and working with customers. Visit www.customerserviceskillsbook.com to visit one such blog written by the author of this book.

Color

Although color is not as important as some other factors related to nonverbal communication in the customer service environment, the way in

Etiquette and manners can send powerful nonverbal signals about your professionalism and background. By fine-tuning your basic dining and etiquette skills, you can positively influence your customers. *In what ways have you seen poor etiquette or manners in various situations influence your opinions of others?*

which you use various colors in decorating a workspace and in your clothing can have an emotional impact on customers. You should at least consider the colors you choose when dressing for work. Much research has been done by marketing and communication experts to determine which colors evoke the most positive reactions from customers. In various studies involving the reaction people had to colors, some clear patterns evolved. Figure 4.3 lists various colors and the possible **emotional messages of color** they can send.

emotional messages of color Research-based use of color to send nonverbal messages through advertisements and other elements of the organization.

KNOWLEDGE CHECK

1. What are the four forms of body language discussed in the text and why are they important in customer service?

2. What are the five vocal cues that can send unintentional nonverbal messages to your customers?

3. How do appearance and grooming affect the level of customer service that you provide?

4. What are the four spatial distances and how might they impact your ability to effectively serve your customers?

5. How do environmental cues send messages to others?

6. What are some of the miscellaneous cues discussed in the text and what role do they have in customer service?

FIGURE 4.3

The Emotional Messages of Color: Emotion or Message

Red	Stimulates and evokes excitement, passion, power, energy, anger, intensity. Can also indicate "stop," negativity, financial trouble, or shortage.
Yellow	Indicates caution, warmth, mellowness, positive meaning, optimism, and cheerfulness. Yellow can also stimulate thinking and visualizing.
Dark blue	Depending on shade, can relax, soothe, indicate maturity, and evoke trust and tranquility or peace.
Light blue	Projects a cool, youthful, or masculine image.
Purple	Projects assertiveness or boldness and youthfulness. Has a contemporary "feel." Often used as a sign of royalty, richness, spirituality, or power.
Orange	Can indicate high energy or enthusiasm. Is an emotional color and sometimes stimulates positive thinking.
Brown	An earth tone that creates a feeling of security, wholesomeness, strength, support, and lack of pretentiousness.
Green	Can bring to mind nature, productivity, positive image, moving forward or "go," comforting, growth, or financial success or prosperity. Also, can give a feeling of balance.
Gold and silver	Prestige, status, wealth, elegance, or conservatism.
Pink	Projects a youthful, feminine, or warm image.
White	Contains all the colors of the color spectrum. Typically used to indicate purity, cleanliness, honesty, and wholesomeness. Is visually relaxing.
Black	Lack of color. Creates sense of independence, completeness, and solidarity. Often used to indicate financial success, death, or seriousness of situation.

LO 4-3 The Role of Gender in Nonverbal Communication

CONCEPT Research indicates that boys and girls and men and women behave differently. Young children are sometimes treated differently by their parents because of their gender preference (either male or female may be the preferred gender, no matter the gender of the parent).

There has been a lot of research on the topic of gender communication in the past couple of decades. As a result, a lot of crucial information has been discovered and written about concerning differences in the way males and females interact and communicate in personal and business situations.

gender communication Term used to refer to communication between genders.

Gender communication is an important factor for you to consider before dealing with others, by better understanding the nuances often exhibited when people of the opposite gender come into contact. For example, some researchers have found that females are more comfortable being in close physical proximity with other females than males are being close to other males. Although similarities exist between the ways in which males

WORK IT OUT 4.5

Gender Communication

To get a better idea of how males and females communicate and interact differently, go to a library or to the Internet and gather information on the topic. Look specifically for information on the following topics:

Brain differences between men (males) and women (females) and the impact of these differences on communication and relationships.

Differences in nonverbal cues used by men (males) and women (females).

Base for the communication differences in the workplace or business world between men (males) and women (females).

and females relate to one another, there are distinct differences in behavior, beginning in childhood and carrying through into adulthood.

Many books have been written that hypothesize that boys and girls are different in many ways, are acculturated to act and behave differently, and have some real biological differences that account for their actions (and inactions), which are examined from a number of perspectives. These books often reference various studies that have found that boys and girls typically learn to interact with each other, and with members of their own gender, in different ways. Females generally tend to learn more nurturing and relationship skills early, whereas males approach life from a more aggressive, competitive stance. Females often search for more "relationship" messages during an interaction and strive to develop a collaborative approach; males typically focus on competitiveness or "bottom-line" responses in which there is a distinct winner. Obviously, these differences in approaches to relationship building can have an impact in the customer service environment, where people of all walks of life come together based on cultural differences.

The lessons learned early in life usually carry over into the workplace and affect customer interactions. If you fail to recognize the differences between the sexes and the gender roles assigned to them in any given culture and do not develop the skills necessary to interact with both men and women, you could experience some breakdowns in communication and ultimately in the customer-provider relationship.

The basis for gender differences is the fact that the brains of males and females develop at different rates and focus on different priorities throughout life. Some research studies indicate that women often tend to be more bilateral in the use of their brain. They can switch readily between the left [analytical, logical, factual, facts-and-figures-oriented] and right [emotional, creative, artistic, romantic, and expressive of feelings] brain hemispheres in various situations. Men, on the other hand, tend to be more lateral in their thinking. This means that they typically favor either the left hemisphere or the right hemisphere. This results in a difference in the way each gender communicates, relates to others, perceives, and deals with various situations.

Another factor that influences the manner in which a man or woman interacts with the opposite gender is behavioral preferences. Again, a lot

FIGURE 4.4

In North America men and women differ in their approach to relationships. Here are some general behavioral differences that are seen in many men and women.

	Females	Males
Body	Claim small areas of personal space (e.g., cross legs at knees or ankles).	Claim large areas of personal space (e.g., use figure-four leg cross).
	Cross arms and legs frequently.	Use relaxed arm and leg posture (e.g., over arm of a chair).
	Sit or stand close to same sex.	Sit or stand away from same sex but closer to females.
	Use subdued gestures.	Use dramatic gestures.
	Touch more (both sexes).	Touch males less, females more.
	Nod frequently to indicate receptiveness.	Nod occasionally to indicate agreement.
	Glance casually at watch.	Glance dramatically at watch (e.g., with arm fully extended and retracted to raise sleeve).
	Hug and possibly kiss both sexes upon greeting.	Hug and possibly kiss females upon greeting.
	Use high inflection at end of statements (sounds like a question).	Use subdued vocal inflection.
Vocal	Speak at faster rate.	Speak at slower rate.
	Express more emotion.	Express less emotion.
	Use more polite "requesting" language (e.g., "Would you please?")	Use more "command" language (e.g., "Get me the . . .).
	Focus on relationship messages.	Focus on business messages.
	Use vocal variety.	Often use monotone.
	Interrupt less; more tolerant of interruptions.	Interrupt more, but tolerate interruptions less.
	Maintain eye contact.	Glance away frequently.
	Smile frequently.	Smile infrequently (with strangers).
Facial	Use expressive facial movements.	Show little variation in facial expression.
	Focus more on details.	Focus less on details.
	Are more emotional in problem solving.	Are analytical in problem solving (e.g., try to find cause and fix problem).
Behavior	View verbal rejection as personal.	Do not dwell on verbal rejection.
	Apologize after disagreements.	Apologize less after disagreements.
	Hold grudges longer.	Do not hold grudges.
	Commonly display personal objects in the workplace.	Commonly display items symbolizing achievement.
	Use bright colors in clothing and decorations.	Use more subdued colors in clothing and decorations.
Environmental	Use patterns in clothing and decoration.	Use few patterns in clothing.

of research has been done to try to figure out why some individuals prefer working with people while others prefer to work alone or focus on tasks. This research stretches back thousands of years to biblical times and continues today as researchers try to better understand the human psyche.

Figure 4.4 lists some basic behavioral differences between females and males.

KNOWLEDGE CHECK

1. How does gender impact customer service?

LO 4-4 The Impact of Culture on Nonverbal Communication

CONCEPT To be successful in a global economy, you need to be familiar with the many cultures, habits, values, and beliefs of a wide variety of people.

Cultural diversity is having a significant impact on the world and the customer service environment. The number of service providers and customers with varied backgrounds is growing at a rapid pace. This trend provides a tremendous opportunity for expanding your personal knowledge and interaction with people from cultures you might not otherwise encounter. However, with this opportunity comes challenge. If you are to understand and serve people who might be different from you, you must first become aware that they are also very similar to you. In addition, if you are to be successful in interacting with a wide variety of people, you will need to understand the **impact of culture** by learning about many behaviors, habits, values, and beliefs from around the world. The Internet is a fertile source for such information. Take advantage of it, or visit your local library to check out books on different countries and their people. Join the National Geographic Society, and you will receive its monthly magazine, which highlights different cultures and people from around the globe.[2]

To become more skilled at dealing with people from other cultures, develop an action plan of things to learn and explore. At a minimum, familiarize yourself with common nonverbal cues that differ dramatically from one culture to another. Specifically, look for cues that might be perceived as negative in some cultures so that you can avoid them. Learn to recognize the different views and approaches to matters such as time, distance, touching, eye contact, and use of colors so that you will not inadvertently violate someone's personal space or cause offense.

impact of culture Refers to the outcome of people from various countries or backgrounds coming into contact with one another and potentially experiencing misunderstandings or relationship breakdowns.

KNOWLEDGE CHECK

1. How can an awareness of the varying cultures in a service environment help or hinder your service delivery?

LO 4-5 Negative Nonverbal Behaviors

CONCEPT You should be aware of habits or mannerisms that can send annoying or negative messages to customers.

People develop unproductive nonverbal behaviors without even realizing it. These may be nervous habits or mannerisms carried to excess (scratching, pulling an ear, or playing with hair). In a customer service environment, you should try to minimize such actions because they might send a negative or annoying message to your customers. An easy way to discover whether you have such behaviors is to ask people who know you well to observe you for a period of time and tell you about anything they observe that could be a problem. The following are some more common behaviors that can annoy people and cause relationship breakdowns or comments about you and your organization.

UNPROFESSIONAL HANDSHAKE

Hundreds of years ago, a handshake was used in many cultures to determine whether a person was holding a weapon. Later, a firm handshake became a show of commitment, of one's word, or of "manhood."

Traditional palm-to-palm handshakes are used and expected in most Western business environments and in Westernized business environments around the world. *Have you ever been caught off guard when someone tried a different handshake version (other than traditional palm-to-palm) when you first met? How did that feel?*

Today, in Western cultures and many others in which the Western way of doing business has been adopted, both men and women in the workplace are expected to convey greeting and/or commitment with a firm handshake. Failure to shake hands appropriately (palm-to-palm), with a couple of firm pumps up and down, can lead to an impression that you are weak or lack confidence or that you do not respect the other person. The grip should not be overly loose or overly firm. An overly firm handshake has its own problems. You may inadvertently injure a person who has specific medical issues (arthritis) with an overly powerful handshake. This type of handshake can be just as much a turn-off as a limp or clammy handshake.

When doing business in other countries or with people from other cultures, it is often helpful to know about their traditional forms of greeting so that you can greet people appropriately, depending on where you are serving them. If handshakes are exchanged, and are not the type to which you might be accustomed based on your cultural background, remember that all cultures do not traditionally adhere to this form of greeting. The other person may just be shaking hands as a show of respect for your culture, so you should appreciate his or her effort rather than critique or criticize it.

One mistake that some people make in a business setting is to carry their informal forms of greetings over to the workplace. For example, while it may be appropriate for you to greet friends and peers with a "high five," slap of the palm of the hand, or knuckle bump or to grip their hand with fingers curled and a brief hug or chest press, this is not appropriate in a professional environment with a customer. In order to project a positive professional protocol, use the traditional handshake when in the workplace if you are in a Westernized business environment.

FIDGETING

Using some mannerisms can indicate to a customer that you are anxious, annoyed, or distracted, and should therefore be avoided, if possible. Such signals can also indicate that you are nervous or lack confidence. Cues such as playing with or putting hair in your mouth, tugging at clothing, hand-wringing, throat-clearing, playing with items as you speak (pencil, pen, or other object), biting or licking your lips, or drumming your fingers or tapping a surface with a pencil or other object can all send a potentially annoying and/or negative message.

POINTING A FINGER OR OTHER OBJECT

For many people, this is viewed as a very accusatory mannerism and can lead to anger or violence on the part of your customer. If you must gesture toward a customer or toward an area or item, do so with an open flat hand (palm up) in a casual manner. The result is a less threatening gesture that almost invites comment or feedback because it looks as if you are offering the customer an opportunity to speak. Additionally, this is the appropriate means for pointing towards something in many cultures.

RAISING AN EYEBROW

This mannerism is sometimes called the *editorial eyebrow* because some television broadcasters raise their eyebrow. With the editorial eyebrow, only one eyebrow is arched, usually in response to something that the person has heard. This mannerism often signals skepticism or doubt about what you have heard. It can be viewed as questioning the customer's honesty.

PEERING OVER TOP OF EYEGLASSES

Many people who need glasses to read but not to see for distances may forget that they have on glasses when they are interrupted while reading or using them. As a result, they may speak to others while wearing their glasses sitting low on the end of their nose. This gesture might be associated with a professor, teacher, or someone who is in a position of authority looking down on a student or subordinate. For that reason, customers may not react positively if you peer over your eyeglasses at them. Typical nonverbal messages that this cue might send are displeasure, condescension, scrutiny, or disbelief.

Our nonverbal cues tell others a great deal about us, particularly when we display unproductive behaviors. *What are some possible reasons for the behaviors being displayed in this photo?*

CROSSING ARMS OR PUTTING HANDS ON HIPS

Typically viewed as a closed or defiant posture, crossing your arms or putting your hands on your hips may send a negative message to your customer and cause a confrontation. People often view this gesture as demonstrating a closed mind, resistance, or opposition.

HOLDING HANDS NEAR MOUTH

By holding your hands near your mouth, you will muffle your voice or distort your message. If someone is hearing-impaired or uses a language other than your native tongue, and relies partly on reading your lips, he or she may be unable to understand your message. Also, placing your hands over or in front of your mouth can send messages of doubt or uncertainty, or can suggest that you are hiding something.

KNOWLEDGE CHECK

1. What are examples of negative nonverbal behaviors and how might they impact service delivery?

LO 4-6 Strategies for Improving Nonverbal Communication

CONCEPT Nonverbal cues are all around us. Vocal and visual cues related to customers' feelings or needs are important and may mean the difference between a successful or unsuccessful customer service experience.

Nonverbal communication is not a science. That is because each person is a unique combination of factors such as personal backgrounds, educational experiences, cultures, and life experiences. There is no one answer related to what a given nonverbal cue means because each is interpreted differently by the person observing it. This is why learning as much as you can about people and what makes them function and act the way that they do is so crucial in the customer service profession.

The four strategies discussed in this section will help provide some basic tools that can help you improve your nonverbal communication skills if you practice them and try to understand the behavior of others.

SEEK OUT NONVERBAL CUES

Too often, service providers miss important vocal and visual clues related to customer feelings or needs because they are distracted doing other things or not being attentive. These missed opportunities can often mean the difference between successful and unsuccessful customer experiences. Train yourself to look for nonverbal cues by becoming a "student of human nature."

Nonverbal cues are all around you, if you simply open your eyes and mind to them. Start spending time watching people in public places (at supermarkets, malls, airports, bus stops, school, or wherever you have the chance). From your observations, objectively evaluate what works and what doesn't, and then modify your behavior accordingly to mimic the positive things you learn.

Try the following strategies to aid you in focusing on the nonverbal cues sent by others:

- Watch the behavior of others you see and the behavior of the people with whom they are interacting. Try to interpret the results of each behavior. However, keep in mind that human nature is not exact and that many factors affect the nonverbal cues used by yourself and others (culture, gender, environment, and many more).
- Be aware that you may be viewing through your own filters or biases, so evaluate carefully.
- Look at **clusters** of nonverbal behavior and the language accompanying them instead of interpreting individual signals. These clusters might be a combination of positive (smiling, open body posture, friendly touching) or negative (crossed arms, looking away as someone talks, or angry facial expressions or gestures). Evaluating clusters can help you gain a more accurate view of what is going on in a communication exchange.

clusters Groupings of nonverbal behaviors that indicate a possible negative intent (e.g., crossed arms, closed body posturing, frowning, or turning away) while other behaviors (smiling, open gestures with arms and hands, and friendly touching) indicate positive message intent.

CONFIRM YOUR PERCEPTIONS

Let others know that you have received and interpreted their nonverbal cues. Ask for clarification by **perception checking** if necessary. This involves stating the behavior observed, giving one or two possible interpretations, and then asking for clarification of message meaning.

perception checking The process of clarifying a nonverbal cue that was received by stating what behavior was observed, giving one or two possible interpretations, then asking the message sender for clarification.

Perception Checking Example

Suppose that you are explaining the features of a piece of office equipment to a customer and she reacts with a quizzical look. You might respond with a statement such as, "You seem astonished by what I just said. I'm not sure whether you were surprised or whether I was unclear in my explanation. What questions do you have?"

Notice in the example above that the focus of the error is on the service provider (I) rather than the customer (you). It also does not include a potentially accusatory question of "What did you not understand?" This latter type of question potentially implies that the customer may not be smart enough to grasp what you were saying. It can be especially pointed if the person speaks another primary language.

By taking the approach in the example, you focus on the customer's behavior and also provide an opportunity for her to gain additional necessary information.

SEEK CLARIFYING FEEDBACK

In many instances, you need feedback in order to adjust your behavior. You may be sending cues you do not mean to send or to which others may react negatively.

Clarifying Feedback Examples

1. Assume that you are on a cross-functional work team with members of various departments in your organization and have been in a meeting to discuss ideas for creating a new work process.

   During a heated discussion of ideas, you excuse yourself briefly to get a drink of water in order to take a prescribed pill.

Later, a teammate mentions that others commented about your frustration level and the fact that you bolted out of the room.

To determine what behaviors led to the team's reaction, you might ask yourself something like, "What did I do that made people perceive that I was upset?"

If you later find out why people viewed your behavior the way they did, you can offer an explanation in your next team meeting and avoid exhibiting similar behaviors in the future.

2. Another example might be to ask a co-worker whether the clothing you have on seems too formal for a presentation you will give later in the day.

Keep in mind, though, that some people will not give you honest, open feedback. Instead, they tell you what they think you want to hear or what they think will not hurt your feelings. For this reason, it is usually best to elicit information from a variety of sources before making any personal behavior changes, or deciding not to make them.

ANALYZE YOUR INTERPRETATIONS OF NONVERBAL CUES

One way to ensure that you are accurately evaluating nonverbal cues given by a variety of people is to analyze your own perceptions, stereotypes, and biases. This is important because the manner in which you view certain situations or groups of people might negatively affect your ability to provide professional and effective service to all your customers. This is especially true of customers in the groups toward which you feel a bias. Without realizing it, you may send negative nonverbal cues that could cause a relationship breakdown and lead to either a dissatisfied customer or even a confrontation.

> **Street Talk**
>
> Customer service representatives are expected to be dedicated, proactive, self managed, and brand ambassadors.
>
> JENNIFER HARPER

KNOWLEDGE CHECK   ⊘

1. What are four strategies for improving your nonverbal behavior with customers.

LO 4-7 Customer-Focused Behavior

CONCEPT Being customer-focused in your behavior may help you solve a customer's problem or eliminate the opportunity for a problem to develop. The nonverbal cues discussed in this section can help you stay customer-focused.

The nonverbal behavior you exhibit in the presence of a customer can send powerful messages. You should constantly remind yourself of advice you may have heard often: "Be nice to people." One way you can indicate that you intend to be nice is to send customer-focused messages regularly and enthusiastically through your nonverbal cues. Figure 4.5 lists some important

FIGURE 4.5
Courtesy Pays

Because of the competitive nature of business, organizations and customer service professionals should strive to pull ahead of the competition in any positive way possible. Simple courteous nonverbal behavior can be one way to beat the service quality levels of other companies. Why should you be courteous?

- *Image is enhanced.* First impressions are often lasting impressions. A more professional impression is created when you and the organizational culture are customer-focused. When your customers feel comfortable about you and the image projected, they are more likely to develop a higher level of trust and willingness to be more tolerant when things do go wrong occasionally.

- *Employee–customer communication improves.* By treating customers in a professional, courteous manner, you encourage them to freely approach and talk to you. Needs, expectations, and satisfaction levels can then be more easily determined. Additionally, when communication works well, you are less likely to have to deal with dissatisfied customers or have to implement service recovery strategies.

- *Word-of-mouth advertising increases.* Sending regular positive nonverbal messages can help create a feeling of satisfaction and rapport. When customers are satisfied and feel comfortable with you and your organization, they typically tell three to five other people. This increases your customer base while holding down formal advertising costs (newspapers and other publications, television, and radio).

- *Employee morale and esteem increase.* If employees feel that they are doing a good job and get positive customer and management feedback, they will probably feel better about themselves. This increased level of self-esteem affects the quality of service delivered. Keep in mind your role in helping peers feel appreciated. They are often your internal customers and expect the same consideration and treatment that your external customers expect.

- *Complaints are reduced.* When people are treated fairly and courteously, they are less likely to complain. If they do complain, their complaints are generally directed to a lower level (below supervisory level) and are generally expressed with low levels of anger. Simple things like smiling or attentive actions can help customers relax and feel appreciated.

- *Financial losses decrease.* When customers are satisfied, they are less likely to desert to competitors, file lawsuits, steal, be abusive toward employees (who might ultimately resign), and spread negative stories about employees and the organization. Building good rapport through communication can help in this area.

- *Customer loyalty increases.* People often return to organizations where they feel welcome, serviced properly, and respected. Your role as a service provider is to create an atmosphere where people feel comfortable and trust that you and the organization are working in their best interest to provide quality products and services that meet their needs, wants, and expectations.

benefits of customer-focused behavior. It gives some simple ways to accomplish this when you are dealing with internal and external customers.

Stand Up, If Appropriate

Depending on the layout of your work area, if you are seated behind a desk when a customer arrives or approaches you, stand up and greet him or her. Use the customer's name if you know it and extend a handshake. These actions show that you respect the person as an equal and are eager to assist her or him. Obviously, if you are a cashier behind a glass enclosure or have some other physical constraints, this would not apply. Just use common sense based on your environment in such instances.

Act Promptly

The speed with which you recognize and assist customers, gather information, or respond tells them what you think of their importance. If your service to the customer will take longer than planned or will be delayed, notify the customer, tell him or her the reason, and offer service alternatives if they are appropriate and available. If on the telephone and they are on hold, come back on the line every 30 seconds or so to let them know that you are working on their issue or question. An alternative to the latter is to tell them how long it will take to get their information or answer and offer them the options that either they can hold for that period or you can take their phone number and call them back within a specified time frame.

Guide Rather Than Direct

If customers must go to another person or area in the organization, or if they ask directions, personally guide them or have someone else do so, if possible. Do not simply point or direct. If you are on the telephone and you need to transfer a customer, give the extension of the person you're connecting to (in case of disconnection), transfer the call, and stay on the line to introduce the customer to the other service provider. Once the connection is made, excuse yourself and thank the customer for calling; then disconnect quietly.

Be Patient with Customers

Provide whatever assistance is necessary without appearing to push customers away. Patiently take the time to determine whether a customer has additional needs. It is fine to ask questions such as, "Will there be anything else I can do to assist you?" to signal the end of your interaction with a customer. Just be sure that you do it with a smile and pleasant tone so that the customer does not feel "dumped," rushed, or abandoned.

Offer Assistance

Offer to assist with doors, packages, directions, or in other ways, especially if a customer is elderly, has a disability, has numerous packages, or appears to need help. Similarly, if someone needs assistance with a door or in getting from one place to another, offer to help. If the person says, "No, thank you," smile and go on your way but monitor the person periodically in case he or she changes his or her mind or wants to signal to you. Do not assume that someone needs help, grab an arm to guide him or her, or push open a door. Such actions could surprise a person and throw him or her off balance. This is especially true of someone with a mobility or sight impairment who has learned to navigate using canes or other assistance. Upsetting a person's momentum or "system" could cause a fall or injury, which in turn could result in embarrassment and/or a liability situation for you or your organization.

Reduce Customer Wait Times

Nobody likes waiting, so keep waits to a minimum. If long delays are anticipated, inform the customer, offer alternatives, and work to reduce the wait time. If you notice that customers routinely have to wait for service, approach your supervisor about the situation and offer any suggestions for preventing this in the future. Remember that, as a responsible employee, you have a role in ensuring that customers are welcomed and getting the appropriate levels of service that they deserve.

Allow Customers to Go First

Typically, you should encourage and allow customers to precede you through cafeteria lines or doors, onto escalators or elevators, into vehicles, and so on as a show of respect. This is especially important if you are dealing with people from cultures in which the senior or eldest person in the group routinely goes ahead of others (e.g., South Korea and other Asian countries) so that others will be able to identify them based on their status. This projects an air of respect and courtesy. If he or she declines, do not make a scene and insist; simply go first yourself.

Offer Refreshments, If Appropriate

Take care of your "guests" the same way you would at home. Offer to get them something to drink if they come to your office or if they are attending lengthy meetings. You may also want to offer reading materials if they are in a waiting area. Be sure that reading materials in waiting areas are current, are professional-looking, and do not have any offensive material in them, such as scantily clad men or women, offensive jokes, or cartoons that target specific groups. Discard old, worn, and inappropriate materials. Also, if you are in an office, ensure that it is tidy, trash cans are emptied, and it projects a professional image before visitors arrive.

Be Professional

Avoid smirking, making faces, or commenting to other customers or co-workers after a customer leaves or turns his or her back. Such activity is unprofessional and will probably make the second customer wonder what you'll do when he or she leaves.

> **Customer Service Success Tip**
>
> Use a greeting and your customer's name, smile, listen effectively, and allow the customer to share questions, concerns, and issues without being interrupted in order to help say, "I value you." The bottom line is to treat all customers professionally and in a manner that makes them feel welcome, important, and as if you really care about them and their needs.

KNOWLEDGE CHECK ✓

1. What are the actions that you can use to exhibit customer-focused behavior?

Small Business Perspective

Small business owners and employees should uphold the same quality standards and commonsense rules related to nonverbal communication as you just read in this chapter. Because of their size and the fact that they typically have limited resources, it is crucial that each employee in a small company strives to project a strong professional image. Each customer contact is crucial in gaining and maintaining customers who will help add to the organization's revenue base.

(continued)

Customer service training is an important component in making smaller organizations more competitive in a global marketplace. Since funding and resources for training are often limited in small businesses, owners must get creative in helping prepare workers to provide quality service. To accomplish this, if some employees have the benefit of knowledge about effective nonverbal customer service skills because they have attended training or educational classes on the topic while they worked for larger companies in the past, they might be asked to mentor fellow employees. Additionally, supervisors or owners might attend professional development workshops to gain knowledge and skills that they can come back and share with all employees. Another option is for employees to be allowed and encouraged to sign up for online courses or attend local colleges or schools that teach courses on effective nonverbal communication. These courses are often less expensive than professional development seminars or workshops and in many instances held onsite. If small businesses are hiring new workers, they can often receive grants for training from local and state government entities because they are adding to the economy by employing someone and increasing the local tax base.

By sharing the knowledge learned in training with other company employees, owners and employees can help gain a more competitive edge over larger, better trained or equipped organizations.

Impact on Service

Based on personal experience and what you just read, answer the following questions:

1. Why do employees from small businesses need to be aware of the impact of their nonverbal messages. Explain.

2. What personal example can you think of where an employee of a small organization sent you or someone you observed an inappropriate nonverbal message. What was the result?

3. If you worked for a small business, what type of situations might require a sound knowledge of nonverbal cues when dealing with customers? Explain.

Key Terms

Mc Graw Hill Education **connect**

appearance and grooming

articulation, enunciation, or pronunciation

body language

clusters

emotional messages of color

environmental cues

etiquette and manners

gender communication

hygiene

impact of culture

interferences

malapropism

miscellaneous cues

nonverbal messages

paralanguage

pauses

perception checking

pitch

posture

proxemics

pupilometrics

rate of speech

semantics

silence

spatial cues

time allocation

verbal fillers

vocal cues

voice quality

volume

Summary

Once you become aware of the potential and scope of nonverbal communication, it can be one of the most important ways you have of sharing information and messages with customers. Numerous messages can be conveyed through a look, a gesture, a posture, or a vocal intonation. To be sure that the messages received are the ones you intended to send, be vigilant about what you say and do and how you communicate. Also, watch carefully the responses of your customers. Keep in mind that gender, culture, and a host of other factors affect the way you and your customers interpret received nonverbal cues.

To avoid distorting customer messages, or sending inappropriate messages yourself, keep these two points in mind: (1) Use a nonverbal cue you receive from others as an indicator and not as an absolute message. Analyze the cue in conjunction with the verbal message to more accurately assess the meaning of the message. (2) Continually seek to improve your understanding of nonverbal signals.

One final point: Remember that you are constantly sending nonverbal messages. Be certain that they complement your verbal communication and say to the customer, "I'm here to serve you."

Review Questions

1. What are six categories of nonverbal cues?
2. What are some of the voice qualities that can affect message meaning?
3. What are some examples of inappropriate workplace attire?
4. How can grooming affect your relationship with customers?
5. What are the four spatial distances observed in Western cultures, and for which people or situations is each typically reserved?
6. What are some of the miscellaneous nonverbal cues that can affect your effectiveness in a customer environment?
7. What are some ways in which men and women differ in their nonverbal communication?
8. What are some examples of unproductive communication?
9. List four strategies for improving nonverbal communication.
10. What are five examples of customer-focused behavior?

Search It Out

www.mhhe.com/customerservice

Search the Internet to Further Your Knowledge of Nonverbal Communication

Now that you have learned some of the basics of nonverbal communication and the impact it can have on your customer relationships, search the Internet to explore the topic further.

1. Select two topics from the following list, check out as many reputable sites as you can find, and prepare a report of at least two pages in length to present to your peers.

Body language

Nonverbal cues

Gender communication

Spatial distances

The impact of color on people

The role of vocal cues in nonverbal communication

Professional appearance and grooming for the workplace

The impact of culture on nonverbal cues

2. Go online and research communication differences between men and women. Use your new knowledge of how males and females differ to improve your service by structuring your communication and approach to their preferences; however, remember that each person is unique, so service customers individually.

3. Search the website for this textbook www.mhhe.com/customerservice for additional activities, reference materials, and support materials.

Listening to the Customer

The most basic of all human needs is the need to understand and be understood. The best way to understand people is to listen to them.
—Ralph Nichols

LEARNING OUTCOMES

After completing this chapter, you will be able to:

5-1 Describe why listening is important to customer service.

5-2 Define the four steps in the listening process.

5-3 List the characteristics of a good listener.

5-4 Recognize the causes of listening breakdown.

5-5 Develop strategies to improve your listening ability.

5-6 Use information-gathering techniques learned to better serve customers.

5-7 Apply concepts discussed to generate meaningful responses to your questions from customers.

To assist you with the content of this chapter, we have added additional review questions, activities, and other valuable resource material at www.mhhe.com/customerservice.

IN THE REAL WORLD TRANSPORTATION—SOUTHWEST AIRLINES

Southwest Airlines had a rocky road to its startup. Incorporated in 1967, it never actually started flying until June of 1971 because of lengthy legal challenges by other major airlines. When it finally started services between Dallas and Houston, Texas, and Dallas and San Antonio, Texas, it used three Boeing 737 aircraft and offered $20 one-way fares. In October of that same year, they offered 14 every-hour flights between Dallas and Houston and seven bi-hourly flights between Dallas and San Antonio and in November added scheduled flights between Houston and San Antonio. That same month they introduced a $10.00 "night fare." Needless to say, the competition was a bit worried about this young upstart airline that began taking business away from them in these three markets and had the potential to expand into other areas. In 1973 Braniff Airlines began a "fare war" that resulted in $13 fares for both airlines, with Southwest upping the stakes by offering customers a choice of a $13.00 fare or a free bottle of premium liquor with every $26.00 full-fare ticket. The result was that Southwest ended the year with its first profits since starting operation and started developing a loyal customer base. By January 1974 it had carried its one-millionth passenger.

Fast forward to 1979, when Southwest got approval to fly to other states after lengthy court battles and began service to Louisiana. This was the first venture outside the state of Texas and was followed by expansion eastward into numerous other states.

As they entered their second decade of service, the airline had over 2,000 employees and over $34 million in revenue. They also launched their successful "Loving you is what we do" customer campaign. As the decade progressed, the airline continued efforts to attract flyers from competing airlines and endear itself to customers by initiating policies such as a senior fare between the hours of 9:00 A.M. and 3:00 P.M. Monday through Friday for people over the age of 65. In 1986, the airline introduced their "Fly Now, Pay Less" fare that lowered all long-distance fares across its 25-city system to a ceiling of $98 each way. By the end of their second decade of operation, Southwest

was winning accolades and awards. According to their website, "For an unprecedented second time since the DOT began keeping records on the performance of the nation's largest carriers, Southwest captured the top rating in all three categories of the DOT operating statistics report." That same year, they reported a net income of over $71 million, with 94 aircraft and over 7,700 employees. They also were given major carrier status by the U.S. Department of Transportation, which meant that they had operating revenue exceeding $1 billion in a 12-month period.

By the 1990s, Southwest had become well established as a major passenger carrier with popular campaigns that focused on families such as the "Family Fare" from Salt Lake City, Utah, to anywhere Southwest flew. Anyone purchasing a full-fare adult ticket could take up to seven other people traveling with them for half price. They also implemented programs that offered to military families and dependents one-way fully-refundable leisure fares that did not require advance purchase. By the end of the decade, the airline had entered the Internet age with online booking and had generated over $478 million in net revenue, had 312 aircraft, and had over 27,000 employees. They had also been ranked fourth on *Fortune* magazine's "100 Best Companies to Work For" list.

By 2000, the company had moved up to number 2 on Forbes List and had expanded the Rapid Rewards program for customers that it had started several years earlier. Beyond that, as the decade progressed and moved into the second decade of the century, Southwest instituted a number of other discount flight initiatives that encouraged air travel and expanded its customer reach. For their efforts they won additional accolades, including the 2012 Top Military Friendly Employer award.

To learn more about Southwest Airlines, visit their website at www.swamedia.com/channels/By-Date/pages/history-by-date or scan the QR Code with your Smartphone application.

www.southwest.com

Think About It

1. Based on what you read here and learned on the airline's website, what are the company's strengths related to customer service?

2. Would you fly Southwest, if you have not already? Why or why not?

3. As a current or potential customer of the airline, what would you expect as a service experience from the airline?

Quick Preview

Before reviewing the chapter content, respond to the following questions by placing a "T" for true or an "F" for false on the rules. Use any questions you miss as a checklist of material to which you will pay particular attention as you read through the chapter. For those you get right, congratulate yourself, but review the sections they address in order to learn additional details about the topic.

_____ 1. Listening is a passive process similar to hearing.

_____ 2. Listening is a learned process.

_____ 3. During the comprehending stage of the listening process, messages received are compared and matched to memorized data in order to attach meaning to the messages.

_____ 4. The two categories of obstacles that contribute to listening breakdowns are personal and professional.

_____ 5. Biases sometimes get in the way of effective customer service.

_____ 6. A customer's inability to communicate ideas effectively can be an obstacle to effective listening.

_____ 7. A faulty assumption arises when you react to or make a decision about a customer's message on the basis of your past experiences or encounters.

_____ 8. A customer's refusal to deal with you, coupled with a request to be served by someone else, could indicate that you are viewed as a poor listener.

_____ 9. Many people can listen effectively to several people at one time.

_____ 10. By showing a willingness to listen and eliminate distractions, you can encourage meaningful customer dialogue.

_____ 11. Two types of questions that are effective for gathering information are reflective and direct.

_____ 12. Open-end questions elicit more information than closed-end questions do because they allow customers to provide what they feel is necessary to answer your question.

Answers to Quick Preview can be found at the end of the chapter.

LO 5-1 Why Is Listening So Important?

CONCEPT To be a better customer service professional, it is necessary to improve your listening skills.

listening An active, learned process consisting of four phases: receiving/hearing the message, attending, comprehending/assigning meaning, and responding.

Customer Service Success Tip

Stop doing other tasks and focus on what your customers are saying in order to increase your listening efficiency. Ask clarifying questions where appropriate.

Listening effectively is the primary means that many customer service professionals use to determine the needs of their customers. Many times, these needs are not communicated to you directly but through inferences, indirect comments, or nonverbal signals. A skilled listener will pick up on a customer's words and these cues or nuances and conduct follow-up questioning or probe deeper to determine the real need.

Most people take the listening skill for granted. They incorrectly assume that anyone can listen effectively. Unfortunately, this is untrue. Many people are complacent about listening and only go through the motions of listening.

In a classic study on listening conducted by Dr. Ralph G. Nichols, who is sometimes called the *father of listening*, data revealed that the average white-collar worker in the United States typically has only about a 25 percent efficiency rate when listening. This means that 75 percent of the message is lost. Think about what such a loss in message reception

To effectively deal with customers, you must listen to their needs, wants, and issues. *What do you do to show others that you are listening as they speak?*

Opportunities	Action Taken	Impact
100 customers a day, each with a $10 order	25 orders were filled successfully	Loss of $750 per day ($273,750 per year)
1,000 customers went to a store in one day	250 were serviced properly	750 were dissatisfied
1,000,000 members were eligible for membership renewal in an association	250,000 returned their applications after receiving a reminder call	750,000 members were lost

FIGURE 5.1

Missed Opportunities (Based on a 25 Percent Efficiency Rate)

could mean in an organization if the poor listening skills of customer service professionals led to a loss of 75 percent of customer opportunities. Figure 5.1 gives you some idea of the impact of this loss.

KNOWLEDGE CHECK

1. Why is effective listening so important as a service provider?

LO 5-2 What Is Listening?

CONCEPT Listening is a learned process, not a physical one.

True listening is an active learned process, as opposed to hearing, which is the physical action of gathering sound waves through the ear canal. When you listen actively, you go through a process consisting of various

Figure 5.3 gives some suggested questions you might ask yourself to check on your listening skills. Figure 5.4 provides questions for a self-assessment of your skills.

FIGURE 5.3
Questions for the Listener

In analyzing your customer's message(s), ask yourself the following questions:

- Am I practicing active listening skills?
- What message is the customer trying to get across?
- What does the customer want or need me to do in response to his or her message?
- Should I take notes or remember key points being made?
- Am I forming premature conclusions, or do I need to listen further?
- Are there biases or distractions I need to avoid?
- Is the customer failing to provide information needed to make a sound decision?
- What other feedback clues are being provided in addition to words? Are they important to message meaning?
- What questions do I need to ask as a follow-up to the customer's message?

FIGURE 5.4
Listening Self-Assessment

To prepare yourself for effective customer interactions and to quickly assess how good your listening skills are, take a few moments to take the following assessment. Depending on your responses, you may need to develop a listening improvement plan using some of the strategies in this chapter and available from other sources.

Place a check mark in the appropriate column.

	Always	Sometimes	Never
1. When someone speaks to me, I stop what I am doing to focus on what they are saying.			
2. I listen to people even if I disagree with what they are saying.			
3. When I am unsure of someone's meaning, I ask for clarification.			
4. I avoid daydreaming when listening to others.			
5. I focus on main ideas, not details, when someone speaks to me.			
6. While listening, I am also conscious of nonverbal cues sent by the speaker.			
7. I consciously block out noise when someone speaks to me.			
8. I paraphrase the messages I receive in order to ensure I understood the speaker's meaning.			
9. I wait until I have received a person's entire message before forming my response.			
10. When receiving negative feedback (e.g., a customer complaint), I listen with an open mind.			

Rating key: Always = 5   Sometimes = 3   Never = 0
Add your total score. If you rated:

40–50	Your listening is excellent
26–39	Your listening is above average
15–25	Your listening likely falls into the range identified by Dr. Nichols' study (included in this chapter)
Below 15	You have a serious listening problem and should seek additional training or resources to improve

KNOWLEDGE CHECK

1. What are the four phases of the active listening process?

2. How would you describe the process of hearing?

3. What occurs during the attending phase of the listening process?

4. What happens in your brain during the comprehending/assigning meaning phase of listening?

5. Why should you be sure to select the appropriate response during the responding phase of listening?

LO 5-3 Characteristics of a Good Listener

CONCEPT Listening will improve as you "learn" in the customer's shoes.

Successful listening is essential to service excellence. Like any other skill, listening is a learned behavior that some people learn better than others. Some common characteristics possessed by most effective listeners are discussed in the following sections. The characteristics of effective and ineffective listeners are summarized in Figure 5.5.

Empathy. By putting yourself in the customer's place and trying to relate to the customer's needs, wants, and concerns, you can often reduce the risk of poor service. Some customer service professionals neglect the customer's need for compassion, especially when the customer is dissatisfied. Such negligence tends to magnify or compound the effect of the initial poor service the customer received.

Understanding. The ability to listen as customers verbalize their needs, and to ensure that you understand them, is essential in properly servicing the customer. Too often, you hear people say, "I understand

FIGURE 5.5

Characteristics of Effective and Ineffective Listeners

Many factors can indicate an effective or ineffective listener. Over the years, researchers have assigned the following characteristics to effective and ineffective listeners:

Effective Listeners	Ineffective Listeners
Focused	Inattentive
Responsive	Uncaring
Alert	Distracted
Understanding	Unconcerned
Caring	Insensitive
Empathetic	Smug/conceited
Unemotional	Emotionally involved
Interested	Self-centered
Patient	Judgmental
Cautious	Disorganized
Open	Defensive

what you mean," when it is obvious that they have no clue as to the level of emotion being felt. When this happens while a customer is upset or angry, the results could be flared tempers, loss of business, bad publicity, and, at the far end of the continuum, acts of violence. Some techniques for demonstrating understanding will be covered later in this chapter.

Patience.   Keep in mind that it is your job to serve the customer. Not everyone communicates in the same manner. Each customer has different needs and expectations based on age, gender, behavioral style, preference, background, and other factors. That is why you must never try to use a cookie-cutter approach to delivering service where you assume all people are the same and respond to the same approach in service delivery. Take the time to ask questions and actively listen to their responses before choosing a course of action.

Do your best to listen well so that you can get at the customer's meaning or need. Don't rush a customer who seems to be processing information and forming opinions or making a decision. This is especially important after you have presented product information and have asked for a buying decision. Answer questions and provide additional information requested, but don't push. Doing so could frustrate, anger, and ultimately alienate the customer. You could end up with a complaint or lost customer.

Patience is especially important when a language barrier or speech disability is part of a customer's situation. Your job is to take extra care to determine the customer's needs and then respond appropriately. In some cases, you may have to resort to the use of an interpreter or written communication in order to determine the customer's needs.

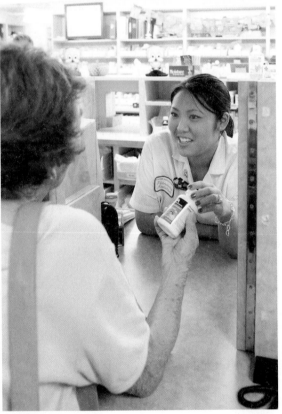

Active listening involves complete attention, a readiness and willingness to take action, and an open mind to evaluate customers and determine their needs. *What should customer service professionals do to achieve these goals of active listening?*

Attentiveness.   By focusing your attention on the customer, you can better interpret his or her message and satisfy his or her needs. Attentiveness is often displayed through nonverbal cues (nodding or cocking of the head to one side or the other, smiling, or using paralanguage). When you are reading, talking on the phone to someone while servicing your customer, or doing some other task while "listening" to your customer, you are not really focusing. In fact, your absorption rate will fall into the 25 percent of listening efficiency category about which you read earlier.

Objectivity.   In dealings with customers, try to avoid subjective opinions or judgments. If you have a preconceived idea about customers, their concerns or questions, the environment, or anything related to the customers, you could mishandle the situation. Listen openly and avoid making assumptions. Allow customers to describe their needs, wants, or concerns in their own words, and then analyze them fairly before taking appropriate action.

KNOWLEDGE CHECK

1. Name the five characteristics possessed by most effective listeners and describe their relationship to customer service.

LO 5-4 Causes of Listening Breakdown

CONCEPT Poor customer service may result from a breakdown of the listening process.

Many factors contribute to ineffective listening. Some are internal or in your brain, but others are external and you cannot control them. The key is to recognize actual and potential factors that can cause ineffective listening and strive to eliminate them. The factors discussed in the following sections are some of the most common.

PERSONAL OBSTACLES

As a listener, you may have individual characteristics or qualities that get in the way of listening effectively to the customer. Some of these **personal obstacles** are discussed in the following sections.

Biases

Your opinions or beliefs about a specific person, group, situation, or issue can sometimes cloud your ability to listen objectively to what is being said. These **biases** may result in preconceived and sometimes incorrect assumptions. They can also lead to service breakdown, complaints, angry or lost customers, or even violence.

Often personal biases are a result of things learned earlier in life and not even recognized on a conscious level. Everyone has such biases to some degree because children repeat what they hear from caregivers, in the media, through music, and via other sources. Unfortunately, some of the things they hear are inappropriate negative stereotypes about individuals or groups of people. Repeating such comments helps lock them into long-term memory; as adults we have these retained images or "tapes" continually playing in the back of our subconscious mind. This is why many people who do not consider themselves as racist or biased against other people whom they perceive to be different will sometimes shout or use slurs or derogatory comments based on race or some other aspect of a person (e.g., weight, color, dialect, or physical condition) in emotional situations. For example, someone cuts them off in traffic, bumps into them in a crowded store, or acts in a way that the person believes is "typical" of "those" people. In such instances, they might react with a derogatory remark or nonverbalized thought because of the mental "tape" or memories in their head.

As a service provider, it is crucial that you never allow such biases to impact the way you listen to or deal with others. Often we see this occur when a service provider has an emotional exchange with a customer and after the customer leaves or hangs up the phone, the provider makes a

personal obstacles Individual factors that can limit performance or success in life. Examples are disabilities, lack of education, attitude, and biases.

biases Beliefs or opinions that a person has about an individual or group. Often based on unreasonable distortions or prejudice.

derogatory comment to him- or herself or to a co-worker that is overheard by others. This portrays the provider in a negative light and potentially degrades the reputation of the organization, especially if another customer or co-worker hears the comment.

Psychological Distracters

psychological distracters
Refers to mental factors that can cause a shift in focus in interacting with others. Examples are state of health and personal issues.

Your psychological state can impede effective listening. **Psychological distracters**, such as being angry or upset, or simply not wanting to deal with a particular person or situation, may negatively affect your listening. Think about a time when you had a negative call or encounter with a customer or someone else and you became frustrated or angry. Did your mood, and possibly your voice tone, change as a result? Did that emotion then carry over and affect another person later?

Often when people become upset, time is needed to cool off before they deal with someone else. If you do not cool off, the chance that you will raise your voice or become frustrated with the next person you encounter is increased greatly. And, if this second encounter escalates because of the person's reaction to a negative tone or attitude, you might respond inappropriately. Thus, a vicious cycle is started. You get angry at a person; your tone carries over to a second, who in turn gets upset with your tone; your emotions escalate; you carry that mood to a third person; and so on. All of this lessens your ability to listen and serve customers effectively.

> ### Street Talk
>
> Empower each customer service representative to make a decision that will bring closure for the customer, leaving them feeling good about the organization and how he or she was treated by the service provider.
>
> SHARON MASSEN, PH.D, CAP *Massen and Associates*

Physical Condition

Another internal factor that can contribute to or detract from effective listening is your state of wellness and fitness. When you are ill, fatigued, in poor physical condition, or just not feeling well, listening can suffer. Because of the hectic pace of today's world, the prevalence and easy access of television, and the belief by many people that they "need" to check their e-mail, text, or voice messages immediately when communication arrives, we are a world of tired people. All of this can cause problems when trying to effectively listen to others or function effectively each day. According to the National Sleep Foundation, "people now sleep about 20 percent less than they did a century ago."[1] Further, "A recent study from the National Health Interview Survey which examined the sleep duration of individuals across several occupations ranging from manufacturing to public administration found that the percent of workers who reported a sleep duration of 6 hours or less per night increased from 24 to 30% in the last 20 years."[2]

We often hear that a good diet and exercise are essential to good health. They are also crucial for effective listening. Try not to skip meals when you are working, stay away from foods high in sugar content, and get some form of regular exercise. These all affect physical condition. Try something as simple as using the stairs rather than the elevator or escalator. Another option is a brisk walk at lunchtime. All of these can help you maintain your "edge" so that you will be better prepared for a variety of customer encounters. Also, avoiding meals that are heavy in carbohydrates can aid you in staying more alert.

When a customer service professional gets angry, his or her tone and mood may likely carry over to a customer. *How do you feel when a customer service professional is angry and raises his or her voice?*

Circadian Rhythm

All people have a natural 24-hour biological pattern (**circadian rhythm**) by which they function. The physiological cycle is associated with the earth's rotation. It affects metabolic and sleep patterns in humans as day replaces night. This "clock" often establishes the body's peak performance periods. Some people are said to be morning people; their best performance typically occurs early in the day. They often wake early, "hit the ground running," and continue until after lunch, when the natural rhythm or energy level in their body begins to slow down. For such people afternoons are often a struggle. They may not do their best thinking or perform physically at peak during that point in the day. According to the National Sleep Foundation, "The circadian rhythm dips and rises at different times of the day, so adults' strongest sleep drive generally occurs between 2:00–4:00 a.m. and in the afternoon between 1:00–3:00 p.m., although there is some variation depending on whether you are a 'morning person' or 'evening person.' The sleepiness we experience during these circadian dips will be less intense if we have had sufficient sleep, and more intense when we are sleep deprived."[3]

Evening people often have just the opposite pattern of energy. They struggle to get up or perform in the morning; however, during the afternoon and in the evening they are just hitting their stride. They often stay awake and work or engage in other activities until the early hours of the next day, when the morning people have been sound asleep for hours. From a listening standpoint, you should recognize your own natural body pattern so that you can deal with the most important listening and other activities during your peak period if possible. For example, if you are a morning person, you may want to ask your boss to assign you to customer contact or to handling problem situations early in the day. At that time, you are likely to be most alert and productive, less stressed, and less apt to become frustrated or irritated by abusive or offensive behavior by others.

circadian rhythm The physiological 24-hour cycle associated with the Earth's rotation that affects metabolic and sleep patterns in humans as day displaces night.

Personal Habits

Take a few minutes to think about your personal nutritional (e.g., how many meals a day you eat, snacks, quantities, and when you eat) and exercise (e.g., how often, duration, and type of exercise) habits since these can affect attention span and your ability to listen effectively; then create a list of the ones that are positive and negative.

Preoccupation

In recent years, many people have become distracted from work and listening activities by personal factors (e.g., financial issues, relationship or family problems, schooling, or stress because of issues at home) that override their efforts to do a good job each day. When you have personal or other matters on your mind, it sometimes becomes difficult to focus on the needs and expectations of the customer and your job tasks. This can frustrate both you and your customers. It is difficult to turn off personal problems, but you should try to resolve them before going to work, even if you must take time off to deal with them. Many companies offer programs to assist employees in dealing with their personal and performance issues. Through **employee assistance programs (EAPs)**, organizations are providing counseling in such areas as finance, mental hygiene (health), substance abuse, marital and family issues, smoking cessation, weight loss, and workplace performance problems. Check with your supervisor or human resources department to identify whether such resources are available in your organization. Also, if you are applying for a new job, ask during the interview process if the company offers EAP.

employee assistance program (EAP) Benefit package offered to employees by many organizations that provides services to help employees deal with personal issues that might adversely affect their work performance (e.g., legal, financial, behavioral, family, and mental health counseling services).

Hearing Loss

Many people suffer from hearing loss caused by physiological (physical) problems or extended exposure to loud noises. Sometimes they are not aware that their hearing is impaired. Often, out of vanity or embarrassment, people take no action to remedy the loss. If you find yourself regularly straining to hear someone, having to turn an ear toward the speaker, or asking people to repeat what they said because you didn't get the entire message, you may have a hearing loss. If you suspect that you have hearing loss, go to your physician or an audiologist (hearing specialist) quickly to avoid complications or further loss of hearing. Failure to do so could lead to issues where your supervisor perceives that listening issues in the workplace are being caused by a poor attitude or some other issue that could result in negative performance ratings for you.

LISTENING SKILL LEVEL

People communicate on different levels, depending on their knowledge and experiences in the area of communication. Adults are influenced by the

FIGURE 5.6
Indicators of Poor Listening

You cannot afford the luxury of failing to listen to your customer. Periodically, you should do a self-check on your listening style to see whether you need to improve. If any of the following events occur, you may need to refocus.

- Customers specifically ask to speak to or be served by someone else.
- You find yourself missing key details of conversations.
- You regularly have to ask people to repeat information.
- You end phone calls or personal encounters not knowing for sure what action is required of you.
- Customers often make statements such as, "Did you hear what I said?" "Are you listening to me?" or "You're not listening."
- You find yourself daydreaming or distracted as a customer is speaking.
- You miss nonverbal cues sent by the customer or others as the two of you communicate.
- You answer a question incorrectly because you didn't actually "listen" to it.

experiences they had as children; that is, they are likely to repeat behavior they learned during childhood. For example, if you grew up in an environment where the people around you practiced positive skills related to listening, providing feedback and using nonverbal communication and effective interpersonal skills for dealing with others, you will likely use similar techniques as an adult (Figure 5.6 shows some indicators of poor listening skills). On the other hand, if your childhood experiences were negative, where active conversation with multiple people talking simultaneously was normal, or you did not have good communication role models, the chances are that you struggle in listening to others effectively.

As you read earlier, listening is the primary skill most people have for gathering information. Unfortunately, in the United States (and other countries), the skill of listening is not routinely taught in most public school systems. People learn the proper techniques involved in the skill only if they take the personal initiative to read, listen to professional development recordings, watch videos, and attend seminars or college courses on listening. Too often, even though an adult's intentions might be well meant, techniques used to teach listening to children are often ineffective.

Thought speed and faulty assumptions that we have about others or a situation can often create barriers to listening effectiveness.

Thought Speed

Your brain is capable of comprehending messages delivered at rates of as much as four to six times faster (**thought speed**) than the speed at which the average adult speaks. In the United States, this rate is approximately 125 to 150 words per minute (wpm), while in other countries or cultures this rate might vary. The difference between the two rates can be referred to as a **lag time** or **listening gap** during which the mind is actually momentarily idle or focused on another activity. The result is that your brain does other things to occupy itself (for example, daydreaming). To prevent or reduce such distraction, you must consciously focus on your customer's message, look for key points, ask pertinent questions, and respond appropriately. One way to help yourself focus is to take notes about an issue,

thought speed The rate at which the human brain processes information.

lag time The term applied to the difference in the rate at which the human brain can receive and process information and at which most adults speak.

listening gap The difference in the speed at which the brain can comprehend communication and the speed at which the average adult speaks in the United States.

suggestion, or complaint as your customer speaks. You then have something to which you can refer or provide feedback from once the customer stops talking. Another benefit of this technique is that you can demonstrate to customers that you are truly interested in their ideas or subject of the conversation.

Ethical Dilemma 5.1

A customer comes into your office at the Department of Water and Sewer on a Tuesday following a three-day holiday weekend. She has a toddler and a five-year-old daughter with her and is very upset. She is cursing and screaming that she was promised on the previous Thursday that her water, which was turned off due to nonpayment of her bill for two months, was supposed to be turned back on Friday afternoon, but was not. She states that she and her two infant children had no water or bathroom to use all weekend.

You know that no turnoffs/turnons are routinely scheduled on Fridays since maintenance staff members have mandatory in-service training every Friday afternoon.

In checking your database, you find that she had promised to come in last Wednesday to give a money order for the delinquent bills but never showed up. You also see that she has a history of nonpayment.

1. What would you say to this customer? Explain.
2. What actions would you take to remedy the situation and get her water back on so that she and her children would have access to services?

Faulty Assumptions

faulty assumptions Service provider projections made about underlying customer message meanings based on past experiences.

Because of past experiences or encounters with others, you may be tempted to make **faulty assumptions** about your customer's message(s). Don't. Each customer and each situation is different and should be regarded as such. Because you had a certain experience with one customer does not mean that you will have a similar experience with another. For example, because one customer lies about an issue with your organization's products or services does not mean that everyone who complains is lying. Take the time to effectively gather information in each customer encounter so that you can make an informed decision on the correct course of action, then make a judgment on what needs to be done to remedy the situation.

EXTERNAL OBSTACLES

external obstacles Factors outside an organization or the sphere of one's influence that can cause challenges in delivering service.

You cannot remove all barriers to effective listening, but you should still try to reduce them when dealing with customers. Some typical examples of **external obstacles** include the following.

Information Overload

information overload Refers to having too many messages coming together and causing confusion, frustration, or an inability to act.

Each day you are bombarded with information from many sources. You get information in meetings, from the radio and television, from customers, and in a variety of public places. In many instances, you spend as much as 5 to 6 hours a day listening to customers, co-workers, family members, friends, and strangers. Such **information overload** can result in stress,

Employees rarely have control over external distractions in the workplace. *What are some strategies to help cope with a noisy work environment?*

inadequate time to deal with individual situations, and reduced levels of customer service.

Other People Talking

It is not possible for you to give your full attention to two speakers simultaneously. In order to serve customers effectively, deal with only one person at a time. If someone else approaches, smile, acknowledge him or her, and say, "I'll be with you in just a moment" or at least signal that message by holding up your index finger to indicate "1 minute" while you smile. If after a minute it appears that you will need more time with your current customer, either call for assistance or ask the waiting person if he or she just has a simple question that you might answer. If he or she indicates this to be the case, ask the current customer if he or she would mind your answering a question. Should you determine that the second customer's question is going to take some time to address, either ask that customer to continue waiting or call for assistance.

Ringing Phones

Ringing telephones can be annoying, but you shouldn't stop helping one customer to get into a discussion with or try to serve another customer over the phone. This creates a dilemma, for you cannot ignore customers or others who depend on you to serve their needs over the telephone.

Several options are available in such instances. You might arrange with your supervisor or co-workers to have someone else take the calls. Those people can either provide service or take messages, depending on the business your organization conducts. Another option is the use of a voice mail

provide service to customers who might become agitated or violent. Some examples of situations when you might want a physical barrier include

- City or state clerks who deal with people who have been charged with traffic or other violations of the law.
- Public utility employees who deal with people who are complaining about service problems.
- Employees in motor vehicle offices where people may have frustrating problems with drivers' licenses or vehicle registration.

ADDITIONAL OBSTACLES TO EFFECTIVE LISTENING

In addition to the issues you just read, customers themselves can negatively affect communication—through their inability to convey a message to you.

Although it is not specifically a listening issue, if customers are unable to deliver their message effectively, you may be unable to receive and properly analyze their meaning. No amount of dedication and effort on your part will make up for a language barrier, a disability (speech, physical) that limits speech and nonverbal body language, or poor communication skills. In these situations, it is often necessary to seek out others to help (translators, signers) or to use alternative means of communication [gestures, written, symbols, or a text telephone (TTY/TDD)] to discover the customers' meaning and satisfy their needs.

By recognizing these limiting factors, you can improve your chances of communicating more effectively. Use Worksheet 5-4 (see www.mhhe.com/customerservice) to evaluate listening distractions in your environment.

KNOWLEDGE CHECK

1. What are six personal obstacles that might cause a listening breakdown?
2. How do thought speed and faulty assumptions impact your listening skill level?
3. What can be done to reduce the external obstacles you just read about?

LO 5-5 Strategies for Improved Listening

CONCEPT You can improve your listening skills in several different ways. One important way is to listen more than you talk.

Numerous techniques can be used to become a more effective listener. The following tips can be used as a basis for improvement.

WORK IT OUT 5.6

Correcting Common Listening Problems

Here are some common listening problems. Work in a small group with other students to try to think of one or two means for reducing or eliminating these problems in your customer service.

Listening to words, not concepts, ideas, or emotions.

Pretending interest in a customer's problem, question, suggestion, or concern.

Planning your next remarks while the customer is talking.

Being distracted by external factors.

Listening only for what you perceive is the real issue or point.

Reacting emotionally to what the customer is saying.

STOP TALKING!

You cannot talk and actively listen at the same time. When the customer starts talking, the first thing you should do is stop talking and listen carefully. One common mistake that many people make is to ask a question, hesitate, and if no answer is immediately offered, ask a second question or "clarify" their meaning by providing additional information. A habit like this is not only confusing to the listener, but rude. Some people (e.g., people who speak a different language, have certain **behavioral styles**, are elderly, or have certain disabilities) take a bit more time to analyze and respond to messages they receive. Others may be simply trying to formulate just the right answer before responding. If you interrupt with additional information or questions, you may interfere with their thought patterns and cause them to become frustrated or forget what they were going to say. The end result is that the listener may not speak or respond at all because he or she believes that you aren't really listening or interested in the response anyhow, or because he or she is embarrassed or confused.

Listening behavior like you just read about could lead to a complaint to your supervisor because of what a customer believes to be rude, uncaring, or an unprofessional service attitude. To avoid such a scenario, plan what you want to say, ask the question, and then stop speaking. You might ask, "Mr. Swanson, how do you think we might resolve this issue?" Once you have asked the question, stop talking and wait for a response. If a response does not come in a moment or so, or the customer states that he or she is unsure or seems confused by what you said, try asking the question another way (paraphrase), possibly offering some guidance to a response and concluding with an open-end question (one that encourages the listener to give opinions or longer responses). You might say, "Mr. Swanson, I'd really like to help resolve this issue. Perhaps we could try _____ or _____. How do you think that would work?"

behavioral styles Descriptive term that identifies categories of human behavior identified by behavioral researchers. Many of the models used to group behaviors date back to those identified by Carl Jung.

of higher satisfaction, lower frustration, and a sense of being cared for on the customer's part.

SHOW EMPATHY

Put yourself in the customer's place by empathizing, especially when the customer is complaining about what he or she perceives to be poor service or inferior products. This is sometimes referred to as "walking a mile in your customer's shoes." For example, if a customer complains that she was expecting a specific service by a certain date but didn't get it, you might respond as follows: "Mrs. Ellis, I apologize that we were unable to complete _____ on the tenth as promised. We dispatched a truck, but the driver was involved in an accident. Can we make it up to you by _____? (Offer a gift, suggest an alternative such as hand delivery, and so on.) This technique, known as **service recovery**, is a crucial step in delivering quality service and remaining competitive into the twenty-first century.

service recovery The process of righting a wrong or correcting something that has not gone as promised involving provision of a product or service to a customer. The concept involves not only replacing defective products, but also going the extra step of providing compensation for the customer's inconvenience.

LISTEN FOR CONCEPTS

Instead of focusing on one or two details, listen to the entire message before analyzing it and responding. Instead of trying to respond to one portion of a message, wait for the customer to provide all the details. Then ask any questions necessary to get the information you need to respond appropriately. For example, assume that a customer (Mr. Chi), who works for a manufacturing company, has requested a special fabricated part to replace one they currently have for a new machine assembly that his company is working on. The part is a special order and not one currently in your company's inventory. He indicates that their development budget for the part is $10,000.

After he explains his need, you might respond with something like, "Mr. Chi, if I understand you correctly, you'd like us to build a new prototype part to replace the one currently being used in the assembly. You're looking for a total cost for development and manufacture not to exceed $10,000. Is that correct?"

LISTEN OPENLY

Avoid the biases discussed earlier. Remember that you don't have to like everyone you encounter, but you do have to respect and treat customers fairly and impartially if you want to maintain a positive business relationship. For example, whenever you encounter a person who is rude or is the type of person for whom you have a personal dislike, try to maintain your professionalism. Remember that you represent your organization and that you are paid by your employer to serve the customer

Note taking can help focus listening and later aid recall of what was discussed. *What system do you use to take notes while talking on the phone or to follow up on customer issues?*

(whoever he or she is). If a situation arises that you feel you cannot or prefer not to handle, call in a co-worker or supervisor. However, be careful in taking this action because you may potentially reveal a personal preference or bias that could later be held against you when you apply for other positions in your organization or positions in other companies. Try to work through your differences or biases rather than let them hinder your ability to deal with others or your career potential. Your ability to serve each customer fairly and competently is important to your job success.

SEND POSITIVE NONVERBAL CUES

Be conscious of the nonverbal messages you are sending. Even when you are verbally agreeing or saying yes, you may be unconsciously sending negative nonverbal messages. When sending a message, you should make sure that your verbal cues (words) and nonverbal cues (gestures, facial expressions) are in **congruence**. For example, if you say, "Good morning. How may I help you?" in a gruff tone, with no smile, and while looking away from the customer, that customer is not going to feel welcome or believe that you are sincere in your offer to assist.

congruence In communication, this relates to ensuring that verbal messages sent match or are in agreement with the nonverbal cues used.

DON'T ARGUE

Do you remember the "did not"/"did too" quarrels you might have witnessed when you were a child and one person accused the other of doing something? Such verbal exchanges often got heated, voices were raised, tempers might have escalated, and someone might have started hitting or pushing. Who won? The answer is—no one. You should avoid similar childish behaviors in dealing with others—especially your current or potential customers. Don't let these memories, or "tapes" in your head, get in the way of good service.

When you argue, you become part of the problem and cannot be part of the solution. Learn to phrase responses or questions positively. Keep in mind that even when you go out of your way to properly serve customers, some of them will respond negatively. Some people seem to enjoy conflict. In such situations, maintain your composure (count to 10 silently before responding), listen, and attempt to satisfy their needs. If necessary, refer such customers to your supervisor or a peer for service rather than let the encounter turn confrontational or emotional.

Street Talk

Do what you say you're going to do. Always show up as promised and always answer phone calls.

GARY GOLDBERG *Owner, Weeding by Hand*

TAKE NOTES, IF NECESSARY

Most people do not have a photographic memory and cannot remember all details about a discussion or situation. If information is complicated, or if names, dates, numbers, or numerous details are involved in a customer encounter, you may want to take notes for future reference and to ensure accuracy. Notes can help prevent your forgetting or confusing information. Once you have made your notes, verify your understanding of the facts with your customer before proceeding. For example, in a client or customer meeting, you may want to jot down key issues, points, follow-up actions, or questions. Doing so shows that you are indeed listening and committed to getting things right or taking appropriate action.

KNOWLEDGE CHECK

1. What is the first thing you must do in order to actively listen?
2. What are seven active listening strategies that can send a message of "I care"?
3. What can you do to ensure that your verbal and nonverbal messages are in congruence?

LO 5-6 Information-Gathering Techniques

CONCEPT Use questions to sort out facts from fiction.

Your purpose in listening to your customers is to gather information about their needs or wants on which you can base decisions on how to best satisfy them. Sometimes, you will need to prompt your customers to provide additional or different types of information.

Use questions to determine customer needs and to verify and clarify information received. This will ensure that you thoroughly understand the customer's message prior to taking action or responding. For example, when you first encounter a customer, you must discover his or her needs or what is wanted. Through a series of open-end questions and closed-end questions you can gain useful information.

OPEN-END QUESTIONS

This type of questioning follows the time-tested approach of the five Ws and one H used by journalists, who ask questions that help determine who, what, when, where, why, and how about a given situation. Basically, **open-end questions** establish a number of facts and are used to seek substantial amounts of information and encourage dialogue. They:

open-end questions Typically start with words like who, when, what, how, and why and are used to engage others in conversation or to gain input and ideas.

customer needs Motivators or drivers that cause customers to seek out specific types of products or services. These may be marketing-driven by advertising they have seen or may tie directly to Dr. Abraham Maslow's hierarchy of needs theory.

Identify Customer Needs

By asking questions, you can help determine **customer needs** and what he or she wants or expects. This is a crucial task because some customers are either unsure of what they need or want or do not adequately express their needs or wants.

Examples

"Ms. Deloach, for what type of car are you looking?"

"Mr. Petell, why is an extended warranty important to you?"

Gather a Lot of Information

Open-end questions are helpful when you're just beginning a customer relationship and aren't sure what the customer has in mind or what's important. By uncovering more details, you can better serve your customer.

Example

"Mr. and Mrs. Milton, to help me better serve you, could you please describe what your ideal house would look like if you could build it?"

Uncover Background Data

When a customer calls to complain about a problem, often he or she has already taken unsuccessful steps to solve it. In such cases, it is important to find out the background information about the customer or situation. By asking open-end questions, you allow customers to tell you as much information as they feel is necessary to answer your question. This is why open-end questions are generally more effective for gathering data than are closed-end questions. If you feel you need more information after your customer responds to an open-end question, you can always ask further questions.

Example

"Mrs. Chan, will you please tell me the history behind this problem, including all of your previous contacts with this office?"

Uncover Objections during a Sale

If you are in sales or cross-selling or upselling products or services (getting a customer to buy a higher quality or different brand of product or extend or enhance existing service agreements) to current customers as a service representative, you will likely encounter **objections**. The reasons for a customer not wanting or needing your product and/or service can be identified through the use of open-end questions.

> **objections** Reasons given by customers for not wanting to purchase a product or service during an interaction with a salesperson or service provider (e.g., "I don't need one," "I can't afford it," or "I already have one").

Such questions can be used to determine whether your customer has questions or objections. Many times, people are not rejecting what you are offering outright; they simply do not see an immediate need for the product or cannot think of appropriate questions to ask. In these cases, you can help them focus their thinking or guide their decision through the use of open-end questions. Be careful to listen to your customer's words and tone when he or she offers objections. If the customer seems adamant, such as, "I really don't want it," don't go any further with your questions. The customer will probably become angry because he or she will feel that you are not listening. A fine line exists between helping and pushing, and if you cross it, you could end up with a confrontation on your hands. Often active listening and experience will help you determine what course of action to take.

Example

"Ms. Williams, from what you told me, all the features of the new RD10 model that we talked about will definitely ease some of your workload, so let me get the paperwork started so you can take it home with you. What do you think?"

Give the Customer an Opportunity to Speak

Although it is important to control the conversation in order to save time and thus allow you to serve more customers, sometimes you may want to give the customer an opportunity to talk. This is crucial if the customer is upset or dissatisfied about something. By allowing a customer to "vent" as you listen actively, you can sometimes reduce the level of tension and help solve the problem. You might also discover other details that will more appropriately allow you to address the situation.

It is important for service providers in any environment to ask appropriate questions in order to determine what the customer wants, needs, and expects. *What types of questions do you typically ask your customers to get the information you need to ensure their satisfaction?*

Examples of Open-End Questions

"What suggestions for improving our complaint-handling process should I present to my supervisor?"

"Why is this feature so important to you?"

"How has the printer been malfunctioning, Jim?"

"What is the main use of this product?"

"What are some of the common symptoms that you have been experiencing?"

"When would you most likely need to have us come out each month?"

"Where have you seen our product or similar ones being used?"

"Why do you feel that this product is better than others you've tried?"

"How do you normally use the product?"

"How has the new hearing aid been performing for you?"

"Mr. O'Connell, I can see you're unhappy. What can I do to help solve this problem?"

CLOSED-END QUESTIONS

closed-end questions Inquiries that typically start with a verb; solicit short, one-syllable answers (e.g., yes, no, one word, or a number); and can be used for such purposes as clarifying, verifying information already given, controlling conversation, or affirming something.

Open-end questions are designed to draw out a lot of information. Traditionally, **closed-end questions** start with verbs such as *do, did, are,* and *will*; elicit short, one-syllable responses; and gain little new information. Many closed-end questions can be answered yes or no or with a specific answer, such as a number or a date. Closed-end questions can be used for:

Verifying Information

Closed-end questions are a quick way to check what was already said or agreed on. Using them reinforces that you're listening and also helps prevent you from making mistakes because you misinterpreted or misunderstood information.

Example

"Mr. Christopherson, earlier I believe you said that you saw Doctor Naglapadi about this problem in the past. Is that correct?"

Closing an Order

Once you've discovered needs and presented the benefits and features of your product and service, you need to ask for a buying decision. This brings closure to your discussion. Asking for a decision also signals the customer that it is his or her turn to speak. If the customer offers an objection or declines to make a purchase, you can try to use the open-end questioning format discussed earlier in order determine the reason for his or her hesitancy. Just remember in such situations to LISTEN to their words and tone when they respond. No often means NO. If you fail to recognize the difference between uncertainty and a decision not to purchase, you might irritate or offend the customer and the situation could escalate negatively.

Example

"Mr. Jones, this tie will go nicely with the new suit you are purchasing. May I wrap it for you as well?"

Gaining Agreement

When there has been ongoing dialogue and closure or commitment is needed, closed-end questions can often bring about that result.

Example

"Veronica, with everything we've accomplished today, I'd really like to be able to conclude this project before we leave. Can we work for one more hour?"

Clarifying Information

Closed-end questions can also help ensure that you have the details correct and thus help prevent future misunderstandings or mistakes. Closed-end questions also help save time and reduce the number of complaints and/or product returns you or someone else will have to deal with.

Example

"Ms. Jovanovich, if I heard you correctly, you said that the problem occurs when you increase power to the engine. Is that as soon as you turn the ignition key or after you've been driving the car for a while?"

Examples of Closed-End Questions

"Do you agree that we should begin right away?" (obtaining agreement).

"Mrs. Leonard, did you say this was your first visit to our restaurant?" (verifying understanding).

"Mr. Morris, did you say you normally travel three or four times a month and have been doing so for the past 10 years?" (verifying facts).

"Is the pain in your tooth constant or just periodic?" (gathering information).

"So, shall I wrap these items for you so that you can make that appointment you mentioned, Mr. Carroll?" (closing an order).

Think About It

1. Why do you think Trader Joe's might have such a loyal customer base?

2. Based on what you read above, on their website, and on an Internet search for the company, what do think about their approach to satisfying customer needs?

3. Is this a company that you would patronize as a customer? Why or why not?

4. Would you want to work for this company? Why or why not?

Quick Preview

Before reviewing the chapter content, respond to the following questions by placing a "T" for true or an "F" for false on the rules. If you do not know an answer, put a question mark. Use any questions you miss as a checklist of material to which you will pay particular attention as you read through the chapter. For those you get right, congratulate yourself, but review the sections they address in order to learn additional details about the topic.

_____ 1. Understanding behavioral styles can aid in establishing and maintaining positive customer relationships.

_____ 2. You should treat others as individuals, not as members of a category.

_____ 3. People whose primary behavioral style category is "E" focus their energy on working with people.

_____ 4. People whose primary behavioral style category is "D" focus their energy on tasks or getting the job done.

_____ 5. Some behavioral styles are better than others.

_____ 6. People who exhibit the "D" style often tend to move slowly and speak in a low-key manner.

_____ 7. People who exhibit the "E" style often tend to be highly animated in using gestures and speaking.

_____ 8. People who exhibit the "R" style often tend to be very impatient.

_____ 9. People who exhibit the "I" style often tend to express their emotions easily.

_____ 10. You should attempt to determine a customer's behavioral style and then tailor your communication accordingly.

_____ 11. To deliver total customer satisfaction, you need to make your customers feel special.

_____ 12. When you say no to a customer, it is important to let him or her know what you cannot do and why.

_____ 13. Service to your customers should be seamless; customers should not have to see or deal with problems or process breakdowns.

_____ 14. Perceptions are based on education, experiences, events, and interpersonal contacts, as well as a person's intelligence level.

_____ 15. Once you've made a perception, you should evaluate its accuracy.

Answers to Quick Preview can be found at the end of the chapter.

LO 6-1 What Are Behavioral Styles?

CONCEPT Behavioral styles are actions or reactions exhibited when you and others deal with tasks or people. As a customer service professional, you need to be aware that everyone is not the same.

For thousands of years, people have devised systems in an attempt to better understand why people do what they do and how they accomplish what they do—and to categorize behavioral styles. Many of these systems are still in use today.

Behavioral styles are observable tendencies (actions that you can see or experience) that you and other people exhibit when dealing with tasks or people. As you grow from infancy, your personality forms based on your experiences and your environment. These form the basis of your behavioral style preference(s).

Have you ever come into contact with someone with whom you simply did not feel comfortable or someone with whom you felt an immediate bond? If so, you were possibly experiencing and reacting to the effect of

behavioral styles Descriptive term that identifies categories of human behavior identified by behavioral researchers. Many of the models used to group behaviors date back to those identified by Carl Jung.

behavioral style. As a customer service professional, you need to be aware that everyone is different. Not everyone behaves as you do, yet many still demonstrate behaviors that are similar to yours. For this reason, you should strive to provide service in a manner that addresses not only the behaviors that you prefer, but also those that fulfill the needs and desires of others as well.

Part of being a customer service professional is that you need to understand human behavioral style characteristics. The more proficient you become at identifying your own behavioral characteristics and those of others, the better you will be at establishing and maintaining positive relationships with customers. Self-knowledge is the starting point. To help in this effort, we will examine some common behaviors that you exhibit and that you may observe in customers.

When dealing with your customers, you should recognize that someone else doing something or acting differently from the way you do doesn't mean that the person is wrong. It simply means that they approach situations differently. Relationships are built on accepting the characteristics of others.

In customer service, adaptability is crucial, for many people do not always act the way you want them to. As you will read later in this chapter, there are many strategies that can be used to help modify and adapt your behavior so that it does not clash with that of your customers. This does not mean that you must make all the concessions when behaviors do not mesh. It simply means that, although you do not have control over the behavior of others, you do have control over your own behavior. Use this control to deal more effectively with your customers.

> **Customer Service Success Tip**
>
> Take the time to obtain one or more of the commercial self-assessment surveys available on the Internet (e.g., DiSC, DISC, or Myers-Briggs Type indicator) in order to learn more about yourself and be better equipped to interact with others in the workplace.

KNOWLEDGE CHECK

1. What are behavioral styles?

LO 6-2 Identifying Behavioral Styles

CONCEPT Each contact in a customer service environment has the potential for contributing to your success. Each person should be valued for his or her strengths and not belittled for what you perceive as shortcomings.

Through an assessment questionnaire, you can discover your own behavioral tendencies in a variety of situations. An awareness of your own style preferences can then lead you to a better understanding of customers, since many also possess similar style preferences. By understanding these characteristics, you can improve communication, build stronger relationships, reduce conflict and misunderstandings, and offer better service to the customer.

Many self-assessment questionnaires and much of the research related to behavioral styles are based on the work begun by psychiatrist Carl Jung and others in the earlier part of the twentieth century. Jung explored human personality and behavior. He divided behavior into two "attitudes" (introvert and extrovert) and four "functions" (thinking, feeling, sensing, and intuitive). These attitudes and functions can intermingle to form eight psychological types; knowledge of these types is useful in defining and describing human behavioral characteristics.

From Jung's complex research (and that of others) have come many variations, additional studies, and a variety of behavioral style self-assessment questionnaires and models for explaining personal behavior. Examples of these questionnaires are the Myers-Briggs Type Indicator (MBTI) and the Personal Profile System (DiSC). While these assessments are typically sold and administered by trained consultants, several organizations allow you to complete similar free surveys online. You can find such tools by searching the Internet for the topics and websites listed in the Search It Out section at the end of this chapter.

primary behavior pattern
Refers to a person's preferred style of dealing with others.

Although everyone typically has a **primary behavior pattern** (the way a person acts or reacts under certain circumstances) to which he or she reverts in stressful situations, people are a combination of various behavioral styles that they pull from as situations change. Because of this, your customers have characteristics in common and regularly demonstrate similar behavioral patterns. Identifying your own style preferences helps you understand and relate to behaviors in others.

To informally identify some of your own behavioral style preferences, complete Work It Out 6.1. This is not a validated behavioral survey but will give a strong indication of your behavioral preferences in dealing with others. Keep in mind that your behavior is adaptable based on a given situation in which you find yourself.

Note: The questionnaire in Work It Out 6.1 is only a quick indicator. A more thorough assessment, using a formal instrument (questionnaire), will be better at predicting your style preferences. For more information or to obtain written or computer-based surveys and reports, do an Internet search as suggested in the Search It Out section at the end of this chapter.

Because of the complexities of human behavior, you should not try to use behavioral characteristics and cues as absolute indicators of the type of person you are dealing with. You and others have some of the characteristics listed for all four style categories shown in this chapter; you simply have learned through years of experience which behavior you are most comfortable with and when adaptation is helpful or necessary. Generally, most people are adaptable and can shift style categories or exhibit different characteristics depending on the situation. For example, a person who is normally very personable and amiable can revert to more directive behavior, if necessary, to manage an activity or process for which he or she will be held accountable. Similarly, a person who normally exhibits controlling or task-oriented behavior can socialize and react positively in "people" situations.

An important point to remember about this short questionnaire, and any other behavioral survey that you use, is that there is no "best" or "worst" style. Each person should be valued for his or her strengths and not belittled because of what you perceive as shortcomings. In a customer environment, each contact has the potential for contributing to your success and that of your organization. By appreciating the behavioral characteristics of people with whom you interact, you can avoid bias or prejudice and better serve your customers.

How can a person who demonstrates one of the four styles be described? How might this person act, react, or interact? Some generalizations about behavior are listed in this section. Remember that even though people have a primary style, they have all four behavioral style characteristics within

WORK IT OUT 6.1

Describing Your Behavior

As a quick way to determine your behavioral style preference, make a copy of this page and then complete the following survey.

Step 1

Read the following list of words and phrases and rate yourself by placing a number (from 1 to 5) next to each item. A 5 means that the word is an accurate description of yourself in most situations, a 3 indicates a balanced agreement about the word's application, and a 1 means that you do not feel that the word describes your behavior well. Before you begin, refer to the sample assessment in Figure 6.1.

5	Relaxed R	5	Competitive E
4	Logical I	5	Enthusiastic R
|3	Decisive D	5	Sincere I
4	Talkative E	4	Accurate D
3	Consistent R	3	Pragmatic (practical) E
5	Nonaggressive I	2	Popular R
	(avoids conflict) D	4	Patient I
1	Calculating E	4	Detail-oriented D
5	Fun-loving R	4	Objective E
5	Loyal I	1	Optimistic R
4	Quality-focused D		

TOTAL R =   I =   D =   E =

Step 2

Once you have rated each word or phrase, start with the first word, Relaxed, and put the letter

"R" to the right of it. Place an "I" to the right of the second word, a "D" to the right of the third word, and an "E" to the right of the fourth word. Then start over with the fifth word and repeat the "RIDE" pattern until all words have a letter at their right.

Step 3

Next, go through the list and count point values for all words that have an "R" beside them. Put the total at the bottom of the grid next to "R =." Do the same for the other letters. For example, if the words *relaxed, consistent, loyal, sincere,* and *patient* all had a number "4" by them, the total would be 20 and that number would go in the total area next to R =.

Once you have finished, one letter will probably have the highest total score. This is your natural style tendency. For example, if "R" has the highest score, your primary style preference is *rational*. If "I" has the highest score, you exhibit more *inquisitive* behavior. "D" indicates *decisive*, and "E" is an *expressive* style preference.

If two or more of your scores have the same high totals, you probably generally put forth similar amounts of effort in both these style areas. As a result, you likely exhibit numerous characteristics listed under both style categories on a fairly regular basis depending on the situation. Most people have primary and secondary styles.

them and demonstrate other style behaviors too depending on the situation in which they find themselves.

By becoming familiar with the style characteristics in Figure 6.1, recognizing them in yourself, and observing how others display them, you can begin to learn how to better adapt to various behaviors. When interacting with others, make sure that you monitor their overall actions and behavior in order to get a better perception of their style preferences rather than react to one or two actions. Also recognize that these characteristics are generalities and not absolutes when dealing with others. People can and do adapt and change behavior depending on a variety of circumstances. There

FIGURE 6.1

Sample Completed Self-Assessment

Your Numerical Rating Value	Behavior Trait	Your Letter Value
5	Relaxed	R
3	Logical	I
1	Decisive	D
4	Talkative	E
5	Consistent	R
3	Nonaggressive (avoids conflict)	I
5	Calculating	D
3	Fun-loving	E
5	Loyal	R
1	Quality-focused	I
3	Competitive	D
2	Enthusiastic	E
5	Sincere	R
1	Accurate	I
3	Pragmatic (practical)	D
1	Popular	E
5	Patient	R
2	Detail-oriented	I
1	Objective	D
2	Optimistic	E
TOTAL	**R = 25** **I = 10** **D = 13**	**E = 12**

is also the possibility that based on your perceptions, you might misinterpret their actions or behaviors.

While there is no definitive research related to preferences based on gender or cultural background, these factors obviously play a role in how someone dresses, acts, and communicates. When dealing with others, consider all possible factors and analyze the situation objectively. When all else fails, use your positive verbal communication skills to ask if your perception is correct.

The following descriptions of the four behavioral style categories are general. Since people are a combination of all four styles, they may exhibit some, but not all, of these characteristics at any given time. They may also exhibit characteristics from other style categories based on a given situation or their emotional state.

R: RATIONAL

rational style One of four behavioral groups characterized by being quiet, reflective, task-focused, and systematic.

People who have a preference for the **rational style** may tend to

- Listen and observe more than they talk (especially in groups).
- Be very patient.
- Wait or stand in one place for periods of time without complaining, although they may be internally irritated about a breakdown in the system or lack of organization.
- Exhibit congenial eye contact and facial expressions.
- Prefer one-on-one or small-group interactions over large-group ones.

- Seek specific or complete explanations to questions (e.g., "That's our policy" does not work well with an "R" customer).
- Dislike calling attention to themselves or a situation.
- Avoid conflict and anger.
- Often wear subdued colors and informal, conservative, or conventional clothing styles and accessories.
- Ask questions rather than state their opinion.
- Communicate more in writing and like the use of notes, birthday cards, or thank-you cards just to stay in touch.
- Like to be on a first-name basis with others.
- Have intermittent eye contact, with a brief, businesslike handshake.
- Have informal, comfortable office spaces, possibly with pictures of family in view.
- Like leisure activities that involve people (often family).

People who exhibit the rational behavioral style preference are congenial and often prefer to seek explanations for actions you take, rather than accepting that "policy says." *How might you serve such a person effectively?*

inquisitive style One of four behavioral groups, characterized by being introverted, task-focused, and detail-oriented.

I: INQUISITIVE

People who have a preference for the **inquisitive style** may tend to

People with a primary behavioral preference of inquisitive are often more intrapersonal and focus on details, facts, and practicality. *How would you address a customer who exhibits these characteristics?*

- Rarely volunteer feelings freely.
- Ask specific, pertinent questions rather than make statements of their feelings.
- Rely heavily on facts, times, dates, and practical information to make their point.
- Prefer to interact in writing rather than in person or on the phone.
- Prefer formality and distance in interactions. They often lean back when talking, even when emphasizing key points.
- Use formal titles and last names as opposed to first names. They may also stress the use of full names, not nicknames (e.g., Cynthia instead of Cindy or Charles instead of Chuck).
- Use cool, brief handshakes, often without a smile. If they do smile, it may appear forced.
- Wear conservative clothing although their accessories are matched well.
- Be impeccable in their grooming but may differ in their choice of styles from those around them (e.g., hair and makeup).
- Be very punctual and time-conscious.

LO 6-3 Communicating with Each Style

CONCEPT Each behavior style features various indicators of this style in practice. Remember, these cues are indicators, not absolutes, as you begin to use them to interact appropriately with others.

Once you recognize people's style tendencies, you can improve your relationships and chances of success by tailoring your communication strategies. As you examine Figure 6.2, think about how you can use these strategies with people you know in each style category. Keep in mind that these and other characteristics outlined in this chapter are only general in nature. Everyone is a mixture of all four styles and can change to a different style to address a variety of situations. Use these examples as indicators of style and not as absolutes. Also, be careful *not* to label a person as being one style (for example, Toni is a high "R") since people use all four styles—and most people do not appreciate stereotypes and labeling.

FIGURE 6.2   Communicating with Different Personality Styles

Style	Behaviors Exhibited	Provider Response	Customer Relationship Strategies
RATIONAL	***Nonverbal Cues*** Gentle handshake; flowing, nondramatic gestures. Fleeting eye contact.	Return firm, brief handshake; avoid aggressive gestures. Make intermittent (3 to 5 seconds) eye contact.	• Work to maintain peace and group stability. • Focus on his or her need for security and amiable relationships. • Show a sincere interest in the customer and his or her views.
	Verbal Cues Steady, even delivery. Subdued volume. Slower rate of speech. Keeps communication brief. Communication follows a logical pattern (e.g., step 1, step 2).	Mirror their style somewhat. Relax your message delivery. Slow your rate if necessary; be patient. Ask open-end questions to draw out information. Use structured approach in communications.	• Organize your information in a logical sequence and provide background data, if necessary. • Take a slow, low-key approach in recommending products or services. • Use open-end questions to obtain information. • Explain how your product or service can help simplify and support the customer's relationships and systems.
	Additional Cues Avoids confrontation.	Attempt to solve problems without creating a situation in which they feel challenged or obliged to defend themselves.	• Stress low risk and benefits to him or her. • Encourage the customer to verify facts, and so on, with others whose opinions he or she values. • When change occurs, explain the need for the change and allow time for the customer to adjust. • Provide information on available warranties, guarantees, and support systems.

FIGURE 6.2 (*Continued*)

Style	Behaviors Exhibited	Provider Response	Customer Relationship Strategies
INQUISITIVE	**Nonverbal Cues** Deliberate body movements. Uses little physical contact. Correspondence is formal and includes many details.	Use careful, restrained body cues. Avoid touching. Respond similarly.	• Often desire quality, efficiency, and precision. • Focus on the customer's need for accuracy and efficiency by methodically outlining steps, processes, or details related to a product or service.
	Verbal Cues Quiet, slow-paced speech (especially in groups). Minimal vocal variety.	Mirror rate and pattern. Use subdued tone and volume.	
	Additional Cues Values concise communication. Uses details to make points. Prefers confirmation and backup in writing. Uses formal names instead of nicknames.	Use brief, accurate statements. Provide background information and data. Respond in writing and provide adequate background information. Address them by title and last name unless told otherwise.	• Tie communication into facts, not feelings. • Prepare information in advance and be thoroughly familiar with it. • Approach encounters in a direct, businesslike, low-key manner. • Avoid small talk and speaking about yourself.
	Additional Cues Sharing of personal information is minimal. Focus on task at hand.	Communicate on business level unless they initiate personal conversation. Organize thoughts before responding.	• Have documentation available to substantiate your claims. • Don't pressure his or her decisions. • Follow through on promises.
DECISIVE	**Nonverbal Cues** Steady, direct eye contact. Writing tends to be short and specific. Gestures tend to be autocratic (e.g., pointing fingers or hands on hips).	Return eye contact (3 to 5 seconds) and smile. Respond in similar fashion; minimize small talk and details. Stand your ground without antagonizing. Maintain a professional demeanor.	• Often want to save time and money. • Focus on the customer's need for control by finding out what he or she wishes to do, what he or she wants or needs, or what motivates him or her. • Provide direct, concise, and factual answers to the customer's questions. • Keep explanations brief and provide solutions, not excuses.
	Verbal Cues Forceful tone. Speaks in statements. Direct and challenging (short, abrupt). Fast rate of speech.	Don't react defensively or in a retaliatory manner. Use facts and logic and avoid unnecessary details. Listen rather than defend. Match rate somewhat.	• Avoid trying to "get to know him or her." The customer often perceives this as a waste of time and may distrust your motives. • Be conscious of time, by making your point and then concluding the interaction appropriately. • Provide opportunities for the customer to talk by alternately providing small bits of information and asking specific questions aimed at solving the problem and serving the customer.

(*Continued*)

FIGURE 6.2 (*Concluded*)

Style	Behaviors Exhibited	Provider Response	Customer Relationship Strategies
	Additional Cues Short attention span when listening. Very direct and decisive.	Keep sentences and communication brief. Support opinions, ideas, and vision.	• Be prepared with information, necessary forms, details, warranties, and so on, before the customer arrives. • When appropriate, provide options supported by evidence and focus on how the solution will affect the customer's time, effort, and money. • Focus on new, innovative products or services, emphasizing especially those that are environmentally sensitive or responsive.
EXPRESSIVE	*Nonverbal Cues* Enthusiasm and inflection in voice. Active body language. Very intense, dramatic Writing tends to be flowery and includes many details.	Listen and respond enthusiastically. Use open, positive body language and smile easily. Return firm, professional one-hand shake. Acknowledge but use caution in returning touch (this action could be misinterpreted by them or others). Show interest and ask pertinent questions. When writing, use a friendly reader-focused style.	• Typically people-oriented and want to be around people. • Focus on the customer's need to be liked and accepted by appealing to his or her emotions. • Give positive feedback, acknowledging the customer's ideas. • Listen to his or her stories and share humorous ones about yourself. • Use an open-ended, friendly approach. • Ask questions such as "What attracted you to this product or service?" • Keep product details to a minimum unless the customer asks for them. • Describe how your product or service can help the customer get closer to his or her goals or to fulfilling his or her needs.
	Verbal Cues Excessive details when describing something. Fast rate of speech. Emphasizes storytelling and fun.	Ask specific open-end questions to help them refocus. Mirror or match their rate and excitement where appropriate. Relax, listen, laugh, and respond as appropriate.	• Explain solutions or suggestions in terms of the impact on the customer and his or her relationships with others. • If appropriate, provide incentives to encourage a decision.
	Additional Cues Inattentive to details in tasks. Shares personal information and virtually anything else freely.	Ask questions to involve them. Reciprocate if you are comfortable doing so; however, stay focused on the task at hand.	• Provide information verbally and in writing to ensure details are not missed. • Provide solid examples and success stories to emphasize the value and importance of products or services.

KNOWLEDGE CHECK

1. What nonverbal cues might someone with a primary style of rational exhibit?

2. What nonverbal cues might someone with a primary style of inquisitive exhibit?

3. What nonverbal cues might someone with a primary style of decisive exhibit?

4. What nonverbal cues might someone with a primary style of expressive exhibit?

5. What verbal cues might someone with a primary style of rational exhibit?

6. What verbal cues might someone with a primary style of inquisitive exhibit?

7. What verbal cues might someone with a primary style of decisive exhibit?

8. What verbal cues might someone with a primary style of expressive exhibit?

LO 6-4 Building Stronger Relationships

CONCEPT Sometimes building stronger customer relationships means that you discover customer needs, seek opportunities for service, and respond appropriately to customers' behavioral styles. Occasionally you will need to deemphasize a no and say it as positively as you can.

Recognizing and relating to customers' behavioral styles is just the first step in providing better service. To deliver total customer satisfaction, you will need to make the customer feel special, which often requires skills such as relationship building through effective communication and **problem solving**.

Whether a situation involves simply answering a question, guiding someone to a desired product or location, or performing a service, customers should leave the interaction feeling good about what they experienced. Providing this feeling not only is good business sense on your part but also helps guarantee the customers return or spread favorable word-of-mouth advertising.

There are many ways of partnering with either internal or external customers to solve problems and produce a **win-win situation** (one in which both the customer and you and your organization succeed and feel good about the outcome). Whatever you do to achieve this result, your customers should realize that you are their advocate and are acting in their best interests to solve their problems. Some suggestions for building stronger customer relationships follow.

problem solving The system of identifying issues, determining alternatives for dealing with them, then selecting and monitoring a strategy for resolution.

win-win situation An outcome to a disagreement in which both parties walk away feeling that they got what they wanted or needed.

People send verbal and nonverbal clues to their behavioral style preference. Observe your customers' eye contact, their level of directness or evasiveness, how quickly or slowly they speak, and their level of warmth versus formality. Once you can read these clues, you'll be better able to individualize the customer service you can provide. *Can you think of a person in your life who exhibits clues to his or her other behavioral style?*

DISCOVER CUSTOMER NEEDS

Using sound listening and verbal and nonverbal communication skills, engage customers in a dialogue that allows them to identify what they really want or need. If you can determine a customer's behavioral style, you can tailor your communication strategy to that style. Keep in mind that some customer needs may not be expressed aloud. In these instances, you should attempt to validate your impressions or suspicions by asking questions or requesting feedback. Gather information about a customer from observing vocal qualities, phrasing, nonverbal expressions and movements, and emotional state. Also, look for signs that help identify his or her primary behavioral style preference. For example, while providing service to Mr. Delgado, you told him that the product he was ordering would not arrive for three weeks. You noticed that he grimaced and made a concerned sound of "Um." At this point, a perception check would have been appropriate. You could have said, "Mr. Delgado, you looked concerned or disappointed when I mentioned the delivery date. Is that a problem for you?" You might have discovered that he needed the item sooner but resigned himself to the delay and didn't ask about other options. In effect, he was exhibiting "I" or possibly "R" behavior (silence and low-key reaction). Rather than have a confrontation, he accepted the situation without voicing disappointment or concern. A potential outcome in such situations might be that your customer decides to check a competitor to see if they have what is wanted or needed. By reacting positively to the customer's nonverbal signals in this scenario, you could identify and address a concern and thus prevent a dissatisfied and/or lost customer.

SAY "YES"

If you must decline a request or cannot provide a product or service, do so in a positive manner. Deemphasizing what you cannot do and providing an alternative puts the customer in a power position. That is, even though she

WORK IT OUT 6.2

Monitoring Behavior

To practice matching behavior with styles, try this activity. Make four or five copies of Worksheet 6.1 (see www.mhhe.com/customerservice). Select four or five friends or co-workers whom you see and interact with regularly. Write one of their names at the top of each worksheet copy. Covertly (without their knowledge) observe these people for a week or so in various settings and make notes about their behavior under each category listed on the worksheet. Focus specifically on the following areas:

Writing pattern or style

Interpersonal communication style (e.g., direct, indirect, specific or nonspecific questions, good or poor listener)

Body movements and other nonverbal gestures

Dress style (e.g., flashy, conservative, formal, informal)

Surroundings (e.g., office decorations or organization, car, home)

Personality (e.g., activities and interactions preferred—solitary, group, active, passive)

At the end of the week, decide which primary and/or secondary style of behavior each person exhibits most often. Then ask these people to assist you in an experiment that will involve them completing the quick style assessment that you did earlier (Figure 6.1).

After they have rated themselves, explain that you have been observing them for the past week.

Compare their ratings to the characteristics described in this chapter, and to your own assessment. Were you able to predict their primary or, at least, their secondary style?

may not get her first request, she is once again in control because she can say yes or no to the alternative you have offered, or she can decide on the next step. For example, when a customer requests a brand or product not stocked by your organization, you could offer alternatives. You might counter with, "Mrs. Hanslik, although we don't stock that brand, we do have a comparable product that has been rated higher by *Consumer Reports* than the one you requested. May I show you?" This approach not only serves the customer but also (sometimes) results in a sale and is important if the person is primarily a high "D" behavioral type and prefers to take the lead in situations.

Figure 6.3 provides some strategies to use when responding to customer complaints and solving problems involving people who demonstrate the four behavioral styles you have learned about. By tailoring customer service strategies to individual style preferences, you address the customer's specific needs. Active listening is a key skill in any service situation. As you review these strategies, think of other things you might do to better serve each behavioral type.

SEEK OPPORTUNITIES FOR SERVICE

View complaints as a chance to create a favorable impression by solving a problem. Watch the behavioral characteristics being exhibited by your customer. Using what you see and hear, take appropriate action to adapt to the customer's personality needs and solve the problem professionally. For example, Mrs. Minga complained loudly to you that the servicewoman who

FIGURE 6.3

Strategies for Responding to Customer Problems

Style	Behaviors	Strategies
RATIONAL	Seeks systematic resolution to the situation. Avoids conflict or disagreement. Strives for acceptance of ideas. Intermittent eye contact. Uses hand and subdued body movements and speech to emphasize key points.	Stress resolution and security of the issue. Smile, when appropriate. Provide references or resources. Listen actively; make eye contact. Focus on personal movements to convey your feelings about the incident (e.g., "How do you feel we can best resolve this problem?").
INQUISITIVE	Listens to explanations. Demands specifics. Mild demeanor. Intermittent eye contact. Gives list of issues, in chronological order. Exhibits patience. Seeks reassurance. Focuses on facts.	Focus on the problem, not the person. Have details and facts available. Approach in nonthreatening manner. Listen actively, make eye contact, and focus on the situation. Be specific in outlining actions to be taken by everyone. Follow through on commitments. Offer guarantees of resolution if possible. Give facts and pros and cons of suggestions.
DECISIVE	Seeks to avoid conflict; just wants resolution. Loud voice. Finger pointing or aggressive body gestures. Firm, active handshake. Directly places blame on service provider. Direct eye contact. Sarcasm. Impatient. Demanding verbiage (e.g., "You'd better fix this"; "I want to see the manager *now*!"). Irrational assertions (e.g., "You people *never* or *always* . . .").	Use low-pitched, unemotional speech; be patient; listen. Be patient; listen empathetically. Don't internalize; he or she is angry with the product or service, not necessarily you. Return a firm businesslike handshake. Be brief; tell him or her what you can do; offer solutions. Be formal, businesslike. Don't take a happy-go-lucky or flippant approach. Be time-conscious; time is money to a "D." Project competence; find the best person to solve the problem. Ask questions that focus on what he or she needs or wants (e.g., "What do you think is a reasonable solution?").
EXPRESSIVE	Threats (e.g., "If you can't help, I'll go to a company that can."). Intermittent smiling along with verbalizing dissatisfaction. Uses nonaggressive language (e.g., "I'd like to talk with someone about . . .").	Reassure; say what you can do. Be supportive; tell the customer what you can do for him or her. Allow him or her to vent frustrations or verbalize thoughts.

Style	Behaviors	Strategies
	Steady eye contact.	Smile, if appropriate; return eye contact while conversing.
	Elicits your assistance and follow-up (e.g., "I really don't want to run all over town searching. Will you please call . . .").	Take the time to offer assistance and comply with his or her requests, if possible.
	Shows sincere interest.	Focus on feelings through empathy (e.g., "I feel that . . .").
	Enthusiastic active handshake.	Return a firm businesslike handshake.
	Enthusiastically explains a situation.	Patiently provide active listening; offer ideas and suggestions for resolution.

FIGURE 6.3
(Concluded)

installed her new washing machine tracked oil onto the dining room carpet. As she is speaking, Mrs. Minga is pointing her finger at you, raising her voice, and threatening to go to the manager if you do not handle this situation immediately. You can take the opportunity to solve the problem and strengthen the relationship at the same time. You might try the following. Make direct eye contact (no staring), smile, and empathize by saying, "Mrs. Minga, I'm terribly sorry about your carpet. I know that it must be very upsetting. If you'll allow me to, I'll arrange to have your dining room carpet cleaned, and for your inconvenience, while they're at it we'll have them clean the carpets in adjoining rooms at no cost to you. How does that sound?" In reacting this way, you have professionally and assertively taken control of the situation. This is important because Mrs. Minga is exhibiting high "D" behavior. Responding in a less decisive manner might result in an escalation of her emotions and a demand to see someone in authority or whom she feels can do something about the issue.

Customers should not be kept waiting because your systems or processes break down. By striving for seamless service delivery, customers of all behavioral styles are more likely to be satisfied. *What can you do on a daily basis to enhance the service that your customers receive?*

FOCUS ON PROCESS IMPROVEMENT

Customers generally do not like being kept waiting when your system is not functioning properly. They rightfully view their time as valuable. In today's "I want it and I want it now" society, inconveniencing your customers will likely lead to emotional reactions, complaints, and customer defection to a competitor. To expect them to patiently wait while a new cashier tries to figure out the register codes, someone gets a price check because the product was coded incorrectly, you have to call the office for information or approvals, and so on, is unfair and unreasonable.

Defects in your system or processes or delays should be handled when the customer is not present. You should strive to provide **seamless service** to customers. This means that they should get great service and never have to worry about your problems or breakdowns. When breakdowns do occur, they should be fixed quickly, and the customer relationship smoothed over. In addition, it is important to recognize that customers with different behavioral styles will react differently to such breakdowns. Here are some examples of how each style might react:

seamless service Service that is done in a manner that seems effortless and natural to the customer. Processes and systems are fully functional, effective, and efficient. Service representatives are well-trained and proficient in delivering service, and there is no inconvenience to the customer.

- "R" style customers are likely to complain in an inoffensive manner and may even smile, but also may seek out a supervisor.
- "I" style individuals may seem to be patient and not say anything or cause a confrontation, but will possibly request directions to the supervisor's office and/or later send a detailed letter or e-mail message of complaint.
- "D" style people may get loud, aggressive, and vocal and demand a supervisor after only a brief delay.
- "E" behavioral types may get upset but will often make the best of their time complaining to other customers and comparing notes on similar past experiences.

No matter what style the customer exhibits, you should strive to reduce or eliminate customer inconvenience and distress.

In all cases, after an extensive delay you may want to compensate the customer for the inconvenience. At the least, such a situation warrants a sincere apology. Such an occurrence might be handled in the following manner: "Mr. Westgate, I am sorry for the delay. We've been experiencing computer problems all day. I'd like to make up for your inconvenience by giving you a 10 percent discount off your meal check. Would that be acceptable?" Although this is not a significant offering, your intention is to show remorse and to placate the customer so that he or she will continue to use your products and/or services.

After you have dealt with the situation, your next concern should be to personally fix the process that caused the breakdown or make a recommendation to your supervisor or other appropriate person. Quality service and **process improvement** are the responsibility of all employees.

process improvement Refers to the process of continually evaluating products and services to ensure that maximum effectiveness, efficiency, and potential are being obtained from them.

MAKE CUSTOMERS FEEL SPECIAL

Most people like to feel special and appreciated. Creating that feeling in others is what stellar customer service is all about. Through simple things like a warm smile, pleasant tone, and welcoming words, you can make your customers feel like the most important people in the world to you . . . because at that moment they should be.

By creating a bond with your customers through positive words and actions, you can easily help them feel as if there is no other place they would rather be or with whom they would rather do business. With a few simple gestures or phrases, you can be on the way to developing a sound customer–provider relationship that not only results in a loyal customers, but is also likely to generate positive word-of-mouth advertising from the customer to other people that they know.

Keep in mind that when customers feel good about themselves as a result of something you did or said, they are likely to better appreciate what you and your organization can offer them. Small tokens of appreciation can be worth their weight in customer gold. For example, to demonstrate appreciation for long-term patronage, you may want to recognize a customer as follows: "Mr. and Mrs. Hoffmeister, we really appreciate your loyalty. Our records indicate that you've been a patient in our office for over 20 years. In recognition, on behalf of Dr. Naglapadi, here is a complimentary dinner certificate for $25. Please accept it with our compliments." Consider how unusual it is to have a customer's loyalty for 20 years and how much revenue such a relationship brings—not just from the customer, but also referrals. Such a reward would likely surprise and amaze most patients since many doctor's offices have a reputation of not valuing a patient's time or business. This type of strategy goes a long way in guaranteeing customer loyalty.

> **Customer Service Success Tip**
>
> Go out of your way to make your customers feel appreciated by recognizing the value of those with whom you come into contact. Do this by communicating with customers effectively, asking questions essential to discovering their needs and expectations, listening to their needs, and providing valid feedback designed to show that you value them and their issues and are willing to help them. All of this can help raise their self-esteem and result in a better customer–provider relationship.

BE CULTURALLY AWARE

The reality of a multicultural customer service environment further challenges your ability to deal with behaviors. This is because, in today's multicultural business environment, it is likely that you will come into contact with someone of a different background, belief system, or culture. Many challenges that develop in these encounters are a result of diversity ignorance.

Even after you master the concepts of behavioral styles, you must remember that because values and beliefs vary from one culture to another, behavior is also likely to vary. For example, in many countries or cultures, the nonverbal gestures that North Americans use have completely different meanings. Also, the reactions to such gestures will differ based on the recipient's personality style. Variations of symbols such as joining the thumb and index finger to form an O, signaling "Okay," have sexual connotations in parts of several countries (e.g., Germany, Sardinia, Malta, Greece, Turkey, Russia, the Middle East, and parts of South America). Likewise,

FIGURE 7.2

Typical Customer Expectations

Customers come to you expecting that certain things will occur in regard to the products and services they obtain. Customers typically expect the following:

Expectations Related to People

Friendly, knowledgeable service providers

Respect (they want to be treated as if they are intelligent)

Empathy (they want their feelings and emotions to be recognized)

Courtesy (they want to be recognized as "the customer" and as someone who is important to you and your organization)

Equitable treatment (they do not want to feel that one individual or group gets preferential benefits or treatment over another)

Expectations Related to Products and Services

Easily accessible and available products and services (no lengthy delays)

Reasonable and competitive pricing

Products and services that adequately address needs

Quality (appropriate value for money and time invested)

Ease of use

Safe (warranty available and product free of defects that might cause physical injury)

State-of-the-art products and service delivery

Easy-to-understand instructions (and follow-up assistance availability)

Ease of return or exchange (flexible policies that provide alternatives depending on the situation)

Appropriate and expedient problem resolution

Customer Service Success Tip

Be prepared and conscientious and think like a customer in order to identify and satisfy customer needs and expectations.

Ethical Dilemma 7.1

You are an employee of a local retail organization that typically closes at 6:00 p.m. At 5:52 p.m., your supervisor tosses you the keys to the front door and tells you to lock up for the evening because he wants to get out early so that he can pick up his wife. They have tickets for a play and are going out to dinner to celebrate their anniversary.

As you lock the door and start to return to your cash register to begin your end-of-day activities, you hear a frantic knock on the front door. An obviously distraught customer is yelling that she needs to buy a gift for her son's birthday and is pointing to the clock on the wall next to your register that indicates 5:56 p.m. There is a sign on the door that lists the closing time as 6:00 p.m.

1. What would you do in this situation?
2. How do you think the customer will view this matter?
3. Are there possible repercussions from a service standpoint? If so, what are they?

KNOWLEDGE CHECK

1. What is a service breakdown?
2. What is the difference between a customer need and a want?
3. How can customer expectations impact the perceived level of product or service quality that they receive?

LO 7-2 The Role of Behavioral Style

CONCEPT Behavioral preferences have a major effect on the interactions of people. The more you know about style tendencies, the better you will understand your customers.

Behavioral style preferences play a major part in how people interact. Styles also affect the types of things people want and value. Depending on how a customer approaches a given situation, they may have a perception that you will or will not take certain actions while serving them. They might also expect that products will perform in a specific manner based on their knowledge, background, research, or experience. If you or your products and services fail to meet those expectations, you can find yourself in the midst of a service breakdown and have to deal with an emotional situation that you might not be prepared to handle. For example, those customers with high expressive behavioral tendencies (e.g., outgoing, flexible, and people-oriented) will probably buy more colorful and people-oriented items and may be more willing to accept alternative suggestions from you than someone who has high decisive (e.g., formal, direct, status and task–oriented people) behavioral tendencies.

The more you know about behavioral style preferences, the easier it becomes to deal with people in a variety of situations and to help match their needs with the products and services you and your organization can provide. Keep in mind that everyone possesses one or a combination of the four following different behavioral styles:

- *Rational.* Prefer one-on-one or small-group interaction, are congenial and patient, avoid conflict, and dislike calling attention to themselves.
- *Inquisitive.* Rarely volunteer feelings, ask "why" questions, desire facts and figures, and are formal, task-oriented, conservative, and punctual.
- *Decisive.* Are decisive, directive, task- and goal-focused, confident, and competitive; seek immediate gratification or results; and talk more than listen.
- *Expressive.* Are open, laid back, flexible, positive, enthusiastic, and informal; prefer dealing with people; and easily share feelings and emotions.

Because customers can display various types of behavior from time to time, you should carefully observe their behavior and learn about each style as an indicator of the type of person with whom you are dealing. Just remember that human beings are complex and react to stimuli in various ways—so adapt your approach as necessary. For that reason, do not use information you learn about behavioral styles as the definitive answer for resolving the situation. In addition, learn to deal with your emotions so that you can prevent or resolve heated emotional situations that might arise when dealing with a personality different from your own.

> **Street Talk**
>
> When talking with a client, I try to put myself in his/her position. What is most important to her? What communicates that I understand? What is one thing I can do right now to better his situation?
>
> PATRICIA CHARPENTIER *Owner, Writing Your Life/LifeStory Publishing*

KNOWLEDGE CHECK

1. How might the four behavioral styles play a role in the perceived level of service received by a customer?

> ### ⚙ WORK IT OUT 7.2
>
> ### Service Breakdown Examples
>
> **What examples of service breakdown have you experienced or can you recall from someone else's story?** List and then discuss them with classmates. After discussing your lists, brainstorm ways that the organization did or could have recovered.

LO 7-3 Difficult Customers

CONCEPT Successful service will ultimately be delivered through effective communication skills, positive attitude, patience, and a willingness to help the customer.

difficult customers People who challenge a service provider's ability to deliver service and who require special skills and patience.

You may think of **difficult customer** contacts as those in which you have to deal with negative, angry, demanding, or aggressive people. These are just a few of the types of potentially difficult interactions that you may encounter as a service representative. From time to time, you will also be called upon to help customers who can be described in one or more of the following ways:

- Are dissatisfied with your service or products.
- Are indecisive or lack knowledge about your product, service, or policies.
- Are rude or inconsiderate of others.
- Are talkative.
- Are internal customers with special requests.
- Speak a primary language other than yours.
- Are elderly and need extra assistance.
- Are young and inexperienced who might need to be guided in making a good choice.
- Have some type of a disability.

Each of the above categories can be difficult to handle, depending on your knowledge, experience, and abilities. A key to successfully serving all types of customers is to treat each person as an individual. If you stereotype people, you will likely damage the customer–provider relationship and might even generate complaints to your supervisor or legal action against you and your organization based on perceived discrimination. Avoid labeling people according to their behavior. Do not mentally categorize people (put them into groups) according to the way they speak, act, or look—and then treat everyone in a "group" the same way.

Ultimately, you will deliver successful service through your effective communication skills, positive attitude, patience, knowledge, service experience, and willingness to help the customer. Your ability to focus on the situation or problem and not on the person will be a very important factor in your success. Making the distinction between the person and the problem is especially important when you are faced with difficult situations in the service environment. Although you may not understand or approve of a person's behavior, he or she is still your customer. Try to make the interaction a positive one, and if necessary ask for assistance from a co-worker or refer the problem to an appropriate level in your operational chain of command.

Many difficult situations you will deal with as a service provider will be caused by a perceived failure to meet your customer's needs, wants, and expectations. You will read about service challenges in this chapter, along with their causes and some strategies for effectively dealing with them.

Handling difficult customers will be one of your biggest challenges, so be prepared. *How would you deal with an unhappy customer?*

DEMANDING OR DOMINEERING CUSTOMERS

Customers might be **demanding or domineering** for a number of reasons. Many times, domineering behavior is part of a personality style or simply behavior that they have learned. In other instances, it could be a reaction to past customer service encounters and an expectation that the customer now has about what should or should not occur. A demanding customer may feel a need to be or stay in control, especially if he or she has felt out of control in the past. Often, such people are insecure or have a behavioral style that lends itself to wanting to be in control or to "win." Some strategies for effectively handling demanding customers are discussed in the following sections:

demanding or domineering customers Customers who have definite ideas about what they want and are unwilling to compromise or accept alternatives.

- *Be professional.* Don't raise your voice or retaliate verbally. Children engage in name-calling, which often escalates into shoving matches. Unfortunately, some adults "regress" to childish behavior. Your customer may revert to negative behavior learned in the past. Both you and the customer lose when this happens.

- *Respect the customer.* You do not necessarily have to like your customer, but you should show respect. This does not mean that you must accommodate your customer's every wish. It means that you should make positive eye contact (but not glare), remain calm, use the customer's name, apologize when appropriate and/or necessary, and let the customer know that he or she is important to you and your organization. Also let the customer know that you are there to assist him or her or make the situation right and work positively toward an acceptable resolution of the problem. If accommodations are appropriate and possible, consider making them. If they are not, perhaps you might explain why something cannot be done. Most adults can be reasoned with if you take the time to talk to them on a professional and equal level.

- *Be firm and fair and focus on the customer's needs.* Assertive behavior is an appropriate response to a domineering or demanding person; aggression is not. Also, remember the importance of treating each

---

Customer Service Success **Tip**

Put yourself in a customer's situation when he or she is demanding and trying to control you. Ask yourself, "Is there something that I have said or done that might have escalated or added to this situation?" If the answer is "yes," apologize, listen, and move toward resolution. If you do not believe that you are at fault, engage the customer with nonthreatening but firm language and explain that your goal is to help the customer, but that you need that person to calmly explain the issue so that you can figure out what needs to be done. If all else fails, you may eventually have to call in a supervisor or other employee to handle the customer's issue.

---

customer as an individual. If you are dealing with a customer who is being unreasonable, contact your supervisor, then try to get the customer to accompany you to a more private location where the three of you can discuss the issue in an unemotional manner out of sight of other customers, if possible.

- *Tell the customer what you can do.* Don't focus on negatives or what can't be done when dealing with your customers. Stick with what is possible and what you are willing to do. Be flexible and willing to listen to requests. If something suggested is possible and will help solve the problem, compliment the person on his or her idea (e.g., "Mr. Hollister, that's a good suggestion, and one that I think will work"), and then try to make it happen. Doing this will show that you are receptive to new ideas, are truly working to meet the customer's needs and expectations, and value the customer's opinion. Also, remember that if you can psychologically partner with a customer, he or she is less likely to attack. You do need to make sure that your willingness to assist and comply is not seen as giving in or backing down. If it is, the customer may make additional demands or return in the future with similar demands. To avoid this, you could add to the earlier statement by saying something like, "Mr. Hollister, that's a good suggestion, and although we cannot do this in every instance, I think that your suggestion is one that will work out this time." This puts the customer on alert that although he or she may get his or her way this time, it will not necessarily happen in the future. Another strategy is to make a counteroffer in an effort to find a win-win solution in which the customer and your organization get partial satisfaction and needs fulfillment.

By being thoroughly familiar with your organization's policies and procedures and your limits of authority, you will be prepared to negotiate with demanding customers. If they want something you cannot provide, you might offer an alternative that will satisfy them. Remember that your goal is complete customer satisfaction, but not at the expense of excessive loss to your organization.

INDECISIVE CUSTOMERS

You will encounter people who cannot or will not make a decision. In some instances this may be a result of their behavioral style or it might be due to

---

⚙ **WORK IT OUT 7.3**

Handling the Demanding Customer

Survey customer service professionals in various professions to see how they handle demanding or domineering customers. Make a list for future reference and role-play a variety of scenarios involving demanding customers with a peer.

McGraw Hill Education **connect**

---

something in their background from which they learned such behavior. Such customers sometimes spend long periods of time vacillating between several options as they seemingly struggle to choose one over the other. They might even leave and come back later to continue their decision-making effort. Sometimes, they will even bring along a friend or family member on the second visit to help facilitate a decision. In some cases, **indecisive customers** truly do not know what they want or need, as when they are looking for a gift for a special occasion. In other instances, such customers are afraid that they will choose incorrectly or need reassurance that the product has the features they really need or will use later. In the latter situation, use all your product or service knowledge and communication skills to provide them with the information they need to make a buying decision. Otherwise, indecisive customers will occupy large amounts of your time and detract from your ability to do your job effectively or to assist other customers.

An important point to keep in mind is that some people really are just looking or researching a product or service as they check out sales, kill time

indecisive customers People who have difficulty making a decision or making a selection when given choices of products or services.

Indecisive people can be frustrating as you try to serve their needs. *What steps would you take to help a customer make a decision?*

between appointments, or relax, or they may simply be lonely and want to be around others. Strategies for dealing with an indecisive person are

- ***Be patient.*** Do not forget that although indecisive people can be frustrating, especially if you have a high decisive or "D" behavioral style preference, they are still customers.
- ***Ask open-end questions.*** Just as you would do with a customer who is dissatisfied, try to get as much background information as possible. The more data you can gather, the easier it is for you to evaluate the situation, determine needs, and assist in the solution of any problems.
- ***Listen actively.*** Focus on verbal and nonverbal messages for clues to determine emotions, concerns, and interests.
- ***Suggest other options.*** Offer alternatives that will help in decision making and reduce the customer's anxiety. Pointing out a warranty or exchange option available on a product or service may make the customer more secure in the decision-making process.
- ***Guide decision making.*** By assertively, not aggressively, offering suggestions or ideas and providing product and/or service information, you can help customers make a decision. Remember that you are helping them, not making the decision for them. If you push your preferences on them, they may be dissatisfied later or have buyer's remorse, where they regret their decision and return the item or even complain that you pressured their decision. Then you or someone else will have to potentially deal with an unhappy customer.

DISSATISFIED AND ANGRY CUSTOMERS

dissatisfied customer Someone who either does not (or perceives that he or she does not) receive promised or quality products or services.

Occasionally, you will encounter **dissatisfied customers** or angry ones. They may feel that they are not being treated fairly, that you or someone else is lying to or taking advantage of them, or that they are not getting the service they want or expect. Possibly they have been improperly served by you or one of your peers, or by a competitor in the past, and have a preconceived idea about anyone who is in the sales or service profession. Think of how many people stereotypically feel about telemarketers or used car salespeople.

The challenge is that in instances where you encounter a dissatisfied or angry customer, and were not personally involved in his or her previous experience, you represent the organization or you may be considered "just like that last service employee." Unfair as this may be, you have to try to calm these customers and make them happy. To do so, try the following strategies:

- ***Listen*** with an open mind to try and discover the basis for their anger or dissatisfaction.
- ***Remain positive and flexible*** while showing a willingness to work with the customer or negotiate.
- ***Smile, give your name, and offer assistance.*** By projecting a "can do" attitude and lowering defenses, you can potentially get the customer to do likewise and salvage the situation and customer–provider relationship.
- ***Be compassionate and empathize without making excuses.*** Angry or dissatisfied customers typically want and expect that you will try to see their side of the situation and will make concessions in order to appease them. This does not mean that you should bow down to them if the

⚙ WORK IT OUT 7.4

Dealing with Angry Customers

Work with a partner. Discuss situations in which you had to deal with an angry person. Think about what made the person angry and what seemed to reduce tension. Make a list of these factors and be prepared to share your list with the class. Use the results of this discussion to develop strategies to help calm angry people in the future.

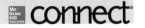

situation was truly not your fault or that of your organization. It does mean that you should try to understand their position and work to bring them back around to a point where you can work together to resolve the issue.

- ***Ask open-end questions and verify information.*** The only way to start to resolve the issue is to find out what caused it in the first place. Ask open-end questions that allow your customers to talk and vent while providing the degree of information needed to identify what went wrong and offer potential solutions.

- ***Take appropriate action.*** Once you have gotten the customer to lower his or her emotions to the point where the two of you can intelligently discuss the situation, you will be on your way to a solution. If you know your organization's policies and procedures and are knowledgeable about products and services, you have the tools to potentially get the relationship back on track and resolve the issue.

Remember: if you get defensive, you become part of the problem and not part of the solution. By maintaining a positive approach and using positive language, you are more likely to bring about a successful outcome when dealing with an angry or dissatisfied person. Figure 7.3 shows some examples of negative wording and some possible alternatives.

Dealing with angry people requires a certain amount of caution. For you to effectively serve an **angry customer**, you must move beyond the emotions to discover the reason for his or her anger. *Note:* Before dealing with customers, check with your supervisor to find out what your policies are

angry customers Customers who become emotional because either their needs are not met or they are dissatisfied with the services or products purchased from an organization.

FIGURE 7.3
Positive Wording

When faced with a customer encounter that isn't going well, remain positive in language. This will help you avoid escalating the situation.

Negative Words or Phrases	Positive Alternatives
Problem	Situation, issue, concern, challenge
No	What I (or we) can do is . . .
Cannot	What I (or we) can do is . . .
It's not my job (or my fault)	Although I do not normally handle that, I'm happy to assist you.
You'll have to (or you must . . .)	Would you mind . . . ? Would you please . . . ?
Our policy says . . .	While I'm unable to . . . , what I can do is . . .

and what level of authority you have in making decisions. This relates to empowerment discussed earlier in the book. By having this information before a customer encounter, you will have the tools and knowledge necessary to handle your customers effectively and professionally. Here are some possible tactics:

- *Be positive.* Tell the customer what you can do rather than what you cannot do.

- *Acknowledge the customer's feelings or anger.* By taking this approach, you've addressed the customer's emotional state, demonstrated a willingness to assist, and encouraged the customer to participate in solving the problem. For example, "Mr. Philips, I can see that you are obviously upset by _____ and I want to help find a solution to this issue; however, I need your assistance to do that. Can you please explain what _____?"

- *Reassure.* Indicate that you understand why he or she is angry and that you will work to solve the problems. For example, "Ms. O'Hara, based on what you have explained, I can see why you are not satisfied with this product. I am going to immediately see what we can do to repair or replace the unit."

- *Remain objective.* In most instances, angry customers are usually upset with the organization, product, or service that you represent, not at you.

- *Listen actively; determine the cause.* Whether the customer is "right" or "wrong" makes no difference in situations like these. Actively listening and trying to discover the problem without attempting to place blame will assure the customer that you are trying to take care of it for him or her.

- *Reduce frustrations.* Don't say or do anything that will create further tension. Do your best to handle the situation with this customer before serving another.

- *Negotiate a solution.* Elicit ideas or negotiate an alternative with the customer. Be willing to compromise, if appropriate or needed.

- *Conduct a follow-up.* Contact your customer as soon as possible after your attempted resolution contact in order to show the customer that you are truly concerned that the issue was correctly resolved and that you value the relationship with him or her. Don't assume that the organization's system will work as designed or intended and that all is well. If the customer was not really satisfied or other issues remain, you may lose a customer and generate negative word-of-mouth publicity as the customer shares his or her story with others.

underpromise and overdeliver A service strategy in which service providers strive for excellent customer service and satisfaction by doing more than they say they will do for the customer or exceeding customer expectations.

Customer Service Success Tip

Strive to do the unexpected and provide quality service to create a memorable customer experience—**underpromise and overdeliver** and do whatever you can (within your authority) to rectify a situation in which a customer is dissatisfied with your product or service in order to ensure customer satisfaction.

⚙ WORK IT OUT 7.5

Responding to Rudeness

Working with a partner, develop a list of rude comments that a customer might make to you. For example, the comment might be, "If you're not too busy, I'd like some assistance." Also list the responses you might give; for example, "If you could please wait, I'll be happy to assist you as soon as I finish, sir (or madam). I want to be able to give you my full attention and don't want to be distracted."

RUDE OR INCONSIDERATE CUSTOMERS

Some people seem to go out of their way to be offensive or to get attention. Although they seem confident and self-assured outwardly, they are often insecure and defensive. Some behaviors they might exhibit are raising the voice; demanding to speak to a supervisor; using profanity; cutting in front of someone else in a line; being verbally abrupt (snapping back at you) even though you're trying to assist; calling you by your last name, which they see on your name tag (e.g., "Listen, Smith"); ignoring what you say; or otherwise going out of the way to be offensive or in control. Try the following strategies for dealing with **rude or inconsiderate customers**:

- ***Remain professional.*** Just because the customer is exhibiting inappropriate behavior does not justify your reacting in kind. Remain calm, assertive, and in control of the situation. For example, if you are waiting on a customer and a rude person barges in or cuts off your conversation, pause, make direct eye contact, smile, and firmly say, "I'll be with you as soon as I finish with this customer, sir (or madam)." If he or she insists, repeat your comment and let the person know that the faster you serve the current customer, the faster you can get to the person waiting. Also, maintaining decorum may help win over the person or at least keep him or her in check.

- ***Don't resort to retaliation.*** Retaliation will only infuriate this type of customer, especially if you have embarrassed him or her in the presence of others. Remember that such people are still customers, and if they or someone else perceives your actions as inappropriate, you could lose more than just the battle at hand.

> **rude or inconsiderate customers** People who seem to take pleasure in being obstinate and contrary when dealing with service providers and who seem to have their own agenda without concern for the feelings of others.

Before you can deal with a customer's business needs, you must first address the customer's emotional issues and try to calm him or her. *What would you do to calm such a customer?*

TALKATIVE CUSTOMERS

Some people phone or approach you and then spend excessive amounts of time discussing irrelevant matters

FIGURE 7.4
Emotion-Reducing Model

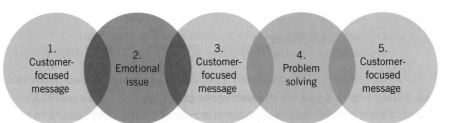

1. Customer-focused message
2. Emotional issue
3. Customer-focused message
4. Problem solving
5. Customer-focused message

emotion-reducing model
Process for reducing customer emotion in situations when frustration or anger exists.

example, "Ms. Hernandez, I can appreciate why you are so frustrated about the service you have received thus far. It seems as if we truly did make an error on your order and I sincerely apologize for that. You are important to us and I am going to do my best to resolve this issue as quickly as possible."

The key to helping resolve any service breakdowns is to frame your problem resolution with customer-focused messages through use of the emotion-reducing model (Figure 7.4). Here's how the **emotion-reducing model** works: Assume a customer has a problem. As the customer approaches (or when you answer the telephone), greet him or her with "Good morning (or afternoon)," a smile, and open body language and gesturing (1. customer-focused message). Then, as the customer explains the issue (2. emotional issue), you can offer statements such as, "I see," "I can appreciate your concern (or frustration, or anger)," or "I understand how that can feel" (3. customer-focused message). Such statements can help you connect psychologically with the customer. Continue to use positive reinforcement and communication throughout your interaction. Once the problem has been defined and resolved (4. problem solving), take one more opportunity at the end of your interaction to send a customer-focused message by smiling and thanking the customer for allowing you to assist. Also, one last apology may be appropriate for inconvenience, frustration, mistreatment, and so on (5. customer-focused message).

KNOWLEDGE CHECK ✓

1. What are the five phases of the emotion-reducing model?

LO 7-5 Reasons for Customer Defection

CONCEPT Failing to meet the customer's needs, handling problems inefficiently, treating the customer unfairly, and using inadequate systems are reasons for the customer to leave you and go elsewhere.

customer defection Customers often take their business to competitors when they feel that their needs or wants are not met or if they encounter breakdown in customer service or poor quality products.

Following a service breakdown, there is often a possibility that you may never see the customer again. This is potentially disastrous to your organization because it costs five to six times as much to win a new customer as it costs to retain a current one. And, as we saw earlier in this chapter, a dissatisfied customer is also likely to tell other people about the bad experience. Thus, you and others in your organization must be especially careful to identify reasons for **customer defection** (Figure 7.5) and remedy potential and actual problems before they negatively affect customers.

FIGURE 7.5

Reasons for Customer Defection

- *Poor service and complacency.* If customers perceive that you and/or your organization do not sincerely care about them or about solving their problems, they may go elsewhere. If a concern is important enough for the customer to verbalize (formally or informally) or to write down, it is important enough for you to take seriously. You should immediately address the problem by listening, gathering information, and taking appropriate action. Customer comments might be casual, for example, "You know, I sure wish you folks stocked a wider variety of rose bush colors. I love shopping here, but your selection is so limited." In this instance, you might write down the customer's name, phone number, and address and then follow up with your manager or buyers about it. Also, practice your questioning skills by asking, "What color did you have in mind?" or "What is your favorite color?" If the customer has a specific request, you could pass that along. You or someone else should try to obtain the item and then contact the customer to discuss your efforts and findings. Sometimes the obvious solutions are the ones that are overlooked, so be perceptive when dealing with customers and look for little clues such as these. It could mean the difference in continued business and word-of-mouth advertising by your customer.

- *Inappropriate complaint resolution.* The key thing to remember about complaint resolution is that it is the customer's perception of the situation, not yours, that counts. If customers believe that they were not treated fairly, honestly, in a timely manner, and in an appropriate fashion, or if they are still dissatisfied, your efforts failed. Remember that only a small percentage of your customers complain. Second attempts at resolution by customers are almost unheard of.

- *Unmet needs.* Customers have very specific needs to which you must attend. When these needs are not addressed or are unsatisfactorily met, the customer is likely to seek an alternative source of fulfillment.

So often, service providers make the mistake of trying to project their personal needs onto others. Their feeling is that "I like it, so everybody should like it." However, today's diverse world requires you to be more knowledgeable and accepting of the ideas, values, beliefs, and needs of others. Failure to be sensitive to diversity may set you, your organization, and your customers on a collision course. Remember what you have read about trust and how quickly it can be destroyed in relationships.

KNOWLEDGE CHECK

1. What are three reasons that customers defect to competitors?

LO 7-6 Working with Internal Customers (Co-workers)

CONCEPT Relationships with your internal customers are important. You should meet your commitments and build a professional reputation.

If you are a service provider, you have external customers who purchase or use your products or services. In addition to these external customers or organizations, if you are a service provider and work in any type of organization that has more than one employee, you also have to deal with internal

Effective relationships with internal customers allow you to gain access to information and services that you need to better serve your external customers. *What are some things that you can do better to serve your internal customers and build stronger relationships with them?*

customers. The bottom line is that, if you give information, products, or services to another person or entity (e.g., team, department, division, or subsidary), you are a service provider and have customers. If you receive information, products, or services from another person or entity, you are a customer to them.

Although your interactions with internal customers may not be difficult, they can often be more sensitive than your dealings with outsiders. This is because if someone within your organization becomes irritated or dissatisfied with you, he or she doesn't necessarily go away. Instead, he or she might tell co-workers or your supervisor about the encounter, which can damage your reputation and even put your standing in the organization in jeopardy. The customer might also withdraw, which means that you might lose access to knowledge, information, or support that you need from him or her in the future.

After all, you see peers and co-workers regularly, and because of your job, office politics, and protocol, your interactions with them are ongoing. Therefore, extend all the same courtesies to internal customers that you do to external ones—in some cases, more so.

The importance of effective internal customer service cannot be underestimated. That is because your relationships with individuals and departments within your organization have far-reaching effects on the organization. Sound internal customer service practices can help to boost employee communication and morale while helping to enhance processes and procedures, reduce costs, increase productivity, and replace interdepartmental competition with interdepartmental cooperation. Through such internal collaboration, external customer service is enhanced because employees have access to information and services they need to better serve external customers. Some suggestions that might help you enhance your interactions with internal customers are given below.

STAY CONNECTED

Since relationships within the organization are so important, go out of your way to regularly make contact with internal customers. You can do this by dropping by their work area to say hello, sending an e-mail, texting, or leaving a voice mail message. You might also friend one another on Facebook, join together on LinkedIn, or otherwise tap into social media channels to get to know one another better outside the workplace and build a more solid relationship.

If you know of a special occasion for a co-worker (e.g., birthday, anniversary, or the birth or adoption of a child), consider sending a card or an e-card to congratulate him or her. This helps strengthen the relationship and can keep the door to communication open so that if service does break down someday, you will have a better chance of hearing about it and solving the problem amiably.

You might describe your co-workers as your "normal" internal customers, but do not forget the importance of your relationships with other organizational employees, such as the cleaning crew (they service your office and work area), security force (they protect you, your organization, and your vehicle), support staff (who provide services like purchasing, payroll, travel, mail, and print services and logistical assistance), and the information technology people (they maintain computer equipment). All these groups or individuals and many others within the organization add value and might be a big help to you at some point. If nothing else, they have connections with other people who might aid in your service delivery efforts. Go out of your way to build and maintain strong interpersonal relationships with others in the workplace, especially if you have a behavioral style to which personal interactions are not second nature or as comfortable. A little extra effort to say good morning or do something nice for others can pay big dividends in the future. For example, if you have good rapport with co-workers and are someday downsized, you still have a support network of people who may know other people in the industry where you might find another job.

MEET ALL COMMITMENTS

Too often, service providers forget the importance of internal customers. Because of familiarity, they sometimes become lax and tend to not give the attention to internal customers that they would give to external customers. This can be a big mistake. For example, if you depend on someone else to obtain or send products or services to external customers, that relationship is as crucial as the ones you have with external customers. Don't forget that if you depend on internal suppliers for materials, products, or information, these people can negatively affect your ability to serve external customers by delaying or withholding the items you need. Such actions might be unintentional or intentional, depending on your relationship. Either way, your external customers suffer and your reputation and that of the organization are on the line.

To prevent, or at least reduce, the possibility of such breakdowns, honor all commitments you make to internal customers. If you promise to do something, do your best to deliver, and in the agreed-upon time. If you can't do something, say so when your internal customer asks. If something comes up that prevents you from fulfilling your commitment, let the customer know of the change in a timely manner.

Remember, it is better to exceed customer expectations than not meet them. If you beat a deadline, they will probably be pleasantly surprised and appreciative.

Ethical Dilemma 7.2

A co-worker promised to help you complete a project where you were to compile information and mail it to customers on Tuesday even though it was not her job. You have helped her in similar situations in the past. It is now Thursday and the co-worker still has not come to your aid and you are now behind schedule.

1. How would you handle this situation? Why?
2. Would you report the situation to your supervisor? Why or why not?
3. What effect might her behavior have on your relationship? Why?

DON'T SIT ON YOUR EMOTIONS

Some people hold on to anger, frustration, and other negative emotions rather than getting their feelings out into the open and dealing with them. Not only is this potentially damaging to health, for it might cause stress-related illnesses, but it can also destroy working relationships. Whenever something goes wrong or you are troubled by something, go to the person and use feedback skills to talk about the situation. Failure to do so can result in disgruntled internal customers, damage to the customer–supplier relationship, and damage to your reputation. Don't forget that you will likely have to continue to rely on your customers in the future, so you cannot afford a relationship problem.

Customer Service Success **Tip**

Be proactive in dealings with individuals and departments in your organization. This can go a long way to building and strengthening relationships and support. Instead of waiting for someone to ask for information, anticipate needs and provide it before he or she needs it. As you read articles or attend training programs, think of information, data, statistics, or pertinent information that would benefit others in the organization and share it with them. Most people will appreciate your interest and initiative and will likely reciprocate.

BUILD A PROFESSIONAL REPUTATION

Through your words and actions, go out of your way to let your customer and your supervisor know that you have a positive, can-do, customer-focused attitude. Let them know that you will do whatever it takes to create an environment in which internal and external customers are important.

Part of projecting a professional image is to regularly demonstrate your commitment to proactive service. This means gathering information, products, and other tools before coming into contact with a customer so that you are prepared to deal with a variety of situations and people. It also means doing the unexpected for customers and providing service that makes them excited about doing business with you and your organization.

ADOPT A GOOD-NEIGHBOR POLICY

Take a proactive approach to building internal relationships so that you can head off negative situations. If your internal customers are in your department, act in a manner that preserves sound working relationships. You can accomplish this in part by adopting the following work habits:

- *Avoid gatherings of friends and loud conversation in your work-space.* This can be especially annoying if the office setup consists of cubicles, as sound travels easily. Respect your co-workers' right to work in a professional environment. If you must hold meetings or gatherings, go to the cafeteria, conference room, or break room or some other place away from the work area.

- *Maintain good grooming and hygiene habits.* Demonstrate professionalism in your dress and grooming. Avoid excessive amounts of colognes and perfumes. This is important because some people have severe allergies to such products and if you are creating an environment where they cannot work, their performance and health suffer.

- *Don't overdo call forwarding.* Sometimes you must be away from your workspace. Company policy may require that you forward your calls. Do not overdo forwarding your calls, especially if you are actually in your office and use that practice as a way to avoid interruptions and focus on a work task. Your co-workers may be inconvenienced and resentful if you do.

- *Avoid unloading personal problems.* Everyone has personal problems now and then. Do not bring personal problems to the workplace and burden co-workers with them. If you have personal problems and need assistance, go to your supervisor, team leader, or human resources department and ask for some suggestions. Many organizations have professionally trained counselors available through their employee assistance programs (EAP). If you get a reputation for often having personal problems that interfere with your effectiveness and efficiency—and bringing them to the workplace—your career could suffer.

Trending NOW

Due in part to the recession, and to some degree with overall dissatisfaction with a lower level of service effectiveness, a number of companies have reversed the trend of offshoring service jobs to countries such as India, the Philippines, and other nations. Instead they are "homesourcing" jobs back to their own country in an effort to make customers feel more comfortable with the service they are receiving and to reduce communication breakdowns.

While sending jobs to countries where salaries are lower and labor issues are reduced makes sense financially, many organizations have found that there is a disconnect with their customers. This is due in part to language differences, but more so to a breakdown with service contractors not effectively understanding the values, expectations, and needs of their customers. It is not enough to be technically proficient and have a knowledge of products and services. To effectively serve customers, service providers must be able to connect on an emotional and intellectual level with their clients.

In gathering data, you should also do a quick assessment of how serious the problem is. You may be hearing about one incident of a defective product or inefficient service. In fact, there may be many unspoken complaints. Also, look for patterns or trends in complaints.

Once you have collected information through questioning and from other sources, spend some time looking over what you have found. If time permits and you think it necessary or helpful (e.g., the customer is not standing in front of you or on the telephone), ask for the opinions of others (e.g., co-workers, team leader/supervisor, technical experts). Ultimately, what you are trying to do is determine alternatives available to you that will help satisfy the customer and resolve the issue.

3. IDENTIFY THE ALTERNATIVES

Let the customers know you are willing to work with them to find an acceptable resolution to the issue. Tell them what you can do, gain agreement, then set about taking action.

Since you are just being brought into the situation when a customer notifies you of a problem or his or her dissatisfaction, you can offer an objective, outside perspective. In effect you are performing as an outside consultant. Use this perspective to offer suggestions or viewpoints that the customer may not see or has overlooked. Additionally, make sure you consider various possibilities and alternatives when thinking about potential resolutions.

Look out for the best interests of your customer and your organization. To do this, be willing to listen to the customer's suggestions and to "think outside of the box" for ideas other than the ones that you and your organization typically use. Don't opt for convenience at the risk of customer satisfaction. If necessary, seek any necessary approval from higher authority to access other options (e.g., to make a special purchase of an alternative item from a manufacturer for the customer, or to give a refund even though the time frame for refunds has expired according to organizational policy).

4. EVALUATE THE ALTERNATIVES

Once all the facts have been collected, look at your alternatives or possible options. While you should certainly strive to hold down costs to your organization, be careful not to let cost be the deciding factor. A little extra time and money spent to resolve an issue could save a customer and prevent recurring problems later. Consider the following factors in this evaluation process:

What is the most efficient way to solve this problem?

Which are the most effective options for solving this problem?

Which options are the most cost-effective?

Will the options being considered solve the problem and satisfy the customer?

Will the selected alternative create new issues?

5. MAKE A DECISION

On the basis of the questions in step 4, and any others you wish to use in evaluation, make a decision on what your course of action will be. To do this, ask the customer, "Which option would you prefer?"

This simple question now puts the customer into the decision-making position and he or she feels empowered. It now becomes his or her choice, and recurring problems may be avoided. If the customer's request is reasonable and possible, proceed and resolve the issue. If not, negotiate a different alternative.

6. MONITOR THE RESULTS

Once you have made a decision, monitor the effect or results. Do not assume that your customer is satisfied, especially if any negotiation occurred between the two of you.

You can monitor the situation with a follow-up call, by asking if the customer needs anything else when you next see or speak to him or her, or by sending a written follow-up (e.g., a thank-you letter with a query concerning satisfaction, a service survey, or an e-mail).

If you determine that your customer is not satisfied or additional needs are present, go back to step 1 and start over.

KNOWLEDGE CHECK

1. What are the six steps of the problem-solving model?

LO 7-9 Implementing a Service Recovery Strategy

CONCEPT The job of a service provider is to return the customer to a satisfied state. Not listening, poor communication, and lack of respect are roadblocks to service recovery.

Humans make mistakes. As a service provider, mistakes often appear glaring to customers, who can be very demanding and unforgiving at times. The best you can hope for when something goes wrong is that you can identify the cause and remedy it quickly to your customers' satisfaction.

The primary purpose of any good service recovery program should be to return the customer–provider relationship to its normal state. When this is done well, a disgruntled customer can often become one who is very loyal and who acts as a publicist for the organization.

Some typical reasons that necessitate service recovery action are

- A product or service did not deliver as expected.
- A promise was not kept (such as failure to follow up).
- A deadline was missed.
- Customer service was not adequately provided (the customer had to wait excessively or was ignored).
- A service provider lacked adequate knowledge or skills to handle a situation.

- Actions taken by you or the organization inconvenienced the customer (e.g., a lab technician took blood during a patient's visit and the sample was mishandled, requiring the patient to return for a retest).
- A customer request or order was not handled properly (e.g., wrong product or service delivered).
- Attempts to return or exchange an item were hampered by policy or an uncooperative employee.
- A customer was given the "runaround," being transferred to various employees or departments and being required to explain the situation to each individual.
- The customer was treated (or perceived he or she was treated) unprofessionally or in a rude manner.
- Corrective action was taken for any of the above reasons and the customer is still not satisfied.

Actually, there are numerous factors in the service process that can lead to a failure to meet customer expectations. Ultimately, they can all influence service recovery.

According to a consumer survey by the internationally known training company AchieveGlobal of Tampa, Florida, customers—regardless of industry, geography, or product/service—want the service they receive to be

- *Seamless.* The company is able to manage behind-the-scenes service factors so that they remain invisible to the customer.
- *Trustworthy.* The company provides what is promised, dependably and with quality.
- *Attentive.* The company provides caring, personalized attention to customers, recognizing both their human and business needs.
- *Resourceful.* The company efficiently provides flexible and creative solutions.

Typically, there are five phases to the service recovery process (see Figure 7.8).

1. APOLOGIZE, APOLOGIZE, AND APOLOGIZE AGAIN

Showing sincere remorse throughout the recovery cycle is crucial. Listen carefully. Empathize with the customer as he or she explains and do not make excuses, interrupt, or otherwise indicate (verbally or nonverbally) that you do not have time for the customer. You want to retain the customer and have an opportunity for recovery. You must demonstrate that you care for the customer and that he or she is very important to you and your organization. Interestingly, many service providers do not accept responsibility and/or apologize when customers become dissatisfied. Such an apology should come immediately after the discovery of the customer's dissatisfaction and should be delivered in person, if possible. The phone is a second option. Written apologies are the last choice.

FIGURE 7.8
Service Recovery Process

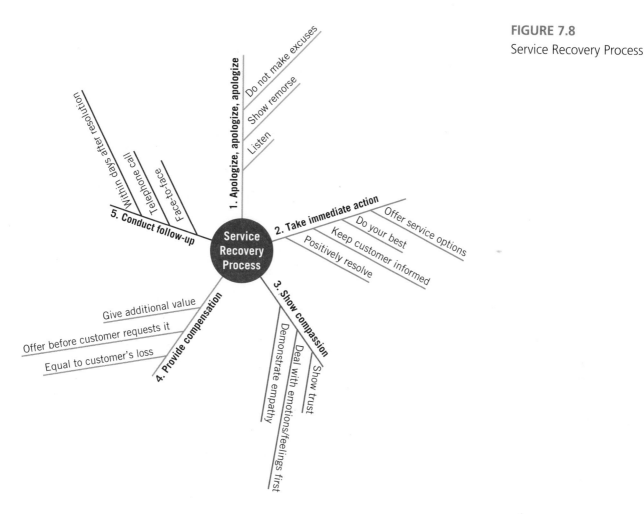

2. TAKE IMMEDIATE ACTION

As soon as your customer has identified a problem, you must set about positively resolving it. As you proceed, it is crucial that you keep the customer informed of actions, barriers encountered, or successful efforts. Even if you are unable to make a quick resolution, the customer may be satisfied if he or she perceives your efforts as sincere and ongoing. You must convince customers through your actions and words that you are doing your best to solve the problem in a timely manner. Also, do not forget what you read earlier in the book about avoiding having to say no without offering **service options**. Remember that your customers want to hear what you can do for them, not what you cannot.

Certainly, there may be times when, even though you want to give customers exactly what they want, you will not be able to do so because of regulations or **prohibitions** (e.g., local, state, or federal laws or regulations). In such cases, it is important to use all the interpersonal skills discussed throughout this book (e.g., active listening, empathizing, and providing feedback) to let customers know that you are prohibited from fulfilling their needs. It is also important to explain the "why" in such situations rather than just saying, "I'm sorry; the law won't let me do that." This type of response sounds as if you are not being truthful, do not want to assist, and are hiding behind an invisible barrier.

service options Alternatives offered by service providers when an original request by a customer cannot be honored because of such restrictions as governmental statutory regulations, nonavailability of products, or inability to perform as requested.

prohibitions Local, state, or federal regulations that prevent a service provider from satisfying a customer's request even though the provider would normally do so.

An example of a prohibition would be when the sister of a patient goes to a doctor's office to get a copy of her brother's medical records. Without specific permission, this would be against the law (Health Insurance Portability and Accountability Act [HIPAA] of 1996) because of a patient's right to privacy and confidentiality between patient and doctor. If you were the receptionist in a doctor's office and someone made such a request, your response might be: "Ms. Ramsey, I apologize for your inconvenience in coming in for nothing. I know it's frustrating. However, although I would love to assist you, I cannot because of state and federal regulations that protect a patient's privacy and confidentiality. If you can get me a signed medical release from your brother, I would be happy to copy his file for you. Can you do that? And, so you won't have to make another trip in here, if you have a fax number, I can get them to you that way." In this instance, you have empathized with the customer, stated what you cannot do, explained why, and offered a way to resolve the problem along with a recovery strategy (e.g., fax). The customer is still not likely to be 100 percent satisfied, but under the circumstances, she will probably appreciate your efforts to help and reduce further effort on her part.

In some situations, you may want to help a customer but cannot because your abilities, time constraints, resources, or the customer's timing of a request prevent fulfillment. Here are some examples of such situations, along with possible responses to your customer:

Example 1: Your Abilities

You work in a pet supply store, you are the only person in the store, and you have a severe back injury that prevents you from lifting anything over 25 pounds. A customer comes in and buys 50 bags of chicken feed, each weighing 100 pounds. She asks that you help her load the bags onto her truck.

Your Response

"Ms. Saunders, we appreciate your business. I know your time is valuable and I'd love to help you. However, I have a back injury and the doctor told me not to lift anything over 25 pounds. I'm the only person working here during the lunch hour. If you can come back in half an hour, I'll have two guys who will load bags for you in no time. Would that be possible? For your inconvenience, I'll even take $10 off your order total."

Example 2: Time Constraints

You work in a bakery and a distraught customer comes in at 3 p.m. Apparently he had forgotten that he was supposed to stop by on the way to work this morning to order a chocolate cake for his daughter's first birthday party, which is at 5 p.m. He wants you to make him a two-layer chocolate cake with her name and butterflies on it.

Your Response

"Mr. Simon, that first birthday party sounds exciting, and I want to help you make it a success. However, realistically, it just cannot be done. We sold our last chocolate cake half an hour ago, and if I bake a new one, it will still have to cool before I can decorate it. You will never make it by five o'clock. I know it's frustrating not to get exactly what you want. However, since your daughter is only one year old and won't know the difference in the type of cake, can I suggest an alternative? We have virtually any other kind of cake you could want, and I can put on chocolate icing and decorate it for you in less than 15 minutes. Would that work?"

Example 3: Available Resources

You are in North Carolina, near the coastline. A customer comes into your lumberyard in search of plywood to board up his house a day before a major hurricane is predicted to hit the area. Since the impending hurricane was announced on the news, you have been overwhelmed with purchases of plywood and sold out two hours ago.

Your Response

"Mr. Rasheed, I can appreciate the urgency of your need. Unfortunately, as you know, everyone in town is buying plywood and we sold out two hours ago. However, I do have a couple of options for you. I can call our store in Jacksonville to find out whether any plywood is left. If there is some, I can have it held if you want to drive over there. The other option is that we have a shipment on the way that should arrive sometime around midnight. I'll be here and can hold some for you if you want to come back at that time. Would either of those options work for you?"

Example 4: Timing

It is April 13 and you are an accountant. With the federal tax filing deadline two days away, you and the entire staff of your firm have been working 12- to 14-hour days for weeks. A regular customer calls and wants to come in in the next couple of days to discuss incorporating her business and to get some information on the tax advantages for doing so.

Your Response

"Ruth, it's great that you are ready to move forward with the incorporation. I think you will find that it will be very beneficial for you. However, with tax deadlines two days away, we are swamped and there is just no way I can take on anything else. Since your incorporation is not under a deadline, can we set up our meeting some time around the first of next week? That will give me time to wrap up taxes, take a breather, and then give you the full attention you deserve."

In all of these instances, you show a willingness to assist and meet the customers' requests even though you are prevented from doing so. You also partner with them and offer alternatives for consideration. This is important, since you do not want to close the door on customer opportunities. Doing so will surely send customers to a competitor.

There might be other occasions when you or your organization does not meet a customer's request even though it is possible to do so. In such cases, company restrictions keep you from fulfilling the customers' request. In this type of situation, you sometimes hear service providers hide behind a phrase such as "Policy says . . . ." The reality is that someone in the organization has decided for business reasons that certain actions cannot or should not be taken. If you encounter such "policies" that prohibit you from delivering service to customers, bring them to the attention of your team leader or management for discussion. These restrictions will most likely cost your organization some customers and result in bad word-of-mouth publicity. An example of such a situation, along with a possible response, is described below:

Example

You work in a gas station in a major tourist area that has a policy that prohibits accepting out-of-town checks. A tourist from another state has her family with her and fills her car with gas. She then comes to you to pay for her purchase. She tells you that she has only personal checks and $2 in cash with her. She is leaving town to return home at this time.

Your Response

"I know that this is an inconvenience, and I apologize. However, because of problems we've had in the past, we do not accept checks from banks out of this area. We will gladly accept major credit cards, travelers' checks, or cash. Does anyone else in your car have a credit card or cash? We also have an ATM machine where you can use a bank debit card to get cash."

3. SHOW COMPASSION

To help the customer see that your remorse and desire to solve a problem are genuine, you must demonstrate empathy. Expressions such as "I can appreciate your frustration," "I understand how we have inconvenienced you," or "I can imagine how you must feel" can go a long way in soothing and winning the customer over. Before you can truly address the customers' problem, however, you must deal with their emotions or feelings. If you disregard their feelings, customers may not give you a chance to help resolve the breakdown. Also, keep in mind what you read about trust in an earlier chapter: you must give it to receive it.

4. PROVIDE COMPENSATION

Prove to customers that they are valuable and that you are trying to make up for their inconvenience or loss. This penance or symbolic self-punishment should be significant enough that the customer feels that you and your organization have suffered an equal loss. The value or degree of your atonement should equal the customer's loss in time, money, energy, or frustration. For example, if a customer's meal was cooked improperly and the customer and others in the party had to wait, you might give the customer a free meal and free coffee or tea to everyone in the group. If you forgot a vegetable that was ordered and it came much later, a free dessert might suffice. The key is to make the offer without the customer having to suggest or demand it.

Not only must the recovery compensate original loss, it should give additional value. For example, if a customer had an oil change done on his or her car and oil was spilled on the carpet, an appropriate gesture might be to give the oil change free and have the carpet cleaned at your company's expense. This solution compensates for inconvenience and lost time while providing added value (saving the cost of the oil change).

5. CONDUCT FOLLOW-UP

The only way to find out whether you were successful in your recovery efforts or whether the customer is truly satisfied is to follow up. The preferable methods are face-to-face questioning or a phone call. This contact should come within a few days after the complaint was resolved. It could take the form of a few simple statements or questions (e.g., "I am following up in case you had any additional questions" or "I'm calling to make sure that it is now working as it should be. Is there anything else we can do to assist you?").

This last step in the recovery process can be the deciding factor in whether the customer returns to you or your organization. It is the phase that reemphasizes the message "We truly care."

KNOWLEDGE CHECK

1. According to AchieveGlobal, what four things do customers want service they receive to be?

2. What are the five phases of the service recovery process?

LO 7-10 Disaster Planning Initiatives in the Service Recovery Process

Hurricanes Katrina and Sandy, the Oklahoma tornadoes of 1999 and 2013, the 2013 earthquake and typhoon in the Philippines, the 2004 earthquake and tsunami in the Indian Ocean, and other similar natural catastrophes all have one thing in common—they devastated homes and businesses on a massive scale.

For organizations that did not have an active disaster preparedness or contingency plan, the results were dramatic and paralyzing financially and from an operational standpoint. Not only were physical structures lost in the devastation, but organizational records and assets were lost and customer service was virtually stopped. Customers had limited access to cell and landline phone service, Internet service was severed or radically disrupted, and there was little or no way to contact companies and businesses for needed services. Call centers were offline or totally destroyed and employees stayed home to deal with their own personal calamity and loss. All of this had a crippling effect on the ability of affected organizations to communicate with and deliver any degree of service.

In the chaos that followed, companies struggled for weeks and months to regain any semblance of their previous operational effectiveness. Businesses were closed; employees were out of work with no income; many people struggled with the loss of precious items and, in many instances, with the loss of a loved one; insurance companies scrambled to appraise the damage and pay insured claims; and utter confusion was the word of the day.

The U.S. Small Business Administration suggests that organizations take at least the following actions to prepare for potential disaster situations in order to remain functional or to more effectively recover should a catastrophe strike:

- Create a preparedness program for the business.
- Identify critical business functions and systems.
- Create an emergency communications plan.
- Test preparedness systems regularly.
- Build a disaster preparedness kit.

As a result of such unthinkable destruction, many organizations have taken proactive measures to create and rehearse disaster preparedness and contingency plans. They store vital information and data at reinforced offsite facilities in various geographic regions and via cloud technology. They also train their employees about the need to think proactively and decide what information is crucial for storage and how they might better prepare in the event of emergencies from a service and personal perspective.

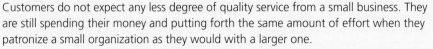

Small Business Perspective

Customers do not expect any less degree of quality service from a small business. They are still spending their money and putting forth the same amount of effort when they patronize a small organization as they would with a larger one.

The challenge for small businesses in service recovery is that they typically do not have training available for employees on the process, and because of the limited number of employees, they typically do not have the luxury of a customer service department to handle follow-ups. Additionally, small businesses do not have large budgets and in some cases have limited liquid assets or money that they can apply to service recovery efforts. Even so, recovery efforts are equally as important, if not more so, to small businesses because they really count on every customer and sale to survive.

To compensate for limited resources, every employee must take responsibility for providing quality service in order to reduce the need for service recovery. When something does go wrong, the service representative making contact with the customer must assume responsibility and do his or her best to follow the steps of the problem-solving model. If situations escalate, the service representative should immediately contact a supervisor or the owner, as appropriate, to bring the issue to management's attention and ask for guidance.

If you work for a small company, you should still strive to be the most competent, conscientious, and professional service provider that you can be.

Impact on Service

Based on personal experience and what you just read, answer the following questions:

1. Why do you think that service recovery efforts are often limited in small companies? Explain.
2. What could be done to better prepare employees of small businesses to better handle service breakdowns? Explain.
3. If you were an employee of a small business and a customer received the wrong product, what would you do to appease the customer? Explain.

Key Terms

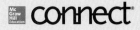

angry customers

customer defection

customer expectations

demanding or domineering customers

difficult customers

dissatisfied customers

emotion-reducing model

indecisive customers

needs

problem-solving model

prohibitions

rude or inconsiderate customers

service breakdowns

service options

strategies for preventing dissatisfaction

talkative customers

underpromise and overdeliver

wants

LEARNSMART

Summary

Dealing with various types of people can be frustrating, but it can also be very satisfying. Many times, you will have to deal with a variety of external and internal customers, including those who are angry, indecisive, dissatisfied, demanding, domineering, rude, or talkative. Your goal in all your efforts should be to work harmoniously with all customers. Whenever you can address customer needs in a variety of situations and find acceptable solutions, you, the customer, and the organization win. To assist customers effectively doesn't take magic; all it takes is a positive attitude, preparation, and a sincere desire to help others. If you use the techniques outlined in this chapter, and others in this book, you're on your way to providing stellar customer service and satisfying customer needs. Whenever a customer experiences an actual or perceived breakdown in service, prompt, appropriate recovery efforts may be your only hope of retaining the customer. In a profession that has seen major strides in quality and technology as well as increased domestic and global competition, service is often the deciding factor. Customers often expect and demand their rights. When they are disappointed, they simply go elsewhere. Your role in the process is to remain vigilant, recognize customer needs, and provide service levels that will keep them coming back.

Review Questions

1. What is meant by the term *service breakdown*? Define.

2. What causes customers to become dissatisfied?

3. What tactics can you use to deal with angry customers?

4. What can you do to assist indecisive people in coming to a decision?

5. Why might some customers feel they have to demand things from others?

6. How can you effectively deal with rude or inconsiderate customers?

7. What are some strategies for refocusing a talkative customer?

8. What are some strategies for preventing customer dissatisfaction? List them.

9. How does the emotion-reducing model work?

10. Why do customers defect?

11. What strategies can you use to build strong relationships with co-workers?

12. List the strategies for effective problem solving.

13. What is service recovery and when do you need to implement it?

Search It Out

1. Search the Internet for Information on Problem Solving

Search the Internet and locate information on providing customer service to irate customers. Also look for information on the following topics:

Conflict resolution

Problem solving

Handling stressful situations

Service breakdown

Service recovery

Be prepared to share what you find with your classmates at the next scheduled class.

2. Contingency Planning

Give some thought to what it would mean to your organization if a natural disaster struck your area and what that would mean to you personally and to your customers. With this in mind, spend some time on the Internet searching information about what organizations are doing to prepare for catastrophic events or disasters.

Once you gather the information, prepare a checklist of things that you could do as a service provider to prepare for such a catastrophe. Also, think of what recommendations you could offer your supervisor for developing contingencies to keep service flowing to your customers.

Be prepared to share your thoughts with your classmates.

You can start your search with these websites: http://search.yahoo.com/search;_ylt=Av0JWlH6nRxrGYSMjY_q4n6bvZx4?p=organziations+with+disaster+preparedness+or+contingency+plans&toggle=1&cop=mss&ei=UTF-8&fr=yfp-t-900-1.

3. Additional Resources

Search the website for this textbook, www.mhhe.com/customerservice, for additional activities, reference materials, and support materials.

Collaborative Learning Activity

Role-Playing Difficult Customer Situations

Work with a partner and role-play one or more of the following scenarios. Each of you should choose at least one scenario in which you will play the service provider role. The other person will play the customer. In each instance, discuss what type of difficult customer you are dealing with and how such an encounter might go. At the end of each role-play, both persons should answer the following questions and discuss ideas for improvement:

Scenario 1

Terry Welch entered your shoe store over 30 minutes ago and seems to be having trouble deciding the style and color of shoes she wants.

Scenario 2

Chris Dulaney is back in your lawn mower repair shop. This is the third time in less than two weeks that he has been in for repairs on a riding mower. Chris is getting upset because the problem stems from a defective carburetor that has been repaired on each previous visit. He is beginning to raise his voice, and his frustration is becoming evident.

Scenario 3

You are a telephone service representative for a large retail catalog distribution center. You've been at work for about an hour when you receive a call from Pat Mason, who immediately starts making demands (e.g., "I've only got a few minutes for you to tell me how to order." "Look, I've read all the articles about the scams telemarketers pull. I'll tell you what I want, and you tell me how much it will cost." or "Listen, what I want you to do is take my order and get me the products within the next two days. I need them for a conference.").

Scenario 4

You are a cashier in the express lane at a supermarket. As you are ringing up a customer's order, a second customer approaches, squeezes past several people in line, and says, "I'm in a hurry. All I have is a quart of milk. Can you just tell me how much it costs, and I'll leave the money right here on the register."

Scenario 5

You are a very busy switchboard operator for ComTech, a large corporation. A vendor whom you recognize from previous calls has just called to speak with your purchasing manager. As in previous calls, the vendor starts a friendly conversation about the weather, how things are going, and other topics not related to business.

Questions

1. How well was service provided?

2. Were any negative or unclear messages, verbal or nonverbal, communicated? If so, discuss.

3. How can you incorporate the improvements you have identified into a real customer service encounter?

4. What open-end questions were used to discover customer needs? What others could have been used?

Face to Face

Handling Service Breakdowns at AAA Landscaping

Background

You are the owner of AAA Landscaping, a small company in Orlando, Florida, that specializes in resodding and maintenance of lawns. Much of your business is through word-of-mouth advertising. Once a contract is negotiated, portions of it are subcontracted out to other companies (e.g., sprinkler system repair and pesticide services). Recently, you went to the home of Stu Murphy to bid on resodding Stu's lawn. Several other bids were obtained, but yours was the lowest. You arranged for work to begin to remove old grass and replace it with St. Augustine grass sod.

As part of the contract, Stu had asked that some basic maintenance be done (e.g., hedge and tree trimming, hauling away of old decorative wooden logs from around flower beds, and general sprucing up of the front area of the house). Also, fertilizer and pesticide were to be applied within two weeks. The contract was signed on Wednesday, and the work was to be completed by Saturday, when Stu had planned a party.

Your Role

You were pleased to get the contract, worth over $1,200. This is actually the third or fourth contract in the same subdivision because of word-of-mouth advertising. The initial sod removal and replacement, weeding, and pruning were completed on Saturday, and you received full payment on Monday.

Later in the week you received a call from Stu stating that several trees were not trimmed to his satisfaction,

debris covering decorative rocks along hedges was not removed as agreed, and bags of clippings had been left behind. Because of other commitments, it was several days before you sent someone out to finish the job. A day later, Stu left another message on your answering machine stating that there was still an untrimmed tree, the debris remained, and the clippings were still in the garage. You didn't get around to returning his call. Over a week later Stu called again, repeating the message he'd left before and reminding you that the contract called for pesticide and fertilizer to be applied to the lawn. You called back and said that someone would be out later in the week. Again, other commitments kept you from following through. Stu called on Saturday and left a fourth message on your answering machine. He said that he was getting irritated at not getting callbacks and action on his needs. Without returning Stu's call, you responded by sending someone out on Tuesday to take care of the outstanding work.

It's been several days since the work was completed, and you assume that Stu is now satisfied since you have heard nothing else from him.

Critical Thinking Questions

1. Based on information in this chapter, how have you done on providing service to Stu? Explain.

2. What were Stu's needs in this case?

3. Could you have done anything differently?

4. Are you sure that Stu will give a good recommendation to neighbors or friends in the future? Why or why not?

Planning to Serve

To help better prepare yourself to deal with difficult customer service situations and to help you to prevent service breakdown or to aid in service recovery, respond to the following statements. On the basis of your responses, seek out resources (e.g., materials, training

programs, and people) that can help broaden your knowledge on these topics. Try to discuss these questions—and your answers—with your co-workers or classmates. This can ultimately help improve your own skills, employee morale, and service to customers.

1. I approach what I believe to be a difficult customer with a positive attitude and believe that I can turn the situation around. **Yes**　**No**

2. In dealing with customers, I seek to determine their true needs before offering a service solution. **Yes**　**No**

3. What actions or circumstances have you noticed lead to service breakdowns in organizations where you were either a customer or service provider?

4. When you were a customer and service broke down, what recovery strategies were effectively used to help "make you whole"?

5. I consciously monitor my language, and elicit feedback from peers on it to ensure that I typically use positive words and phrases when communicating. **Yes**　**No**

6. When dealing with the types of difficult customers described in this chapter, I maintain my professionalism and actively listen in order to better serve their needs. **Yes**　**No**

7. When working with co-workers, I afford the same courtesies and professionalism that is required for external customers. **Yes**　**No**

8. When you were a customer and service broke down, what ineffective recovery strategies did you experience?

Quick Preview Answers

1. T	3. F	5. T	7. T	9. T	11. T
2. F	4. F	6. T	8. T	10. T	12. T

Ethical Dilemma Summary

Ethical Dilemma 7.1 Possible Answers

1. What would you do in this situation?

   You are in an awkward situation. Your boss wants to leave and has made that clear, yet your customer is in need of service. An appropriate strategy would be to call your supervisor, make him aware of the situation, and ask him how you should handle it.

2. How do you think the customer will view this matter?

   In effect, you are violating your own store policy regarding closing times. Customers have a legitimate expectation that if you have a written policy displayed (the time on the door); that you will follow it. By failing to adhere to posted times, you are not only potentially violating your customer's trust, but also creating a situation where you lose merit in their eyes and the organization will likely sustain negative word-of-mouth publicity as they recount the story to many others and likely on social media.

3. Are there possible repercussions from a service standpoint? If so, what are they?

If you allow the customer to come in to get the item(s) needed, she will likely be thankful and less stressed, although the fact that you locked up earlier than announced may play a role in future end-of-day visits. In the future, she might opt to go elsewhere in similar circumstances. If you do not allow her to shop, you will likely lose her future business and she will spread word of the incident to anyone who will listen to her. She might even call or send a letter or e-mail to the store manager to complain.

Ethical Dilemma 7.2 Possible Answers

1. How would you handle this situation? Why?

   This is a touchy situation in which you basically asked the co-worker to do you a favor and she agreed to do so. Rather than jump to conclusions, it is probably best to approach the co-worker in a friendly and nonthreatening manner, using some strategies you read about in Chapters 3 and 4. Ask why she failed to assist as she agreed and listen to her response rationally. Depending on what she tells you, let her know that you are disappointed that she failed to either help or come to you before now to explain that she could not do so. Also, let her know how you feel about her failure to come forward. The last is important because people often do not realize the effect their behavior has on others and how it might impact relationships.

2. Would you report the situation to your supervisor? Why or why not?

   Since this was not a task assigned to both of you, it is probably best not to go to your supervisor or to point fingers and blame your co-worker for your missing the deadline. After all, it is your job and not hers.

3. What effect might her behavior have on your relationship? Why?

   Because relationships are built on trust, your co-worker's behavior could certainly negatively affect your relationship in the future, depending on her reason for failing to assist you. Even if she has a good reason, the fact that she did not at least let you know of the obstacle could influence how you feel toward her and your ability to trust and work with her effectively in the future.

Customer Service in a Diverse World

Diversity is the one true thing we all have in common. Celebrate it every day.
—Anonymous

LEARNING OUTCOMES

After completing this chapter, you will be able to:

8-1 Recognize that diversity is not a bad thing.

8-2 Describe some of the characteristics that make people unique.

8-3 Embrace the need to treat customers as individuals.

8-4 Determine actions for dealing with various types of people.

8-5 Identify a variety of factors that make people diverse and that help to better serve them.

8-6 Communicate effectively with a diverse customer population.

To assist you with the content of this chapter, we have added additional review questions, activities, and other valuable resource material at www.mhhe.com/customerservice.

IN THE REAL WORLD MANUFACTURING—JOHNSON & JOHNSON

Johnson & Johnson (J&J) was founded in New Brunswick, New Jersey (where it is currently headquartered), in 1886 by three Johnson brothers to produce antiseptic wound medications. The company later began developing products such as baby products, sanitary napkins for women, dental care products, bandages, and other wound dressings. In 1924 J&J expanded to an international platform by opening an operation in England. By the middle of the twentieth century, J&J had expanded into pharmaceuticals and had become a household name with products such as baby shampoo, Tylenol, AcuVue disposable contact lenses, and coronary stents leading its extraordinary product and distribution growth worldwide.

Today, J&J employs more than 128,000 employees in 275 companies operated in 275 different countries. Their corporate family includes

- The world's largest and most diverse medical devices and diagnostics company.
- The world's sixth-largest biologics company.
- The world's sixth-largest consumer health company.
- The world's eighth-largest pharmaceuticals company.

Since its founding, J&J has been a leader in the areas of healthcare, wellness, medicine, and health education. The company's ethical commitment to customers, employees, communities, and stockholders is outlined in the J&J credo and has been the driving force behind its success for over 100 years. The four main tenets of their credo are summarized here:[1]

- **"We believe our first responsibility is to the doctors, nurses and patients, to mothers and fathers and all others who use our products and services."** Part of this commitment is ensuring that products are of a high quality and reasonable price and that they are delivered to customers promptly and accurately while providing a fair profit for suppliers.

- **"We are responsible to our employees, the men and women who work with us throughout the world."** J&J believes in treating employees as individuals and with dignity and based on their own merit. Part of this is fair compensation in a safe working environment where people feel secure in their jobs and that their opinions matter. Additionally, employees should have equal opportunity and be managed in a just, ethical manner. All of this should be done in a manner that allows employees the opportunity to also fulfill their family obligations.

- **"We are responsible to the communities in which we live and work and to the world community as well."** Part of the J&J philosophy is to be a good citizen of their communities and the world by supporting charities and paying their fair share of taxes. They encourage civic involvement and health and education programs while doing their part to protect the environment and natural resources.

- **"Our final responsibility is to our stockholders. Business must make a sound profit."** Ultimately, J&J has a responsibility to stockholders to make a fair profit. All efforts related to new research, implementation of new processes, and purchases of assets and facilities are done in a mindful manner. These efforts help maintain revenue reserves for emergencies while providing a fair return on investment for shareholders.

Even though J&J has experienced serious challenges and threats in the past (e.g., Tylenol poisoning in 1982), the company's proactive approach to business has allowed it to recover and thrive where other organizations have floundered. By taking a visionary approach to product and service development and continually working to maintain customer respect and trust, J&J is able to move forward and expand even in dire economic times.

www.jnj.com

For more information about Johnson & Johnson, do an Internet search and either visit their website (www.jnj.com/connect/home?presentationtemplate=nonflash) or scan the QR code with your smartphone application to get to their site.

Think About It

1. What do you currently know about J&J and the products and services it provides?

2. How does J&J compare to other companies of which you are aware from the standpoint of commitment to customers, employees, and community?

3. Why do you think J&J has survived and thrived since 1886 when other companies often have much shorter lifespans?

4. As a customer, do you trust J&J brands? Why or why not?

Quick Preview

Before reviewing the chapter content, respond to the following questions by placing a "T" for true or an "F" for false on the rules. Use any questions you miss as a checklist of material to which you will pay particular attention as you read through the chapter. For those you get right, congratulate yourself, but review the sections they address in order to learn additional details about the topic.

_____ 1. Diversity is an important aspect of everyone's life that can present many positive opportunities or negative challenges depending on your knowledge of other people and groups.

_____ 2. Many people only associate the term *diversity* with the word *cultural*, which describes the differences between groups of people from various countries and with differing beliefs.

_____ 3. The diverse nature of your customer population requires you to be aware of the various ways people from different cultures interact in the business setting.

_____ 4. Values are the "rules" that people use to evaluate situations, make decisions, interact with others, and deal with conflict.

_____ 5. In some cultures, direct eye contact is often discouraged, for it suggests disrespect or overfamiliarity.

_____ 6. Today, all cultures use less formality in the business environment and do not stress the importance of using titles and family names as often as they did in the past.

_____ 7. When encountering someone who speaks a language other than yours, you should avoid jokes, words, or acronyms that are tied to sports, historical events, or specific aspects of your own culture.

_____ 8. In serving customers from some cultures, it is important to avoid the use of the word "no" because this word may cause the customer to become embarrassed or experience a "loss of face."

_____ 9. According to the U.S. Census Bureau, over 54 billion Americans have some level of disability.

_____ 10. When a customer has a disability, the disability should be deemphasized by thinking of the person first and the disability second.

_____ 11. When dealing with an elderly customer, you should always be respectful.

_____ 12. Younger customers are as valuable as those in any other group and should be served professionally.

Answers to Quick Preview can be found at the end of the chapter.

LO 8-1 The Impact of Diversity

CONCEPT   Diversity is an important aspect of everyone's life. Encounters with others give us an opportunity to expand our knowledge of others.

As the world grows smaller economically and otherwise (e.g., in world trade, international travel, outsourcing and offshoring of jobs, worldwide Internet access, international partnerships between organizations, and technologically transmitted information exchange), the likelihood that you will have contact on the job with people from other cultures, or who are different from you in other ways, increases significantly. This likelihood also carries over into your personal life. **Diversity** is encountered everywhere (e.g., over the telephone, on Internet, in supermarkets, in religious organizations, and on public transportation) and is an important aspect of everyone's life. Although it presents challenges in making us think of differences

diversity The characteristics, values, beliefs, and factors that make people different, yet similar.

and similarities, it also enriches our lives—each encounter we have with another person gives us an opportunity to expand our knowledge of others and build relationships, while growing personally.

One significant impact that diversity has on customer service is that people from varied backgrounds and cultures bring with them expectations based on the "norm" of their country or group. Whether this diversity pertains to cultural or ethnic differences, beliefs, values, religion, age, gender, ability levels, or other factors, a potential breakdown in customer satisfaction can occur if people get other than what they want or expect.

Part of creating a positive diverse customer business environment is to train each service provider on the nuances of dealing with people who have backgrounds that are different from their own. Additionally, this effort involves each employee taking ownership for enhancing his or her knowledge and skills related to working with a diverse customer base.

As you begin your journey through the concept of dealing with diverse customers in this chapter, stop and think about the following questions.

- How do you define *diversity*?
- What do you already know about diverse cultures around the world?
- In what ways do your cultural beliefs and values differ from those of cultures with which you have contact as a service provider?
- In what ways are your cultural beliefs and values similar to those of cultures with which you have contact as a service provider?
- How do the beliefs and expectations of people from a gender other than your own impact your ability to serve them effectively?

The people of the world are becoming more increasingly integrated each day as ease of travel and the Internet close the distance gap between them. *What are you doing to educate yourself about differences in gender, generations, and other factors that influence the way the diverse customers that you will encounter think and act?*

- What is your personal interest in learning about other cultures or diverse groups?
- What training or research have you done on diversity and how has that impacted your views or perspectives towards others who may be different from you?

KNOWLEDGE CHECK

1. What does the term *diversity* mean to you?

LO 8-2 Defining Diversity

CONCEPT Diversity is not a simple matter; it is not difficult to deal with if you are fair to people and keep an open mind.

cultural diversity The different racial, ethnic, and socioeconomic varieties, based on factors such as values, beliefs, and experiences, that are present in people grouped together in a given situation, group, or organization.

The word *diversity* encompasses a broad range of differences. Many people only associate the term *diversity* with **cultural diversity**, which has to do with the differences between groups of people, depending on their country of origin, backgrounds, and beliefs. They fail to recognize that diversity is not just cultural. Certainly, diversity occurs within each cultural group; however, many other characteristics are involved. For example, within a group of Japanese people are subgroups such as males, females, children, the elderly, athletes, thin people, gay or lesbian people, Buddhists, Christians, grandparents, and married and single people, to mention just a few of the possible diverse characteristics, beliefs, and values.

Customer Service Success Tip

A key point to remember is that the concept of treating others as you would like to be treated (a value common in many religions—e.g., the Golden Rule) can lead to service breakdowns. This is because your customers are unique and may not value what you do or want to be treated as you do.

To better ensure service success, find out what customers want and treat them as they want to be treated. This concept has been termed the **Platinum Rule**.[2]

Platinum Rule Term coined by speaker and author Tony Alessandra related to going beyond the step of treating customers the way you want to be treated, to the next level of treating them the way they would like to be treated.

Diversity is not a simple matter, yet it is not difficult to deal with. Start your journey to better understanding of diversity by being fair to people and keeping an open mind when interacting with them. In fact, when you look more closely at, and think about, diversity, it provides wonderful opportunities because people from varying groups and geographic locations bring with them special knowledge, experience, and value. This is because even though people may have differences or potentially look different, they also have many traits in common. Their similarities form a solid basis for successful interpersonal relationships if you are knowledgeable and think of people as individuals; you can then capitalize on their uniqueness. If you cannot think of the person instead of the group, you may

---

⚙ WORK IT OUT 8.1

Encountering Diversity

Take a few minutes to think about diversity and what it means to you. Write your own definition of diversity.

During the past week, in what situations have you encountered someone from a different culture, group, or background in the workplace or at school (someone whose values or beliefs differed from yours or who looked or dressed differently from you or your group)? Make a list of the diverse people that you met (e.g., where they were from, why they were different from you, and how they were similar to you) and the situations encountered.

Once you have created your responses, form a group with two to three other students, share your responses, and discuss the implications of providing quality service to customers who are different from you.

---

stereotype people—lump them together and treat them all the same. This is a recipe for interpersonal disaster, service breakdown, and organizational failure.

The basic customer service techniques related to communication found in this book can be applied to many situations in which you encounter customers from various groups. Coupled with specific strategies for adapting to special customer needs, these techniques provide the tools you need to provide excellent customer service.

Some factors that make people different are innate, that is, they are born with them, such as height, weight, hair color, gender, skin color, physical and mental condition, and sibling birth order. All these factors contribute to our uniqueness and help or inhibit us throughout our lives, depending on the perceptions we and others have. Other factors that make us unique are learned or gained through our environment and our life experiences. Examples of these factors include religion, **values, beliefs**, economic level, lifestyle choices, profession, marital status, education, and political affiliation. These factors are often used to assign people to categories. Caution must be used when considering any of these characteristics, since grouping people can lead to stereotyping and possible discrimination.

The bottom line is that all of these factors affect each customer encounter. Your awareness of differences and of your own preferences is crucial in determining the success you will have in each instance.

values Long-term appraisals of the worth of an idea, person, place, thing, or practice held by individuals, groups, or cultures. They affect attitudes and behavior.

beliefs Perceptions or assumptions that individuals or cultures maintain. These perceptions are based on past experiences, memories, and interpretations and influence how people act and interact with certain individuals or groups.

✓ KNOWLEDGE CHECK

1. How does cultural diversity differ from diversity?

2. In what ways might a customer's values and beliefs impact your ability to deliver effective service to them?

LO 8-3 Customer Awareness

CONCEPT Applying your own cultural practices and beliefs to a situation involving someone from another culture can result in frustration, anger, poor service, and lost business.

Aren't all customers alike? Emphatically, no! No two people are alike, no two generations are alike, and no two cultures are alike. In addition, each customer has needs based on his or her own perceptions and situation.

In our highly mobile, technologically connected world, it is not unusual to encounter a wide variety of people with differing backgrounds, experiences, religions, modes of dress, values, and beliefs within the course of a single day. Many of these factors can affect customer needs, wants, and expectations and potentially create situations in which you must be alert to the verbal and nonverbal messages that indicate those needs. Moreover, the diverse nature of your customer population requires you to be aware of the various ways people from different cultures or groups interact in the business setting. Applying your own cultural practices and beliefs to a situation involving someone from another culture can result in frustration, anger, poor service, and lost business.

With a changing customer world come potential differences in the way some people perceive factors such as time, communication style, gender roles, religion, dress, and members of other countries and cultures. By better understanding other cultures and contexts, you have a prime opportunity for building a solid customer–provider relationship. You also significantly reduce the chance for communication and service breakdowns due to differing perspectives and expectations.

Because people from various cultures approach situations in different ways, you run the risk of misunderstanding that can occur due to the way people deal with communication, conflict, problem solving, task completion, and decision making. This is why cultural awareness training and research are so crucial to your job success and effective customer service.

KNOWLEDGE CHECK ✓

1. How can better understanding the cultural differences of your customers potentially assist in enhancing the customer service you provide?

LO 8-4 The Impact of Cultural Values

CONCEPT Values often dictate which behaviors and practices are acceptable or unacceptable. These values may or may not have a direct bearing on serving the customer.

Although many cultures have similar values and beliefs, specific cultural values are often taught to members of particular groups starting at a very young age. This does not mean that a particular group's values and beliefs are better or worse than those of any other culture; they are simply important to that particular group. These values often dictate which behaviors and practices are acceptable or unacceptable. They may or may not have a direct bearing on serving the customer, but they can have a very powerful influence on what the customer wants, needs, thinks is important, and is willing to seek or accept. Values can also influence your perceptions and actions toward others. Being conscious of differences can lead to a better understanding of customers and potentially reduce conflict or misunderstandings in dealing with them.

Many service providers take values for granted. This is a mistake. Values are the "rules" that people use to evaluate issues or situations, make decisions, interact with others, and deal with conflict. As a whole, a person's value system often guides thinking and helps him or her determine right from wrong or good from bad. From a customer service perspective, values often strongly drive customer needs and influence the buying decision. Values also differ from one culture to another, depending on its views on ethics, morals, religion, and many other factors. For example, if customers perceive clothing as either too sexy or too conservative, they may not purchase the items, depending on what need they are trying to meet. Or they may not buy a house because it's in the perceived "wrong" neighborhood.

Values are based on the deeply held beliefs of a culture or subculture. These beliefs might be founded in religion, politics, or group mores. They drive thinking and actions and are so powerful that they have served as the basis for arguments, conflicts, and wars for hundreds of years.

To be effective in dealing with others, service providers should not ignore the power of values and beliefs, nor should they think that their value system is better than that of someone else. The key to service success is to be open-minded and accept that someone else has a different belief system that determines his or her needs. With this in mind you, as a service provider, should strive to use all the positive communication and needs identification you have read about thus far in order to satisfy the customer.

Education, cultural nuances, family backgrounds, and other factors cause people to behave based on their own experiences. The more informed you are about similarities and differences that people from various cultures have, the greater the likelihood that you will provide quality service. *How should you provide customer service to someone of another culture?*

Cultural values can be openly expressed or subtly demonstrated through behavior. They can affect your interactions with your customers in a variety of ways. In the next few pages, consider the connection of values with behavior, and how you can adjust your customer service to ensure a satisfactory experience for diverse customers. Keep in mind that the degree to which customers have been acculturated to prominent cultural standards will determine how they act.

Your goal is to provide excellent service to the customer. In order to achieve success in accomplishing this goal, you must be sensitive to, tolerant of, and empathetic toward customers. You do not need to adopt the beliefs of others, but you should adapt to them to the extent that you provide the best service possible to all of your customers. As mentioned earlier, apply the Platinum Rule of service when dealing with customers.

MODESTY

modesty Refers to the way that cultures view propriety of dress and conduct.

Modesty is exhibited in many ways. In some cultures (e.g., Muslim and Quaker), conservative dress by women is one manifestation of modesty. For example, in some cultures women demonstrate modesty and a dedication to traditional beliefs by wearing a veil or headdress. Such practices are tied to religious and cultural beliefs that originated hundreds of years ago. In other cultures, nonverbal communication cues send messages. For example, direct eye contact is viewed as an effective communication approach in many Westernized cultures, and lack of eye contact could suggest dishonesty or lack of confidence to a Westerner. In some cultures (India, Iran, Iraq, and Japan), direct eye contact is often discouraged, in particular between men and women or between people who are of different social or business status, for it is considered disrespectful or rude. Modesty is encouraged between sexes. Often a sense of modesty is instilled into people at an early age (more so in females). This value may be demonstrated by covering the mouth or part of the face with an open hand when laughing or speaking, or through avoiding direct eye contact in certain situations.

Another way that you might offend someone's modesty is through your environment. For example, if you have a waiting room that has magazines that show advertisements with scantily clad models or a television or radio station broadcasting for customers that contains sexual situations (e.g., soap operas) or racy talk show hosts, you may want to rethink the situation to potentially avoid offense to some customers.

Impact on Service

When encountering examples of modest behavior, evaluate the situation for the true message being delivered. The person may really be exhibiting suspicious behavior. However, instead of assuming that the customer is being evasive or dishonest, consider the possible impact of culture as part of your assessment of the situation. If you suspect illegal intentions, certainly call your risk management staff or a supervisor; however, do not unnecessarily force the issue or draw undue attention to a customer's nonverbal behavior, cultural dress, or beliefs being demonstrated. Instead, continue to verbally probe for customer needs and address them. In addition, provide the same quality of friendly service as you would to others who display behavior or cultural characteristics that do not differ from your own.

EXPECTATIONS OF PRIVACY

expectations of privacy The belief that personal information provided to an organization will be safeguarded against inappropriate or unauthorized use or dissemination.

Based on your personality and prior life experiences, you may be more or less likely to disclose personal information, especially to people you do not know well. You should be aware that disclosing personal information about oneself is often a cultural factor and that **expectations of privacy** vary. For example, many people who are British, German, Australian, Korean, or Japanese may display a tendency to disclose less about themselves than many North Americans do.

Ethical Dilemma 8.1

Assume that you are an employee in a lingerie store at a local shopping mall, and you and a fellow employee have been discussing world events because of a news story about a terrorist bombing you saw on the television this afternoon. You were talking about how, in a post-9/11 world, there is ongoing scrutiny and reevaluation of handling different situations because of security concerns worldwide. Airports limit what can be carried onto planes, people are checked by security personnel and devices (e.g., metal detectors and scanners), and organizational policies and procedures related to service and various situations have been modified (e.g., entrance into buildings, background checks for current and new employees, and access to certain types of data and equipment).

Shortly after your conversation with the other employee, a male customer or client comes in carrying a paper bag. Based on the man's mode of dress, you and another employee debate on what country he is from before you approach him to offer assistance. When you do, he states that he is "just killing time while his wife has her hair done." You observe him leave your store, wander into several others and then return a second time about an hour later. Your fellow employee jokes that, "He is probably a terrorist casing the place to blow it up."

1. Does the man's dress or the other employee's comments make a difference in this situation? Explain why or why not.

2. What action should you take, if any? Why or why not?

3. Does the conversation that you had with your co-worker have any bearing on the course of action you choose in this situation? Explain.

4. What are possible repercussions if you either act or decide not to act?

5. If the person was dressed differently, would you take a different course of action? Explain.

Impact on Service

If you tend to be gregarious and speak freely about virtually any topic, you should curtail this tendency in the customer service environment. Failure to do so could make some customers feel uneasy and uncomfortable. Their discomfort may result from the fact that if you are conducting business in a Western culture, when someone asks a question or shares information, there is often an expectation that the other party will reciprocate. Reluctance to do so may be perceived as being unfriendly or even rude. A good rule of thumb is to stay focused on the business of serving your customer in an expeditious and professional manner. Keeping your conversations centered on satisfying the customers' needs can accomplish this. This should not be construed to mean that you should totally avoid "small talk"; just keep it under control and watch customer reactions closely. Talking about the weather, traffic, or some other impersonal topic might be fine. Avoid controversial topics that might be emotional hot buttons or sensitive to other people (e.g., politics, religion, or perspectives on birth control).

FORMS OF ADDRESS

Although many North Americans often pride themselves on their informality, people from other countries may see informality as rudeness, arrogance, or overfamiliarity. For example, if you were from the United States

Forms of address and greetings differ around the world. When meeting someone from another culture, it may be appropriate to use their cultural greeting format rather than a handshake, depending on the situation. *What do you know about greetings used by other cultures and how might a lack of knowledge or cultural insensitivity hinder perceptions of your level of service to some customers?*

wai Traditional gesture in Thailand used in conjunction with a slight bow as a greeting to say "thank you" or "sorry" (pronounced "why"). It is executed by placing the palms and fingers of both hands together as in a prayer position in the center of the chest. Holding the hands higher in relation to the face is an indication of more respect or reverence to the other person

namaste Traditional greeting gesture in India (pronounced "NAH-mes-tay") that is performed with a slight bow and by placing the palms and fingers of both hands together as in a prayer position in the center of the chest

acculturated The cultural and psychological changes that often occur as a person or group of people are integrated into another culture or country and adopt the habits and beliefs of their new environment.

form of address Title used to address people. Examples are Mister, Miss, and Doctor.

and failed to greet the customer appropriately (e.g., with a slight bow, sign of the **wai, namaste,** or other traditional greeting) or called customers from a more formal culture by their first name without their permission (e.g., in a doctor's office or a waiting area), you might possibly irritate or anger them.

When meeting someone from another culture who has not been **acculturated** into your own, you might greet the customer according to his or her cultural background. This demonstrates sensitivity and respect to the customer and his or her culture and can create an instant bond. For example, many cultures (e.g., Argentina, many European countries, China, and other parts of Asia) stress formality in greeting someone in the business environment and place importance on the use of titles and family names when addressing others.

To further confuse the issue of how to address a customer, some cultures have differing rules on how family names are listed and used. For example, in parts of China and Taiwan, many people are given a family name, a generational name (for the period during which they are born), and a personal name at birth. The generational and personal names might be separated by a hyphen or space [e.g., a female might be named Li (family name) Teng (generational name) Jiang (personal name), or Li Teng-Jiang]. Women typically do not take their husband's surnames. When addressing someone from the Chinese culture, use an appropriate title such as *Mr.* or *Mrs.* followed by the family name (Mrs. Li) unless you are asked to use a different **form of address**.

Many service providers from other cultures who move to a Westernized culture often adopt a Western first name (e.g., Amanda or Richard) when they immigrate to, or work with, people from that culture. This makes it easier for their customers and co-workers to pronounce their names.

In Argentina (and most **Hispanic**, **Chicano,** and **Latino cultures**), people have two surnames: one from their father (listed first) and one from their mother (e.g., Jose Ricardo Gutierrez (father's surname) Martinez (mother's surname). Usually, when addressing the person, use a title only with the father's surname (e.g., Mr. or Mrs. Gutierrez).

Impact on Service

A customer's preference for a particular name or form of address can have an impact upon your ability to effectively deal with him or her. If you start a conversation with someone and immediately alienate the person by incorrectly using his or her name, you may not be able to recover. Moreover, informality or improper use of family names could send a message of lack of knowledge or concern for the customer as an individual or as being important to you.

RESPECT FOR ELDERS

In most cultures, some level of respect is paid to older people. Often this **respect for elders** is focused more on males (when older men are viewed as revered, as among Chinese). This arises from a belief that with age come knowledge, experience, wisdom, authority, and, often, higher status. Thus, respect for or deference to elders is normal. Also, in many cultures age brings with it unique privileges and rights (such as the right to rule or to be the leader). For example, this is true in many Native American cultures.[3]

Impact on Service

You must be careful to pay appropriate respect when speaking to older customers (of both sexes). Further, you should be sensitive to the fact that if the customer demands to speak to a senior person or to the manager or owner, he or she may simply be exhibiting a customary expectation for his or her culture or generation. If you can assist without creating conflict in such situations, do so; if not, honor the request when possible.

> **Customer Service Success Tip**
>
> Ask your customer his or her preference for being addressed rather than assume familiarity and make the choice yourself. The latter can lead to a service relationship breakdown.

Hispanic culture Refers to people who were born in Mexico, Puerto Rico, Cuba, or Central or South America.

Chicano culture Refers primarily to people with a heritage based in Mexico.

Latino culture Refers to people of Hispanic descent.

respect for elders A value held by people from many cultures.

Trending NOW

Many organizations and employees have realized the importance of creating a fair and equal environment in which everyone feels respected and valued. This is especially important in a service environment where employees encounter customers who have different characteristics daily.

To ensure that you are ready for potential situations in which you will be serving people of different ages, genders, abilities, cultural and religious backgrounds, and numerous other diversity factors, consider participating in the following initiatives:

1. Honestly evaluate your own biases towards people from a given group and develop some strategies for overcoming them.

2. Visit a restaurant that serves ethnic foods other than that of your native culture.
3. Share your own story with someone from a different group (e.g., age, gender, ethnic background, or religion) and see how their life experiences compare or differ from yours.
4. Identify at least one resource for diversity information and visit it each month.
5. Take a language course to learn a new language.
6. Visit a religious institution, museum, or historical monument of a culture different from your own.
7. Volunteer to work with people whose race, gender, or cultural backgrounds are different from your own.

IMPORTANCE OF RELATIONSHIPS

In many Asian, Latin American, and Middle Eastern cultures, the building of a strong **interpersonal relationship** is extremely important before business is conducted. For example, in China, Egypt, El Salvador, Indonesia, Korea, Japan, and Myanmar (Burma), it is not unusual to have a number of meetings with people in an organization before coming to an agreement. Lunch, dinner, and office meetings often occur for weeks before an agreement is reached. Also, unless you reach the right level of management in the organization for these meetings, all your efforts may be wasted. Figure 8.1 shows a partial listing of some of the world's more relationship-focused countries where building relationships before conducting business is often crucial.

Impact on Service

Failure to establish support or an environment of trust could lead to a breakdown in service and/or lost customers. This does not mean that you should hesitate to assume a quicker familiarity with customers from such cultures. This could also alienate them. Instead, when you will be having ongoing contact or doing repeat business, follow the customers' lead. Get to know them and share information about your organization and yourself that can lead to mutual respect and trust. You may find that you also have to take time at the beginning of each encounter with your established customers to reestablish the relationship. This may involve spending time in conversations related to nonbusiness topics (e.g., their health, sports, hobbies, pets, or other topics in which the customer is interested). Just remember to familiarize yourself with cultural manners and etiquette for the customer's country before meeting in order to avoid cultural taboos. For example, it is inappropriate for a male to ask a male counterpart from many Middle Eastern countries about his wife or daughter.

Relationship building may also involve presenting gifts to persuade various people in the organization that you are a friend and have their interests at heart. Only then can you proceed to determine needs and provide service. People from many countries view this as an appropriate form of etiquette, while others may label such gratuities as bribes. Whatever your belief, if the practice is a cultural norm, you may do well to follow it when dealing with customers from other regions of the world.

FIGURE 8.1
Relationship-Focused Countries (Partial Listing)

Bangladesh	Indonesia	Myanmar	Saudi Arabia
Brazil	Iran	Pakistan	Singapore
China	Iraq	Philippines	South Korea
Colombia	Japan	Poland	Thailand
Egypt	Kuwait	Qatar	Turkey
Greece	Malaysia	Romania	Vietnam
India	Mexico	Russia	

GENDER ROLES

Culturally and individually, people view the role of men and women differently. Although **gender roles** are continually evolving throughout the world, decision making and authority are often clearly established as male prerogatives within many cultures, subcultures, or families. For example, in many Middle Eastern, Asian, South American, and European countries, women have often not gained the respect or credibility in the business environment that they have achieved in many parts of North America.

gender roles Behaviors attributed to or assigned by societal norms.

In some countries it is not unusual for women to be expected to take a "seen and not heard" role or to remain out of business transactions. In Korea and other Pacific Rim countries, it is rare for women to participate in many business operations. Men often still have higher social status than females. You do not have to agree with these practices, but you will need to take them into consideration when facing them in some customer encounters.

When serving customers from different countries, you would do well to remember that people may leave a country, but they take their cultural norms and values with them. Failure to consider alternative ways of dealing with people in certain instances might cause you to react negatively to a situation and nonverbally communicate your bias.

Impact on Service

If you are a female dealing with a male whose cultural background is like one of those just described, he may reject your assistance and ask for a male service provider. If you are a male dealing with a male and female from such a culture, do not be surprised if your conversation involves only the male. Attempts to draw a woman into such a transaction or make direct eye contact and smile may embarrass, offend, or even anger customers and/or their family members who are present. Generally, people who have lived or worked in Western cultures for longer periods will acculturate and not take offense to more direct behaviors that are meant to convey friendliness and to engage customers (e.g., smiling, engaging in small talk about families, or complimenting on dress).

ATTITUDE TOWARD CONFLICT

Conflict is possible when two people come together in a customer environment, but it does not have to happen. By recognizing your biases and preferences, and being familiar with other cultures, you can reduce the potential for disagreement. Certainly, there will be times when a customer initiates conflict. In such instances, all you can do is to use the positive communication techniques described throughout this book.

attitudes Emotional responses to people, ideas, and objects. They are based on values, differ between individuals and cultures, and affect the way people deal with various issues and situations.

Many times, **attitudes** toward conflict are rooted in the individual's culture or subculture and based on behavioral style preference. Some cultures are **individualistic cultures** (emphasis is placed on individuals' goals, as in Western countries), and some are **collective cultures** (individuals are viewed as part of a group, as in Japan or in Native American cultures). Members of individualistic cultures are likely to take a direct approach to

individualistic cultures Groups in which members value themselves as individuals who are separate from their group and responsible for their own destiny.

collective cultures Members of a group sharing common interests and values. They see themselves as an interdependent unit and conform and cooperate for the good of the group.

conflict, whereas people whose culture is collective may address conflict indirectly, using an informal mediator in an effort to prevent loss of face or embarrassment for those involved. Even within subcultures of a society, there are often differing styles of communication and dealing with conflict. Of course, regardless of culture or group, people choose different **conflict resolution styles** based on personality style preferences.

conflict resolution style The manner in which a person handles conflict. People typically use one of five approaches to resolving conflict: avoidance, compromise, competition, accommodation, or collaboration.

Impact on Service

Depending on the individuals you encounter and their cultural background, you and your customers may deal differently with conflict. If you use the wrong strategy, emotions could escalate and customer dissatisfaction could follow. The key is to listen and remain calm, especially if the customer becomes agitated.

THE CONCEPT OF TIME

In relation to time, people and societies are often referred to as being either **monochronic** or **polychronic**. People from monochronic societies tend to do one thing at a time, take time commitments seriously, are often focused on short-term projects or relationships, and adhere closely to plans. On the other hand, polychronic people are used to distractions, juggle multiple things (e.g., conversations) without feeling stressed, consider time as a guide and flexible commodity, work toward long-term deadlines, and base promptness on relationships.

monochronic Refers to the perception of time as being a central focus with deadlines being a crucial element of societal norms.

polychronic Refers to the perception of time as a fluid commodity that does not interfere with relationships and elements of happiness.

concept of time Term used to describe how certain societies view time as either polychromic of monochronic.

People from the United States are typically very time-conscious (monochronic). You often hear such phrases as "time is money," "faster than a New York minute," and "time is of the essence," which stress their impatience and need to maximize time usage. Similarly, in Germany, punctuality is almost a religion, and being late is viewed as very unprofessional and rude. In most business settings in the United States, anyone over 5 minutes late for a meeting is often chastised. In many colleges and universities, etiquette dictates that students wait no longer than 15 to 20 minutes when an instructor (depending on whether he or she is a full or associate professor) is late for a class.

In many instances, North Americans tend to expect people from other cultures to be as time-conscious as they are; however, this is not always the case. For example, it is not unusual for people from Arab countries (polychronic) to be a half hour or more late for an appointment or for a person from Hispanic and some Asian cultures to be an hour late. It is also not unusual for people from such cultures to fail to show up for an appointment at all. A phrase used by some Asian Indians sums up the concept and justifies the lateness: "Indian standard time." Such tardiness is not viewed as disrespect for the time of others or rudeness; it is simply indicative of a cultural value or way of life. Figure 8.2 lists countries according to their **concept of time**.

The perception of time and how it is viewed and used vary between cultures. *What do you know about the ways that various cultures view time, and how might that affect your ability to interact with and serve customers from those groups?*

Impact on Service

In Western and other monochronic cultures, you are expected to be punctual. This is a crucial factor in delivering effective service. Although others may not have the same beliefs and may be late for meetings, you must

FIGURE 8.2
Monochronic and Polychronic Countries

Most cultures can be described as either monochronic or polychronic. Some are both in that people exhibit one focus in the workplace and another with relationships. In some countries, a monochronic approach is prevalent in major urban areas, whereas a polychronic view is taken elsewhere. The following is a sampling of countries and their perspective on time.

Monochronic	Polychronic		Both
Australia	Africa	Latvia	Brazil
Canada	Bahrain	Lebanon	France
Czech Republic	Bangladesh	Mexico	Japan
England	Cambodia	Myanmar	Spain
Germany	China	Native American tribes	
Hungary	Croatia	Pakistan	
The Netherlands	Estonia	Philippines	
New Zealand	Ethiopia	Portugal	
Norway	Greece	Romania	
Poland	India	Russia	
Slovakia	Indonesia	Saudi Arabia	
Sweden	Ireland	Serbia	
Switzerland	Italy	South Korea	
United States	Java	Thailand	
	Jordan	Turkey	
	Kuwait	Ukraine	
	Laos	Vietnam	

observe time rules in order to project an appropriate image and to satisfy the needs of your customers and organization.

OWNERSHIP OF PROPERTY

In many cultures (e.g., Buddhist, certain African tribes, and the Chickasaw Indian Nation), **ownership of property**, or accumulation of worldly goods or wealth, is frowned upon. In the case of the Chickasaw Indians and other native tribes in North America, such things as the earth, nature, natural resources, possessions, and individual skills are shared among the tribal group. They are not to be owned or kept from others, for the Creator gave them.[4] Many devout Buddhists believe that giving away personal belongings to others can help them reach a higher spiritual state. Thus, the amassing of material things is not at all important to them and is often frowned upon.

ownership of property Refers to how people of a given culture view property.

Impact on Service

People have differing levels of needs. Ask customers what their needs are and listen to their responses. Don't persist in upgrading a customer's request to a higher level or more expensive product if he or she declines your suggestion. You may offend and lose a customer. Of course, if you are in sales, you must make a judgment on whether an objection is one that you should attempt to overcome or whether it is culturally based and means no.

Customer Service Success Tip

By being aware of the time values that you and your customers have and proceeding accordingly; you can reduce your own stress level when dealing with customers or clients from other cultures.

Keep Your Message Brief

Avoid lengthy explanations or details that might frustrate or confuse your customer. Use simple one-syllable words and short sentences. But also avoid being too brisk. Make sure you allow time for interpretation of, translation of, and response to your message.

Check Frequently for Understanding

In addition to using short words and sentences, pause often to verify the customer's understanding of your message before continuing. Avoid questions such as "Do you understand?" Not only can this be answered with a "yes" or "no" as you read in an earlier chapter, but it can also offend someone who speaks and understands English reasonably well. The nonverbal message is that the person may not be smart enough to get your meaning. Instead, try tie-in questions such as "How do you think you will use this?" or others that will give you an indication of whether the customer understands the information you have provided. These types of questions help you and the customer visualize how the information will be put to use. They also give you a chance to find out if the person has misunderstood what you explained.

Keep Smiling

Smiling is a universal language; speak it fluently (when appropriate).

CUSTOMERS WITH DISABILITIES

According to the U.S. Census Bureau, one in five Americans or 56.7 million (19 percent of the population), has some type of disability, with more than half that number having a serious disability.[8] This is not just an issue in the United States. Around the world, populations are aging. The future impact on societies is going to be huge because these numbers are projected to continue to grow as populations age.

From a customer service perspective, you will certainly encounter someone in the workplace who has a disability and that may require your assistance in serving him or her.

customers with disabilities
Descriptive phrase that refers to anyone with a physical or mental disability.

Some service professionals are uncomfortable working with **customers with disabilities**. This is often because they have had little prior exposure to people who have special needs, they are uninformed about various disabilities, or they have an unfounded fear or anxiety in relating to them.

Even though you may be unfamiliar with how people with disabilities adapt to life experiences, you should strive to provide excellent service to them. In most cases, customers who have disabilities have learned to accommodate their own personal needs and do not want to be treated differently; they want to be treated equally. Related to this, a point to remember is that many people with disabilities will not disclose the fact out of concern that they might be treated differently or discriminated against. In reality, their disability is the norm for them and they do not see it as big of an issue as someone who does not share their disability or have knowledge about it.

In addition to all the factors you have read about previously, to be effective in dealing with customers in the United States, you must be aware of the **Americans with Disabilities Act of 1990** (ADA), the ADA Amendments Act of 2008, and other legislation passed by Congress to protect individuals and groups.

Legislation similar to the ADA now exists in many other countries as well, so if you work in such an area, you should familiarize yourself with and comply with those laws. You should also understand the court interpretations of these laws that require businesses to provide certain services to customers with disabilities and to make certain premises accessible to them. The laws also often prohibit any form of discrimination or harassment related to a disability.

Since the passage of the ADA, much has been published about the rights of and accommodations for people with disabilities. Figure 8.3 provides general strategies for working with customers and others with disabilities and complying with the ADA. In addition, the following sections discuss specific approaches you can take to work well with people with certain disabilities.

Customers with Hearing Disabilities

Hearing loss is common as people age or because of a medical condition and can be a real challenge in service environments. According to the World Health Organization, over 360 million people (5 percent of the world's population) have some form of disabling hearing loss. Additionally, approximately one-third of people over the age of 65 are affected by a disabling hearing loss.[9] As people age, this issue will become more prevalent.

Americans with Disabilities Act of 1990 A U.S. federal act signed into law in July 1990 guaranteeing people with disabilities equal access to workplace and public opportunities.

Customer Service Success Tip

Do not assume that just because someone has an obvious disability that he or she requires or wants your assistance. Offer assistance, if appropriate, and follow your customer's lead in offering assistance. Unsolicited assistance can be offensive and might even be dangerous if it is unexpected and causes the person to lose his or her balance or distracts him or her.

In addition to the suggestions offered in this chapter for serving customers with specific disabilities, here are some general guidelines for success:

- *Be prepared and informed.* You can find a lot of literature and information about disabilities. Do some reading to learn about the capabilities and needs of customers with various disabilities.

- *Be careful not to patronize.* Refrain from talking "down" to customers with disabilities. Just because they have a physical or mental disability does not mean that they cannot help themselves or understand what you are saying. Customers with disabilities should be valued no less as a customer or person than someone who does not exhibit a disability.

- *Treat them equally, not differently.* Just as you would other customers, work to discover their needs and then set about satisfying them.

- *Refer to the person, not the disability.* Instead of referring to *the blind man,* refer to *the man wearing the red shirt* or *the man who is standing by the . . . ,* or, better yet, *the man who needs . . . .*

- *Offer assistance, but do not rush to help without asking.* Just as you would ask someone without a disability whether you might assist him or her, hold a door, or carry a package, do the same for a person with a disability. If he or she declines, drop the issue and move ahead in your service efforts.

- *Be respectful.* The amount of respect you show to all customers should be at a consistently high level. This includes tone of voice (showing patience), gestures, eye contact, and all the other communication techniques you have learned about.

FIGURE 8.3

General Strategies for Servicing Customers with Disabilities

As the population ages, hearing deficits become more prominent in customers. *How can you ensure that your message is heard and understood when serving someone with a hearing loss?*

hearing disabilities Conditions in which the ability to hear is diminished below established auditory standards.

Remember that customers who have **hearing disabilities** may have special needs, but they also have certain abilities. Do not assume that people who are hearing impaired are helpless. In interactions with such customers, you can do a variety of things to provide effective service:

- Face your customer directly when speaking.
- Speak louder (assuming they only have partial hearing loss).
- Provide written information and instructions where appropriate and possible.
- Use pictures, objects, diagrams, or other such items to communicate more clearly, if appropriate.
- To get the person's attention, use nonverbal cues such as gesturing.
- Use facial expressions and gestures to emphasize key words or express thoughts.
- Enunciate your words and speak slowly so that the customer can see your mouth form words (but do not overexaggerate your mouth's movements).
- Use short sentences and words.
- Check for understanding frequently by using open-end questions to which the customer must provide descriptive answers.
- Communicate in a well-lighted room when possible.
- Watch backlighting (light coming from behind you that can cast a shadow on your face), which may reduce the ability to see your mouth.
- Reduce background noise, if possible.

If you serve customers over the telephone or Internet, you may find yourself interacting with a **Telecommunications Relay Service (TRS)**, also called relay service, relay operator, and IP-relay. Through such services, specially trained operators act as intermediaries between people who are deaf, hard-of-hearing, speech disabled, or deaf and blind and standard telephone users. This is accomplished when a disabled customer uses a keyboard or assistive device to contact the operator service. Those people then add the intended service provider onto the call and translate messages verbally back and forth between the customer and provider. The customer types comments and the operator then relays them to the service provider. When the provider responds, the operator responds back to the customer in writing. As you can imagine, this is a time-consuming process. If you are contacted by such an operator, be patient and speak slowly so your message gets translated properly.

Real-Time IM Relay for Customers with Hearing and Speech Loss services are now available to assist people with hearing loss. The relatively new technology has virtually replaced the previous relay services [telecommunications device for the deaf (TDD) or telephone typewriter (TTY)]. The new system is currently offered exclusively by AT&T and at no cost to people who sign up for AT&T's Relay Services. Users log in to a specialized AOL AIM interface through an Internet connection on a PC and on a wireless device. Specially trained relay operators read the instant messages to hearing callers and then type IMs, which are displayed—in real time—to the hearing-impaired end user.

Unlike with the previous TTY system, instead of having to wait until a relay operator types a full phrase or sentence and sends it to the recipient, IM users can see the text messages word-by-word as they are typed. In effect, this makes conversations being transmitted seem more like a call that a hearing customer might experience.

Like many other aspects of life involving technology these days, there are people who try to abuse "the system." There are many scam artists (e.g., Nigerian-based con artists) who attempt to use the TRS systems to steal from unsuspecting organizations, especially small businesses. This can create a potential trust issue between you and legitimate customers with disabilities who contact you via an assistance system. Provide quality service whenever you are contacted by a relay operator; however, always beware. To protect your organization, make sure that you receive payment in advance via a credit card or a money order or check (ensure the check clears your bank) before shipping products.

Customers with Vision Disabilities

As with hearing loss, many people experience vision loss because of medical conditions or as a result of the aging process. According to the World Health Organization, "285 million people are visually impaired worldwide: 39 million are blind and 246 [million] have low vision."[10] This means that you are likely to encounter someone with a vision impairment or sight loss on any given day.

Like people who have hearing impairments, customers with **vision disabilities** may need special assistance, but they are not helpless. Depending on your organization's product and service focus, you can do things to assist visually impaired customers. Be aware that, depending on the type of impairment, a person may have limited vision that can be used to advantage when serving them.

Here are some strategies to use that can potentially help improve the quality and level of service you provide:

- Talk to a visually impaired person the same way you would talk to anyone else.
- You do not have to raise your voice; the person is visually impaired, not hard of hearing.
- Do not feel embarrassed or change your vocabulary. It is okay to say things like "Do you see my point?" or "Do you get the picture?"
- Speak directly to the customer.
- Speak to the person as he or she enters the room or approach the person so that he or she knows where you are. Also, introduce others who are present, or at least inform the customer of their presence.

Telecommunications Relay Service (TRS) Through such services, specially trained operators act as intermediaries between people who are deaf, hard-of-hearing, speech disabled, or deaf and blind and standard telephone users.

Real Time IM Relay for Customers with Hearing and Speech Loss Instant messaging system that allows people with hearing loss who have signed up for AT&T's free Relay Service to receive real-time instant messages from callers.

vision disabilities Conditions resulting from lost visual acuity or disability.

- If appropriate, ask how much sight he or she has and how you can best assist.
- Give very specific information and directions (e.g., "A chair is approximately 10 feet ahead on your left").
- If you are seating the person, face him or her away from bright lights that might interfere with any limited vision he or she may have.
- When walking with someone who is blind, offer your arm. Do not take the person's arm without permission; this could startle him or her. Let the person take your elbow and walk slightly behind you.
- When helping a blind person to a chair, guide his or her hand to the back of the chair. Also, inform the person if a chair has arms to prevent him or her from overturning the chair by leaning or sitting on an arm.
- Leave doors either completely closed or open. Partially open doors pose a danger to visually impaired people.

Customers with Mobility or Motion Impairments

mobility or motion impairments Physical limitations that some people have, requiring accommodation or special consideration to allow access to products or services.

According to the U.S. Census Bureau, 47 million people in the United States over the age of 15 have difficulty walking or climbing stairs and use a wheelchair, cane, crutches, or a walker.[11] The term "mobility impairment" typically refers to disabilities that impact someone's ability to move without assistance, manipulate objects, and interact with the physical world. Impairments may affect the person's movement of head, hands, body, legs, and/or feet and could impact his or her coordination or balance and sensation or ability to feel. Mobility-impaired users include those who are confined to bed, use a wheelchair or other assistive device to navigate, or have permanently incapacitated or reduced hand movements. Causes range for mobility impairments. Someone might have had an accident or may have a disabling disease such as spina bifida, muscular dystrophy, or cerebral palsy.

Customers who have **mobility or motion impairments** often use specially designed equipment and have had extensive training in how to best use assistive devices to compensate for the loss of the use of some part of their body. You can best assist them by offering to help and then following their lead or instructions. Do not make the assumption that they need your assistance and then set about giving it. You can cause injury if you upset their balance or routine. Here are some strategies for better serving these customers:

The number of people with mobility impairments is on the rise. *What are some strategies that you can use to better serve customers with a mobility impairment?*

- Prior to a situation in which you may have to accommodate someone who uses a walker, wheelchair, crutches, or other device, do an environmental survey of your workplace. Note areas where space is inadequate to permit mobility (a minimum of 36 inches is needed for a standard wheelchair) or where hazards exist. If you can correct the situation, do so. For example, move or bring in a different table or chair or rearrange furniture for better access. Otherwise, make suggestions for improvements to the proper people in your organization. Remind them that the ADA and state regulations require an organization to accommodate customers with such disabilities.

- Do not assume that someone who has such an impairment cannot perform certain tasks. As mentioned earlier, people who have disabilities are often given extensive training. They have learned how to overcome obstacles and perform various tasks in different ways.

- Make sure that you place information or materials at a level that makes it possible for the person to see without undue strain (e.g., eye level for someone in a wheelchair so that he or she does not have to look up).

- Do not push or lean on someone's wheelchair without his or her permission.

> **Customer Service Success Tip**
>
> Stand or sit so that you can make direct eye contact with a person in a wheelchair without forcing the person to look up at an uncomfortable angle for extended periods. This reduces discomfort and neck strain on his or her part.

ELDERLY CUSTOMERS

Being older does not make a person or a customer less valuable. In fact, many older customers are in excellent physical and mental shape, are still employed, and have more time to be active now than when they were younger. Studies show that aging citizens have more disposable income now than at any other time in history. And, as the **baby boomer** population (people born between 1946 and 1964) ages, there are more older Americans than ever (41.4 million in 2011, up from 40.3 million in 2010).[12] Moreover, as the population ages, there will be a greater need for services—and service providers—to care for people and allow them to enjoy a good quality of life. Figure 8.4 shows the U.S. population aged 65 and older between 1900 and 2030. Consider the following strategies when you are interacting with an elderly customer.

baby boomer A term applied to anyone born between 1946 and 1964. People in this age group are called "boomers."

Be Respectful

As you would with any customer, be respectful. Even if the customer seems a bit arrogant, disoriented, or disrespectful, don't lose your professionalism. Recognize that sometimes these behaviors are a response to perceptions based on your cues. When this happens, quickly evaluate your behavior and make adjustments, if necessary. If an older customer seems

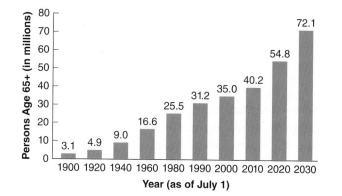

FIGURE 8.4 Number of Persons 65 and Older: 1900 to 2030 (in Millions)

Source: Administration on Aging, Department of Health and Human Services, "A Profile of Older Americans," www.aoa.gov/aoaroot/aging_statistics/profile/2009/4.aspx.

WORK IT OUT 8.2

Identifying Resources

Check with local advocacy groups or on the Internet for information on the types of accommodations you might make for people with various disabilities and how best to interact with people who have specific disabilities (e.g., sight, mobility, hearing impairment). Collect and read literature on the subject. Share the information with other students and/or co-workers (if you currently work in a customer service environment).

What to look for:

Definitions of various disabilities.

Strategies for better communication.

Accommodations necessary to allow customer access to products and services.

Resources available (e.g., tools, equipment, training, or organizations).

Bibliographic information on disabilities (e.g., books or articles).

abrupt in his or her response, think about whether you might have nonverbally signaled impatience because of your perception that he or she was slow in acting or responding.

Customer Service Success Tip

Use the following strategies to help enhance communication with all customers:

- Face the person.
- Talk slowly and enunciate words clearly (but do not overexaggerate your mouth's movements).
- Keep your hands away from your mouth.
- Talk without food or chewing gum in your mouth.
- Observe the customer's nonverbal cues.
- Reword statements or ask questions again, if necessary.
- Be positive, be patient, and practice the good listening skills covered in Chapter 5.
- Stand near good lighting, and keep background noise to a minimum, when possible.
- If an interpreter is with the customer, talk to the customer and not the interpreter. The interpreter will know what to do.

Be Patient

Allow older customers the time to look around, respond, react, or ask questions. Value their decisions. Also, keep in mind that as some people age, their ability to process information lessens and their attention span becomes shorter. Do not assume that this is true of all older customers, but be patient when it does occur.

Answer Questions

Providing information to customers is crucial in order to help them make reasonable decisions. Even though you may have just explained something, listen to the customer's questions, respond, and restate. If it appears that the customer has misunderstood, try repeating the information, possibly using slightly different words.

Try Not to Sound Patronizing

If you appear to talk down to older customers, problems could arise and you could lose a customer. Customers who are elderly should not be treated as if they are senile! A condescending attitude will often cause any customer, elderly or otherwise, to take his or her business elsewhere.

Remain Professional

Common courtesy and professionalism should always be extended to customers without regard for their age. Words such as please, thank you, yes sir/ma'am, and other such pleasantries can go a long way in building customer–provider relationships and show that you respect and appreciate your customers.

Unfortunately, some service representatives get caught up in being over-familiar with customers, especially if they seem easy-going and kind. This is a common error for many people in more informal cultures such as in the United States. Do not let yourself fall into the trap of addressing older customers accompanied by their children or grandchildren with "Good morning, Grandma" or some similar comment just because one of their family members used that language. Such an approach is unprofessional, inappropriate, disrespectful, and rude. It is also likely to offend either the person whom you are addressing or his or her companion.

Guard against Biases

Be careful not to let biases about older people interfere with good service. Don't ignore or offend older customers by making statements such as "Hang on, old timer. I'll be with you in a minute." Such a statement might be in jest, but nonetheless it is potentially offensive to the person, and to others who might hear it. Similarly, do not use such age-based comments when referring to an older co-worker or external customer since these might be overheard by others and may cause people to form opinions about your level of professionalism or your beliefs regarding older people as a result. Either could cause problems in the workplace and ultimately impact service potential.

YOUNGER CUSTOMERS

You have heard the various terms describing the "younger generation"—Generation Y, Nexters, MTV generation, Millennial Generation, or cyber kids. Whatever the term, this group follows Generation X (born 1964–1977) and is now in the workplace in great numbers as employees and consumers.

Financially, the group accounts for billions of dollars in business revenue for products such as clothes, music, videos, electronic entertainment equipment,

> **Street Talk**
>
> Different cultures and different ways of doing things in a business today mean that you need to be a wealth of information about how to work positively with your colleagues, your customers, and the management team in your company. If you work with a diverse population, study the cultures in the resources you can locate in the library or on the Internet.
>
> SHARON MASSEN, PH.D., CAP *Massen and Associates*

Younger customers can often have a completely different set of needs. *What are some effective strategies for handling customers of a younger generation?*

younger customers Subjective term referring to anyone younger than the service provider. Sometimes used to describe members of Generation X (born to baby boomers) or later.

and entertainment consumption. Generation Y is a spending force to be reckoned with, and marketers are going after them with a vengeance. If you don't believe this, pick up a magazine and look at the faces of the models, look at the products being sold, and watch the shows being added to television lineups each year. All of this affects the way you will provide service to this generation of customers. Depending on your own age, your attitude toward them will vary. If you are of Gen Y, you may make the mistake of being overly familiar with your age group in delivering service.

If you are a Gen Xer, you will potentially treat members of this generation as you would your own children. Be careful not to do this or to come across as domineering or controlling since this will likely irritate your customer(s).

If you are a baby boomer or older, you may feel paternalistic or maternalistic or might believe some of the stereotypical rhetoric about this group (e.g., low moral values, fragmented in focus, overprotected by legislation and programs). Although some of these descriptions may be accurate for some members of the group, it is dangerous to pigeonhole any group or individual, as you have read. This is especially true when providing service, since service is based on satisfying personal needs and wants.

Remember when you were young and felt that adults didn't understand or care about your wants or needs? Well, your **younger customers** probably feel the same way and will remember how you treat them. Their memories could prompt them to take their business elsewhere if their experience with you is negative.

If you are older, you may be tempted to talk down to them or be flippant. Don't give in to the temptation. Keep in mind that they are customers. If they feel unwelcome, they will take their business and money elsewhere, and they will tell their friends about the poor treatment they received. Just as with older customers, avoid demeaning language and condescending forms of address (*kid, sonny, sweetie, sugar,* or *young woman/man*).

Additional points to remember when dealing with younger customers is that they may not have the product knowledge and sophistication in communicating that older customers might have. You can decrease confusion and increase communication effectiveness by using words that are appropriate for their age group and by taking the time to explain and/or demonstrate technical points. Keep it simple without being patronizing if you are older than your customers and make sure not to allow any frustration to show in your tone of voice.

WORK IT OUT 8.3

Serving a Variety of Customers

Pair up with a peer and use the following scenarios as the basis of role-plays to give you practice and feedback in dealing with various categories of customers. Before beginning, discuss how you might deal with each customer in a real-life situation. After the role-plays, both persons should answer the following questions and discuss any ideas for improvement.

Questions

1. How well do you feel that service was provided?

2. Were any negative or unclear messages, verbal or nonverbal, communicated? If yes, discuss.

3. What open-end questions were used to discover customer needs? What others could have been used?

4. How can identified areas for improvement be incorporated into a real customer service encounter?

Scenario 1

You are an airport shuttle driver and just received a call from your dispatcher to proceed to 8172 Dealy Lane to pick up Cassandra Fenton. You were told that Ms. Fenton is blind and will need assistance getting her bags from the house to the bus. Upon arrival, you find Ms. Fenton waiting on her front porch with her bags.

Scenario 2

Mrs. Zagowski is 62 years old and is in the library where you are working at the circulation desk. As you observe her, you notice that she seems a bit frustrated and confused. You saw her browse through several aisles of books, then talk briefly with the reference librarian, and finally go to the computer containing the publication listings and their locations. You are going to try to assist her. Upon meeting her, you realize that she has a hearing deficit and has difficulty hearing what you are saying.

Scenario 3

You are the owner of a small hobby shop that specializes in coins, stamps, comics, and sports memorabilia. Tommy Chin, whom you recognize as a regular "browser," has come in while you are particularly busy. After looking through numerous racks of comic books and trading cards, he is now focused on autographed baseballs in a display case. You believe that he cannot afford them, although he is asking about prices and for other information.

KNOWLEDGE CHECK

1. What are some strategies that you might use to ensure effective communication with your customers who speak a primary language other than your own?

2. How can you better assist customers who have a hearing disability?

3. What are some ways that you can better serve customers with vision impairments?

4. What should you remember to do when serving older customers?

5. How should you approach and interact with customers who are younger than you?

LO 8-6 Communicating with Diverse Customers

CONCEPT Many considerations need to be taken into account when you are delivering service to a diverse customer base. Appropriate language usage is a meaningful tool that you should master for good customer service.

Given all this diversity, you must be wondering how to provide service that is acceptable to all of these customer groups. As you've seen, there are many considerations in delivering service to a diverse customer base. Therefore, consider the following basic guidelines for communicating; these tips are appropriate for dealing with all types of customers.

wiki A form of server software that allows nontechnical personnel to create and edit website pages using any web browser and without complex programming knowledge.

blogs Online journals (web logs) or diaries that allow people to add content. Many organizational websites use them to post "what's new" sections and to receive feedback (good and bad) from customers and website visitors.

podcasts A word that is a derivative of Apple® Computer's iPod® media player and the term *broadcasting*. Through podcasts, websites can offer direct download or streaming of their content (i.e., music or video files) to customers or website users.

inclusive The concept of ensuring that people of all races, genders, and religious and ethnic backgrounds, as well as a multitude of other diverse factors, are included in communications and activities in the workplace.

> ### Customer Service Success Tip
>
> Learn as much technology as you can if you plan to effectively provide service to members of Generations X and Y, since they are very technically savvy. Technology examples include smartphones, iPods, iPads, computer hardware and software, Internet options and services, social media, and service delivery technology such as **wikis**, **blogs** (web logs), and **podcasts.**

Be Careful with Your Remarks and Jokes

Comments that focus on any aspect of diversity (religion, sexual preference, weight, hair color, age) can be offensive and should not be made. Also, humor does not cross cultural boundaries well. Each culture has a different interpretation of what is humorous and socially acceptable.

Make Sure That Your Language Is "Inclusive"

When speaking, address or refer to the people from various groups that are present. If you are addressing a group of two men and one woman, using the term *guys* or *fellows* excludes the woman and thus is not **inclusive**.

Respect Personal Preferences When Addressing People

As you read earlier, don't assume familiarity when addressing others. (Don't call someone by her or his first name unless she or he gives permission.) Don't use *Ms.* if a female customer prefers another form of address. Also, avoid derogatory or demeaning terms such as *honey*, *sugar*, and *sweetheart* or other overly familiar language with either gender.

Use General Terms

Instead of singling a customer out or focusing on exceptions in a group, describe people in general terms. That is, instead of referring to someone as a *female supervisor*, *black salesperson*, or *disabled administrative assistant*, say *supervisor*, *salesperson*, or *administrative assistant*.

Recognize the Impact of Words

Keep in mind that certain words have a negative connotation and could insult or offend. Even if you do not intend to offend, the customer's perception is the deciding factor of your actions. For example, using the terms *handicapped* or *crippled*, *boy*, *girl*, *homo*, *retard*, or *idiot* may conjure up a negative image to some groups or individuals and label you as unprofessional, biased, and inconsiderate. Using such terminology can also reflect negatively upon you and your organization and should never be used.

Use Care with Nonverbal Cues

The nonverbal cues that you are familiar with may carry different meanings in other cultures. Be careful when you use symbols or gestures if you are not certain how your customer will receive them. Figure 8.5 lists some cues that are common in Western cultures but have negative meanings in other cultures.

KNOWLEDGE CHECK

1. What are some strategies that you might use to ensure effective communication with all types of customers?

FIGURE 8.5
Nonverbal Cue Meanings

The following are symbols and gestures that are commonly used in the United States but have different—and negative or offensive—meanings in other parts of the world:

American Gesture or Symbol	Meaning in Other Cultures	Country
Beckoning by curling and uncurling index finger*[†]	Used for calling animals or ladies of the evening	Australia, Hong Kong, Indonesia, Malaysia, Yugoslavia
V for victory sign (with palm facing you)*[‡]	Rude gesture	England
Sole of foot pointed toward a person*[‡]	You are lowly (the sole is the lowest part of the body and contacts the ground)	Egypt, Saudi Arabia, Singapore, Thailand
"Halt" gesture with palm and extended fingers thrust toward someone*[†‡]	Rude epithet	Greece
Thumb up (fingers curled) indicating *okay*, *good going*, or *everything is fine**[‡]	The number 5; rude gesture	Australia, Nigeria, Japan
Thumb and forefinger forming an O, meaning *okay*[‡]	Zero or worthless; money; rude gesture	Brazil, France, Greece, Italy, Japan, Malta, Paraguay, Russia, Tunisia, Turkey
Waving good-bye with fingers extended, palm down, and moving the fingers up and down toward yourself*[‡]	Come here	Parts of Europe, Colombia, Myanmar, Peru
Patting the head of a child	Insult; inviting evil spirits	Parts of the Far East
Using red ink for documents	Death; offensive	Parts of China, Korea, and Mexico
Passing things with left hand (especially food)	Socially unacceptable	India, Pakistan

*R. Axtell, *Gestures: The Do's and Taboos of Body Language around the World* (New York: John Wiley and Sons, 1991).
[†] A. Wolfgang, *Everybody's Guide to People Watching* (Yarmouth, MA: International Press, Yarmouth, 1995).
[‡] D. Morris, *Bodytalk: The Meaning of Human Gestures* (New York: Crown Trade Paperback, 1994).

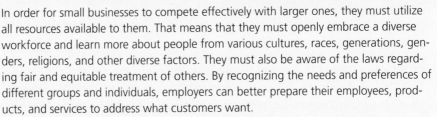

Small Business Perspective

In order for small businesses to compete effectively with larger ones, they must utilize all resources available to them. That means that they must openly embrace a diverse workforce and learn more about people from various cultures, races, generations, genders, religions, and other diverse factors. They must also be aware of the laws regarding fair and equitable treatment of others. By recognizing the needs and preferences of different groups and individuals, employers can better prepare their employees, products, and services to address what customers want.

Part of the initiative to prepare to better deal with diversity involves providing training and job aids that can support employees as they serve customers. Programs such as effective multicultural communication, cultural sensitivity, diversity awareness, behavioral styles, and others that provide insights into how people behave, what they value and believe, their special needs, and any cultural background information are valuable in educating employees about others.

By doing research on the products and services desired and typically used by various groups of customers, small businesses and their employees can become a valuable resource for those seeking specific products and services. This can lead to them being recognized as a prime source or organization that specializes in particular products or in the delivery of culturally and group-specific products and can help themselves stand out from the competitive crowd.

Impact on Service
Based on personal experience and what you just read, answer the following questions:

1. What specific customer needs might employees of a small business have to meet? Explain.

2. How does the changing demographic environment impact the ability of small businesses to compete for customers? Explain.

3. If you worked for a small business, what do you think you would need to know in order to deliver appropriate service to a diverse customer base? Explain.

Key Terms

acculturated

Americans with Disabilities Act of 1990

attitudes

baby boomer

beliefs

blogs

Chicano culture

collective cultures

concept of time

conflict resolution style

cultural diversity

customers with disabilities

diversity

expectations of privacy

face

foreign-born people

form of address

gender roles

hearing disabilities

Hispanic culture

inclusive

individualistic cultures

interpersonal relationship

Latino culture

mobility or motion impairments

modesty

monochromic

namaste

ownership of property

Platinum Rule

podcasts

polychromic

Real-Time IM Relay for Customers with Hearing and Speech Loss

respect for elders

Telecommunications Relay Service (TRS)

values

vision disabilities

wai

wiki

younger customers

Summary

Opportunities to deal with a diverse customer base will increase as the global economy expands. With continuing immigrations, an aging world population, shifts in cultural values, and increased ease of mobility, the only thing certain is that the next customer you speak with will be different from you. Remember, however, that he or she will also be similar to you in many ways and that both of you will have a basis for discussion.

The success you have in the area of dealing with others is totally dependent on your preparation and attitude toward providing quality service. Learn as much as you can about various groups of people in order to effectively evaluate situations, determine needs, and serve all customers on an equal basis.

Review Questions

1. What are some innate qualities or characteristics that make people unique?

2. What external or societal factors affect the way members of a group are seen or perceived?

3. What are values?

4. Do beliefs differ from values? Explain.

5. Why would some people be reluctant to make eye contact with you?

6. When dealing with customers with a disability, how can you best help them?

7. How can recognition of the cultural value of "importance of family" be helpful in customer service?

8. What are some considerations for improving communication in a diverse environment?

9. How can you effectively communicate with someone who has difficulty with the English language?

10. What are some techniques for effectively providing service to older customers?

Search It Out

www.mhhe.com/customerservice

1. Search the Internet for Diversity Information

Search the Internet to locate information and articles related to topics covered in this chapter. Be prepared to share what you found at your next scheduled class or session. The following are some key words you might use in your search:

Any country name (e.g., Australia, Canada, Sri Lanka)

Any religion (e.g., Muslim, Hindu, Buddhist, Christian)

Baby boomers

Beliefs

Cultural diversity

Cultural values

Disabilities

Disability advocacy

Diversity

Elderly

Generation X

Generation Y

Intercultural communication

Intercultural dynamics

IP-Relay

Jellabiya

Population projections

Relay operator

Relay Service

Telecommunications Device for the Deaf (TDD)

Telecommunications Relay Service (TRS)

Telephone typewriter (TTY)

Turban

Ethical Dilemma Summary

Ethical Dilemma 8.1 Possible Answers

1. Does the man's dress or the other employee's comments make a difference in this situation? Explain why or why not.

   Even though we live in a global society where someone can get on a plane and be on the other side of the world within 24 hours, a majority of people in any country have never traveled outside their own borders. They also have little or no contact with people from different ethnic groups or cultures, and have not taken the time to do research on the dress, values, religion, beliefs, and other aspects of other groups. The result is quite honestly ignorance that is often supplanted by negative stereotypes seen in the media, on television, in movies, and from their like-minded, uneducated peers.

   In this instance, the people involved might be reacting to post-9/11 stereotypes that "all of those people" are terrorists simply because they look similar, have the same religion, or come from the same country or geographic region. In reality, nothing is further from the truth. Like any other service situation, this customer should be evaluated based on one-on-one contact and information provided, and not on potentially irrational and unprofessional decisions.

2. What action should you take, if any? Why or why not?

   As a service professional, you should be polite, attentive, and responsive to all customers. Additionally, as an employee of any type of organization (retail or otherwise) you should take ownership of your environment. After all, your employer pays you to be professional and alert on the job. In this situation, the customer seems to be acting in an unusual and possibly suspicious manner. Certainly, security is a concern for anyone these days. You would be correct and prudent to monitor the man's actions and to notify your supervisor, a co-worker, and/or security of the situation just in case the person is up to some unlawful or otherwise inappropriate activity. Because of potential risk, you should not confront such a person yourself, and certainly not alone without others watching the situation.

   Any action you take would likely be precautionary to prevent loss (financial or physical) to your organization yourself and others. Also, in the event that the person is really up to illegal activity, you would likely be doing it out of concern for safety (yours and others).

3. Does the conversation that you had with your co-worker have any bearing on the course of action you choose in this situation? Explain.

   Obviously, such conversations raise awareness and possibilities in your mind; however, since the customer has displayed friendly actions (smiling) and has not done anything other customers might do, you should continue to be professional and courteous.

4. What are possible repercussions if you either act or decide not to act?

   If you fail to act and the person is engaged in some unlawful or mischievous activity, you, others, and the organization could sustain loss, damage, and possible injury. If you do act and the man is not doing anything more than "killing time," the person's perception could be that you are targeting him and potentially could become upset or even claim some sort of discrimination. You could also lose his business and that of anyone to whom he relates his experience.

5. If the person was dressed differently, would you take a different course of action? Explain.

   Truthfully, no matter how a customer is dressed, you should always maintain a positive, attentive, and professional manner. Should other factors (e.g., actions or comments) by the customer indicate that you should treat him or her otherwise, then you should act accordingly (e.g., ask him or her to leave or request assistance from a supervisor, peer, or security).

Ethical Dilemma 8.2 Possible Answers

1. Have you ever witnessed similar situations in the workplace? Explain.

   Spend some time discussing your experience(s) with other students along with the results of such behavior.

2. From a service perspective, is this situation a problem? Explain.

   Even though the customer may not have heard the remarks in this situation, this is unacceptable behavior. You (and possibly others, including customers) may have overheard the remarks. As a service provider, employees represent not only themselves, but also the organization. People form opinions based on what they see workers do and say. This type of incident can lead to lost business, negative word-of-mouth publicity, and claims of defamation and discrimination. Not only is there potential for financial loss, but also damage to the reputation of the service providers involved, other workers, and the organization.

3. What would you do or say about the incident that you just witnessed? Explain.

At the very least, you should intervene to point out that the language is disrespectful, derogatory, and discriminatory and can cause problems for the two employees, others at the organization, and the organization itself. Depending on the reaction you get when approaching the others, you may need to escalate this matter to your supervisor for appropriate action.

4. If you fail to act in this situation, what are possible repercussions? What about if you do act?

Customer Service via Technology

In the world of Internet customer service, it's important to remember that a competitor is only one mouse click away.

—Doug Warner

LEARNING OUTCOMES

After completing this chapter, you will be able to:

9-1 Recognize the role of technology-effective service delivery.

9-2 Describe ways in which technology enhances an organization's service delivery capabilities.

9-3 Discuss ways in which companies are integrating the evolving web-based and mobile technologies into their service strategies.

9-4 Communicate effectively via e-mail, the Internet, and fax.

9-5 Deliver quality service through effective telephone techniques.

To assist you with the content of this chapter, we have added additional review questions, activities, and other valuable resource material at www.mhhe.com/customerservice.

IN THE REAL WORLD TECHNOLOGY—NETFLIX

Netflix is a true turn-around success story. The company was founded in 1997 and is headquartered in California. The company grew and came to dominate the video and Blu-ray disc rental business with its low pricing and fast delivery policies. Companies like Hollywood Video and Blockbuster are two of the casualties that fell by the wayside because they could not compete with the efficiency and popularity of Netflix and other creative video and entertainment providers (e.g., Redbox).

In 2007 Netflix introduced streaming capability. The following year they partnered with Apple and several consumer electronics companies and have since grown to be the leading company streaming videos and TV episodes globally to customers' television sets via Xbox 360, Wii, and PS3 devices and some Internet-connected Blu-ray disc players and HDTVs. Individuals downloading content to their computers can watch it instantly. To capitalize on the latest mobile technology, Netflix created an application (app) that allows iPad, iPhone, and Android and Windows phones and tablets to download content directly to their mobile devices.

There are 900 employees working at the corporate office to serve over 30 million members in the United States, Canada, Latin America, the United Kingdom, Ireland, and the Nordics. The beauty of the technology involved with Netflix is that users do not have to download expensive viewing software to watch movies and television shows they want to see. With streaming video, customers can start accessing content as soon as it is ordered and downloaded.

Compared to cable costs and considering that at a theater a movie for two people, each having popcorn and a drink, can cost upwards of $50 to $60 in some areas, the basic Netflix $7.99 monthly membership price is a true bargain. This service allows members the ability to download an unlimited number of movies or shows and to view them on multiple devices simultaneously. To entice new members, Netflix offers a free one-month trial membership.

Like other major companies before it (e.g., Coke, J.C. Penney, Sears, Kmart, and Pepsi), Netflix leaders made a severe miscalculation related to its products and services in 2011. This error not only cost the company market share and lost customer loyalty, but also put it into a potential death spiral. Briefly, the CEO, Reed Hastings, announced that Netflix was spinning off its DVD-by-mail business into a separate service called Qwikster and raised prices on its service. The result was a huge member outcry, major financial analyst and media criticism, and a drop in stock prices between July 2011 and September 2012 from nearly $300 per share to slightly over $50 per share. Luckily, Mr. Hastings quickly realized that he had erred and reversed the decision, apologized for his bad judgment, and started to get the company back on a comfortable and productive track. The result has been amazing in that stock prices and membership continue to rebound. The company continues its efforts to search out new ways to dominate the video and television entertainment distribution industry. For example, in 2012, they signed a multiyear deal with the Disney Company to exclusively distribute Disney animation and first-run movies. In addition, Netflix started on a path taken by FX, HBO, and AMC and has started developing its own programming. The move is expected to be another success story for the company.

For more information about this organization, visit www.netflix.com or scan the QR code on this page with your smartphone app. Look at their historical and other information about the organization on their website.

Think About It

Based on this organization's profile, answer the following questions and be prepared to discuss your responses.

1. From your personal experiences, what you just read about the company, and what you found on their website, what do you feel are the strengths of the company from an external customer perspective? Explain.

www.netflix.com

2. What societal factors have impacted Netflix and contributed to its popularity and growth? Explain the relationship of these factors to Netflix's growth.

3. What do you think are some future opportunities for growth related to customer service at Netflix? Explain.

4. As a consumer, are you a fan of Netflix and what it has accomplished? Why or why not?

5. How do you feel Mr. Hasting's actions as the CEO have helped or hurt the company? Explain your views.

Quick Preview

Before reviewing the chapter content, respond to the following questions by placing a "T" for true or an "F" for false on the rules. Use any questions you miss as a checklist of material to which you will pay particular attention as you read through the chapter. For those you get right, congratulate yourself, but review the sections they address in order to learn additional details about the topic.

_____ 1. According to the Cellular Telecommunications Industry Association, over 276 million people in the United States subscribe to a wireless telephone service.

_____ 2. E-commerce is a term that means that the commerce of the United States is in excellent condition.

_____ 3. A customer service representative might also have one of the following job titles: associate, sales representative, consumer affairs counselor, consultant, technical service representative, operator, account executive, attendant, or engineer.

_____ 4. The acronym TTY is used by call center staff members to indicate that something is to be done today.

_____ 5. Businesses have not yet learned to harness the power of web-based and mobile technologies to serve their customers.

_____ 6. Many organizations think of technology as a way to reduce staff and save money.

_____ 7. One way to improve your image over the telephone is to continually evaluate your speech.

_____ 8. Jargon, slang, and colloquialisms can distort message meaning.

_____ 9. Adjusting your rate of speech to mirror a customer's rate can aid comprehension.

_____ 10. Quoting policy is one way to ensure that customers understand why you can't give them what they want.

_____ 11. To ensure that accurate communication has taken place, you should summarize key points at the end of a telephone conversation.

_____ 12. Chewing food and gum, drinking, or talking to others while on the telephone can be distracting and should be avoided.

_____ 13. Using voice mail to answer calls is an effective way to avoid interruptions while you are speaking to a customer.

_____ 14. Planning calls and the information you will leave on a voice mail is an effective way to avoid service breakdown.

_____ 15. Because of the cost of technology, small businesses cannot effectively benefit from its use as a customer service tool.

Answers to Quick Preview can be found at the end of the chapter.

LO 9-1 The Role of Technology in Customer Service

CONCEPT Customer service is a 24/7 responsibility, and technology can assist in making it effective.

To say that technology has permeated almost every aspect of life in most developed countries would be an understatement. With the number of Internet users continuing to climb throughout the world, it is no wonder that online sales of products and services continue to rise.

Research conducted by McKinsey and Company "into the Internet economies of the G-8 nations as well as Brazil, China, India, South Korea, and Sweden finds that the web accounts for a significant and growing portion of global GDP. Indeed, if measured as a sector, Internet-related consumption and expenditure is now bigger than agriculture or energy. On average, the

FIGURE 9.1
Impact of the Internet Worldwide

- Various sources track Internet usage throughout the world and report data related to demographics, penetration rates, and other factors. The following are some attention-getting figures:
- 2,405,518,376 Internet users worldwide, www.internetworldstats.com/stats.htm
- 1,076,681,059 users in Asia (highest usage worldwide), www.internetworldstats.com/stats.htm
- 273,785,413 North American users, www.internetworldstats.com/stats.htm
- Top five countries with Internet users (in this order): China, United States, India, Japan, Brazil, www.internetworldstats.com/top20.htm
- Top five languages used on the Internet (in this order): English, Chinese, Spanish, Japanese, Portuguese, www.internetworldstats.com/stats7.htm

Internet contributes 3.4 percent to GDP in the 13 countries covered by the research." Further, "The United States is the largest player in the global Internet supply ecosystem, capturing more than 30 percent of global Internet revenues and more than 40 percent of net income."[1] Imagine the sales potential and impact on customer service if only 25 percent of people worldwide bought online regularly. Obviously, with the high number of users, Internet usage is not just a Generation X or Generation Y tool. Consumers of all ages are using the Internet for many reasons. Figure 9.1 illustrates the impact of the Internet around the world.

Computers and other forms of technology are continually becoming smaller, more complex, and more powerful; we have only started to see the impact that technology will have on shaping the future. Most businesses in

QR Code (Quick Response Code) Similar in concept to the standard barcode that appears on retail products, this code can allow access to virtually any type of stored information about products, services, or organizations.

Trending NOW

QR Codes

A **QR code (Quick Response code)** is similar in concept to the standard barcode that appears on retail products. Those products contain embedded product and price information that can be accessed by handheld readers. Originally, the QR code was used in the automotive industry in Japan but has since moved beyond to other industries due to its faster readability and capacity to store more information. It can allow access to virtually any type of stored information about products, services, or organizations.

Businesses have realized the potential of the code and started to use it other than for product information. As you have seen in this book, by scanning a code with a smartphone or other specially equipped camera device, consumers can be directed to a website where additional information about the book or supplemental resources may be accessed.

In 2011, the Royal Dutch Mint issued a special coin with a three-dimensional image on one side and a QR

Code on the back that, when scanned, takes users to a special website where historical information about the coin can be read. This is just one of the creative uses for this useful technology.

First coin minted in the world with a QR code on one side and a three-dimensional image on the other. Minted by the Royal Dutch Mint in 2011.

The technology of today progresses more rapidly than most people can keep up with. *What are you doing to stay abreast of industry technology changes?*

offshoring Refers to the relocation of business services from one country to another (e.g., services, production, and manufacturing).

outsourcing Refers to the practice of contracting with third-party companies or vendors outside the organization (usually in another country) to deliver products and services to customers or produce products.

the United States are technologically dependent in some form. Calculators, cash registers, maintenance equipment, telephones, radios, cellular phones, pagers, computer systems, and handheld personal planners are typical examples of technology that we rely upon. We have become a 24/7 society (we access technology 24 hours a day, 7 days a week) and can communicate at any time and in virtually any place. Examples of the way that people use technology to give and receive service include students who communicate with their instructors or register and take courses online, arranging to order or return merchandise, and tracking package shipments. According to ChartsBin.com the current worldwide number of mobile cellular telephone subscriptions is 5,371,029,000.[2] The United States has almost 279 million of those users.

As a result, more people are accessing telephone-related customer service and the economies of many countries are being significantly influenced by technology-based customer services. Business is being done more than ever via mobile applications as people use their smartphones to replace personal devices and computers to surf the Internet and place orders. This is especially true of younger consumers, who view e-mail and personal computers as old technology. One study points to 38 percent of retail activity conducted by younger users as an indication that this technology is on the upswing.[3]

There has been some shrinkage in the number and size of call centers in the United States due to the following: **offshoring** call center functions to other countries (e.g., India, Mexico, or the Philippines), **outsourcing** to third-party companies that specialize in call center operations, and the rise in self-service web or speech recognition technologies that allow customers to place their own orders and access information without contacting a customer care representative. However, due to the sagging economy that started around 2007, those numbers will likely stabilize and actually grow in coming years. One factor that could help stimulate the growth of call centers is an increased demand by customers for technology-based ordering and service systems. With a decline in the economy in the first decade of the twenty-first century, and factors such as reduced family incomes and increased gasoline prices, more people are opting to do their shopping and business from the comfort of their own home. Because of the convenience of online shopping, the trend is likely to continue to grow in the future. For example, instead of driving to the bank to check their account or deal with an issue, customers simply log online or call. This saves time and vehicle operating costs.

All of this means that companies that are not prepared to meet the future will lose business as customers migrate to providers that are better prepared. With access to products and services at almost any time through telephones, wireless telephones, e-mail, facsimile machines, and the Internet, customers

Many organizations are striving to find new ways to apply technology to enhance service and connect with customers and others.

FIGURE 9.2

Using Technology to Better Serve

Organization	Application
American Automobile Association www.aaa.com	AAA mobile services are being provided via GPS-enabled wireless telephones. Members can access directions and restaurant and hotel information, and in case of a need for roadside assistance, their vehicle's location can be determined in order to dispatch help.
Travelocity, Expedia, and Priceline www.travelocity.com www.expedia.com www.priceline.com	All three services and others like them act as online discount brokers for hotels, car rental companies, airlines, and other travel-related services. These organizations have pulled together a huge system of discounted travel services that consumers can access and through which they can make reservations for a fee.
Meriwether Lewis Elementary School www.lewiselementary.org/	This school uses blogs as an organization as well as providing a location for educators to create their own blogs related to their classes and extracurricular activities. Parents, staff, students, and other interested parties can access important information 24/7 via the Internet, even when the school is closed.
Barack Obama	During his bid for president of the United States in 2008, Barak Obama's campaign tapped into the power of iPhone, Twitter, social media, a website, and other technology to raise millions of dollars in campaign funds and communicate with supporters in a short period of time. In doing so, he set a new precedent for future political campaigns by showing the power of technology in reaching out to potential contributors.

are in a power position as never before. Many organizations are looking for new service applications for available technology. Figure 9.2 illustrates how some organizations are embracing technology to better serve their customers.

KNOWLEDGE CHECK

1. In what ways are the Internet and technology affecting people and businesses around the world?
2. What is causing the number and size of call centers in the United States to shrink?

LO 9-2 The Customer Contact/Call Center or Help Desk

CONCEPT   Electronic commerce is an expanding and powerful way to employ technology to conduct business.

Because of the expansion of technology used by customer support staff in many organizations, customer contact or customer care centers (called call centers and by other names by some organizations) providing technology-based

Electronic Mail (E-mail)

electronic mail (e-mail) System used to transmit messages around the Internet. This technology is being replaced with instant messaging (IM) in some call centers as many younger consumers embrace it as a primary form of communication.

spamming or spam An abusive use of various electronic messaging systems and technology to send unsolicited and indiscriminant bulk messages to people (also used with instant messaging, web search engines, blogs, and other formats).

facsimile (fax) machine Equipment that converts printed words and graphics into electronic signals and allows them to be transmitted across telephone lines then reassembled into a facsimile of the words and graphics on the receiving end.

fax-on-demand Technology that allows information, such as a form, stored in a computer to be requested electronically via a telephone and transmitted to a customer.

instant messaging Communication technology that allows people to type messages back and forth and see the other person's message as soon as it is sent. They can then respond quickly as if having a conversation over the telephone. This technology has replaced e-mail as a form of written communication in some call centers.

intelligent callback technology Technology that gathers information from the customer and tells the customer when he or she can expect a callback.

interactive kiosks or digital displays Computer terminals that have customized software and hardware and set up in a public area where users can touch a screen display to access application for information, commerce, education, or entertainment.

Electronic mail (e-mail) provides an inexpensive, rapid way of communicating with customers in writing worldwide. It allows customers to access information via telephone and then, through prompting (and using the telephone keypad), have the information delivered to them via e-mail. A big advantage of e-mail is that you can write a single message and have it delivered to hundreds of people worldwide in a matter of minutes at little or no cost. The downside of using this vehicle from a customer standpoint is that **spamming** or sending **spam** by unscrupulous people and organizations has given e-mail advertisers in general a bad reputation.

Facsimile (Fax) Machine

A **facsimile (fax) machine** allows graphics and text messages to be transported as electronic signals via telephone lines or from a personal computer equipped with a modem. Information can be sent anywhere in the world in minutes, or a customer can make a call, key in a code number, and have information delivered to his or her fax machine or computer without ever speaking to a person (**fax-on-demand** system).

In most instances, fax machines have given way to computer technology that allows senders to scan images into their computer and send them as attachments to e-mail messages.

Instant Messaging

Instant messaging is a type of technology that allows online chats in real-time text transmission over the Internet between customers and service representatives. Short messages are typically transmitted between the two parties. Once someone types in his or her message and hits send, the other person sees it immediately and can respond. Some more advanced systems use technology that provides real-time texting in which each character typed is seen simultaneously by the receiver as the message is being written.

Intelligent Callback Technology

Customer expectations continue to grow and change as new technology is introduced into the workplace. One result is that they have become far less tolerant of long wait times to receive service. To address this concern, many organizations have introduced **intelligent callback technology** into their call centers. With this equipment, they are able to allow customers to decide whether they prefer to wait to speak to a representative or would rather receive a scheduled callback. Such technology gathers information from the customer and tells the customer when he or she can expect a callback. Thus, the call center experience becomes more managed by the customer, is more convenient, and potentially provides a greater degree of customer satisfaction.

Interactive Kiosks or Digital Displays

Interactive kiosks or digital displays are an evolving technology that allows customers and customer contact centers equipped with video camera–computer hookups to interact via the computer. Similar to interactive kiosks by companies like INTOUCH Interactive, Four Winds Interactive, or

Symon where customers can view product videos or other product information, this technology allows customers and agents to see one another during their interactions. Many organizations are now using these in lobbies to allow self-service to customers. You may have seen these at airline check-ins, banks (ATMs), or in theme parks or other entertainment venues. Walt Disney World has been using this technology at their theme parks for years to allow guest to use kiosks to make their restaurant reservations upon arrival in the park. Because of privacy concerns or preference, some software allows customers to block their image, yet they still see the agent to whom they are speaking.

Interactive Voice Response (IVR) System or Voice Response Unit (VRU)

An **interactive voice response (IVR) system** or **voice response unit (VRU)** allows customers to call in 24 hours a day, 7 days a week, even when customer service representatives are not available. By keying in a series of numbers on the phone, customers can get information or answers to questions. Such systems perform a text-to-speech conversion to present database information audibly to a caller. They also ensure consistency of information. Banks and credit card companies use such systems to allow customers to access account information.

Internet Callback Technology

Internet callback technology allows someone browsing the Internet to click on words or phrases (e.g., *Call me*), enter his or her phone number, and continue browsing. This triggers a predictive dialing system (discussed later in this chapter) and assigns an agent to handle the call when it rings at the customer's end.

Internet Telephony

Internet telephony allows users to have voice communications over the Internet. Although widely discussed in the industry, call center Internet telephony is in its infancy, lacks standards, and is not currently embraced by consumers. Power outages, quality issues with transmissions, and other technical glitches have prevented this medium from becoming widely used by most organizations.

Media Blending

Media blending allows agents to communicate with a customer over a telephone line at the same time information is displayed over the Internet to the customer. As with Internet telephony, this technology has not yet been taken to its full potential.

Online InformationFulfillment System

Online information fulfillment systems allow customers to go to the World Wide Web, access an organization's website, and click on desired information. This is one of the fastest-growing customer service technologies. Every competitive business will eventually use this system so that customers can get information and place orders.

interactive voice response (IVR) system Technology that allows customers to call an organization 24 hours a day, 7 days a week to get information from recorded messages or a computer by keying a series of numbers on the telephone keypad in response to questions or prompts.

voice response unit (VRU) System that allows customers to call 24 hours a day, 7 days a week by keying a series of numbers on the telephone keypad in order to get information or answers to questions.

Internet callback technology Technology that allows someone browsing the Internet to key a prompt on a website and have a service representative call a phone number provided.

Internet telephony Technology that allows people to talk to one another via the Internet as if they were on a regular telephone.

media blending Technology that allows a service provider to communicate with a customer via telephone while at the same time displaying information to the customer over the computer.

online information fulfillment system Technology that allows a customer to access an organization's website and click on desired information without having to interact with a service provider.

Predictive Dialing System

Predictive dialing systems automatically place outgoing calls and deliver incoming calls to the next available agent. This type of system is often used in outbound (telemarketing/call center) operations. Because of numerous abuses, the government is continually restricting its use.

Screen Pop-Ups

Screen pop-ups are used in conjunction with ANI and IVR systems to identify callers. As a call is received and dispatched to an agent, the system provides information about the caller that "pops" onto the agent's screen before he or she answers the telephone (e.g., order information, membership data, service history, contact history).

Speech or Voice Recognition

Speech- or voice-recognition programs allow a system to recognize keywords or phrases from a caller. These systems can be for routing callers to a representative and for retrieving information from a database. This technology is incorporated into a customer contact center's voice response system. It is typically used by individuals to dictate data directly into a computer, which then converts the spoken words into text. There are a variety of potential applications for voice-recognition systems for all contact centers. Some organizations are recording customers' voices (passwords and phrases) as a means of identification so that customers can gain access to their accounts without allowing unauthorized persons to break into them and steal personal information. With other applications, agents speak into a computer, instead of typing data, and people who have disabilities can obtain data from their accounts by speaking into the computer.

In addition to use in call centers, voice-recognition software is being used by many of the world's largest companies to facilitate customer service and provide services through their products. Examples can be found in Apple products that use their Siri attendant, automotive manufacturers that have telephone and media integration built into many of their cars, and banks (e.g., Wells Fargo and Bank of America) that use it for their automated attendant systems.

Telephone Typewriter System (TTY)

Partly because of the passage of the 1990 Americans with Disabilities Act in the United States, and similar laws in other countries, which required

Trending NOW

Self-Service and Digital Channels Like Chat and E-Mail Are Rising in Popularity

Channel usage rates are also quickly changing: we've seen a 12 percent rise in web self-service usage, a 24 percent rise in chat usage, and a 25 percent increase in community usage for customer service in the past three years. Expect customer service organizations to better align their channel strategy this year to support their company's customers' needs. Expect them to also work on guiding customers to the right channel based on the complexity and time sensitivity of interactions.[4]

that telecommunication services be available to people with disabilities, organizations now have the technology to assist customers who have hearing and speech impairments. By using a **Telephone Typewriter system (TTY)**—a typewriter-like device for sending messages back and forth over telephone lines—a person who has a hearing or speech impairment can contact someone who is using a standard telephone. The sender and the receiver type their messages using the TTY. To do this, the sender or receiver can go through an operator-assisted relay service provided by local and long-distance telephone companies to reach companies and individuals who do not have TTY receiving technology, or the user can get in touch directly with companies that have TTYs. The service is free of charge. Operators can help first-time hearing-disabled users understand the rules in using TTY. Also, local speech and hearing centers can often provide training on the use of TTY in a call center environment.

The federal government has a similar service (Federal Information Relay Service, or FIRS) for individuals who wish to conduct business with any branch of the federal government nationwide.

With the advent of technology in phones, cars, and other electronic devices that can accept, translate, and respond to spoken words, new tools are being developed daily that can enhance the customer experience. *In what ways have you experienced speech recognition technology and how do you think it will impact customer service?*

Voice over Internet Protocol (VoIP)

Another video-based service option for businesses that has been used by individuals for a number of years is known as **Voice over Internet Protocol (VoIP)** and allows voice communications combined with multimedia, such as video images, to be transported over the Internet. This free or low-cost means of communication has been popular with users as an alternative to long-distance calling that does not allow speakers to see one another. Various software and service providers, such as Microsoft's Skype, Linphone, and Google Voice, offer this means for organizations to connect via voice and images with their customers. In addition to video capability, companies can transfer files and conduct videoconferences.

Telephone Typewriter system (TTY) A typewriter-like device used by people with hearing disabilities for typing and sending messages back and forth via telephone lines. It is also known as telecommunications device for the deaf (TDD).

Voice over Internet Protocol (VoIP) Technologies, methodologies, and transmission techniques involved in the delivery of voice and image communication via the Internet.

KNOWLEDGE CHECK

1. How have changes in technology changed the look and operation of call centers?

2. What are some traditional call center technologies and how have they improved customer service?

3. How is customer relationship management software being used in call centers?

Street Talk

When talking on the telephone, be sure that the phone is inactive before commenting on the conversation to a colleague nearby. If the phone call is still active, the customer will hear any comments you may make before the line is inactive.

SHARON MASSEN, PH.D., CAP *Massen and Associates*

of privacy, and concerns that their personal and financial information might be compromised, leading to future issues with their credit.

Informed customers go to great lengths to protect their credit card, merchant account, and social security numbers; addresses; and personal data (e.g., arrest records, medical history, and family data). Many news stories have warned of criminal activity associated with technology. The result is that customers, especially those who are technically naive, have a level of distrust and paranoia related to giving information via the Internet and over the phone to unsolicited callers. This is why many websites involved in e-commerce offer the option of calling a toll-free number instead of entering credit card and other personal information into an Internet order form. If you, as a customer service provider, encounter a lot of this type of reluctance, notify your supervisor. Some systemic issues may be adding to your customers' fears. You have a personal responsibility and a vested interest to improve processes and procedures in the organization. Helping identify these issues and dealing with them can make life easier for you and your customers while helping the organization improve the quality of service delivered and potentially increasing revenue streams. The latter can lead to more available cash for new equipment, facilities, salaries, and benefits.

One thing to remember is that a customer's reluctance to provide you with information is not necessarily a reflection on you or your service-providing peers; it is based more on a distrust in the system. Figure 9.3 lists some strategies you can use to help reduce customer fears related to communicating via technology.

Trending NOW

Wait Time Reduction Technology

According to *The Wall Street Journal*, retail organizations are taking steps towards better customer satisfaction by using technology to reduce service wait times.[9] Some examples of this are

- Kroger Supermarkets have installed infrared body heat-sensing cameras (like those used by the military and law enforcement) known as QueVision at entrances and cash registers of 95 percent of its stores. These devices sense the number of people waiting and signal that new lanes need to be opened. The result is that average wait times have been lowered from four minutes to 26 seconds.

- Chili's Restaurants allow diners to pay at their table with a small flat-screen device so that their credit card never leaves their sight and they do not have to wait for a server's assistance to check out.

- Walmart is testing a "Scan & Go" iPhone application that allows customers to scan bar code items they are buying as they shop and place them in bags. When they get to the register, they hold their phone to the self-checkout screen and the information is wirelessly transferred.

- Nordstrom department stores are using handheld devices that allow customers to pay an associate anywhere in their store, rather than proceeding to a single checkout line.

Avoiding customer concerns is often as simple as communicating effectively. Try some of the following approaches to help reassure your customers about the security of technology:

- Emphasize the organization's policy on security and service. If customers voice concerns about providing a credit card number over the phone or on the Internet, you might respond with "This is not a problem. You can either fax or mail the information to us."
- Stress participation in consumer watchdog or community organizations (e.g., Better Business Bureau or Chamber of Commerce), if your organization participates.
- Direct customers to areas on your website that show your digital certificate or security level (e.g., a Secure Socket Layer [SSL] logo from a third-party certifying source like VeriSign or Thawte) and that indicate the encryption of information entered into the order system and transferred electronically.
- Point out any website page that shows the organization's history and shows how long you have been in business (assuming there has been a period of time since establishment). The longevity of a company can subconsciously allay fears and convince people that you have been around for a while and are not likely to go out of business tomorrow.
- Ask for only pertinent information.
- Answer questions quickly and openly (e.g., if a customer asks why you need certain information, respond in terms of customer service, such as, "We need that information to ensure that we credit the right account.").
- Avoid asking for personal and financial account information when possible.
- Offer other options for data submission, if they are available.
- When using the telephone, smile and sound approachable in order to establish rapport (customers can "hear" a smile over the telephone).
- Listen carefully for voice tones that indicate hesitancy or uncertainty and respond appropriately (e.g., "You sound a bit hesitant about giving that information, Mr. Hopkins. Let me assure you that nothing will be processed until we have actually shipped your order.").
- Communicate in short, clear, and concise terms and sentences. Also, avoid technical or "legal" language that might confuse or frustrate the customer.
- Explain how personal information will be used or stored.

FIGURE 9.3
Reducing Customer Fears about Technology

KNOWLEDGE CHECK

1. What are some reasons why technology has assumed a more dominant role in customer service?
2. What are some trends leading to the expansion of the use of technology to serve customers?
3. How many common call center technologies can you list?
4. In what ways are organizations tapping today's technology to better serve potential and existing customers?
5. What are some advantages of technology related to customer service?
6. List some of the disadvantages of technology related to customer service.

Customer Service Success Tip

Never send financial, proprietary, or confidential information (e.g., credit card numbers, medical information, social security numbers, or personal or employment history information) via e-mail since it is an unsecured method of communicating.

the time and date that a message was opened. The downside of that is that your receivers can cancel the return notification on their end and you will still not know if the message ever arrived.

- *Use organization e-mail for business only.* Many companies have policies prohibiting sending personal e-mail via their system. Some companies have started to actively monitor outgoing messages and many now can use unauthorized use of the e-mail as grounds for dismissal. Avoid violating your company's policy on this. Remember, too, that while you are sending personal messages, you are wasting productive time and your customers may be waiting. Unless you have security software that will decode and mask the information, hackers or others who do not have a right or need to know such information can gain access to it. A good rule of thumb is to never send anything by e-mail that you would not want to see in tomorrow's newspaper.

- *Use blind courtesy copies sparingly.* Most e-mail systems allow you to send a copy to someone without the original addressee knowing it (a blind courtesy copy, or bcc). If the recipient becomes aware of the bcc, your actions might be viewed as suspicious and your motives brought into question. A customer might view your actions as an attempt to hide something from him or her. Thus, a relationship breakdown could occur if the original recipient discovers the existence of the bcc or if the recipient of the bcc misuses the information.

- *Copy only necessary people.* Nowadays, most people are overloaded with work and do not have the time to read every e-mail. If someone does not need to see a message, do not send that person a copy with the "reply to all" function available in e-mail programs. When you do the latter, anyone listed as a recipient or copied will get the return e-mail.

emoticons (emotional icons) Humorous characters that send visual messages such as smiling or frowning. They are created with various strokes of the computer keyboard characters and symbols.

- *Get permission to send advertisements or promotional materials.* As mentioned earlier, people have little time or patience to read lengthy e-mail messages, especially from someone trying to promote or sell them something. This is viewed the same way you probably think of unsolicited junk mail or telemarketing calls at home. Companies should routinely have an "opt-out" check box available when they are soliciting e-mail information from their customers. If your company does not have this option, it might be well for management to consider such an option as a service to their customers and potential customers.

- *Be cautious in using emoticons.* **Emoticons (emotional icons)** are the faces created through the use of computer keyboard characters. Many people believe that their use in business correspondence is inappropriate and too informal. Also, since humor is a matter of personal point of view, these symbols might be misinterpreted and confusing. This is especially true when you are corresponding with someone from a different culture. Figure 9.5 shows examples of emoticons.

It is so easy to send a potentially offensive message via the computer, especially if you are in a hurry. *What do you do to ensure that you follow accepted e-mail protocol and etiquette when sending messages?*

FIGURE 9.5
Sample Emoticons

:-)	Happy	:-}	Embarrassment or sarcasm
:-(	Sad	:-D	Big grin or laugh
;-)	Flirting or wink	<:-)	Stupid question (dunce cap)
O /\	Defiant or determined	O:-)	Angel or saint
:-O	Yelling or surprised	>:-)	Devil
:-x	Lips are sealed	:~/	Really confused

- *Fill in your address line last.* This is a safety mechanism to ensure that you take the time to read and think about your message before you send the e-mail. The message cannot be transmitted until you address it. You will have one last chance to think about the effect of the message on the recipient.

FACSIMILE

As with any other form of communication, there are certain dos and don'ts to abide by when you use a fax machine to transmit messages. Failing to adhere to these simple guidelines can cause frustration, anger, and a breakdown in the relationships between you and your customers or others to whom you send messages.

- *Be considerate of your receiver.* If you plan to send a multipage document to your customer, telephone in advance to make sure that it is OK and a good time to send it. This is especially true if you will be using a business number during the workday or if there is only one line for the telephone and fax machine. It is frustrating and irritating to customers when their fax is tied up because large documents are being transmitted. If you must send a large document, try to do so before or after working hours (e.g., before 9 a.m. or after 5 p.m.). Also, keep in mind geographic time differences. Following these tips can also help maintain good relationships with co-workers who may depend on the fax machine to conduct business with their customers.

- *Limit graphics.* Graphic images that are not needed to clarify written text waste the receiver's printer cartridge ink, tie up the machine unduly, and can irritate your receiver. Therefore, delete any unnecessary graphics (or solid colored areas) including your corporate logo on a cover sheet if it is heavily colored and requires a lot of ink to print. (If appropriate, create a special outline image of your logo for your fax cover sheets.)

- *Limit correspondence recipients.* As with e-mail and memorandums, limit the recipients of your messages. If they do not have a need to know, do not send them messages. Check your broadcast mailing list (a list of people who will receive all messages, often programmed into a computer) to ensure that it is limited to people who "have a need to know." This is also important from the standpoint of confidentiality. If the information you are sending is proprietary or sensitive in any way, think about who will receive it. Do not forget that unless the document is going directly to someone's computer fax modem, it may be lying in a stack of other incoming messages and accessible by people other than your intended recipient.

checking information for the customer on the line and with his or her permission. Your voice quality will alert the customer to the fact that you are otherwise occupied.

- *Answer promptly.* A lot is communicated by the way a phone call is handled. One tip for success is to always answer by the third or fourth ring. This sends a nonverbal message to your customers of your availability to serve them. It also reduces the irritating ringing that you, co-workers, or customers have to hear.

FIGURE 9.7

Transfer Calls and Use the Hold Function Properly

Be sure you understand how the telephone transfer (sometimes called the link) and hold functions work. Nothing is more frustrating or irritating for callers than to be shuffled from one person to the next or to be placed on what seems to be an endless hold. Here are some suggestions that can help to increase your effectiveness in these areas:

- **Always request permission before transferring a caller.** This shows respect for the caller and psychologically gives the caller a feeling of control over the conversation. You can also offer options (you can ask the caller to allow a transfer or let you take a message). This is especially helpful when the customer is already irritated or has a problem. Before transferring the call, explain why you need to do so. You might say, "The person who handles billing questions is Shashandra Philips at extension 4739. May I transfer you, or would you rather I take a message and pass it along to her?" This saves you and the caller time and effort, and you have provided professional, courteous service. If the caller says, "Yes, please transfer me," follow by saying something like, "I'd be happy to connect you. Again, if you are accidentally disconnected, I'll be calling Shashandra Philips at extension 4739."

- **Once you have successfully reached the intended person,** announce the call by saying, "Shashandra, this is (your name), from (your department). I have (customer's name) on the phone. She has a (question, problem). Are you the right person to handle that?" If Shashandra answers yes, connect the caller and announce, "(Customer's name), I have Shashandra Philips on the line. She will be happy to assist you. Thanks for calling (or some similar positive disconnect phrase)." You can then hang up, knowing that you did your part in delivering quality customer service.

  If the call taker is not available or is not the appropriate person, reconnect with the customer and explain the situation. Then offer to take a message rather than trying to transfer to different people while keeping the customer on hold. You would make an exception if the call taker informed you of the appropriate person to whom you should transfer, or if the customer insisted on staying on the line while you tried to transfer to the right person.

blind transfer The practice of transferring an incoming caller to another telephone number.

- **You should avoid making a blind transfer.** This practice is ineffective, rude, and not customer-focused. A **blind transfer** happens when a service provider asks a caller, "May I transfer you to Cathy in Billing?" or may even say, without permission, "Let me transfer you to Tom in Shipping." Once the intended transfer party answers, the person transferring the call hangs up. Always announce your caller by waiting for the phone to be picked up and saying, "This is (your name) in (your department). I have (customer's name) on the line. Can you take the call?" Failure to do this could result in a confrontation between the two people. If the calling customer is already upset, you have just set up a situation that could lead to a lost customer and/or angry co-worker.

- **If you place someone on hold,** it is a good idea to go back on the line every 20 to 30 seconds to let the person know that you have not forgotten the call. This action becomes more important if the phone system you are using does not offer information or music that the customer hears during the holding time.

- **One final word about holds.** Once you return to the phone to take the call, thank the caller for waiting.

- *Use titles with names.* It has been said that there is nothing sweeter than hearing one's own name. However, until you are told otherwise, use a person's title (e.g., Mr., Mrs., Ms., or Dr.) and last name. Do not assume that it is alright to use first names. Some people regard the use of their first name as insolent or rude. This may especially be true of older customers and people from other cultures where respect and use of titles are valued. When you are speaking with customers, it is also a good idea to use their name frequently (don't overdo it, though, or you'll sound mechanical). Repeat the name directly after the greeting (e.g., "Yes, Dr. Carmine, how may I help you?"), during the conversation (e.g., "One idea I have, Mr. Perrier, is to . . ."), and at the end of the call (e.g., "Thanks for calling, Mrs. Needham. I'll get that information right out to you. Is there anything else I can do to assist you today?").

- *Ask questions.* You read about the use of questions earlier in the book. Use them on the telephone to get information or clarify points made by the customer. Ask open-end questions; then listen to the response carefully. To clarify or verify information, use closed-end questions.

- *Use speakerphones with caution.* Speakerphones make sense for people who have certain disabilities and in some environments (where you need free hands or are doing something else while you are on hold or are waiting for a phone to be answered). From a customer service standpoint, they can send a cold or impersonal message, and their use should be minimal. Many callers do not like them and even think that speakerphone users are rude. Also, depending on the equipment used and how far you are from the telephone, the message received by your customer could be distorted, or it might seem as though you are in an echo chamber. Before using a speakerphone, ask yourself whether there is a valid reason for not using a headset or handheld phone.

  When you are using a speakerphone, make sure that your conversation will not be overheard if you are discussing personal, proprietary, or confidential information. Also, if someone is listening in on the customer's conversation, make sure that you inform the customer of that fact and explain who the listener is and why he or she is listening. As you read earlier, some people are very protective of their privacy and their feelings should be respected.

It is important to always project a professional image whether talking to customers face-to-face or by telephone. *How do you project a professional image to your customers over the telephone?*

require a lot of warehouse space and tie up large amounts of revenue if they were stocked internally. Instead, special orders were handled through established business accounts with major manufacturers and distributors who drop-shipped the items ordered by customers around the world when they are ordered via the website, telephone, or fax. When orders arrived, they were processed and a purchase order faxed to the supplier, who in turn shipped the item and invoiced the author's company. That company in turn invoiced or collected payment from the customer who placed the order. There are many small businesses using this process all over the world. According to an article on the U.S. Small Business Administration website, Forrester Research, Inc. estimates that 47.3 million North American households have online access and 43.9 percent have browsed online. Of that 43.9 percent, 65 percent have made purchases. By 2014, the research firm estimates that U.S. online retail sales will grow to $250 billion, up from $155 billion in 2009.[10]

The key to successful e-commerce for a small business is to plan before getting involved. There are many elements that must be considered (e.g., website design, maintenance, and support; merchandise types and sources; marketing; distribution; payment processing; and staffing). To be successful, small businesses need a high-quality computer system with a quality printer, fax machine, telephone, answering machine, and copier. A toll-free number is also valuable and sends a subliminal message that the company is larger and more professional.

Impact on Service

Based on personal experience and what you just read, list three to five small businesses with which you had business dealings within the past month, then answer the following questions about them:

1. What are some of the types of technology that you have witnessed these businesses using to serve their customers?

2. How successful were their employees in using the technology provided to them to service customers? Explain and give examples.

3. In what ways has technology hindered one or more of these companies from delivering effective customer service? Explain.

4. How could these companies improve service with new, different, or upgraded technology?

Key Terms

Mc Graw Hill Education **connect**®

applications or apps

automated attendants

automated computer telephone interviews

automatic call distribution (ACD) system

automatic number identification (ANI) system

blind transfer

bloggers

blogs

chat support

cloud computing

computer telephony integration (CTI)

customer relationship management (CRM) software

electronic mail (e-mail)

emoticons (emotional icons)

Facebook

facsimile (fax) machine

fax on demand

fee-based 900 numbers

help desk

instant messaging

intelligent callback technology

interactive kiosks or digital displays

interactive voice response (IVR) system

Internet callback technology

Internet telephony

media blending

offshoring

online information fulfillment system

outsourcing

Pinterest	social media	Voice over Internet Protocol (VoIP)
podcasts	spamming or spam	voice response unit (VRU)
posts	speech or voice recognition	websites
predictive dialing system	tablets	Wi-Fi
QR code (Quick Response Code)	Telephone Typewriter system (TTY)	wikis
robocall	text messaging or texting	YouTube
screen pop-ups	tweet	
smartphones	Twitter	

≣ILEARNSMART·

Summary

Delivering customer service via technology can be an effective and efficient approach to use to achieve total customer satisfaction. However, you must continually upgrade your personal technology knowledge and skills, practice their application, and consciously evaluate the approach and techniques you use to provide service.

In the quality-oriented organizational cultures now developing in the United States and in many other countries, service will make the difference between survival and failure for individuals and organizations. You are the front line, and you are often the first and only contact a customer will have with your company. Learn as much as you can about the technology that your organization has available to it for service delivery. Strive to use that technology to its fullest potential, but do not forget that you and your peers ultimately determine whether expectations are met in the eyes of your customer.

Whether a company is large or small, technology can help make them successful when properly utilized. Smart and successful managers stay current of trends in society and act quickly to implement strategies that incorporate technology to address evolving customer needs.

Review Questions

1. In what ways can technology play a role in the delivery of effective customer service? Explain.

2. What are some advantages of using technology for service delivery?

3. What are some disadvantages of using technology for service delivery?

4. What are some of the communication skills for success?

5. How can you project a more positive image over the telephone?

6. What information should you always get when taking telephone messages?

7. When transferring calls, what should you avoid and why?

8. When you leave a message on voice mail, what information should you give?

9. What is telephone tag, and how can it be avoided or reduced?

10. How are small businesses benefitting from today's technology?

Search It Out

www.mhhe.com/customerservice

1. Search the Internet for Customer Service Technology

a. Visit www.youtube.com and search the phrase "customer service." Identify and download one example each of a positive and a negative customer service experience that you can share with the class.

b. Search the Internet for sites that deal with customer service and the technology used to deliver quality customer service. Also, look for the websites and organizations that focus on the technology and people involved in the delivery of customer service. Be prepared to share what you find with the class.

to allow delivery of larger shipments via land, air, and sea to supply-chain management and financial business services. The company went public, offering stock in 1999. Since then, UPS has acquired more than 40 companies, including industry leaders in trucking and air freight, retail shipping and business services, customs brokerage, and finance and international trade services. Its focus on the environment and reduction of expenditure of paper and natural resources has escalated in an effort to reduce pollution and ensure the viability of the world in the future.

Think About It

1. What do you personally know about UPS and how does this impact your perspective of the company as a current or potential customer?

2. From a customer perspective, why do you think some companies like UPS have survived and flourished when competitors have not done as well?

3. What role do you think management decisions to improve services since its inception have played in impacting customer service from UPS? Explain.

4. What positive aspects about the company do you think help contribute to its worldwide success and reputation? Explain.

5. Would you like to work for a company like UPS? Why or why not?

Quick Preview

Before reviewing the chapter content, respond to the following questions by placing a "T" for true or an "F" for false on the rules. Use any questions you miss as a checklist of material to which you will pay particular attention as you read through the chapter. For those you get right, congratulate yourself, but review the sections they address in order to learn additional details about the topic.

_____ 1. Customer satisfaction and loyalty are the result of effective product and service delivery, resolution of problems, and elimination of dissatisfaction.

_____ 2. The number of customers with major problems who continue to do business with an organization if their complaint is resolved is about 9 percent.

_____ 3. One way to take responsibility for customer relationships is to personalize your approach when dealing with customers.

_____ 4. Customers usually decide to purchase or repurchase from a supplier on the basis of the quality and performance of the products and services.

_____ 5. Many customers return to organizations because of relationships established with employees even though comparable products and services are available elsewhere.

_____ 6. As customers develop long-term relationships with an organization, they tend to become more tolerant of poor service.

_____ 7. Projecting an enthusiastic "I'm happy to serve you" attitude is one way to have a positive effect on customer relationships.

_____ 8. Customers usually exhibit six common needs that must be addressed by service providers in order to ensure customer loyalty.

_____ 9. Using a customer's name is a good way to personalize your relationship with a customer.

_____ 10. Trust is not a major concern for most customers.

_____ 11. Handling complaints quickly and effectively is a good strategy for aiding customer retention.

_____ 12. An important step often overlooked in dealing with customers is follow-up.

Answers to Quick Preview can be found at the end of the chapter.

LO 10-1 The Role of Trust

CONCEPT Trust is the most important criterion for a relationship. Trust depends on many factors. Communicating effectively, keeping your word, caring, and trusting your customers are some of these factors.

trust Key element in cementing interpersonal relationships.

Trust is at the heart of any relationship, especially when there is an exchange of money for products or services. For a customer to hand over his or her hard-earned cash to you and your organization typically takes a bit of persuasion through advertising or word-of-mouth endorsements from previous customers. All of this is developed by an ongoing investment of time, effort, and money from your organization and commitment and initiative from each service provider.

For trust to start and grow, your customers must believe several things about you and your organization:

1. You and the organization have the customer's best interests in mind before, during, and after the transaction.
2. You and the organization are honest and forthcoming with customers and your goal is to deliver the best products and services possible in a timely manner and at a fair price.
3. You have quality products and services that are backed by a guarantee that should something go wrong, it will be quickly and earnestly taken care of.

For customers to continue doing business with you, they must trust you and your organization. The thing about trust is that it has to be earned, and that does not happen overnight. Only through continued positive efforts on the part of everyone in your organization can you demonstrate to customers that you are worthy of their trust and thereby positively affect customer retention. Through actions and deeds, you must deliver quality products, services, and information that satisfy the needs of your customers. Every touch point with a customer is an opportunity for you and your organization to influence customer loyalty.

Even when you win trust and achieve customer satisfaction, the customer relationship is very fragile. It is easy to destroy trust quickly; an inappropriate tone, a missed appointment, failure to follow through on a promise, a lie, and a misleading statement or information to a customer are just some of the ways you can sabotage this relationship.

The good news for North American businesses is that as the economic recession has started to show signs of slowing down and reversing, **customer satisfaction** levels for a number of industries have begun a slow movement toward improvement on the University of Michigan American Customer Service Index (ACSI) scale of 100 possible points. Even so, there is still a long way to full recovery in the United States and around the world as consumers begin to again trust the government and economic systems that let so many down and resulted in grave financial consequences around the world.

customer satisfaction A marketing term that is used to describe how well an organization is doing in providing products and services that meet or exceed a customer's needs and expectations.

While organizations are starting to gain access to more capital due to loosening of restrictions on lending and other economic factors, the average consumer has yet to experience higher income flows or levels of disposable income. Many are still unemployed or underemployed. Still, recent reports are that the housing industry is starting to rebound to a point where houses are in higher demand and people are actually getting into cash bidding wars and paying as much as $100,000 over the asking price in some geographic locations. This is putting money into people's pockets, and, as a result, other areas of the economy (e.g., automotive, home goods, and clothing) are also starting the road to recovery.

Part of the trust equation is gaining consumer satisfaction with products and services offered by a provider. One UK consumer study on the topic found "Retailers that satisfy consumer demands online are likely to see more return business, and even offline sales, as a result. . . . Of the 10,000 respondents to the survey nearly two-thirds (62%) said they were more likely to return to a retailer's website if they were satisfied with their service. Furthermore, 42% said they would be more likely to make an offline purchase from that retailer."[1]

Being technically proficient at your job is not enough. You also have to build and maintain strong customer relationships in order to be successful. *What can you do to create a lasting relationship with your customers?*

Tuesday. The store guarantees that the photos will be ready on Saturday. If possible, develop the film before Saturday and call to tell the customer it is ready. When he or she comes to pick it up, give a coupon for a discount on the next roll of film. Such proactive actions help secure customer loyalty.

PROVIDE PEACE OF MIND

Be positive and assertive. Assure customers through your words and actions that you are confident, have their best interests at heart, and are in control of the situation. Let them know that their calls or messages, questions, and needs will be addressed professionally and in a timely manner. Reassure them that what they purchase is the best quality, has a solid warranty, will be backed by the organization, and will address their needs while providing many benefits. Also, assure them that their requests and information will be processed rapidly and promises will be met. All of these things can lead them to the belief that they made the right decision in selecting you and your organization and that you will take care of their needs.

BE RESPONSIBLE FOR YOUR CUSTOMER RELATIONSHIPS

Taking a concerned, one-on-one approach to working with customers helps satisfy immediate needs while building a basis for long-lasting relationships. Customers tend to enjoy dealing more with people whom they believe are caring and have their best interests at heart. Interacting with someone they like is a pleasant experience and is likely to encourage trust and an enhanced relationship.

PERSONALIZE YOUR APPROACH

Think of the theme song for the syndicated television show *Cheers*. The idea of the theme song was that *Cheers* was a great place to go because "everyone knows your name." For the most part, people are a social species and need to be around others to grow and flourish. Helping your customers feel accepted can create a bond that will keep them coming back.

To create a social bond with customers, you will need to take time to get to know your regular customers and serve them individually. Recognizing them and using their names while interacting goes a long way toward creating that bond. For new customers, immediately start using the positive interpersonal communication skills you have learned. Treating customers as individuals and not as a number or one in a series is a very important step in building rapport and loyalty.

Customer Service Success Tip

Take the time to personalize your customer interactions and to make each customer feel special. Use a customer's name often during an interaction, listen, smile, ask questions to show interest, and strive to project a positive image. This can all lead to enhanced trust and helps ensure that the customer returns.

⚙ WORK IT OUT 10.2

Problem Solving

Working in teams of three or four members, decide on a course of action to resolve the problem posed in the following scenario. You have been a cashier at Gifts Galore for a little over two months. A customer comes into your gift shop and wants to return a lamp that she says she purchased from your store as a gift for a wedding. Apparently, she discovered later that the intended recipient already had a lamp exactly like the one she bought. She tells you that she remembers the salesperson, Brittney, because her daughter's name is spelled the same way. You know that Brittney used to work at the gift shop but quit about the time you started. The customer has no receipt, and you do not recognize the product as one that your store sells. You are empowered to make exchanges and give refunds up to a product value of $50. The customer says the lamp was $49.95 before tax. Store policy says that the customer must have a receipt if a refund is to be made. What questions would you ask to clarify the situation? How would you handle the problem?

KEEP AN OPEN MIND

To develop and maintain an open mind, make it a habit to assess your attitude about your job, customers, products, and services before making contact with your customers. Make sure that you are positive, objective, prepared, and focused. Don't let negative attitudes block good service. Many service providers, even the more seasoned ones, go through slumps during which they feel down about themselves, their job, supervisors, organizations, customers, and so on. This is normal. Customer service is a stressful job, and external and internal factors (e.g., circadian rhythm, workload, and personal problems) influence one's perceptions of people and the world in general; however, guard against pessimism.

If you are facing personal problems that seem overwhelming, contact your supervisor, human resources, or personnel department, or any other appropriate resource [e.g., employee assistance program (EAP) representative] to help you sort out your problems. Failure to do so could lead to poor customer service or a less-than-professional image.

INDIVIDUALIZE SERVICE

Each customer is unique and has his or her own desires and needs. For that reason, every situation you handle will be slightly different. You should view each person as an individual and not deal with customers on the basis of preconceived ideas or the demographic group of which they are part. By addressing a customer as an individual, listening so that you can discover his or her personal needs and problems, and then working to satisfy the needs or solve the problems, you potentially create a loyal customer. A simple way of accomplishing individualized service is to ask what else the customer would like. For example, in the case of a restaurant server who uses such a question, a customer might respond, "Do you have any (item)?" If the item is available, the server could cheerfully reply, "We certainly do. I'll get it for you right away." If the item is not available,

Showing Respect

Take a few minutes to think of other ways that you can show respect for a variety of customers (e.g., older, younger, people with disabilities, or people of various cultural backgrounds). Discuss how these can positively influence service.

the server might reply, "I'm sorry we do not have (item). However, we do have (alternative item). Would that be acceptable?"

SHOW RESPECT

Even if you don't agree with a customer, respect his or her point of view or need and provide the best possible service. In return, the customer will probably respect and appreciate you and your efforts. A variation of an old adage may help put this concept into perspective: *The customer may not always be right, but he or she is still the customer.*

If you lose sight of the fact that it is the customer who supports the organization, pays your salary, provides for your benefits, and gives you a job, you may want to examine why you are working in your current position. By acknowledging the value of your customers and affording them the respect and service they deserve, you can greatly improve your chances of having a satisfied customer. Some easy ways to show respect to customers include

> **Customer Service Success Tip**
>
> Remember to remain positive when dealing with customers and tell them what you can do, not what you cannot do. This simple strategy can lead to satisfied and loyal customers.

- When addressing the customer, use his or her last name and title. (If you are on the telephone, write down the customer's name along with other pertinent information so that you do not forget.)
- Stop talking when the customer begins to speak.
- Take time to address the customer's questions or concerns.
- Return calls or e-mail messages within reasonable amounts of time.
- Show up on time for scheduled meetings.
- Do what you promised to do, and do it right the first time, within the agreed-upon time frame.

ELICIT CUSTOMER INPUT

> **Street Talk**
>
> Unveil some of your secrets to your customers. Today, customers need to know more about your organization because the word of mouth in the world of business becomes one of the most invaluable referrals. Earn your customer's loyalty with entertaining details like your architectural plan, your new recipe, or a way to save.
>
> **WENDY RICHARD** *HRD Specialist*

Some people actually encourage rewarding customers who complain. Complaints provide feedback that can enable service providers and organizations to rapidly shift resources to fix things that are not working well in an effort to satisfy the customer. By taking the time to ask for customer input and actually listening to what he or she has to say, then acting appropriately upon those comments, you can solidify a bond and further enhance the customer's level of trust in you. If you think about it, this makes sense. You cannot fix what you do not know is broken.

Many times, service providers do not take the time to ask for feedback because they are afraid that it may not be good. In other instances, they simply do not think of asking or care to do so. To increase your own effectiveness and that of your organization, actively and regularly seek input from your customers. No one knows better than the customer what he or she likes or needs. Take the time to ask the customer, and then listen and act upon what you are told. By asking customers questions, you give them an opportunity to express interest, concerns, emotion, and even complaints. There are many ways of gathering this information (e.g., customer satisfaction cards, written surveys, and service follow-up telephone calls; see Figure 10.1). The key is to

FIGURE 10.1
Customer Information-Gathering Techniques

There are many ways to gather information about customer satisfaction levels. Some of the more common include the following.

- *Customer comment cards* are simple 5- x 7-inch (approximately) card stock questionnaires that quickly gather customer reactions to their service experiences. These cards are commonly found on restaurant tables and at point-of-sale locations (e.g., cash registers). They typically consist of four or five closed-end questions that can be answered with yes/no or short answers and have a space for general comments.

- *Toll-free numbers* are often used to obtain customer opinions after a service encounter. Customers are provided a toll-free number on their sales receipt and encouraged to call within 24 hours. As a reward, they are often given discount coupons, bonus frequent guest/user points, or other small incentives.

- *Verbal comments* can be elicited from customers and logged in by service providers. By asking customers for feedback on their experiences and paying heed to them, immediate service adjustments can be made.

- *Follow-up telephone surveys* can be done by employees or consultants using a written list of questions. The key is to be brief, not impose on customers, and ask questions that will gather pertinent information (e.g., open-end questions).

- *Service contact surveys* that are mailed or e-mailed (with permission) to people who have contacted an organization to get information, make a purchase, or use a service can gather more in-depth information.

- *Automated surveys* that can be sent to targeted customers and taken through a link to a website following transactions or events in order to get their opinion. The Internet offers a variety of websites that provide survey services. Some are even free (e.g., www.surveymonkey.com).

- *Exit interviews* conducted by greeters, hosts, or hostesses as customers leave a facility. These are typically one or two quick questions (e.g., "How did you enjoy your stay?," "Were you able to find everything you needed?," or "What can we do to make your next visit more pleasurable?"). The key is to log in responses for future reference.

- *Shopper/customer surveys* that can yield a wealth of information. These are typically longer and more detailed than a comment card. They can be given to a customer as he or she leaves or can be sent to customers later (get names and addresses from checks written). Offer discount coupons or other incentives for returned surveys and provide self-addressed, stamped envelopes.

- *Focus groups* of six to eight internal or external customers can be formed to do in-depth, face-to-face or online (chat) surveys. Often organizations conducting these provide snacks and gifts (e.g., $50) for each participant. Ask open-end questions related to the organization and products and services provided. Often, trained marketing or other facilitators are used to conduct such sessions. They also analyze responses and provide reports to management along with recommendations for improvement.

- *Sales and service records* can provide a wealth of information. They can reflect whether customers are returning and what products and services are being used most, and can show patterns of purchases.

somehow ask the customer, "How well did we do in meeting your needs?" or "What do you think?" If this is not a normal procedure in your place of business, you should consider bringing it up at a staff meeting. It will take extra effort on the part of the customer service employees, but the effort will be well-rewarded in the goodwill it will elicit from your customer base.

> ### KNOWLEDGE CHECK ✓
>
> 1. Why is trust so important to the customer–provider relationship?
> 2. How do recalls impact customer trust in an organization or industry?
> 3. What are some strategies that you can use to build customer trust?
> 4. What are some typical strategies that can be used to gather customer information?

LO 10-2 Customer Loyalty

CONCEPT   Customer and brand loyalty are a crucial element of any organization's success.

customer loyalty Term used to describe the tendency of customers to return to a product or organization regularly because of the service and satisfaction they receive.

touch point Any instance in which a service provider or organization (e.g., face to face, in writing, through technology) comes in contact with a customer; it is an opportunity to influence customer loyalty and enhance the customer relationship.

Customer loyalty is an *emotional* rather than a *rational* thing. Each time there is contact at a **touch point** where the customer and provider come together, there is opportunity for further cementing the customer relationship and loyalty or driving a wedge between the customer and organization due to failure to meet expectations or needs. With every contact, service providers should strive to demonstrate commitment to exceed customer expectations and provide an experience that is beyond anything for which they might have hoped. Tied to commitment, loyalty is typically based on customer interest in maintaining a relationship with your organization. Often, customer interest is created and maintained through one or more positive experiences that lead to a relationship.

An important point to keep in mind about customer loyalty is that it does not happen as a result of a single customer–provider encounter. Nor does it happen just because of periodic special promotions, sales, or passive loyalty programs that provide only minimal rewards. Rather, true customer loyalty stems from an organization's concerted, ongoing efforts that are part of their strategic goals to meet and exceed the expectations and needs of their customers.

Lasting customer relationships are built on trust! The most important thing to remember about trust is that, without it, you have no relationship. This applies to all human situations, not just the customer service environment. In the business world, trust typically results in positive word-of-mouth advertising. This mode of endorsement can be powerful and contribute to organization or product success. In a time when mom and pop shops have shuttered their doors and have been replaced by nationwide chains, consumers still have the most powerful tool for ensuring that they receive the best possible customer service: their mouths.

Customer loyalty has been impacted to some degree by the advent of mobile and other types of electronic communication devices that allow consumers to easily find a way to provide feedback on products and services to others and to reach out for information that helps them make a buying decision. Additionally, with competing products being only a mouse click away, a customer can research numerous sources and make a buying decision within a matter of minutes without ever leaving the comfort of his or her desk chair or chaise lounge. This is one reason why many business owners and marketing professionals tout that customer loyalty is dead. That may be true to some degree based on applying old standards of what loyalty looked like. However, in an era where society and the mechanisms of business have morphed dramatically toward technology integration and a melding of world economies, it is still possible for successful and innovative companies to carve out a niche and have a degree of customer loyalty toward their brands.

Examples of Brand Loyalty

- Cadillac is still very popular with the parents of Baby Boomers (born between 1964 and 1980) who grew up with that icon of quality and prosperity.
- Trader Joe's markets have almost a cult following of people who believe that fresh, natural products are a must to ensure longevity and health.
- The Four Seasons and Ritz Carlton hotel chains have a following of more affluent customers who appreciate luxury when they travel.
- Nordstrom's department stores have die-hard customers who love to be catered to as they shop.

All of these organizations have identified and targeted a specific category and have successfully delivered their message about products and services to them through advertising and ultimately word-of-mouth consumer promotions.

While the use of technology to shop and research information varies between generational and other customer groups, it plays a more significant role than ever might have been imagined in the past and certainly has an impact on overall customer satisfaction and loyalty. By using technology, customers can access product and service experts from around the world in a matter of seconds to find out about a company's reputation, products, and services. They can check forums that focus on and organizations that gather consumer feedback to see if an organization or person is credible and worthy of their trust and business.

For many consumers, the concept of what are acceptable product quality and service level has changed dramatically over the years, along with who they believe. For example, in the case of Millennials (people born between 1980 and 2000—depending on what source you reference) ". . . the definition of 'expert'—a person with the credibility to recommend brands, products, and services—has shifted from someone with professional or academic credentials to potentially anyone with firsthand experience, ideally a peer or close friend. U.S. Millennials also tend to seek multiple sources of information, especially from noncorporate channels, and they're likely to consult their friends before making purchase decisions. . . ."[6]

The key to establishing and maintaining customer loyalty is to put forth an honest and ongoing series of initiatives and efforts that demonstrate to customers that they are important to the organization. Through words and actions, service providers can show that they are truly there to assist customers meet their needs, wants, and expectations.

One way that organizations try to cement relationships and encourage customer loyalty and retention is through loyalty or rewards programs. Such programs have been around since the 19th century when soap manufacturers offered certificates redeemable for color lithographs. Later, merchants created various incentive programs that were designed to give added value and create brand loyalty for products and companies. One of the most recognized incentive initiatives in the late 1800s and up to today in the United States and overseas has been the Sperry and Hutchinson (S&H) Green Stamps program. For decades, millions of customers dutifully collected small green stamps with S&H emblazoned on them from stores and businesses and pasted the stamps into books. The books were later traded for housewares and other items. Stores bought the stamps from S&H and then distributed them with purchases based on criteria that each company set. Customers often chose who to trade with based on the value of the stamps given. S&H went through various iterations due to the economy and a Supreme Court ruling that restricting the distribution of stamps was illegal. The stamps were in use up until the 1990s when the Internet made them obsolete. The company morphed into a system of S&H "greenpoints" that are still in use today to get rewards from Home Depot and other recognizable companies. People who still have green stamps can redeem them through the company's website (www.greenpoints.com/).

Trending NOW

Walt Disney was a visionary and innovator and his company often leads the way with service-related processes and procedures often mimicked by its competitors and other companies. With recent expansions to its theme parks, the company has introduced a new radio frequency wristband device called MagicBands that will eliminate the need for guests at its Walt Disney World Resort to carry room keys, park tickets, passes, or even money and credit cards. These high-tech bracelets will be worn by guests, who can scan them at special kiosks or points of sale to make purchases in their gift shops and food venues, to enter the parks, to access "fast passes" that allow them a designated reservation time for various rides and venues in the parks, to enter their hotel room, and much more.

The devices have a code that securely links to guest information stored in an encrypted database to prevent loss of personal and financial information. The bands then allow access to various locations and to make purchases, if a credit card has been associated with the band at guest services. In the latter case, a personal identification number (PIN) would be required to make a purchase to prevent unauthorized use should the band get lost. Parents also can set dollar limits on what and the amount that children may purchase to avoid overspending.

The implications for use of such devices span many industries where customers stay in one facility or location owned by a company and make purchases or access services; for example, in a hotel resort or on cruise ships, where guests would be able to easily access various services without having to sign for each transaction and end up with a stack of receipts they have to track.

The convenience of high-tech devices such as the MagicBand is one way that Disney is showing that it is always thinking of new ways to make the guest experience seamless, better fortify the customer–provider relationship, and lead to higher levels of satisfaction and brand loyalty.

KNOWLEDGE CHECK ✓

1. What is customer loyalty?

2. What is the most important thing to remember about trust related to customer loyalty?

3. How have mobile and other technologies impacted customer loyalty?

LO 10-3 The Importance of Customer Relationship Management

CONCEPT Long-term relationships are the ones that sustain organizations.

Why bother building relationships with customers? The answer would seem obvious—so that you can stay in business. However, when you examine the question further, you may find that there are more reasons than you think. This is where the **customer relationship management (CRM)** concept comes in. There are actually a number of components in the CRM process:

- Operational (involving sales and service representatives).
- Collaborative (involving interaction with customers through such means as e-mail).
- Web pages and automated voice response, or AVR, systems.
- Analytical (involving analyzing customer data for efforts like marketing and financial forecasting).

Through CRM, organizations and employees get to better know their customers and project needs that can be satisfied through appropriate products and services.

At one point in history, business owners knew their customers personally. They knew their customers' families, what their religious affiliation was, and what was happening in their lives. That was then, and this is now. Our current society is more mobile; people live in large metropolitan areas where relationships are distant, and families live miles apart from one another in many instances. Large multinational organizations provide the products and services once provided by the neighborhood store. All this does not mean, however, that the customer–provider relationship can no longer exist.

Additionally, with B2B (business-to-business), customers are often companies. This makes managing **customer relationships** more difficult because of the number of contacts you might have in an organization and the varying requirements or needs each might have. Also, much of business-to-business service is delivered through technology.

customer relationship management (CRM) Concept of identifying customer needs; understanding and influencing customer behavior through ongoing communication strategies in an effort to acquire, retain, and satisfy the customer.

customer relationships Ongoing friendships with customers focused on making them feel comfortable with an organization and its service providers and enhancing customer loyalty.

Relationships are a crucial part of customer service. By working to build trust and getting to know customer needs, service providers increase their effectiveness. *What techniques do you use to build rapport and trust with customers?*

Numerous service organizations use CRM software to better keep track of customer needs, access multiple sources of customer information (e.g., credit reports, past contacts, and voice and e-mail messages), and record service provided. CRM is a crucial element of customer loyalty.

Typically, many service providers look at customer interactions from a short-term perspective. They figure that a customer calls or comes in (or they go to the customer), they provide service, and then the customer (or the service provider) goes away. This is a shortsighted viewpoint in that it does not consider the long-term implications. This is not the way to gain and sustain customer loyalty.

A more customer-focused approach is to view customers from a relationship standpoint. That does not mean that you have to become intimate friends with all your customers; it simply means that you should strive to employ as many of the positive relationship-building skills that you have learned as possible. By treating both internal and external customers in a manner that leads them to believe that you care for them and have their best interests at heart, you can start to generate reciprocal feelings. Using the interpersonal communication skills you have learned throughout this book and through other sources is a great way to begin doing this.

People usually gravitate toward organizations and people with whom they have developed rapport, respect, and trust, and who treat them as if they are valued as a person. Relationships are developed and enhanced through one-on-one human interaction. This does not mean that people who provide service via technology cannot develop relationships. Those relationships develop on a different level, using the nonverbal skills.

customer retention The ongoing effort by an organization to meet customer needs and desires in an effort to build a long-term relationship and keep the customer for life.

churn rate Refers to the number of customers who leave a supplier during a given time period.

Remember that long-term customer relationships (**customer retention**) are the ones that sustain organizations. In many organizations, particularly those that have contractual customers (e.g., members or subscribers), the **churn rate** is often an indicator of customer dissatisfaction, better targeted marketing and sales efforts or better or cheaper pricing by competitors, or factors related to service provider relationships with customers. No matter the cause, the issue is that organizations that have an ongoing high churn rate are doomed to failure.

The days of a customer adopting one product or company for life are long gone. With easy access and global competitiveness, customers are often swayed by advertising and a chance at a "better deal." Quality levels and features between competing brands and organizations are often comparable. The thing that separates competitors is their level of service. It is not unusual for customers to switch back and forth between products or organizations simply because of pricing. This is sometimes referred to as service **churn**. According to research by Harris Interactive, ". . . the majority of companies lose between 10% to 40% of their customers every year. Other calculations show that the average company loses half of its customer base over a 5-year period."[7]

churn The process of a customer switching between products or companies, often simply to get a better price, contract, rebate, or warranty.

Seeking out new or replacement customers through advertising and other means is a very costly proposition. This is because in addition to having to find new customers, you and your organization have to educate and win them over. You have to prove yourself to newly acquired customers. More than likely, new customers are also going to be more apprehensive, skeptical, and critical than customers who have previous experience with your organization. For these reasons, it is imperative that you and every other member of your organization work to build and strengthen customer relationships and develop loyalty on the part of those customers with whom you have an existing relationship.

Many organizations and industries seem to forget the value of fostering solid customer relationships. They often treat existing customers poorly or not as well as newly acquired ones. Examples of this can be found in

- High maintenance and transaction fees charged by financial institutions.
- High fees charged by hotels for local calls.
- Escalating fees charged by airlines for ticket changes, baggage, seat assignments, snacks/food, and priority boarding.
- Inability for existing cell phone or cable customers locked into contracts to get the same deals as new customers.
- Cancellation fees by doctors' and dentists' offices regardless of the reason.
- Restocking fees charged by many online retailers for returned items.
- Charges at gas stations for air and water for vehicles.
- Fees charged to access Internet connections in hotel rooms.

Major organizations spend millions of dollars on **customer loyalty programs**. Unfortunately, small businesses cannot compete on those levels. What they can do is train all employees to build relationships on an interpersonal level and to take every opportunity to reinforce the value of customers when they interact with them. What this means is that just because a company does not have deep pockets or large staff resources, they can still strive to gain and retain customers the old fashioned way . . . through building strong personal relationships with their customers.

A research study on loyalty related to small and medium-size enterprises (SMEs) by Barclays Bank found that

> . . . the majority of consumers (58%) believe that small independent retailers are in a better or the same position to engender loyalty among their current customers than large, corporate brands—and it's the personal touches which count the most. Nearly two thirds (60%) of consumers said they are always, often or sometimes willing to pay more for a similar product from a small, independent retailer compared to a cheaper product from a large, corporate retailer. It's up to SMEs to convert these sales via customer loyalty.[8]

customer loyalty program An incentive program offered by an organization to reward customers for spending money and purchasing products and services.

BENEFITS OF CUSTOMER RELATIONSHIP MANAGEMENT

When organizations attain a high degree of brand recognition and a reputation for providing quality products and services at a competitive price, while going above and beyond their customers' expectations, they are typically rewarded with customer loyalty and repeat and referral business.

According to a J.D. Powers and Associates North American Hotel Guest Satisfaction Index Study, "The highest-performing hotel brands differentiate themselves by meeting customer expectations consistently, whether it's a guest's first stay with the brand or their fiftieth. . . . By setting and maintaining high brand standards, hotels build a reputation for reliability, which breeds customer loyalty."[9]

FIGURE 10.2
Loyalty Equation

Effective product/service delivery
+ Proactive relationship building
+ Elimination of dissatisfiers
+ Resolution of problems
+ Follow-up
= Customer satisfaction and loyalty

Other direct benefits of going above customer expectations include

• Less need to obtain new customers through marketing because current customers are aware of offerings and take advantage of them.
• Reduced marketing costs because direct mail, follow-up, and other customer recruitment activities are reduced.
• Increased return on investment (ROI) because marketing can target specific customer needs.
• Enhanced customer loyalty due to pricing and product service offerings that meet current customer needs.
• Elevated profitability due to increased sales, customer referrals, and longer customer retention during life cycle.
• Targeted marketing based on statistics on which customers buy more and on high-ticket item sales.

By providing excellent customer service and dealing with dissatisfaction as soon it is identified, you can help ensure that customers remain loyal and keep coming back. Figure 10.2 shows an equation that conveys the loyalty concept.

Technical Assistance Research Program (TARP) Worldwide An Arlington, Virginia–based firm specializing in customer service research studies for call centers and many other industries.

Traditionally, customers will remain loyal to a product, service, or organization that they believe meets their needs. Even when there is an actual or perceived breakdown in quality, many customers will return to an organization that they believe sincerely attempts to solve a problem or make restitution for an error. According to the **Technical Assistance Research Program (TARP) Worldwide** (not associated with the U.S. federal government's Troubled Asset Relief Program), many organizations have found that, when complaints were acted upon and resolved quickly, most customers returned to the organization (see Figure 10.3).

The bottom line is that you and other employees must realize that customer service is everyone's business and that relationships are the basis of that business.

COST OF DISSATISFIED CUSTOMERS

cost of dissatisfied customers Phrase that refers to any formula used to calculate the cost of acquiring a new customer or replacing a current one as a result of having a dissatisfied customer leave an organization.

Many research studies have been conducted to try to determine the **cost of dissatisfied customers**. Too often, service providers look at the loss of a sale when a customer is dissatisfied as a single event. However, as you saw in the last section, one dissatisfied customer can cost your organization a lot.

To get an idea of what one negative customer experience can cost your organization over a 10-year period, consider the following example.

WORK IT OUT 10.4

Personal Customer Relationship Experiences

Think about a service provider with whom you deal frequently and have established a better-than-average customer–provider relationship. Perhaps you have been dealing with the organization for a long period of time or visit frequently. Reflect on the relationship and make a list of positive customer service behaviors exhibited by this person. Then review the list and make it a personal goal to replicate as many of these behaviors as possible when dealing with your own customers.

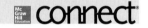

Example

Ms. Ling comes in to return a product that she paid $22 for over a month ago. She explains that the product did not fit her needs and that she had been meaning to return it since the date she purchased it but kept forgetting. She also explains that she comes in at least once a week to make purchases. Your company has a three-day return policy, your manager is out to lunch, and you do not have the authority to override the policy. Ms. Ling is in a hurry and is upset by your inability to resolve the issue. She leaves after saying, "You just lost a good customer!"

Let's assume that Ms. Ling spends at least $22 a week in your store and calculate the potential loss to your organization.

$22 × 52 (number of weeks in a year) = $1,144

10 (number of years as a customer) × $1,144 = $11,440

16 (number of people statistically told of her negative experience) × $11,440 = $183,040

FIGURE 10.3

The Importance of Customer Loyalty

For almost three decades, the research firm TARP has conducted various studies to determine the effects of customer service. The research has revealed the following:

- It will cost an organization at least five times more to acquire a new customer than it will to keep an existing one.
- On average, 50 percent of consumers will complain about a problem to a front-line person. In business-to-business environments, this figure jumps to 75 percent.
- For small-ticket items, 96 percent of consumers do not complain or they complain to the retailer from whom they bought an item. For large-ticket items, 50 percent complain to front-line employees, and 5 to 10 percent escalate the problem to local managers or corporate headquarters.
- At least 50 percent of your customers who experience problems will not complain or contact your organization for help; they will simply go elsewhere.
- Customers who are dissatisfied will tell as many as 16 friends about a negative experience with your organization.
- The average business loses 10 to 15 percent of its customers per year because of bad service.

Source: Technical Assistance Research Program (TARP), 1300 Wilson Boulevard, Suite 950, Arlington, Virginia 22209.

These numbers are the bad news. The good news is that you and every other employee in your organization can reduce a large percentage of customer defections by providing quality service.

KNOWLEDGE CHECK

1. What is customer relationship management (CRM)?
2. What is meant by churn rate?

LO 10-4 The Role of Channel Partner Relationships on Customer Loyalty

CONCEPT Relationship with channel partners is a key component for managing customer loyalty.

channel partner Relationship of two organizations through which partners are able to build a larger and stronger competitive presence in the marketplace.

A key component of managing customer loyalty is for organizations to effectively manage its **channel partner** relationships. Such partners can help gain access to new business opportunities at lower costs, without having to merge or acquire more assets and employees. This means that retail and service pricing can be kept down. This provides a more competitive posture for your organization and potentially attracts and holds customers based on reduced pricing and enhanced product and service availability. Through such relationships, organizations are able to build a larger and stronger competitive presence in the marketplace, which can help enhance customer trust and loyalty. This potentially occurs because customers view the organizations as a larger and stronger supplier or entity.

THREE TYPES OF CHANNEL PARTNERS

There are three types of typical channel partners with which your organization might have a relationship:

1. **Transactional or indirect.** This type of organization provides a distribution outlet or link for your company's products and services. The challenge is that they maintain no specific loyalty and when the opportunity arises to obtain a newer product or service line, or one that is less expensive, they may move to other suppliers or vendors. Examples of transactional partners are online websites (e.g., Amazon.com and Overstock.com), retail stores, or service providers (e.g., plumber, laundry, pest control, masseuse/masseur, and car repair).
2. **Tactical.** This category of partners includes organizations that are intricately meshed with your company's internal operations. Examples of such arrangements include mobile phone service providers that use retail outlets (e.g., Best Buy or mall kiosks).
3. **Strategic.** The third type of channel partnership involves signing agreements through which one organization creates a long-term alliance with another organization to brand, develop, or produce each other's products

or services. As example of this is the code sharing that takes place between airlines where two different airlines can sell seats on a single plane under their own individual flight numbers.

LO 10-5 Provider Characteristics Affecting Customer Loyalty

CONCEPT Personal characteristics of a service provider may affect customer loyalty positively or negatively.

Many of your personal characteristics affect your relationships with customers. In customer service, some circumstances are beyond your control; however, your personal characteristics are not. Some of the most common qualities of service providers that affect customers are described in the next sections.

RESPONSIVENESS

Customers typically like to feel that they are the most important person in the world when they come in contact with an organization (see Figure 10.4). This is a human need. If customers feel that they are not appreciated or not

FIGURE 10.4
Addressing Customer Needs

Everyone has needs that must be met in some fashion. Here are six common customer needs, along with strategies to satisfy them. Keep in mind that no two customer interactions are exactly alike. As a result, you may find yourself using any of the strategies below (or others) to address a need that you identify for a given customer. The key is to remain flexible as you work with customers and adapt to their specific needs and requests.

Customer Need	Strategies for Satisfying the Need
To feel welcome	Use an enthusiastic greeting, smile, and the customer's name; thank the customer; be positive
To be understood	Listen actively, paraphrase, ask key questions, give positive feedback, empathize
To feel comfortable	Use an enthusiastic welcome, relieve anxiety through friendly communication, explain your actions calmly, ensure physical comfort (e.g., seats, refreshments)
To feel appreciated	Thank the customer, follow up, go beyond service expectations, provide "special" offers, remember special details about the customer (e.g., birthdays, favorite colors, facts about their families)
To feel important	Use the customer's name, personalize service, give special treatment when possible, elicit opinions, remember details about him or her (e.g., last purchase made, last visit, preferred styles or foods)
To be respected	Listen, don't interrupt, acknowledge the customer's emotions and concerns, take time to serve, ask advice, elicit feedback

Personal Service Expectations

Think of how you would expect to be treated if you were a customer of the company for which you currently work. List behaviors that you would expect to encounter from customer service employees.

welcome by you or another service provider, they will likely take their business elsewhere. However, they will often first complain to management and will tell anyone who will listen about the poor quality of service they received.

A simple way to demonstrate responsiveness is to attend to customer needs promptly. If you get an e-mail or voice mail message, respond to it immediately, if possible. If that is not possible, try to respond within 4 hours, or certainly within 24 hours. If you have face-to-face customer contact, greet customers quickly (within 10 to 15 seconds), even if you are busy with someone else. If nothing else, at least smile and gesture that you will be with them momentarily.

Once you do get to serve the customer, and before getting to the business at hand, greet the customer with a smile and start the interaction on a friendly note in one or more of the following ways:

Be enthusiastic. Use open body language, vocal cues, and gestures that you have read about previously in this book, coupled with some of the techniques described below to let your customers know that you are glad they have chosen you and/or your organization.

Use the customer's title and name. If you know the customer's name, use it. Remember, though, not to assume familiarity and start using the customer's first name unless you are given permission to do so.

Show appreciation. "Thank you for coming to (organization)." "It's nice to see you this morning." "You have been very patient while I assisted the previous customer. Thank you."

Engage in small talk. "Isn't this weather terrible?" "Is this your first visit to our store?" "Didn't I see you in here last week?" (Say this only if you recognize the customer. If he or she answers yes, thank the person for returning to the store.)

Compliment. "You look like you're having a good day" (assuming the customer is smiling and does look happy). "That color really looks nice on you," "That's a beautiful necktie," or other appropriate compliment.

ADAPTABILITY

In a continually evolving world, you will undoubtedly have many opportunities to deal with customers who have different beliefs, values, perceptions, needs, and expectations. You will also encounter people whose personality styles differ from yours. Each of these meetings will provide an opportunity for you to adapt your approach in dealing with others. By doing so, you increase the likelihood of a successful interaction as well as a satisfied customer emerging from the encounter. Taking measures to adapt your personality style to that of your customers in order to communicate with and serve them effectively is a smart move. Keep in mind that you cannot change the customers; however, you can adapt to them and their approach to a situation.

Another, more subtle, way to show your ability to adapt relates to technology. By quickly learning and mastering new technology systems provided to you by the organization, you can respond faster and more efficiently to customer needs. This is especially true if many of your customers will likely be very technology-literate. If you cannot match their expectations, or at least demonstrate knowledge and effectiveness in using technology, you might frustrate them and drive them away. In turn, you might create negative word-of-mouth publicity about your organization and its employees.

Customers have many choices for service. Each person in the organization must go out of his or her way to project a positive image and work to project a "can do" attitude with customers. *What do you do to show that you are worthy of your customers' patronage and support?*

COMMUNICATION SKILLS

As you have read earlier in this book, your ability to obtain and give information; listen, write, and speak effectively; and deal with emotional situations are keys to successful customer service. By using a variety of effective interpersonal techniques, you can determine customer needs. The most successful service providers are the ones who have learned to interact positively and build rapport with customers. To help ensure the most effective service possible, you should continually strive to improve your ability to interact and communicate with a variety of people. The better your skills are, the more likely you will be able to address different situations that arise in the workplace.

Customer Service Success Tip

Listen to your customer and address his or her needs; don't just talk about yourself, your organization, products, and services. Trust is gained through use of positive relationship-building skills.

Trending NOW

Many marketers are using mobile applications to deliver coupons to customers in an effort to gain new customers and build brand loyalty. One estimate by Juniper Research projects that the total redemption value of such coupons will reach $43 billion globally by 2016.[10]

> ⚙ **WORK IT OUT 10.6**
>
> ## Passing Time
>
> **Partner with someone and try this experiment in order to better realize how customers and service providers might perceive the passing of time differently (e.g., while a customer is on hold).** When your instructor says, "Go," mentally try to determine when 30 seconds have elapsed. When you believe 30 seconds have elapsed, say "Now."
>
> Afterward, you will participate in a discussion led by your instructor about perceptions about time and how your perception and that of your customer can be significantly different depending on the situation.

DECISIVENESS

Decisiveness relates to being able and willing to make a decision and take necessary actions to fulfill customer needs. Taking a wait-and-see approach to customer service often leads to customer dissatisfaction. Just as you probably do, customers value their time. By keeping them waiting while you run to someone else for a decision or answer can be frustrating. Granted, such a situation is sometimes created by a management style that makes it necessary to get certain approvals (e.g., for checks, returns or refunds, or discounts). However, these are internal issues that should be resolved before the customer encounters them. If you face such barriers, think of alternative ways of handling them, and then approach your supervisor with suggestions for improvement. Your ideas may make your life easier by reducing the chances of a frustrating and unproductive service encounter.

Once you have supportive systems in place, gather information effectively by using the listening techniques discussed in Chapter 5, carefully and quickly analyze the situation, and then make a decision on how to solve the problem.

ENTHUSIASM

As discussed earlier, attaining and maintaining a level of excitement about your customers, products, services, organization, and job that says, "I'm happy to help you," is an important step toward establishing a relationship.

If you are enthusiastic about serving your customers, they will often respond by loyally supporting you and the organization. People typically react positively to enthusiastic employees who appear to be enjoying themselves as they work. This should not be interpreted as meaning that providers should act unprofessionally or create an environment in which they have fun at the expense of customer service or attention to their customers. Find a good balance between fun and professionalism. Southwest Airlines has succeeded in finding the right mix. Employees dress casually, are recruited partially on the basis of their personality, and often use jokes and games on flights to reduce some of the stress of air travel in a security-conscious industry. They have been rewarded with continued corporate profits while other airlines often report losses.

The long-term benefit is that if you and your organization can generate return customers through enthusiasm, the potential for organizational growth and prosperity exists. This in turn sets the stage for better benefits, salary, and workplace modifications that lead to higher employee enthusiasm. Once all the elements are connected, all contribute to successful customer service.

As a side note, many employees and employers are trying to find ways to make the workplace less stressful and more enjoyable for themselves and customers. Several resources listed in the Bibliography will help in this quest.

ETHICAL BEHAVIOR

With a heightened incidence of actual or alleged corporate wrongdoing (e.g., Enron, Martha Stewart, and numerous politicians), customers have been sensitized and made wary of organizations, their leaders, and practices. Many organizations have formed ethics committees made up of employees from across their organization to deal with actual or perceived violations of ethical standards or organization codes. Many have adopted a **code of ethics** or codes of conduct that are taught to all employees, new and old, and to which they are held accountable. By having a written standard of conduct, organizations demonstrate to customers that they are concerned for their welfare and have the intention of operating in an ethical manner. This effort can ease customer trepidation or concerns that they are going to be taken advantage of by employees. (See Figure 10.5 for examples of both ethical and unethical behavior.)

> **Customer Service Success Tip**
>
> Even if the organization for which you work does not have such a code, it is crucial that you and your peers guard against any words or actions that might raise scrutiny or customer skepticism.

> **code of ethics** A set of standards, often developed by employees, that guide the conduct of all employees.

FIGURE 10.5

Examples of Ethical and Unethical Behavior

Some examples of ethical behavior follow:

- Before someone complains, a company voluntarily recalls a product that it discovered was defective or potentially dangerous.
- A manager notifies a customer when he or she finds out that an employee has lied to or deceived the customer.
- An employee reports a theft carried out by another employee.
- A truck driver tracks down the owner of a parked car at a mall to identify herself as the person who accidentally scraped a bumper while making a delivery.
- A cab driver finds a wallet in his taxi and turns it in.

Some examples of unethical behavior follow:

- Providing or substituting an inferior or more expensive product for an advertised name brand item.
- Providing inferior or nonstandard parts or repairs on a service call but charging for factory parts.
- Misleading a customer about what is covered on an extended home warranty in order to sell a policy and make a commission.
- Failing to adhere to local, state, or federal regulations (e.g., dumping hazardous waste, such as petroleum or pesticide products, in unauthorized areas or collecting sales taxes but failing to report the taxes).
- Lying to a patient about why he or she has to wait so long before being seen by a technician, nurse, or doctor (e.g., the medical professional came in late or returned late from lunch).

Establishing (and maintaining) high legal, social, and ethical standards in all interactions with customers is imperative. Failure to do so can lead to loss of reputation and business, and/or legal liability. While it is not always easy to take an ethical approach to getting wrong or illegal behavior corrected, it is the morally right thing to do. There will certainly be instances where you or another person brings improper behavior to someone's attention, which then results in personal loss and consequences (e.g., lost employment and income, having to testify in a court case, feeling like an outcast from others). Even so, there is the personal satisfaction of doing the right thing and, often, there are financial rewards for your positive behavior. Still, monitoring and helping correct improper behavior is a personal choice based on your values and beliefs. You cannot control how other people act, but you can control how you act.

Ethical Dilemma 10.2

Your goal is to one day become a licensed real estate broker; however, with recent changes in the economy, you have decided to get a job in a related profession that provides a more stable income and benefits. To help position you for future opportunities in the field while you gain more knowledge and experience about how the profession works, you recently took a job as a professional assistant in a large real estate company.

From your previous research and a course you took at the local community college, you know that there are numerous federal laws pertaining to the real estate profession. One of them is the requirement to disclose known information about any potentially hazardous situations that exist related to a listed property (e.g., the presence of lead-based paint or asbestos).

You recently overheard two senior agents discussing a potential deal in which someone is interested in buying a retail property that has been on the market for some time. The potential buyers want to use the building for a child care facility. Apparently, it is an older building built in the late 1960s and the inside has been repainted several times in the past. Somehow, one of the agents found out that the original lead-based paint was never removed, only covered over.

Coincidentally, you know one of the women who is interested in the building. Her children go to school with your son.

1. Should you say anything to anyone in the office? Explain.
2. Should you say anything to the potential buyer? Explain.
3. If you do not say anything, is there any potential liability? Explain.
4. If you do say something to either the agents, your boss, or the potential buyer, what are the potential repercussions for you?

INITIATIVE

Taking an action related to your job or customer service without having to receive instructions from others is a sign of initiative. Such actions also help to ensure that your customer's needs are identified and met in a timely fashion. Too many service providers take the "It's not my job" or "I can't do that" approach to dealing with customer situations. This can lead to customer dissatisfaction because the provider seems to be lazy or uncaring. To counter such impressions, you should take responsibility when a problem arises. By building a strong knowledge base (as described in the next section) and using the skills discussed in this book, you will have the tools you need to deal effectively with various situations without having to turn to others for assistance. This can expedite service and enhance your reputation in the eyes of your customers, peers, and supervisors.

Initiative does not only apply to external customer situations. What you do around your boss and co-workers (internal customers) also sends powerful messages about you. For example, if you work in a retail store and walk down an aisle and you see a piece of trash on the floor or an item placed in the wrong location, you should take the time to pick it up and put it where it belongs. This sends a message of personal responsibility and the initiative to care about the image presented to external customers. By such a small act, you potentially prevent an external customer from developing a negative impression about your organization and its employees, which might ultimately affect sales and revenue levels. You also potentially gain the respect and appreciation of other employees because you have helped create a more professional work environment. These are the types of actions that often lead to career opportunities, raises, and other potential benefits.

> **Street Talk**
>
> Make the client in front of you the most important person in the world, even if it's just for the duration of a phone call.
>
> PATRICIA CHARPENTIER *Owner, Writing Your Life/LifeStory Publishing*

KNOWLEDGE

Your customers expect you to know what business your organization is in. With all the products and service variations available to customers, the high level of technology, deregulation of industries, and innovations coming on the market daily, customers depend on service providers to educate and guide them in making purchases and decisions. Taking time to learn about policies, procedures, resources, products, services, and other information can help you provide total customer satisfaction in an efficient and timely manner.

If the organization you work for does not provide training or resources, take the initiative to ask supervisors or team leaders for materials and information. Also develop a network with other employees throughout the organization and use that network to gain access to information. Network in other ways as well: organizations involved in your particular product or service can provide general training to you; service organizations can lead you to mentors and other individuals who can help your career; and networking with others in your line of work outside of your company can also help in many ways. Joining an organization whose membership includes people who do what you do for a living can give you different perspectives and add to your knowledge base. You, your organization, and your customers will ultimately benefit from your initiatives.

> **Customer Service Success Tip**
>
> Take the opportunity to get any type of training that becomes available to help develop new workplace knowledge or skills. Many organizations provide training and literature to help employees become more knowledgeable and to stay current. You can also find many free information sources and training modules on the Internet.

PERCEPTIVENESS

Recognizing the need to pay close attention to verbal and nonverbal cues, cultural factors, and the feelings or concerns of others is important. If necessary, you may want to review these topics in Chapters 3, 4, and 8. By

⚙ WORK IT OUT 10.7

Preparing for Contingencies

Take a few minutes to think about a situation in your organization (or one that you have visited) in which a system did not function as it should (e.g., computer crashed, cash register stopped working, website went offline, telephones went dead, products did not arrive from a supplier as expected). What did you (or the service provider) do or say immediately to inform the customer of the situation? How was the problem resolved? How long did it take to fix the

issue? If customers were inconvenienced, was anything done to compensate them? What could have been done differently, and potentially better, to resolve the situation?

Discuss your answers with others and get their thoughts on how they would have felt if they were the customer in the situation you identified. Would they have been satisfied by your actions (or those of the service provider)?

staying focused on customers and the signals they send, you can often recognize hesitancy, interest in a product or adamant rejection, irritation, anxiety, and a multitude of other unspoken messages. Once you have identified customers' signals, you can react appropriately and address their needs.

One way you can address customer needs is to anticipate them, depending on where you work. Suppose that a customer makes a comment like, "Man, is it hot outside. My lips are parched." You might offer a cold drink or direct the customer to a cafeteria or soft drink machine. You might offer a blanket to a family member staying with someone in the emergency room in the middle of the night when it is very cold. Or you might offer a chair to someone who is accompanying a customer while he or she shops and tries on clothing. Such small gestures show that you are astute in noticing their needs and nonverbal cues. Remember, sometimes the little things mean a

Training is usually provided by most organizations to increase employee knowledge and effectiveness with customers. *What training do you think would be useful to you in a new position in customer service?*

lot. Moreover, in all of these examples, by taking care of the customer's basic needs, you might encourage him or her to shop longer.

PLANNING ABILITY

Planning is a crucial skill to possess when operating in today's fast-paced, changing customer service environment, especially in technology-based environments. To prepare for all types of customer situations, you and your organization must have a strategy. This often involves assessing various factors related to your organization, industry, products, services, policies and procedures, resources, and customer base. Remember that a systemic breakdown on your part or that of your organization is not the responsibility or problem of your customers. In fact, most do not care about your issues; they just want fast, efficient, quality service. If you and your organization fail to provide it, they may take their business elsewhere. By being proactive and thinking about such factors, you will be able to provide better service to your customers.

Also, you should consider alternative strategies for dealing with unusual situations (**contingency plans**). Such alternatives are helpful when things do not go as originally planned (e.g., a computer database fails, service is not delivered as promised, or products that were ordered from another organization for a customer do not arrive as promised).

Figure 10.6 shows the **planning process model**, the basic steps of which are

1. *Set a goal*. In a customer service situation, the obvious goal is to prevent problems from occurring. You also want to successfully address customers' needs, have them leave the service experience satisfied, spread positive word-of-mouth advertising, and return in the future.

2. *Examine and evaluate the situation*. In this phase of planning, you should look at all possible factors that could affect a customer interaction (e.g., the environment, policies, procedures, your skills and authority level, management support, and the customer). With these factors in mind, work with your peers and supervisor or team leader to establish criteria for selecting acceptable actions. For example, it might be acceptable to use voice mail if you are dealing with a customer; however, it is not proper to forward incoming messages to voice mail so that you can meet with a peer on a non-work-related issue.

contingency plans Backup systems or procedures that are implemented when regular ones break down or fail to function as intended.

planning process model Five-step process for creating contingency or backup plans to better serve customers when problems arise or things do not go as expected.

Street Talk

A simple technique to ensure you are looking through the lens of the customer is to first identify with their emotions, and then meet their needs. For example, you might say, "I can see you are upset; let me see what I can do to take care of this problem" or "I can hear you are frustrated. Let me review the situation and see what I can do to help you." By identifying with the customer's emotions first, you let him or her feel valued versus feeling as if he or she is processed as just another transaction.

TERI YANOVICH   *President, T. A. Yanovich, Inc*

FIGURE 10.6
Planning Process Model

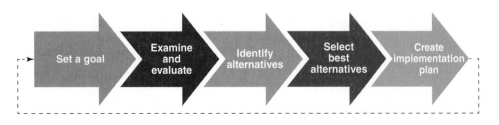

3. *Identify alternatives.* Meet with peers and supervisors or team leaders to develop a list of alternatives for dealing with various customer situations. Consider the advantages and disadvantages of each option.

4. *Select the best alternatives.* After reviewing all the options, select the one (or more) that best addresses the targeted goal of providing quality service to customers. Do not forget to measure this choice against the criteria you established earlier.

5. *Create an implementation plan.* Working with peers and supervisors or team leaders, decide which resources (human and otherwise) will be needed to deliver effective service. Also, develop a system for evaluating success. For example, a customer wants two items, but you have only one in stock. You apologize for not being able to fulfill the customer's needs. Is this "success"? Or would you be successful if, in addition to the apology, you called other stores, located another item, and had it delivered to the customer's house at no cost?

PROBLEM-SOLVING ABILITY

If a customer has a problem, you have a problem. Remembering this simple concept can go a long way in reminding you of your purpose for being a service provider. Your primary job function is to address the needs of your customer. To do this when a customer is dissatisfied or has a concern, you should take responsibility for the problem instead of trying to place blame and defer the issue to someone else. What or who created the problem (e.g., the weather, you, the customer, or the manufacturer) doesn't matter. Your goal is to identify and implement appropriate solutions to the extent that you are authorized to do so. Otherwise, you should seek assistance from the appropriate person according to your organization's policy. To accomplish sound problem solving, you will need a process for gathering and analyzing information. As with the planning process discussed earlier, you should take some specific steps to find a solution to a customer's problem. These steps are described in the following sections. The problem-solving model discussed in Chapter 7 can also be applied when you are trying to encourage and maintain customer loyalty.

Problem resolution is not difficult if it is approached systematically. If you have done the planning described earlier and know what options are available and what authority you have, it becomes much easier.

PROFESSIONALISM

As you have read in previous chapters, projecting a positive personal image—through manner of dress, knowledge, appearance of your work area, and your mental attitude—is a crucial element in communicating an "I care" image to customers and potential customers. By paying close attention to such factors, you better position yourself to establish and maintain a strong customer relationship. This is especially true where attitude is concerned. Attitude can mean success or failure when dealing with customers and can be communicated through the various verbal and nonverbal cues you have read about in other chapters.

KNOWLEDGE CHECK

1. List some of the common qualities of service providers that affect customers.
2. What are six common customer needs?
3. What is a code of ethics and what role does it play in building a stronger customer–provider relationship?
4. What is the risk of an organization failing to demonstrate high ethical standards?
5. Describe the five steps of the planning process model and why each is important in delivering quality customer service.

LO 10-6 Making the Customer Number One

CONCEPT Make a good first impression by establishing rapport; then identify and satisfy your customers' needs. Follow up to obtain repeat business.

Most people like to feel that they are important and valued. By recognizing and acting on that fact, you can go a long way toward providing solid customer service, reducing churn, and building a strong relationship with customers. By being an "I care" person, you can generate much goodwill while meeting customer needs.

Every time you encounter a customer in person or over the phone, you have an opportunity to provide excellent service. Some companies call a service encounter the **moment of truth** or refer to them as **contact points**, in

moment of truth A phrase popularized by Scandinavian Airlines System President Jan Carlzon in his popular 1987 book of the same name. It is defined as any instance when a customer comes into contact with any element or representative of an organization.

contact points Instances in which a customer connects with a service provider or some other aspect of an organization.

Customer loyalty is won by providing extra service for the customer. Organizations must assess individual needs and determine how to meet those needs better than the competition does. In this case, customers who have mobility impairments or limitations will keep coming back to this establishment because they have provided transportation for those with disabilities. *How can you provide extra service for customers with special needs?*

IDENTIFY AND SATISFY CUSTOMER NEEDS QUICKLY

Use the questioning, listening, observing, and feedback skills outlined in this book to focus on issues of concern to the customer. By effectively gathering information, you can then move to the next phase of customer service.

EXCEED EXPECTATIONS

As you can see on the relationship-rating point scale, customers typically expect that, if they pay a certain price for a product or service, they will receive a specific quality and quantity in return. This is not an unusual expectation. The average customer looks for value.

With the Internet and global competition, many products and services are only a mouse click away. If you and your organization fail to deliver as promised or expected, customers may simply go away or move on to another website in search of quality products and services that are competitively priced. Today's customers tend to be better-educated consumers who recognize that if they cannot fulfill their needs in one place, they can easily access the same or similar products and services on the Internet or by visiting a competitor. Therefore, you need to exceed a customer's expectations.

Many terms are used to describe the concept of exceeding expectations—knock-their-socks-off service, positive memorable customer experiences, E-plus service, customer delight, dazzling service, fabled service, and five-diamond or five-star service. All these phrases have in common the concept mentioned before of going above and beyond customer expectations—*under*promise and *over*deliver. By going out of your way not only to satisfy customers but also to "wow" them by doing, saying, or offering the unexpected related to high-quality service delivery, you can exceed expectations. The result could be the reward of continuing patronage or loyalty from the customer.

Here are two examples of unexpected service or going the extra mile and exceeding customer expectations. The author recently bought flooring tiles from a home product warehouse and took them home. Upon opening the box, he discovered that several tiles were broken. After the customer called the store to complain, an employee delivered the replacement tiles and assisted the customer in showing him how to properly lay them. Another example occurred when the author purchased gift cards from three different restaurant chains for special occasions. Each chain rewards customers for their loyalty and encourages them to return. Brio Tuscan Grille, Olive Garden, and Outback Steakhouse are all nationally known restaurant chains that give a free $10 gift card each time a customer purchases a $50 gift card. This provides an instant reward, encourages future purchases, and helps get customers into the restaurants, where they are likely to bring others along and spend additional money.

FOLLOW UP

Service professionals regrettably often overlook this important element of the service process, although it can be one of the most crucial in establishing long-term relationships. Follow-through is a major factor in obtaining repeat business. After you have satisfied a customer's needs, follow up with the customer on his or her next visit or via mail, e-mail, or telephone to ensure that he or she was satisfied. For external customers, this follow-up can be coupled with a small thank-you card, coupons for discounts on future purchases, small presents, or any other incentive to reward their patronage. You can follow up with internal customers by using voice mail or e-mail messages, leaving Post-it® notes on their desks, inviting them for coffee in the cafeteria, or any other of a number of ways. The prime objective is to let them know that you have not forgotten them and appreciate their business and support.

> **Customer Service Success Tip**
>
> Smile, remind the customer you are available to help in the future, give an opportunity for last-minute questions, and invite the customer to return. Just as with your initial impression, you need to close on a high note.

KNOWLEDGE CHECK

1. What are customer-rating points and how do they impact an organization?
2. What is a moment of truth with a customer?
3. How can exceeding customer expectations be beneficial to an organization?

LO 10-7 Enhancing Customer Satisfaction as a Strategy for Retaining Customers

CONCEPT Do the unexpected; deal with one customer at a time; handle complaints efficiently. These are just some of the things you can do to enhance customer satisfaction.

Keeping customers can be difficult in a competitive, global marketplace because so many companies have joined in the race for customers. By providing a personal, professional strategy, you can help ensure that customers return. This is because building good relationships in order to increase customer satisfaction is valuable—it can lead to repeat business—the key to keeping a business productive and profitable. Customers like doing business with those who understand them and their needs and go out of their way to deliver timely and quality services and products at a fair price. This can lead to satisfaction and that is a big factor for many customers in remaining loyal to a brand or organization. In your organization, your efforts could be a deciding factor in customer ratings for the quality of services rendered. The following are tips that can help provide quality service to customers.

PAY ATTENTION

As you listen, focus all your attention on the customer so that you can identify and address his or her needs. If you are serving in person, use positive

Getting customers to visit or contact your organization is just the first step in the customer–provider relationship. Each person must strive to make the experience a positively memorable one so that he or she continues to return and tells others about the great service that he or she received. *What is your role in creating memorable experiences that help retain customers?*

nonverbal cues (e.g., face the customer, smile, use open gestures, make eye contact, stop doing other things, and focus attention on the customer) and language. Ask open-end questions to determine the customer's needs. Also, use the active listening techniques discussed in Chapter 5 to ensure that you get all the information you need to properly address the customer's needs or concerns.

DEAL WITH ONE CUSTOMER AT A TIME

You cannot effectively handle two people (on the phone or in person) simultaneously. When more than one call or customer comes in at the same time, seek assistance or ask one customer either if he or she could wait or if you might get back to him or her at a later time. Then, give personalized attention to the other customer.

KNOW YOUR CUSTOMERS

This is crucial with long-term customers, but it is also important with everyone. You may see or talk to hundreds of customers a week; however, each customer has only one or two contacts with you. Although you might not recall the name of everyone you speak with during a day, your customers will likely remember what was said or agreed upon previously, and expect you to do the same. For that reason, use notes or your computer to keep a record of conversations with customers. You can review or refer to these notes in subsequent encounters. This avoids having customers repeat themselves, and they will feel "special" because you remembered them. Many professionals use database management programs or contact software (e.g., ACT or Maximizer) or customer contact management systems to log and catalog contacts and customers, as well as to keep detailed notes on each contact with a customer. Consider such programs to be your electronic "cheat sheet" to help you remember important details about all your customers, clients, or patients (e.g., spouse names, favorite colors, birthdays, sizes, last purchase, prior conversations, and other valuable information).

GIVE CUSTOMERS SPECIAL TREATMENT

As you read earlier, you should try to take the time for a little small talk once in a while. This will help you learn about your customers and what's important to them (potential needs). Occasionally, paying them compliments also helps (e.g., "That's an attractive tie" or "That perfume is very pleasing").

SERVICE EACH CUSTOMER AT LEAST ADEQUATELY

Take the necessary time to handle your customer's questions, complaints, or needs. If you have a number of customers on the phone or in person, service one at a time and either ask to get back to the others or get help from a co-worker, if possible. You might also suggest alternative information resources to customers, such as fax-on-demand or your website, online information system, or interactive voice response. This may satisfy them and help reduce the calls or visits from customers because they can now get the information they need from alternative sources.

DO THE UNEXPECTED

Do not just provide service; provide exceptional service. Provide additional information, offer suggestions that will aid the customer, send articles that may be of interest, follow up transactions with calls or letters to make sure that needs were met, or send cards for special occasions and to thank customers. These are the little things that mean a lot and can mean the difference between a rating of Average or Exemplary on the relationship-rating point scale.

Example: Give 'Em the Extra Pickle!

An example of doing the unexpected came when Bob Farrell, founder of Farrell's Ice Cream Parlor restaurants, reportedly responded to a customer complaint a number of years ago. Farrell received a letter from a regular customer of many years. The customer had been ordering hamburgers with an extra pickle since he started patronizing Farrell's. At some point, the man went to Farrell's and ordered a hamburger but was told by a new server that the extra pickle would cost an additional 25 cents. When the man protested, the server conferred with her manager and happily reported that the extra pickle would cost only 5 cents. At that point the man left and wrote Farrell, who wrote back enclosing a free coupon, apologizing, and inviting the customer back.

The lesson to be learned here is that when you have a loyal customer whom you might lose because of enforcement of a trivial policy, you should be flexible. When policies inhibit good service and negatively affect customer relationships, they should be pointed out to management and examined for possible modification or elimination.

Customer Service Success Tip

Treat all customers as if they are crucial to the organization—they are! Do whatever is possible and reasonable to maintain a strong customer–provider relationship and keep the customer returning and recommending that others should do likewise. Whether someone is a new or existing customer should make no difference.

HANDLE COMPLAINTS EFFECTIVELY

Treat complaints as opportunities to redeem missed service expectations, and handle them effectively. Acknowledge any error on your part and do everything possible to resolve the problem quickly and to the customer's satisfaction. Thank the customer for bringing his or her concerns to your attention.

SELL BENEFITS, NOT FEATURES

An effective approach to increasing sales is used by most salespeople. They focus on benefits and not features of a product or service. A feature differs from a benefit in that it is a descriptive aspect of a product or service (e.g., has a shorter turn radius, has 27 options, comes in five different colors, has a remote control, and uses less energy than competing models).

Show each customer how your product, service, or information addresses his or her needs. What benefit will result? Stress that although other organizations may offer similar products and services, yours fit their needs best (if they do), and how. If your product or service doesn't fit their needs, admit it and offer any available alternatives (such as referral to a competitor). Your customers will appreciate your honesty, and even if you can't help them, they will probably return in the future because you are trusted.

KNOW YOUR COMPETITION

Stay abreast of what other, similar organizations are offering in order to counter comments about them. This does not mean that you should criticize or belittle your competitors or their products and services. Such behavior is unprofessional and unethical, and will likely cause the customer to lose respect for you. And when respect goes, trust goes.

Staying aware of the competition has the additional benefit of helping you be sure that you can describe and offer the products, services, and features of your organization that are comparable to those being offered by others.

The Marriott hotel chain recognized a need to compete with cheaper reservation rates being offered on the Internet. Marriott announced its "Look No Further Best Rate Guarantee" that matched reservation rates for the same hotel, room type, and reservation dates at all its hotels (excluding Ritz-Carlton) no matter where the customer found them. The chain states as part of its guarantee, "If the lower rate you found qualifies, we will adjust your room rate to reflect that rate, and give you an additional 25% off the lower rate."[11] The hotel chain did this to remain competitive and fill rooms.

KNOWLEDGE CHECK

1. What are some tips that a service provider might follow to enhance customer satisfaction?

LO 10-8 Strive for Quality

CONCEPT A customer's perception of quality service is often one of the prime reasons for his or her return.

A final strategy for helping to increase customer loyalty relates to the quality of service you and your organization provide. So much is written these days about quality—how to measure it and its significance—that there is a temptation to think of it as a fad. In the areas of customer service and customer retention, thinking this way could be disastrous. A customer's perception of quality service is often one of the prime reasons for his or her return.

Terms such as **total quality management (TQM)** and **continuous quality improvement (CQI)** are often used in many industries and by manufacturers to label the goal of improvement. Basically, quality service involves efforts and activities that are done well and that meet or exceed customer needs and expectations. In an effort to achieve quality service, many organizations go to great lengths to test and measure the level of service provided to customers.

On a personal level, you can strive for quality service by working to achieve an Exemplary rating on the relationship-rating point scale. Your organization's ability to deliver quality service depends on you and the others who provide front-line service to customers. If you do not adopt a professional attitude and continually strive to improve your knowledge, skills, and efforts in dealing with customers, failure and customer dissatisfaction can result.

total quality management (TQM) and continuous quality improvement (CQI) Systematic approaches to identifying and quantifying best practices in an organization and/or industry in order to make improvements in effectiveness and efficiency.

Small Business Perspective

The Small Business Administration reported that

- Small businesses continue to be incubators for innovation and employment growth during the current recovery. The net job gains of small businesses matched those of larger businesses during the last half of 2010, and the gross job gains of small business outpaced those of large businesses by about 3 to 1.

- Data for 2009 and 2010 indicated that both large and small businesses were hit hard by the 2007 recession. The data further indicate that the small business share of GDP held steady in early 2009, but fell further in 2010, as corporate businesses (large-business centric) recovered more quickly than non-corporate businesses (small business centric).

- The construction industry, a sector predominately made up of small businesses, was especially affected by the downturn, and has declined as a share of the overall economy.

- The health care industry, on the other hand, is made up of about 50 percent small businesses, and has grown as a share of the overall economy, partly offsetting the overall losses in employment in other industries.[12]

Like most organizations at the end of the first decade of the 21st century, the small business sector was been hit hard financially. In addition, small businesses have to face competition and strive to maintain customer loyalty on three fronts. First, they have to effectively compete with local small business competitors. Second, they have to stave off competition from large chain stores and organizations that maintain a local presence and have large advertising budgets. Finally, they must compete with similar organizations worldwide on the Internet.

Building and maintaining customer loyalty is no easy task for small business owners, who typically have limited financial and human resources. Not only must they be concerned with the day-to-day business operations, but they also must continually monitor

(continued)

competitive practices and trends in society that might impact their bottom line. Without the buying clout of larger organizations, they often struggle to maintain a profitable business model while looking for ways to continue to maintain or grow their business. Rising product and distribution costs, fees from banks and credit card processing companies, insurance, state and local taxes, employee expenses, and myriad other expenses work to eat away profit margins. These are major reasons why entrepreneurs and small business owners need to focus so heavily on customer loyalty. Those who take a reactive "next" approach to dealing with customers, where they wait for someone to click on their website or walk through the door, are doomed to failure. Successful businesspeople continually look for new and innovative approaches to serving their customers. This includes using an integrated approach to doing business (e.g., face-to-face, telephone, computers, and other available technology). Customers expect that anyone who provides products and services will be competitive and prepared to match the service and delivery systems of others in their industry. Those organizations that cannot meet these standards are typically the ones that close their doors.

The cost of getting new customers versus maintaining current ones has traditionally been higher. According to TARP Worldwide, "the real ratio of cost to win a new customer vs. retaining a current customer varies from 2 to 1 to 20 to 1 (this depends on the size and value of the customer to the company/industry); and that it costs five times as much to win a new customer as to keep a current customer. This formed the basis for establishing many of the customer service 800 numbers in the early 1980s."[13]

A prudent business strategy for any size business is to keep the customers you have and try to bring in new ones with low- or no-cost initiatives (e.g., referral programs, incentives, discount coupons, brand recognition, and positive word-of-mouth publicity). Typically, some of the factors that can help sustain a loyal customer population for retail organizations include

- Service representatives who are knowledgeable and helpful, have excellent communication skills, and care about their job and customers.
- Service and assistance that are readily available and easily accessible 24/7/365 and in a variety of formats (e.g., telephone, fax, Internet, face-to-face).
- Unique products that differentiate you from competitors.
- Creation of a one-stop shopping experience where customers can obtain multiple types of products and services at one location.
- High-quality products that require lower levels of maintenance and follow-up service.
- A flexible, "no-hassle" return or exchange policy.

Service organizations also should be concerned about customer loyalty. Some factors that can assist in customer satisfaction and retention include

- Staff who are experienced, knowledgeable, trustworthy, and reliable and possess a "can-do" attitude.
- The ability to create a true partnership with clients where the success of the customer is a prime consideration as opposed to just fulfilling the requirements of a contract or project.
- The ability to see beyond the obvious and come up with customized, unique strategies and interventions to address client needs.
- Flexibility in dealing with clients who are experiencing a changing environment or situation.

Impact on Service

Based on personal experience and what you just read, answer the following questions:

1. How well do small businesses do in delivering quality service and retaining customers?
2. What factors have you seen small businesses faced with in the past couple of years?
3. What technology have you witnessed small business owners using to gain and retain customers?
4. Are there issues related to customer service and retention that are faced more by small businesses than large ones? Explain.

Key Terms

channel partner
churn
churn rate
code of ethics
contact points
contingency plans
cost of dissatisfied customers
customer loyalty
customer loyalty program

customer relationship management (CRM)
customer relationships
customer retention
customer satisfaction
moment of truth
planning process model
relationship-rating points
relationship-rating point scale

Technical Assistance Research Program (TARP) Worldwide
total quality management (TQM) and continuous quality improvement (CQI)
touch point
trust

Summary

Building enduring, strong customer relationships is based on the principles of trust, responsibility, loyalty, and satisfying customer needs. These are all crucial elements of success in an increasingly competitive business world. Retaining current customers is less expensive and more effective than finding and developing new ones. The key is to provide courteous, professional service that addresses customer needs. Although many factors potentially affect your ability to deliver quality service, you can apply specific methods and strategies to keep your customers coming back.

Too often, service providers lose sight of the fact that they are the organization and that their actions determine the outcome of any customer–provider encounter. By employing the strategies outlined in this chapter, and those you read about previously, you can do much to ensure customer satisfaction and organizational success.

Review Questions

1. How can you build customer trust?
2. What are some key reasons why customers remain loyal to a product, a service, or an organization?
3. What are some of the provider characteristics that affect customer loyalty?
4. What are the steps in the planning process model? Describe.
5. What are six common customer needs?
6. What are ways for service providers to take responsibility for customer relations?
7. What are some techniques for making the customer feel that he or she is No. 1?

Search It Out

www.mhhe.com/customerservice

1. Search the Internet for Information on Customer Loyalty

Search the Internet for additional information related to customer loyalty. Select one of the following projects:

a. Go to the websites of organizations that deal with customers and service. Identify research data, articles, bibliographies, and other reference sources

(e.g., videotapes) related to customer loyalty and create a bibliography similar to the one at the end of this book. Here are a few sites to get you started:

www.ICSA.com
www.SOCAP.com
www.CSR.com

www.Amazon.com

www.Barnes&Noble.com

b. Go to various search engines to locate information and articles on *customer loyalty*. To find information, enter terms related to concepts covered in this chapter or locate websites dealing with such issues. Here are a few to get you started:

Customer loyalty

Customer satisfaction

Customer retention

Customer Service Review magazine

Total quality management in customer service

Cost of customer service

2. Additional Resources

Search the website for this textbook, www.mhhe.com/customerservice, for additional activities, reference materials, and support materials.

Collaborative Learning Activities

Building Loyalty

Here are three options for activities that you and others can use to reinforce the concepts of building loyalty that you read about in this chapter.

1. Working with a partner, think of times when you have both been frustrated or dissatisfied with service received from a provider. Make a list of characteristics the service provider(s) exhibited that had a negative impact on you. Once you have a list, discuss the items on the list, and then honestly say whether either (or both) of you exhibit any of these negative behaviors when dealing with others. For the ones to which you answered yes, jointly develop a list of strategies to improve each behavior.

2. Take a field trip around your town. Walk through and/or past as many establishments as possible. Look for examples of actions that organizations are doing to encourage and discourage customer loyalty. List the examples on a sheet of paper and be prepared to discuss them in groups assigned by your instructor when you return to class. Some examples of encouragement might be free samples of a product being distributed at a food court, discount coupons, acceptance of competitor coupons, or free

refills on drinks. Negative examples might be signs that say "Restrooms for customers only" or "No change given," and policies that allow discounts only on certain days and no refunds on purchases (exchanges only).

3. Do a survey of at least 20 people of different age groups and cultural and ethnic backgrounds. Ask the following questions related to customer retention and loyalty, then report your findings in class:

• What is the most important thing that a service provider can do to get you to return to a store, organization, or website?

• When shopping for a product or service, what referral source do you value most when making a buying decision (e.g., website, consumer article or media channel, newspaper, family member, or friend)?

• If you are trying to decide where to purchase a product or service and the only two differentiators are slightly higher cost and a better approach to service, which would you choose?

• If you could choose between buying an identical product locally or on the Internet, which source are you more likely to select?

Face to Face

Assessing the Need for Reorganization at Get Away

Background

After over 9 years in business, the Get Away travel agency in Des Moines, Iowa, is feeling the pinch of competition. During the past 14 months, the owners, Marsha Henry and Consuela (Connie) Gomez, have seen business profits dwindle by 18 percent. Employee attrition was also over 50 percent in the past 6 months. Neither Marsha nor Connie can figure out what has happened. Although travel reservationists have had to deal with airline fee caps, customers making more reservations on the Internet, and the fact that many industry travel providers are cutting back, competing agencies don't seem to be suffering as much as Get Away. The problem is especially worrisome because Marsha and Connie recently took out a second mortgage on their office building so that they could put more money into promotion and customer acquisition efforts. The more efforts they make at gaining exposure, the more customers they lose, it seems. Recently, they lost a major corporate client that accounted for over $100,000 in business a year. Out of desperation, they have decided to hire you, a seasoned travel agency manager, to try to stop their descent and turn the operation around.

Your Role

As the new manager at Get Away, you have been given the authority to do whatever is necessary to salvage the agency. By agreement with Marsha and Connie, they are delaying the announcement of your hiring to other agency employees. Your goal is to objectively assess the operation by acting as a customer.

Your first contact with the agency came on Thursday morning, when you placed a phone call to the office at 9:00 a.m. posing as a customer. The phone rang 12 times and was curtly answered with, "Hello. Please hold (click)." After nearly 5 minutes, an agent, Sue, came on the line and stated, "Sorry for the wait; we're swamped. Can I get your name and number and call you right back?" Two-and-a-half hours later, you got a call from Tom. He said that Sue had gone home for the day because she was sick, and he was doing her callbacks. Sue would follow up when she came in the next day. You

had asked a friend to make a similar call yesterday (Wednesday), and she had similar results.

On Thursday afternoon, you stopped by the office at 1:55 p.m. Of four agents who should have been there, only Claudia was present. Apparently Tom and Sue were still at lunch. Two customers were waiting as you arrived. Aisha greeted you with a small smile and asked you to "take a number and have a seat." You looked around the office and saw desks piled high with materials, an overflowing trash can, and an empty coffeepot in the waiting area bearing the sign "Please have a cup on us." In talking to your fellow "customers," you learned that one had been there for over 45 minutes. Both were irritated at having to wait, and, eventually, one left. You left after 30 minutes and passed Tom and Sue, who came in laughing. You thought you detected an odor of alcohol on Tom. Neither acknowledged you. From the office, you proceeded to a meeting with Marsha and Connie.

Critical Thinking Questions

1. What impressions of the travel agency did you have as a result of your initial phone call?

2. How did your office visit affect you?

3. What will you tell Marsha and Connie about employee professionalism?

4. What customer needs are being overlooked in this scenario?

5. In what ways can this situation be improved?

Planning to Serve

To help enhance customer retention and foster customer loyalty efforts of any organization, think about the following questions:

1. What are some strategies that can be used to show customers that their business is valued?

2. What obstacles exist to customer loyalty and how might they be removed?

3. What are some of the things that positively impact customer loyalty in many organizations?

4. What are some things that differentiate organizations and that can be accentuated to build customer retention and loyalty?

5. When a customer becomes dissatisfied, what can be done to appease and retain that customer's business?

6. What is the most difficult aspect of customer retention in your mind? Explain.

Quick Preview Answers

1. T	3. T	5. T	7. T	9. T	11. T
2. F	4. T	6. F	8. T	10. F	12. T

Ethical Dilemma Summary

Ethical Dilemma 10.1 Possible Answers

1. What would you say or do to the pharmacist?

   Because of the serious nature of this incident, you should not become part of a potentially litigious and health-threatening situation. Tell the pharmacist that you do not feel comfortable not telling the patient the truth and ask him to handle it himself.

2. Should you notify anyone else about the incident? Explain.

   Because of the serious nature of this event, you should definitely report it to the store manager and, depending on the reaction that you get, you may want to consider whether this organization is really somewhere that you want to continue working. If the situation is not properly resolved with the disciplining and/or removal of the pharmacist, there are going to be major legal and other problems in the future. If it is not handled at a local level, you can always contact the regional store manager and, if necessary, corporate headquarters. If all else fails, each state has governmental agencies that license and oversee pharmacies and pharmacists. You can report the incident to them for investigation.

3. What do you do or say to the patient? Explain.

   In the immediate instance, you should probably defer discussion of the matter and explain that the pharmacist or someone else will be right with the customer.

4. What are the ethical issues here and how would you deal with them?

   This is certainly a very awkward, sensitive, and serious issue with which to deal. If you fail to share with the pharmacist your concerns and feelings about the way the situation is being handled, it will possibly be repeated, and potentially have serious medical repercussions or worse. The pharmacist is not only acting unprofessionally, unethically, and potentially illegally, he is also potentially putting himself and the organization in a litigious situation and endangering the lives of patients. Granted, this may have been a legitimate mistake on the part of the pharmacist; however, that does not make it any less serious.

   On the other hand, if you refuse to do as the pharmacist tells you, your job and future opportunities might be in jeopardy. This could be a reality; however, remember that federal law protects whistleblowers from retaliation. Also, you have an option of going to the store manager to discuss the issue. The bottom line is that this is a very serious medical issue.

5. How do such instances potentially affect customer loyalty?

   There have been many media reports of similar incidents in recent years and, as a result, consumers are very skeptical and leery about going to pharmacies. Typically, when these cases arise, there is an exodus from the involved pharmacies to their competitors. The old adage of "buyer beware" is certainly the watchword for many patients these days. Also, there are many watchdog groups monitoring such cases.

Ethical Dilemma 10.2 Possible Answers

1. Should you say anything to anyone in the office? Explain.

   In a situation where you are the "new kid on the block," it is likely that your inclination is to keep your mouth shut, especially since you do not yet have a strong rapport with co-workers. In such situations, most people would not feel comfortable approaching anyone to share their views. However, if you fail to say something to the agents or your supervisor, there is a chance that federal Environmental Protection Agency (EPA) guidelines are going to be violated and children are going to be put in potential physical danger. This is based on research that shows young children assimilate almost 50 percent of any lead that they might ingest (e.g., from eating paint chips they find on the floor). This can lead to mental and physical medical conditions.

   You could try approaching the agents casually (in the break room) and sharing some interesting "research" that you read (go online in advance to read about the EPA rulings) about the effect of lead-based paint in buildings. Ask them how agents normally handle situations where they know about such paint in properties that are listed. This can put the agents on notice without accusing them and might even result in your finding that they were not aware of the EPA guidelines.

   Another alternative would be to approach your supervisor and let him or her know that you have heard of a property the agency has listed that might violate EPA guidelines for lead-based paint and ask what types of disclosures agents have to warn potential buyers about. Again, you could do this in a nonaccusatory fashion.

If neither of these approaches has any direct corrective impact, you have a number of additional options. Some of these include

- Confronting the agents about the conversation that you overheard and ask them to inform the potential buyer.

- Telling your supervisor of the conversation and asking him or her to speak to the agents.

- Telling the potential buyer of the situation.

- Reporting the incident to the EPA if a sale is made and no legal disclosure was done.

- Quitting your job and saying nothing.

2. Should you say anything to the potential buyer? Explain.

Before approaching a customer, you should always try to resolve the issue internally within the organization at the lowest possible level.

3. If you do not say anything, is there any potential legal liability? Explain.

If a sale is made and legal disclosure is not made as required by law, the organization and agents could be held legally and potentially civilly liable.

4. If you do say something to either the agents, your boss, or the potential buyer, what are the potential repercussions for you?

There are a number of potential results if you speak up:

- You might be thanked for bringing the issue to the attention of the agents, boss, or buyer.

- You might also be ostracized by your peers for intervening.

- You might be fired by your boss, if he or she is aware of the practice and wants to keep the illegal activity under wraps.

READER'S CUSTOMER SERVICE SURVEY—*Customer Service Skills for Success, 6th Edition*

Name _____

Title _____

Organization/School _____

Address (where you want booklet mailed)

_____

City/State/Zip _____

Phone ( ) _____

Customer feedback is crucial for delivering effective service and addressing specific needs. For us to make necessary additions, deletions, or corrections to this book, we need your help. Please take a few minutes to provide feedback in the following areas and return this questionnaire to the address noted at the end. In exchange for your thoughts and time, we'll send you a free booklet written by the author, titled *Communicating One-to-One*, on effective interpersonal communication techniques. (Photocopy this questionnaire if you prefer.) All the information indicated above is needed to receive the free booklet.

Thank you.

1. Describe yourself in terms of customer contact experience:
   ____ Entry level (Up to one year) ____ Mid-level (2–5 years) ____ Senior (5+ years)

2. Are you currently working in a customer contact position in a business or organization? Yes _____ No _____

3. In what industry do you currently work or intend to work once you graduate?

   _____

4. The information provided in this book was clearly written and easy to read.
   1 _____ 2 _____ 3 _____ 4 _____ 5 _____ 6 _____ 7 _____
   Strongly   Neutral   Strongly
   Disagree   Agree

5. The examples and techniques outlined in this book are realistic and useful.
   1 _____ 2 _____ 3 _____ 4 _____ 5 _____ 6 _____ 7 _____
   Strongly   Neutral   Strongly
   Disagree   Agree

6. The supplemental materials (website materials, figures, activities, questions, references) reinforced key concepts and chapter objectives.
   1 _____ 2 _____ 3 _____ 4 _____ 5 _____ 6 _____ 7 _____
   Strongly   Neutral   Strongly
   Disagree   Agree

7. The design of this book was logical, efficient, effective, and easy to follow.
   1 _____ 2 _____ 3 _____ 4 _____ 5 _____ 6 _____ 7 _____
   Strongly   Neutral   Strongly
   Disagree   Agree

8. The level of information was well targeted to entry- and mid-level customer contact personnel.

1 _____ 2 _____ 3 _____ 4 _____ 5 _____ 6 _____ 7 _____
Strongly   Neutral   Strongly
Disagree   Agree

9. The text included real-world examples and scenarios related to a variety of industries that helped make chapter content more relative to the workplace.

1 _____ 2 _____ 3 _____ 4 _____ 5 _____ 6 _____ 7 _____
Strongly   Neutral   Strongly
Disagree   Agree

10. I can apply information or ideas learned directly to my current or future job.

1 _____ 2 _____ 3 _____ 4 _____ 5 _____ 6 _____ 7 _____
Strongly   Neutral   Strongly
Disagree   Agree

11. This book compares well to other textbooks I have used.

1 _____ 2 _____ 3 _____ 4 _____ 5 _____ 6 _____ 7 _____
Strongly   Neutral   Strongly
Disagree   Agree

12. I will recommend this book to others.

1 _____ 2 _____ 3 _____ 4 _____ 5 _____ 6 _____ 7 _____
Strongly   Neutral   Strongly
Disagree   Agree

13. What chapter was most valuable to you? Why? _____
_____

14. Please tell us one additional concept or topic area related to customer service that you would like to have seen added to this book.

_____
_____

15. In your mind, what is the most critical issue facing customer service professionals today? Why?

_____
_____

16. If you rated any question less than "5" above, please explain why you did so.

_____
_____

17. What other topics related to customer service are of interest to you? Why?

_____

18. Did you use any of the supplemental website content created for this book? If so, what did you use?

_____

Thank you for taking time to provide feedback.

Send form to: Bob Lucas, Principal
Robert W. Lucas Enterprises
P.O. Box 180487
Casselberry, Florida 32718-0487
PH: (407) 695-5535
E-mail: blucas@robertwlucas.com
www.robertwlucas.com

GLOSSARY

A

acculturated The cultural and psychological changes that often occur as a person or group of people are integrated into another culture or country and adopt the habits and beliefs of their new environment.

acknowledgment A communication technique for use with customers who have a complaint or are upset. It involves recognizing the customer's level of emotion before moving on to help resolve the issue.

Americans with Disabilities Act of 1990 (ADA) A U.S. federal act signed into law in July 1990 guaranteeing people with disabilities equal access to workplace and public opportunities.

angry customers Customers who become emotional because either their needs are not met or they are dissatisfied with the services or products purchased from an organization.

appearance and grooming Nonverbal characteristics exhibited by service providers that can send a variety of messages that range from being a professional to having a negative attitude.

applications or apps Software that can process information and perform various tasks on smartphones, tablets or electronic devices, and computers using Internet wireless (Wi-Fi) and wired connections.

articulation, enunciation, or pronunciation Refers to the manner or clarity in which verbal messages are delivered.

assertiveness Involves projecting a presence that is assured, confident, and capable without seeming to be aggressive or arrogant.

assigning meaning The phase of the listening process in which the brain attempts to match a received sound or message with other information stored in the brain in order to recognize or extract meaning from it.

attending The phase of the listening process in which a listener focuses attention on a specific sound or message being received from the environment.

attitudes Emotional responses to people, ideas, and objects. They are based on values, differ between individuals and cultures, and affect the way people deal with various issues and situations.

automated attendants Provide callers with a menu of options from which they can select by pressing a key on their telephone keypad.

automated computer telephone interview A voice recognition computer mechanism that queries survey respondents with questions and stores their responses. Depending upon answers received, the system can branch and follow scripted prompts.

automatic call distribution (ACD) system Telecommunications system used by many companies in their call centers and customer care facilities to capture incoming calls and route them to available service providers.

automatic number identification (ANI) system A form of caller identification system similar to home telephone caller ID

systems. ANI allows incoming customers to be identified on a computer screen with background information so that they can be routed to an appropriate service representative for assistance.

B

baby boomer A term applied to anyone born between 1946 and 1964. People in this age group are called "boomers."

behavioral styles Descriptive term that identifies categories of human behavior identified by behavioral researchers. Many of the models used to group behaviors date back to those identified by Carl Jung.

beliefs Perceptions or assumptions that individuals or cultures maintain. These perceptions are based on past experiences, memories, and interpretations and influence how people act and interact with certain individuals or groups.

biases Beliefs or opinions that a person has about an individual or group. Often based on unreasonable distortions or prejudice.

blind transfer The practice of transferring an incoming caller to another telephone number and hanging up once someone answers without announcing who is calling.

bloggers Individuals who write content that is posted on blogs on the World Wide Web.

blogs or web logs Online journals or diaries that allow people to add content. Many organizational websites use them to post "what's new" sections and to receive feedback (good and bad) from customers and website visitors.

body language Nonverbal communication cues that send powerful messages through gestures, vocal qualities, manner of dress, grooming, and many other cues.

broadband Internet access Refers to a very fast connection to the Internet that is made possible by technology that can communicate up to 40 times the amount of data or information possible with the old phone dial-up Internet connections. With broadband, users can download images, video clips, and music; send e-mail; and perform other functions at a much faster speed.

burnout A category of stress that encompasses personal exhaustion, lack of enthusiasm, reduced productivity, and apathy toward the job and customers.

business-to-business (B2B) Refers to business-to-business customer service.

C

channel Term used to describe the method through which people communicate messages. Examples are face-to-face, telephone, e-mail, written correspondence, and facsimile.

channel partner Relationship of two organizations through which the partners are able to build a larger and stronger competitive presence in the marketplace.

chat support   An online support system that provides customers with access to a "real person" to get answers and help resolve issues. By going to an organization's website that has chat capability, a customer can avoid having to navigate a cumbersome toll-free phone system that often requires him or her to sit on hold for endless amounts of time waiting for a service representative to become available.

Chicano culture   Refers primarily to people with a heritage based in Mexico.

churn   The process of a customer switching between products or companies, often simply to get a better price, rebate, or warranty.

churn rate   Refers to the number of customers who leave a supplier during a given time period.

circadian rhythm   The physiological 24-hour cycle associated with the Earth's rotation that affects metabolic and sleep patterns in humans as day displaces night.

closed-end questions   Inquiries that typically start with a verb and solicit short, one-syllable answers (e.g., yes, no, one word, or a number) and can be used for such purposes as clarifying, verifying information already given, controlling conversation, or affirming something.

cloud computing   Technology that allows for remote storage of a user's data that can then be accessed through a web browser using a mobile application on the user's tablet, mobile device (e.g., smartphone), laptop computer, or desktop computer. The term relates to storing information "off in the electronic clouds" rather than on a user's storage device.

clusters   Groupings of nonverbal behaviors that indicate a possible negative intent (e.g., crossed arms, closed body posturing, frowning, or turning away) while other behaviors (smiling, open gestures with arms and hands, and friendly touching) indicate positive message intent.

code of ethics   A set of standards, often developed by employers, that guide the conduct of all employees.

Cold War   A period of military, economic, and political tension and competition between the United States and the former Soviet Union that lasted from the 1940s through the 1990s.

collective cultures   Members of a group sharing common interests and values. They see themselves as an interdependent unit and conform and cooperate for the good of the group.

comprehending   The phase of the listening process in which the brain attempts to match a received sound or message with other information stored in the brain in order to recognize or extract meaning from it or assign meaning to it.

computer telephony integration (CTI)   A system that integrates a representative's computer and phone to facilitate the automatic retrieval of customer records and other information needed to satisfy a customer's needs and requests.

concept of time   Term used to describe how certain societies view time as either polychronic or monochronic.

conflict   Involves incompatible or opposing views and can result when a customer's needs, desires, or demands do not match service provider or organizational policies, procedures, and abilities.

conflict resolution style   The manner in which a person handles conflict. People typically use one of five approaches to resolving conflict: avoidance, compromise, competition, accommodation, or collaboration.

congruence   In communication, this relates to ensuring that verbal messages sent match or are in agreement with the nonverbal cues used.

contact points   Instances in which a customer connects with a service provider or some other aspect of an organization.

contingency plans   Backup systems or procedures that are implemented when regular ones break down or fail to function as intended.

cost of dissatisfied customers   Phrase that refers to any formula used to calculate the cost of acquiring a new customer or replacing a current one as a result of having a dissatisfied customer leave an organization.

cottage industries   Term adopted in the early days of customer service when many people started small businesses in their homes or cottages and bartered products or services with neighbors.

crisis manager   A person who waits until the last minute to address an issue or take an action. The result is that others are then inconvenienced and have to shift their priorities to help resolve the issue.

cultural diversity   The different racial, ethnic, and socioeconomic varieties, based on factors such as values, beliefs, and experiences, that are present in people grouped together in a given situation, group, or organization.

customer-centric   A term used to describe service providers and organizations that put their customers first and spend time, effort, and money identifying and focusing on the needs of current and potential customers. Efforts are focused on building long-term relationships and customer loyalty rather than simply selling a product or service and moving on to the next customer.

customer contact center   A central point within an organization from which all customer service contacts are managed via various forms of technology.

customer defection   Customers often take their business to competitors when they feel that their needs or wants are not met or if they encounter breakdown in customer service or poor-quality products.

customer expectations   The perceptions that customers have when they contact an organization or service provider about the kind, level, and quality of products and services they should receive.

customer-focused organization   A company that spends energy and effort on satisfying internal and external customers by first identifying customer needs, then establishing policies, procedures, and management and reward systems to support excellence in service delivery.

customer-friendly systems   Refers to the processes in an organization that make service seamless to customers by ensuring that things work properly and the customer is satisfied.

customer loyalty   Term used to describe the tendency of customers to return to a product or organization regularly because of the service and satisfaction they receive.

customer loyalty program   An incentive program offered by an organization to reward customers for spending money and purchasing products and services.

customer needs   Motivators or drivers that cause customers to seek out specific types of products or services. These may be marketing-driven by advertising they have seen or may tie directly to Dr. Abraham Maslow's hierarchy of needs theory.

customer relationship management (CRM)   Concept of identifying customer needs: understanding and influencing customer behavior through ongoing communication strategies in an effort to acquire, retain, and satisfy the customer. The ultimate goal is customer loyalty.

customer relationship management (CRM) software Software designed for use by organizations to assist their marketing, sales, and service professionals to better manage their relationship with current and potential customers by providing a database function for storage and retrieval of information about customers, products, and services.

customer relationships Ongoing friendships with customers focused on making them feel comfortable with an organization and its service providers and on enhancing customer loyalty.

customer retention The ongoing effort by an organization to meet customer needs and desires in an effort to build long-term relationships and keep them for life.

customer satisfaction A marketing term that is used to describe how well an organization is doing in providing products and services that meet or exceed a customer's needs and expectations.

customer service The ability of knowledgeable, capable, and enthusiastic employees to deliver products and services to their internal and external customers in a manner that satisfies identified and unidentified needs and ultimately results in positive word-of-mouth publicity and return business.

customer service environment An environment made up of and influenced by various elements of an organization. Examples are delivery systems, human resources, service, products, and organizational culture.

customers with disabilities Descriptive phrase that refers to anyone with a physical or mental disability.

D

decisive style One of four behavior style groupings characterized by a direct, no-nonsense approach to people and situations.

decoding The stage in the interpersonal communication process in which messages received are analyzed by a receiver in an effort to determine the sender's intent.

deliverables Products or services provided by an organization.

delivery system The method(s) used by an organization to provide services and products to its customers.

demanding or domineering customers Customers who have definite ideas about what they want and are unwilling to compromise or accept alternatives.

deregulation Occurs when governments remove legislative or regulatory guidelines that inhibit and control an industry (e.g., transportation, natural gas, and telecommunications).

difficult customers People who challenge a service provider's ability to deliver service and who require special skills and patience.

disparate treatment Term meaning deliberate discrimination against a person based on his or her age, race, sex, ethnicity, or ability level.

dissatisfied customer Someone who either does not (or perceives that he or she does not) receive promised or quality products or services.

distress Pain or worry brought on by either internal or external physical or mental strain.

diversity The characteristics, values, beliefs, and factors that make people different, yet similar.

downsizing Term applied to the situation in which employees are terminated or empty positions are left unfilled once someone leaves an organization.

E

e-commerce An entire spectrum of companies that market products and services on the Internet and through other technology, and the process of accessing them by consumers.

electronic mail (e-mail) System used to transmit messages around the Internet. This technology is being replaced with instant messaging (IM) in some call centers as many younger consumers embrace it as a primary form of communication.

e-mail management System of providing organizational guidelines for effective use of e-mail systems.

emoticons (emotional icons) Humorous characters that send visual messages such as smiling or frowning. They are created with various strokes of the computer keyboard characters and symbols.

emotional messages of color Research-based use of color to send nonverbal messages through advertisements and other elements of the organization.

emotion-reducing model Process for reducing customer emotion in situations when frustration or anger exists.

employee assistance program (EAP) Benefit package, offered to employees by many organizations, that provides services to help employees deal with personal problems that might adversely affect their work performance (e.g., legal, financial, behavioral, and mental counseling services).

employee expectations Perceptions about positive and negative aspects of the workplace.

employee roles Task assignments that service providers assume.

empowerment The word used to describe the giving of decision-making and problem-resolution authority to lower-level employees in an organization. This precludes having to get permission from higher levels in order to take an action or serve a customer.

encoding The stage in the interpersonal communication process in which the sender decides what message will be sent and how it will be transmitted along with considerations about the receiver.

environmental cues Any aspect of the workplace with which a customer comes into contact. Such things as the general appearance of an area, clutter, unsightly or offensive items, or general disorganization contribute to the perception of an environment.

ethical behavior Acting in a manner that sends a message of positive morality and good values when confronted with a customer situation or problem.

ethics The term comes from the Greek word *ethos*, meaning character. Ethics involves right and wrong or good and evil and is illustrated by the way one responds to situations or acts.

etiquette and manners Includes the acceptable rules, manners, and ceremonies for an organization, profession, or society.

eustress A term coined by psychologist Dr. Hans Seyle to describe the positive stress that people sometimes experience when they set goals or objectives and the exhilaration that are essential for personal expansion and growth.

expectations of privacy The belief that personal information provided to an organization will be safeguarded against inappropriate or unauthorized use or dissemination.

expressive style One of four behavior groups, characterized as being people-oriented, fun-loving, upbeat, and extroverted.

external customers   Those people outside the organization who purchase or lease products and services. This group includes vendors, suppliers, people on the telephone, and others not from the organization.

external obstacles   Factors outside an organization or the sphere of one's influence that can cause challenges in delivering service.

F

face   Refers to the important concept of esteem in many Asian cultures. In such cultures, one tries not to cause embarrassment or otherwise create a situation in which someone looks bad in the eyes of others.

Facebook   A social networking site founded in 2004 by Mark Zuckerburg and his college roommates as a social networking tool to allow students at Harvard University to network socially. It quickly expanded to other major educational institutions and then to the world. It is open for use by anyone over the age of 13 to share information, send messages, and network socially.

facsimile (fax) machine   Equipment that converts printed words and graphics into electronic signals and allows them to be transmitted across telephone lines, then reassembled on the receiving end into a facsimile of the words and graphics.

faulty assumptions   Service provider projections made about underlying customer message meanings based on past experiences.

fax on demand   Technology that allows information, such as a form, stored in a computer to be requested electronically via a telephone and transmitted to a customer.

fee-based 900 number   A premium telephone number provided by organizations and individuals that, when called, can provide information and services that are billed back to the caller's local telephone bill.

feedback   The stage of the interpersonal communication process in which a receiver responds to a sender's message.

feel, felt, found technique   A process for expressing empathy and concern for someone and for helping him or her understand that you can relate to his or her situation.

fight or flight syndrome   A term used by scientists to describe the body's reaction to stressors in which the heart starts pumping the chemical adrenaline into the bloodstream and the lungs start taking in more oxygen. This provides the fuel needed to deal with the situation. (See also stressors.)

filters   Psychological barriers in the form of personal experiences, lessons learned, societal beliefs, and values through which people process and compare information received to determine its significance.

foreign-born people   Refers to people not born in a given country.

form of address   Title used to address people. Examples are Mister, Miss, and Doctor.

G

gender communication   Term used to refer to communication between males and females.

gender roles   Behaviors attributed to or assigned by societal norms.

globalization   The term applied to an ongoing trend of information, knowledge, and resource sharing around the world. As a result of a more mobile society and easier access to transportation and technology, more people are traveling and accessing products and services from international sources than ever before.

global terms   Potentially inflammatory words or phrases used in conversation. They tend to inappropriately generalize behavior or group people or incidents together (e.g., always, never, everyone, everything, all the time).

H

hearing   A passive physiological process of gathering sound waves and transmitting them to the brain for analysis. It is the first phase of the listening process.

hearing disabilities   Conditions in which the ability to hear is diminished below established auditory standards.

help desk   Term used to describe a service provider trained and assigned to assist customers with questions, problems, or suggestions.

hierarchy of needs theory   Developed by Dr. Abraham Maslow. In studies, Maslow identified five levels of needs that humans possess: physiological (basic), safety, social, esteem, and self-actualization.

Hispanic culture   Refers to people who were born in Mexico, Puerto Rico, Cuba, or Central or South America.

human resources   Refers to the employees of an organization.

hygiene   The healthy maintenance of the body through such practices as bathing regularly, washing hair, brushing teeth, cleaning fingernails, and using commercial products to eliminate or mask odors.

I

"I" or "we" messages   Messages that are potentially less offensive than the word "you," which is like nonverbal finger-pointing when emotions are high.

impact of culture   Refers to the outcome of people from various countries or backgrounds coming into contact with one another and potentially experiencing misunderstandings or relationship breakdowns.

inclusive   The concept of ensuring that people of all races, genders, and religious and ethnic backgrounds, as well as a multitude of other diverse factors, are included in communications and activities in the workplace.

indecisive customers   People who have difficulty making a decision or making a selection when given choices of products or services.

individualistic cultures   Groups in which members value themselves as individuals who are separate from their group and are responsible for their own destiny.

inflection   The change in tone of the voice as one speaks. This quality is also called pitch and adds vocal variety and punctuation to verbal messages.

information overload   Refers to having too many messages coming together and causing confusion, frustration, or an inability to act.

inquisitive style   One of four behavioral groups, characterized by being introverted, task-focused, and detail-oriented.

insourcing   The opposite of outsourcing, this occurs when organizations decide to have internal employees assume functions and perform work instead of contracting out to third parties or outsourcing it.

instant messaging   Internet communication technology that allows two or more people to type messages back and forth and see the other person's message as soon as it is sent (real-time communication). They can then respond quickly as if having a conversation over the telephone. This technology has replaced e-mail as a form of written communication in some call centers. More advanced forms allow voice calling, video chat, and hyperlinks to various media.

intelligent callback technology   Technology that gathers information from the customer and tells the customer when he or she can expect a callback.

interactive kiosks or digital displays   Computer terminals that have customized software and hardware and are set up in a public area where users can touch a screen display to access applications for information, commerce, education, or entertainment. Many organizations are now using these in lobbies to allow self-service to customers. You may have seen these at airline check-ins, in banks (ATMs), or in theme parks or other entertainment venues.

interactive voice response (IVR) system   Technology that allows customers to call an organization 24 hours a day, 7 days a week to get information from recorded messages or a computer by keying a series of numbers on the telephone keypad in response to questions or prompts.

interferences   Noises that can interfere with messages being effectively communicated between two people.

internal customers   People within the organization who either require support and service or provide information, products, and services to service providers. Such customers include peers, co-workers, bosses, subordinates, and people from other areas of the organization.

Internet callback technology   Technology that allows someone browsing the Internet to key a prompt on a website and have a service representative call a phone number provided. These systems allow someone browsing the Internet to click on words or phrases (e.g., *Call me*), enter his or her phone number, and continue browsing. This triggers a predictive dialing system and assigns an agent to handle the call when it rings at the customer's end.

Internet telephony   Technology that allows people to talk to one another via the Internet as if they were on a regular telephone.

interpersonal relationship   Focuses on the need for service providers to build strong bonds with customers.

interpersonal skills   The skills used by people to relate to and communicate effectively with others. Examples are verbal and nonverbal communication skills and the ability to build trust, empathy, and compassion.

J

job factors affecting stress   Refer to the elements of a job that frustrate or pressure someone.

job stress   Term coined to describe the impact of the internal and external elements of the workplace that cause service providers to feel mentally and physically pressured or to become ill.

L

lag time   The term applied to the difference in the rate at which the human brain can receive and process information and at which most adults speak.

Latino culture   Refers to people of Hispanic descent.

learning organizations   A term used by Peter Senge in his book *The Fifth Discipline* to describe organizations that value knowledge, education, and employee training. They also learn from their competition, industry trends, and other sources and develop systems to support continued growth and development in order to remain competitive.

listening   An active, learned process consisting of four phases: receiving/hearing the message, attending, comprehending/assigning meaning, and responding.

listening gap   The difference in the speed at which the brain can comprehend communication and the speed at which the average adult speaks in the United States.

M

malapropism   The unintentional misuse or distortion of a word or phrase that sounds somewhat like the one intended but with a different context. This often has humorous results.

media blending   Technology that allows agents to communicate with a customer over a telephone line at the same time information is displayed over the Internet to the customer. As with Internet telephony, this technology has not yet been taken to its full potential.

memory   The ability to gain, store, retain, and recall information in the brain for later application. Short-term memory stores small bits of information (seven items, plus or minus two) for approximately 20 seconds while long-term memory can store much larger quantities of information for potentially unlimited duration.

mentors   Individuals who dedicate time and effort to befriend and assist others. In an organization, they are typically people with a lot of knowledge, experience, skills, and initiative and have a large personal and professional network established.

message   A communication delivered through speech or signals, or in writing.

miscellaneous cues   Refers to factors used to send messages that impact a customer's perception or feelings about a service provider or organization. Examples are personal habits, etiquette, and manners.

mission   The direction or focus of an organization that supports day-to-day interactions with customers.

mission statement   An organization's mission statement that defines its purpose or objectives and *how* it will attain them. It is committed to writing and publicly shared with employees and customers.

mobility or motion impairments   Physical limitations that some people have, requiring accommodation or special consideration to allow access to products or services.

modesty   Refers to the way that cultures view propriety of dress and conduct.

moment of truth   A phrase popularized by Scandinavian Airlines System President Jan Carlzon in his popular 1987 book of the same name. It is defined as any instance when a customer comes into contact with any element or representative of an organization.

monochronic   Refers to the perception of time as being a central focus with deadlines being a crucial element of societal norms.

N

namaste   Traditional greeting gesture in India (pronounced NAH-mes-tay) that is performed with a slight bow and by placing the palms and fingers of both hands together as in a prayer position in the center of the chest.

needs   Motivators or drivers that cause customers to seek out specific types of products or services. These may be marketing-driven, may be based on advertising they have seen, or may tie directly to Abraham Maslow's hierarchy of needs theory.

networking   The active process of building relationships and sharing resources.

noise   Refers to physiological or psychological factors (physical characteristics, level of attention, message clarity, loudness of message, or environmental factors) that interfere with the accurate reception of information. It can also include environmental factors (e.g., external sounds or room acoustics) that inhibit communication and listening.

nonverbal feedback   Messages sent to someone through other than spoken means. Examples are gestures, appearance, and facial expressions.

nonverbal messages   Consist of such things as movements, gestures, body positions, vocal qualities, and a variety of unspoken signals sent by people, often in conjunction with verbal messages.

North American Free Trade Agreement (NAFTA)   A trade agreement entered into by the United States, Canada, and Mexico to help, among other things, eliminate barriers to trade, promote conditions of fair trade across borders, increase investment opportunities, and promote and protect intellectual property rights.

O

objections   Reasons given by customers for not wanting to purchase a product or service during an interaction with a salesperson or service provider (e.g., "I don't need one," "I can't afford it," or "I already have one").

offshoring   Refers to the relocation of business services from one country to another (e.g., services, production, and manufacturing).

online information fulfillment system   Technology that allows a customer to access an organization's website and click on desired information without having to interact with a service provider.

onshoring   The opposite of offshoring, this is the practice of keeping or bringing jobs back within the borders of an organization's home country.

open-end questions   Typically start with words like who, when, what, how, and why and are used to engage others in conversation or to gain input and ideas.

organizational culture   Includes an element of an organization that a customer encounters.

outsourcing   Refers to the practice of contracting with third-party companies or vendors outside the organization (often in another country) to deliver products and services to customers or produce products.

ownership of property   Refers to how people of a given culture view property.

P

paralanguage   Consists of voice qualities (e.g., pitch, rate, tone, or other vocal qualities) or noises and vocalizations (e.g., "Hmmm" or "Ahhh") made as someone speaks that let a speaker know that his or her message is being listened to and followed.

paraphrase   The practice of a message receiver giving back in his or her own words what he or she believes a sender said.

pauses   A verbal technique of delaying response in order to allow time to process information received, think of a response, or gain attention.

perception checking   The process of clarifying a nonverbal cue that was received by stating what behavior was observed, giving one or two possible interpretations, then asking the message sender for clarification.

perceptions   How someone views an item, situation, or others.

personal factors affecting stress   Refer to issues that someone has related to family, finances, or other elements of life that can create pressure or frustration.

personal obstacles   Individual factors that can limit performance or success in life. Examples are disabilities, lack of education, attitude, and biases.

pet peeves   Refer to factors, people, or situations that personally irritate or frustrate a service provider and that, left unchecked, can create a breakdown in effective service.

Pinterest   A pin- or corkboard type of social media forum where users can share photos and images on various themes or interests.

pitch   Refers to the change in tone of the voice as one speaks. This quality is also called inflection and adds vocal variety and punctuation to verbal messages.

planning process model   Five-step process for creating contingency or backup plans to better serve customers when problems arise or things do not go as expected.

Platinum Rule   Term coined by speaker and author Tony Alessandra related to going beyond the step of treating customers the way you want to be treated, to the next level of treating them the way they would like to be treated.

podcasts or podcasting   A word that is a derivative of Apple® Computer's iPod® media player and the term broadcasting. Through podcasts, websites can offer direct download or streaming of their content (e.g., music or video files) to customers or website users.

polychronic   Refers to the perception of time as a fluid commodity that does not interfere with relationships and elements of happiness.

posts   Articles or other content published on blogs for site visitors to read, comment on, share, or download.

posture   Refers to how one sits or stands in order to project various nonverbal messages.

predictive dialing system   System that automatically places outgoing calls and delivers incoming calls to the next available agent. This system is often used in outbound (telemarketing/call center) operations. Because of numerous abuses, the government is continually restricting its use.

primary behavior pattern   Refers to a person's preferred style of dealing with others.

prioritizing time   Relates to how someone decides the importance of various tasks and the order in which they are dealt with.

problem solving   The system of identifying issues, determining alternatives for dealing with them, then selecting and monitoring a strategy for resolution.

problem-solving model   The process used by a service provider to assist customers in determining and selecting appropriate solutions to their issues, concerns, or needs.

process improvement   Refers to the process of continually evaluating products and services to ensure that maximum effectiveness, efficiency, and potential are being obtained from them.

product   Something produced or an output by an individual or organization. In the service environment, products are created to satisfy customer needs or wants.

prohibitions   Local, state, or federal regulations that prevent a service provider from satisfying a customer's request even though the provider would normally do so.

protégé   Typically less experienced recipients of the efforts of mentors.

proxemics   Relates to the invisible barrier surrounding people in which they feel comfortable interacting with others. This zone varies depending on the level of relationship a person has with someone else.

psychological distracters   Refers to mental factors that can cause a shift in focus in interacting with others. Examples are state of health and personal issues.

pupilometrics   The study of pupil reaction to stimuli.

Q

QR Code (Quick Response Code)   Similar in concept to the standard barcode that appears on retail products, this code can allow access to virtually any type of stored information about products, services, or organizations.

R

rapport   The silent bond built between two people as a result of sharing common interests and issues and demonstrating a win-win, I care attitude.

rate of speech   Refers to the number of words spoken per minute. Some research studies have found that the average rate of speech for adults in Western cultures is approximately 125–150 words per minute (wpm).

rational style   One of four behavioral groups, characterized by being quiet, reflective, task-focused, and systematic.

Real-Time IM Relay for Customers with Hearing and Speech Loss   AT&T instant messaging system that allows people with hearing loss who have signed up for AT&T's free Relay Service to receive real-time instant messages from callers.

receiver   One of the two primary elements of a two-way conversation. Gathers the sender's message and decides how to react to it.

recognition   A process that occurs in thinking when a previously experienced pattern, event, process, image, or object that is stored in memory is encountered again.

relationship management   The process of continually monitoring interactions with a customer in order to strengthen ties and retain the customer.

relationship-rating points   Values mentally assigned by customers to a service provider and his or her organization. They are based on a number of factors starting with initial impressions and subsequently by the quality and level of service provided.

relationship-rating point scale   The mental rating system that customers apply to service and service providers. Ratings range from exemplary to unsatisfactory, with an average rating being assigned when service occurs as expected.

respect for elders   A value held by people from many cultures.

responding   Refers to sending back verbal and nonverbal messages to a message originator.

road rage   A term used to describe the practice of a driver or passenger in a vehicle verbally and/or physically assaulting others as a result of the frustrations experienced while driving (e.g., driver failing to signal, cutting into a lane abruptly, or tailgating).

robocall   A term used to describe a type of automated phone auto-dialer that delivers a personalized, prerecorded message to recipients. Often these callers are scammers who offer fraudulent offers to unsuspecting recipients in an effort to get them to send money or to extract personal information from them. They are robotic in nature, thus the name. These calls are illegal to individuals on the Do Not Call Registry unless the caller falls into certain categories (e.g., political organizations or emergency agencies).

rude or inconsiderate customers   People who seem to take pleasure in being obstinate and contrary when dealing with service providers and who seem to have their own agenda without concern for the feelings of others.

RUMBA   An acronym for five criteria—realistic, understandable, measurable, believable, and attainable—used to establish and measure employee performance goals.

S

screen pop-ups   Used in conjunction with ANI and IVR systems to identify callers. As a call is received and dispatched to an agent, the system provides information about the caller that "pops" onto the agent's screen before he or she answers the telephone (e.g., order information, membership data, service history, contact history).

seamless service   Service that is done in a manner that seems effortless and natural to the customer. Processes and systems are fully functional, effective, and efficient. Service representatives are well-trained and proficient in delivering service, and there is no inconvenience to the customer.

semantics   The scientific study of relationships between signs, symbols, and words and their meaning. The way words are used or stressed often affects their perceived meaning.

sender   One of the two primary elements of a two-way conversation. Originates messages to a receiver.

service breakdowns   Situations when customers have expectations of a certain type or level of product or service that are not met by a service provider.

service culture   A service environment made up of various factors, including the values, beliefs, norms, rituals, and practices of a group or organization.

service delivery systems   The mechanisms or strategies used by an organization to provide service to customers.

service economy   A term used to describe the trend in which businesses have shifted from primarily production and manufacturing to more service delivery. As part of this evolution, many organizations have developed specifically to provide services to customers.

service industry   A term used to describe businesses and organizations that are engaged primarily in service delivery. *Service sector* is a more accurate term because many organizations provide some form of service to their customers even though they are primarily engaged in research, development, and manufacture of products.

service measurement   Techniques used by organizations to determine how customers perceive the value of services and products received.

service options   Alternatives offered by service providers when an original request by a customer cannot be honored because of such restrictions as governmental statutory regulations, nonavailability of products, or inability to perform as requested.

service philosophy   The approach that an organization takes to providing service and addressing the needs of customers.

service recovery   The process of righting a wrong or correcting something that has not gone as promised involving provision of a product or service to a customer. The concept involves not only replacing defective products, but also going the extra step of providing compensation for the customer's inconvenience.

service sector   Refers to organizations and individuals involved in delivering service as a primary product.

setting priorities   The process of deciding which factors or elements have greater importance and placing them in a hierarchy.

silence   Technique used to gain attention when speaking, to allow thought, or to process information received.

Skype   Refers to a software application that is a division of Microsoft® and provides free or paid service that allows people to connect with other Skype subscribers anywhere in the world with voice, video, or text messages.

Small Business Administration (SBA)   U.S. governmental agency established to assist small business owners.

small talk   Dialogue used to enhance relationships, show civility, and build rapport.

smartphones   Mobile telephones that are built with a mobile operating system similar to a computer that allows them to perform a myriad of functions using what are called applications or apps.

social media   Websites through which users come together as "communities" of friends, relatives, and like-minded individuals for social networking and microblogging (blogging) and to share ideas, content (e.g., videos or images), and personal and other information. Examples of social media include Facebook, Twitter, Tumblr, Instagram, Pinterest, LinkedIn, Google Plus, Dribble, and Reddit.

spamming or spam   An abusive use of various electronic messaging systems and technology to send unsolicited and indiscriminant bulk messages to people (also used with instant messaging, web search engines, blogs, and other formats).

spatial cues   Nonverbal messages sent on the basis of how close or far someone stands from another person.

speech or voice recognition   The ability of a machine or software program to identify words and phrases in spoken language and convert them to a machine-readable format that can respond to vocal prompts and branch to optional responses.

stereotype   Generalization made about an individual or group and not based on reality. Similar people are often lumped together for ease in categorizing them.

strategies for preventing dissatisfaction   Techniques used to prevent a breakdown in needs fulfillment when you are dealing with customers.

strategies for reclaiming time   Techniques used to eliminate time wasters and to become more effective and efficient.

stressors   Factors in a person's life that cause him or her to react positively or negatively to a situation that caused the pressure. (See also fight or flight syndrome.)

T

tablet   A personal computer (PC) that is a hybrid between a notebook or laptop computer and a personal digital assistant (PDA) and has a flat-screen viewing panel. Users can navigate the functions on a tablet by using a plastic-tipped stylus to tap icons or swiping and tapping on the screen with their finger.

talkative customers   Customers exhibiting extroverted behavior who are very people-oriented.

Technical Assistance Research Program (TARP) Worldwide   An Arlington, Virginia–based firm specializing in customer service research studies for call centers and many other industries.

Telecommunications Relay Service (TRS)   Through such services, specially trained operators act as intermediaries between people who are deaf, hard-of-hearing, speech disabled, or deaf and blind and standard telephone users.

telecommuting   A trend seen in many congested metropolitan areas and government offices. To reduce traffic and pollution and to save resources (e.g., rent, telephone, and technology systems), many organizations allow employees to set up home offices and from there electronically communicate and forward information to their corporate offices.

telephone management   Strategies for the effective use of the telephone and associated equipment in communicating.

Telephone Typewriter system (TTY)   A typewriter-like device used by people with hearing disabilities for typing messages back and forth via telephone lines. [Also known as a Telecommunications Device for the Deaf (TDD).]

text messaging or texting   The process of someone typing and sending a brief electronic message to another person over a phone network using a mobile phone or fixed or portable device.

thought speed   The rate at which the human brain processes information.

time allocation   Amount of attention given to a person or project.

time management   The systematic practice of categorizing daily activities, identifying and eliminating factors that interfere with efficiency, and developing effective strategies for getting the most out of the time available.

time management and technology   Refers to the ability to use technology to improve effectiveness and efficiency in a service environment.

time management face-to-face   Techniques for increasing time efficiency when dealing with customers.

time management on the run   Strategies for using downtime effectively to accomplish small tasks or be creative.

time perception   The manner in which time is viewed as being either polychronic or monochronic.

time reality   Acceptance of the fact that each person has only a finite amount of time each day to accomplish tasks and to enhance its usage.

time wasters   Events, people, items, and other factors that create unnecessary loss of time.

total quality management (TQM) and continuous quality improvement (CQI)   A systematic approach to identifying and quantifying best practices in an organization and/or industry in order to make improvements in effectiveness and efficiency.

touch point   Any instance in which a service provider or organization (e.g., face-to-face, in writing, through technology) comes in contact with a customer; it is an opportunity to influence customer loyalty and enhance the customer relationship.

trust   Key element in cementing interpersonal relationships.

tweets   Messages limited to 140 characters sent via Twitter to other mobile equipment and computer users.

Twitter   An online social networking service and microblogging service that enables its users to send and read text-based messages.

two-way communication An active process in which two individuals apply all the elements of interpersonal communication (e.g., listening, feedback, positive language) in order to effectively exchange information and ideas.

U

underpromise and overdeliver A service strategy in which service providers strive for excellent customer service and satisfaction by doing more than they say they will for the customer or exceeding customer expectations.

V

values Long-term appraisals of the worth of an idea, person, place, thing, or practice held by individuals, groups, or cultures. These affect attitudes and behavior.

verbal feedback The response given to a sender's message that allows both the sender and the receiver to know that a message was received correctly.

verbal fillers Verbal sounds, words, or utterances that break silence but add little to a conversation. Examples are uh, um, ah, and you know.

vision disabilities Conditions resulting from reduced or lost visual acuity or ability.

vision statement A vision statement communicates an organization's values and purpose and explains *what* the organization wants to be.

vocal cues Qualities of the voice that send powerful nonverbal messages. Examples are rate, pitch, volume, and tone.

voice mail management System for creating outgoing messages and leaving messages on an answering system effectively.

Voice over Internet Protocol (VoIP) Technologies, methodologies, and transmission techniques involved in the delivery of voice and image communication via the Internet.

voice quality Refers to the sound of one's voice. Terms often attributed to voice quality are raspy, nasal, hoarse, and gravelly.

voice response unit (VRU) System that allows customers to call 24 hours a day, seven days a week by keying a series of numbers on the telephone keypad to get information or answers to questions.

volume Refers to loudness or softness of the voice when speaking.

W

wai Traditional gesture in Thailand (pronounced "why") used in conjunction with a slight bow as a greeting and to say "thank you" or "sorry." It is executed by placing the palms and fingers of both hands together as in a prayer position in the center of the chest. Holding them higher in relation to the face is an indication of more respect or reverence to the other person.

wants Things that customers typically desire but do not necessarily need.

websites A series of electronic "pages" that are hosted on a web server and provide vital organizational, product, and service information and multiple ways for consumers to get in touch with key company representatives via the Internet.

what customers want Things that customers typically desire but do not necessarily need.

Wi-Fi Technology that enables electronic devices such as smartphones, computers, and tablets to send and receive data wirelessly (using radio waves) over a computer network.

wiki An interactive website where users are free to add, modify, or delete information. Because of the casual and flexible nature of such sites, many people, especially educators, do not consider them a valid resource.

win-win situation An outcome to a disagreement in which both parties walk away feeling that they got what they wanted or needed.

workplace violence A trend that has developed and escalated in the past decade, spawned by many changes in the workplace, shifting societal values and beliefs, and a variety of other factors.

Y

Y2K bug The term applied to a programming error made in many software packages that would cause a computer to fail to recognize the year 2000 at midnight on December 31, 1999. In instances where the oversight occurred, computers would cease to function at that hour. Billions of dollars were spent to correct the error worldwide.

younger customers Subjective term referring to anyone younger than the service provider. Sometimes used to describe members of generation X (born to baby boomers) or later.

YouTube The largest video-sharing website on the Internet where users can upload, share, and view videos.

NOTES

Chapter 1

1. Jeremy Twitchell, "From Upstart to $1 Billion Behemoth, Zappos Marks 10 Years," *Las Vegas Sun*, June 16, 2009, www.lasvegassun.com/news/2009/jun/16/upstart-1-billion-behemoth-zappos-marks-10-year-an/.
2. Louis D. Johnston, "History Lessons: Understanding the Decline in Manufacturing, MinnPost, February 22, 2012, www.minnpost.com/macro-micro-minnesota/2012/02/history-lessons-understanding-decline-manufacturing.
3. C. Brett Lockhart and Michael Wolf, "Employment Outlook: 2010–2020: Occupational Employment Projections to 2020," *Monthly Labor Review* (January 2012), pp. 84–108, U.S. Department of Labor, Bureau of Labor Statistics. www.bls.gov/opub/mlr/2012/01/art5full.pdf.
4. *Ibid*.
5. Bureau of Labor Statistics, U.S. Department of Labor, "Projections Overview," *Occupational Outlook Handbook*, March 29, 2012, www.bls.gov/ooh/About/Projections-Overview.htm.
6. *Ibid*.
7. "Work Is a Verb," Global Workplace Analytics, n.d., www.teleworkresearchnetwork.com/home/work-is-a-verb-not-a-noun.
8. Sandy Smith, "Rethinking Priorities: Consumers Sustain Careful Spending Habits," *NRF Stores*, February 2012, www.stores.org/STORES%20Magazine%20February%202012/rethinking-priorities#.UWSU47nD-zm.
9. Mitra Toossi, "Employment Outlook: 2010–2020: Labor Force Projections to 2020: A More Slowly Growing Workforce," *Monthly Labor Review* (January 2012), pp. 43–64, www.bls.gov/opub/mlr/2012/01/art3full.pdf.
10. *Ibid*.
11. "Computer and Internet Use in the United States: 2010," U.S. Census Bureau, n.d., www.census.gov.
12. Chad Brooks, "Technology Firms Outsourcing More Jobs Than Ever," *Business News Daily*, March 22, 2013, www.businessnewsdaily.com/4191-more-tech-firms-outsourcing-jobs.html.
13. Toossi, "Employment Outlook," tab. 1.
14. Bureau of Labor Statistics, "Projections Overview," chart 2.
15. U.S. Census Bureau, U.S. Department of Commerce, "Quarterly Retail E-Commerce Sales 4th Quarter 2012," news release, February 15, 2013, www.census.gov/retail/mrts/www/data/pdf/ec_current.pdf.
16. Caroline Fairchild, "Recession Generation Opts to Rent Not Buy Houses to Cars," Bloomberg.com, August 7, 2012, www.bloomberg.com/news/2012-08-08/recession-generation-opts-to-rent-not-buy-houses-to-cars.html.
17. Bureau of Labor Statistics, U.S. Department of Labor, "Employee Tenure Summary," news release, September 18, 2012, www.bls.gov/news.release/tenure.nr0.htm.
18. "Small Business Trends: Small Business Is BIG!," U.S. Small Business Administration, n.d., www.sba.gov/content/small-business-trends.
19. Zoe Galland, "A Stew of Small Biz Stats," *Bloomberg Businessweek*, May 2, 2006, www.businessweek.com/stories/2006-05-02/a-stew-of-small-biz-statsbusinessweek-business-news-stock-market-and-financial-advice.

Chapter 3

1. Papa John's Pizza, www.papajohns.com/about/index.shtm.
2. "Statistics about Business Size (including Small Business)," U.S. Census Bureau, www.census.gov/epcd/www/smallbus.html.

Chapter 4

1. Julius Fast, *Body Language* (New York: Pocket Books, 1960).
2. National Geographic Society, www.nationalgeographic.com.

Chapter 5

1. National Sleep Foundation, "Fatigue and Excessive Sleepiness," www.sleepfoundation.org/article/sleep-related-problems/excessive-sleepiness-and-sleep.
2. Centers for Disease Control and Prevention, "Insufficient Sleep Is a Public Health Epidemic," www.cdc.gov/features/dssleep/.
3. National Sleep Foundation, "How Much Sleep Do Adults Need?," www.sleepfoundation.org/article/white-papers/how-much-sleep-do-adults-need (internal citation omitted).

Chapter 6

1. Desmond Morris, *Bodytalk: The Meaning of Human Gestures* (New York: Crown Trade Paperbacks, 1994), pp. 118–19, 130–31.
2. Ibid., p. 142.

Chapter 7

1. L. Stampler, "The Ten Most Valuable Brands in the World," *Business Insider*, http://finance.yahoo.com/news/the-10-most-valuable-brands-in-the-world-161307417.html.
2. Coca-Cola, "Mission, Vision and Values," www.coca-colacompany.com/our-company/mission-vision-values.

Chapter 8

1. Johnson & Johnson, Credo, http://www.jnj.com/connect/about-jnj/jnj-credo/.
2. Tony Alessandra and Michael J. O'Connor, *The Platinum Rule* (New York: Warner Books, 1996).
3. American Indian Policy Center, www.airpi.org/research/tdlead.html.
4. Chickasaw Nation, www.chickasaw.net/site06/heritage/250_965.htm.
5. "How Many People in the World Speak English 2013?," Exploredia, February 25, 2011, http://exploredia.com/how-many-people-in-the-world-speak-english-2013/.
6. Bureau of Labor Statistics, U.S. Department of Labor, "Labor Force Characteristics of Foreign-Born Workers Summary," May 22, 2013, www.bls.gov/news.release/forbrn.nr0.htm.
7. National Geographic Society, http://nationalgeographic.com.

8. U.S. Census Bureau, U.S. Department of Commerce, "Nearly 1 in 5 People in the U.S. Have a Disability, U.S. Census Bureau Reports," July 25, 2012, www.census.gov/newsroom/releases/archives/miscellaneous/cb12-134.html.

9. World Health Organization, "Deafness and Hearing Loss," February 2013, www.who.int/mediacentre/factsheets/fs300/en/.

10. World Health Organization, "Visual Impairment and Blindness," June 2012, www.who.int/mediacentre/factsheets/fs282/en/.

11. U.S. Census Bureau, U.S. Department of Labor, "Anniversary of Americans with Disabilities Act: July 26," July 25, 2013, www.census.gov/newsroom/releases/archives/facts_for_features_special_editions/cb12-ff16.html.

12. U.S. Census Bureau, U.S. Department of Labor, "Older Americans Month: May 2013," March 7, 2013, www.census.gov/newsroom/releases/archives/facts_for_features_special_editions/cb13-ff07.html?sf12522919=1&sf12575013=1&sf12575381=1&sf12890316=1.

Chapter 9

1. M. Pélissié du Rausas, J. Manyika, E. Hazan, J. Bughin, M. Chui, and R. Said, "Internet Matters: The Net's Sweeping Impact on Growth, Jobs, and Prosperity, McKinsey Global Institute, Insights & Publications, May 2011, www.mckinsey.com/insights/high_tech_telecoms_internet/internet_matters.

2. ChartsBin, "Number of Mobile Subscribers by Country," 2011, http://chartsbin.com/view/1880.

3. G. Sterling, "Report: Nearly 40 Percent of Internet Time Now on Mobile Devices," February 26, 2013, http://marketingland.com/report-nearly-40-percent-of-internet-time-now-on-mobile-devices-34639.

4. K. Leggett, "Forrester's Top 15 Trends for Customer Service in 2013," January 14, 2013, http://blogs.forrester.com/kate_leggett/13-01-14-forresters_top_15_trends_for_customer_service_in_2013.

5. D. Clarkson et al., "Making Proactive Chat Work," Forrester, June 4, 2010, www.forrester.com/Making+Proactive+Chat+Work/fulltext/-/E-RES57054?objectid=RES57054.

6. Baymard Institute, "22 Cart Abandonment Rate Statistics," July 28, 2013, http://baymard.com/lists/cart-abandonment-rate.

7. "Deal with It! Discounts Drive Brand Love on Social Media," Nielsen Newswire: Consumer, November 3, 2011, www.nielsen.com/us/en/newswire/2011/deal-with-it-discounts-drive-brand-love-on-social-media.html.

8. Pinterest, Wikipedia, http://en.wikipedia.org/wiki/Pinterest.

9. J. Jargon, "Retailers Wage War Against Long Lines," *The Wall Street Journal*, May 1, 2013, http://online.wsj.com/article/SB10001424127887323798104578453293807869744.html.

10. "eCommerce, The Newest Business Frontier: It's Time to Get Connected," U.S. Small Business Administration, www.sba.gov/content/ecommerce-resources.

Chapter 10

1. H. Leggatt, "ForeSee: UK Online Shoppers More Satisfied with Experience," BizReport, January 4, 2012, www.bizreport.com/2012/01/foresee-uk-online-shoppers-more-satisfied-with-experience.html.

2. American Customer Satisfaction Index, "Quarterly Update on U.S. Overall Customer Satisfaction," May 2013, http://marketing.theacsi.org/acton/attachment/5132/f-0009/1/-/-/-/-/file.pdf.

3. Dr. S. Shane, "The US Egg Industry and the Salmonella Recall," WATTAgNet, December 15, 2010, www.wattagnet.com/19497.html.

4. "*Deepwater Horizon* Oil Spill," http://en.wikipedia.org/wiki/Deepwater_Horizon_oil_spill.

5. A. McInnes, "Customers' Problems Are Companies' Loyalty Opportunities," Forrester Blogs, December 6, 2012, http://blogs.forrester.com/andrew_mcinnes/10-12-06-customers_problems_are_companies_loyalty_building_opportunities.

6. C. Barton, J. Fromm, and C. Egan, "The Millenial Consumer: Debunking Stereotypes," The Boston Consulting Group, April 2012, p. 6, www.brandchannel.com/images/papers/536_BCG_The_Millennial_Consumer_Apr_2012%20(3)_tcm80-103894.pdf.

7. Harris Interactive, "Churn Management and Winback," www.harrisinteractive.com/services/loyaltyCPI.asp.

8. D. Hunter, "Customer Loyalty Boosts Small Business Profitability," May 30, 2013, www.freshbusinessthinking.com/news.php?CID=0&NID=18475&PGID=1#.UaeKlbnD-Uk.

9. J.D. Power and Associates, "2009 North America Hotel Guest Satisfaction Index Study," January 1, 2009, www.jdpower.com/corporate/news/releases/pressrelease.aspx?ID=2009133.

10. J. Hanslip, "Press Release: Mobile Coupon Redemption Values to Exceed $43bn Globally by 2016, Driven by Better Targeting and Mobile Apps," November 1, 2011, http://juniperresearch.com/viewpressrelease.php?pr=269.

11. Marriott, "Frequently Asked Questions," www.marriott.com/hotel-prices/faqs.mi.

12. K. Kobe, "Small Business GDP: Update 2002–2010, SBA Office of Advocacy, January 2012, www.sba.gov/sites/default/files/rs390tot_1.pdf.

13. TARP Worldwide, "Customer Mine Blog," November 9, 2008, http://blog.tarp.com/?m=20081109.

BIBLIOGRAPHY

Aguilar, Leslie, and Linda Stokes. *Multicultural Customer Service: Providing Outstanding Service across Cultures.* New York: McGraw-Hill/Irwin, 1996.

Alessandra, Tony, and Michael J. O'Connor. *The Platinum Rule: Discover the Four Basic Business Personalities and How They Can Lead You to Success.* New York: Grand Central Publishing, 2008.

Andersen, Peter A. *The Complete Idiot's Guide to Body Language.* New York: Penguin Group, 2004.

Anderson, Kristin, and Carol Kerr. *Customer Relationship Management.* New York: McGraw-Hill, 2002.

Anderson, Kristin, and Ron Zemke. *Knock Their Socks Off Answers.* New York: AMACOM, 1995.

Axtell, Roger E. *Gestures: The Do's and Taboos of Body Language around the World.* New York: Wiley, 1991.

Barlow, Janelle, and Paul Stewart. *Branded Customer Service: The New Competitive Edge.* San Francisco, CA: Berrett-Koehler, 2006.

Bosworth, Michael T., and John R. Holland. *Customer Centric Selling.* New York: McGraw-Hill, 2004.

Bowden, Mark. *Winning Body Language: Control Conversation, Command Attention, and Convey the Right Message—Without Saying a Word.* New York: McGraw-Hill, 2010.

Bowman, Judith. *Don't Take the Last Donut: New Rules of Business Etiquette.* Franklin Lakes, NJ: Career Press, 2007.

Burgoon, Judie K., Laura K. Guerrero, and Kory Floyd. *Nonverbal Communication.* Upper Saddle River, NJ: Pearson, 2009.

Calero, Henry H. *The Power of Nonverbal Communication: How You Act Is More Important Than What You Say.* Los Angeles: Silver Lake Publishing, 2005.

Capodagli, Bill, and Lynn Jackson. *The Disney Way: Harnessing the Management Secrets of Disney in Your Company.* New York: McGraw-Hill, 2007.

Disney Institute. *Be Our Guest: Perfecting the Art of Customer Service.* New York: Disney Editions, 2001.

Evensen, Renée. *Customer Service Training 101: Quick and Easy Steps That Get Results.* 2nd ed. New York: AMACOM, 2010.

Ford, Lisa, David McNair, and Bill Perry. *Exceptional Customer Service: Going Beyond Your Good Service to Exceed the Customer's Expectation.* Avon, MA: Adams Media, 2001.

Gee, Val, and Jeff Gee. *Super Service: Seven Keys to Delivering Great Customer Service.* New York: McGraw-Hill, 1999.

Greenberg, Paul. *CRM at the Speed of Light.* 4th ed. New York: McGraw-Hill, 2009.

Gudykunst, William B. *Bridging Differences: Effective Intergroup Communication.* 4th ed. Thousand Oaks, CA: Sage, 2003.

Gundling, Ernest, and Anita Zanchettin. *Global Diversity: Winning Customers and Engaging Employees within World Markets.* Boston, MA: Nicholas Brealey International, 2007.

Hicks, Rick, and Kathy Hicks. *Boomers, Xers, and Other Strangers: Understanding the Generational Differences That Divide Us.* Wheaton, IL: Tyn Dale, 1999.

Karp, Hank, Connie Fuller, and Danilo Sirias. *Bridging the Boomer Xer Gap.* Palo Alto, CA: Davies-Black, 2002.

Lebon, Paul. *Escape Voicemail Hell: Boost Your Productivity by Making Voicemail Work for You.* Highland Village, TX: Parleau, 2000.

Leland, Karen, and Keith Bailey. *Customer Service for Dummies.* 3rd ed. New York: Wiley, 2007.

Lucas, Robert W. *How to Be a Great Call Center Representative.* Watertown, MA: American Management Association, 2001.

Lucas, Robert W. *Please Every Customer: Delivering Stellar Customer Service across Cultures.* New York: McGraw-Hill Professional, 2011.

National Restaurant Association. *Customer Service Competency Guide.* Upper Saddle River, NJ: Prentice Hall, 2007.

Pease, Allan, and Barbara Pease. *The Definitive Book of Body Language.* New York: Bantam Dell, 2004.

Quinlan, Kathryn A. *Customer Service Representative.* Mankato, MN: Capstone Press, 1999.

Remland, Martin S. *Nonverbal Communication in Everyday Life.* 3rd ed. Boston, MA: Houghton Mifflin, 2008.

Richardson, Will. *Blogs, Wikis, Podcasts and Other Powerful Tools for Classrooms.* Thousand Oaks, CA: Corwin Press, 2006.

Satterwhite, Marilyn, and Judith Olson-Sutton. *Business Communication at Work.* New York: Glencoe/McGraw-Hill, 2000.

Solomon, Charlene M., and Michael S. Schell. *Managing across Cultures: The Seven Keys to Doing Business with a Global Mindset.* New York: McGraw-Hill, 2009.

Solomon, Micah. *High-Tech High-Touch Customer Service: Inspire Timeless Loyalty in the Demanding New World of Social Commerce.* New York: AMACOM, 2012.

Sterne, Jim. *Customer Service on the Internet: Building Relationships, Increasing Loyalty, and Staying Competitive.* 2nd ed. New York: Wiley, 2000.

Stinnett, Bill. *Think Like Your Customer: A Winning Strategy to Maximize Sales by Understanding How and Why Your Customers Buy.* New York: McGraw-Hill, 2005.

Timm, Paul R., and Christopher G. Jones. *Technology and Customer Service: Profitable Relationship Building.* Upper Saddle River, NJ: Pearson Education, 2005.

Toister, Jeff. *Service Failure: The Real Reasons Employees Struggle with Customer Service and What You Can Do About It.* New York: AMACOM, 2012.

Trompenaars, Fons, and Charles Hampden-Turner. *Riding the Waves of Culture: Understanding Diversity in Global Business.* 2nd ed. New York: McGraw-Hill, 1998.

Wainwright, Gordon R. *Teach Yourself Body Language.* Chicago: Contemporary Books, 2003.

Wolvin, Andrew D. *Listening and Human Communication in the 21st Century.* Chichester, West Sussex, United Kingdom: Wiley-Blackwell, 2010.

Zemke, Ron, and Chip Bell. *Service Magic: The Art of Amazing Your Customers.* Dearborn, MI: Dearborn Trade Publishing, 2003.

Zemke, Ron, Claire Raines, and Bob Filipczak. *Generations at Work: Managing the Clash of Veterans, Boomers, Xers, and Nexters in Your Workplace.* New York: AMACOM, 2000.

Zimmerman, Scott, Ronald Finklestein, and Tony Alessandra. *The Platinum Rule for Small Business Mastery.* New York: Morgan James Publishing, 2007.

CREDITS

Photos

Part One

Opener: © Robert W. Lucas.

Chapter 1

Opener: © Ethan Miller/Getty Images; p. 7: © Corbis; p. 13: © Klaus Tiedge/Blend Images LLC RF; p. 21: © Tim McGuire/Corbis; p. 26: © Chuck Savage/Corbis.

Chapter 2

Opener: © Toby Talbot/AP Photo; p. 47: © klenger/Getty Images RF; p. 50: © KEMAL BA/Getty Images RF; p. 55: © Spiderstock/ Getty Images RF; p. 58: © Terry Vine/Getty Images RF; p. 67: © Image Source/Getty Images RF; p. 72: © Tanya Constantine/ agefotostock RF; p. 76: © Gene Chutka/Getty Images RF.

Part Two

Opener: © Robert W. Lucas.

Chapter 3

Opener: © Taro Yamasaki/Time Life Pictures/Getty Images; p. 93: © Cultura/Nancy Honey/Getty Images; p. 103: © Terry Vine/ Blend Images/Corbis RF; p. 111: © Stockbroker xtra/ agefotostock RF; p. 112(1): © Design Pics/Don Hammond RF; p. 112(2): © Bartosz Hadyniak/Getty Images RF; p. 112(3): © 2009 Jupiterimages Corporation RF; p. 112(4): © GoodSportHD.com/Alamy RF; p. 112(5): © Rob Daly/ agefotostock RF; p. 112(6): © Kelly Fajack/Getty Images; p. 112(7): © George Doyle/Getty Images RF; p. 112(8): © Don Tremain/Getty Images RF.

Chapter 4

Opener: Courtesy of Fields Auto Group; p. 133: © Troels Graugaard/Getty Images RF; p. 137: © Comstock/Punchstock RF; p. 141: © Anton Kovalenko/Alamy; p. 142: © Photodisc/ Getty Images RF; p. 147: © Ron Chapple Stock/Alamy RF; p. 152: © Somos/SuperStock RF; p. 153: © Eyecandy Images/ agefotostock RF; p. 162(1): © Photodisc/Getty Images RF; p. 162(2): © Nick Koudis/Getty Images RF; p. 162(3): © Photodisc/Getty Images RF; p. 162(4): © Nick Koudis/ Getty Images RF.

Chapter 5

Opener: © Jack Hobhouse/Alamy; p. 169: © Clerkenwell/Getty Images RF; p. 174: © Spencer Grant/PhotoEdit; p. 177: © Monkey Business/agefotostock RF; p. 181: © Digital Vision/Getty Images RF; p. 186: © ImageShop/Corbis RF; p. 188: © Comstock/Getty Images RF; p. 192: © Comstock Images/SuperStock RF.

Part Three

Opener: © Robert W. Lucas.

Chapter 6

Opener: © TJP/Alamy; p. 209(top): © Paul Barton/Corbis; p. 209(bottom): © XiXinXing/Getty Images RF; p. 210: © Thinkstock/Jupiterimages RF; p. 211: © Ingram Publishing RF; p. 216: © John Henley/Corbis; p. 219: © Claudia Dewald/ Getty Images RF; p. 226(left): © Blend Images/Moxie Productions/Getty Images RF; p. 226(right): © Digital Vision/ Getty Images RF.

Chapter 7

Opener: © The McGraw-Hill Companies, Inc./Jill Braaten, photographer; p. 239: © Montgomery Martin/Alamy RF; p. 241: © Getty RF; p. 245: © Getty Images/Image Source RF; p. 250: © Kali Nine LLC/Getty Images RF; p. 255: © NuStock/ Getty Images RF; p. 258: © Robert W. Lucas.

Chapter 8

Opener: © Emile Wamsteker/Bloomberg via Getty Images; p. 277: © Punchstock/Digital Vision RF; p. 281: © Stewart Cohen/ Pam Ostrow/Blend Images/Corbis RF; p. 284(left): © PhotosIndia.com LLC/Alamy RF; p. 284(right): © ranplett/ Getty Images RF; p. 288: © Stockbyte/Getty Images RF; p. 292: © 2009 Jupiterimages Corporation RF; p. 298: © N. Vasuki Rao/Getty Images RF; p. 300: © Wavebreakmedia Ltd/The Agency Collection/Getty Images RF; p. 304: © Digital Vision/Getty Images RF.

Chapter 9

Opener: © M4OS Photos/Alamy; p. 317: Courtesy of the Royal Dutch Mint; p. 318: © Vladyslav Starozhylov/Alamy RF; p. 321(left): © BananaStock RF; p. 321(right): © Stockbyte/ Punchstock RF; p. 323: © Images.com/Corbis; p. 327: © Nihat Dursun/Getty Images RF; p. 330: © Tetra Images/Corbis RF; p. 331: © Pankaj Kumar/agefotostock RF; p. 338: © YAY Media AS/Alamy RF; p. 344: © Damir Karan/Getty Images RF; p. 349: © Tom Grill/Corbis RF; p. 353: © Jose Luis Pelaez Inc/Blend Images LLC RF.

Chapter 10

Opener: © The McGraw-Hill Companies, Inc./John Flournoy, photographer; p. 369: © Don Emmert/AFP/Getty Images; p. 374: © Eric Audras/Onoky/Corbis RF; p. 381: © Joey Foley/ Getty Images for Payless ShoeSource; p. 389: © mangostock/ agefotostock RF; p. 394: © JLP/Jose L. Pelaez/Corbis; p. 397: © Libby Welch/Alamy; p. 402: © Fotosearch Premium/Getty Images RF.

INDEX